# Ref on INFINITY

## An Introduction to Kabbalah

### RAOUL NASS

EDITED BY
**KALMAN SERKEZ**

JASON ARONSON INC.
*Northvale, New Jersey*
*Jerusalem*

This book was set in 11 pt. New Baskerville by Alpha Graphics of Pittsfield, NH and printed and bound by Book-mart Press of North Bergen, NJ.

Copyright © 1999 by The Mazel Project

10 9 8 7 6 5 4 3 2 1

All rights reserved. No part of this book may be used or reproduced in any manner whatsoever without written permission from Jason Aronson Inc. except in the case of brief quotations in reviews for inclusion in a magazine, newspaper, or broadcast.

**Library of Congress Cataloging-in-Publication Data**

Nass, Raoul.
  Reflections on infinity : an introduction to Kabbalah / by Raoul Nass.
    p.  cm.
  Includes bibliographical references and index.
  ISBN 0-7657-6062-2
  1. Cabala—History.        I. Title.
BM526.N37   1999
296.1'6—dc21                                                                99-15797
                                                                                  CIP

Printed in the United States of America on acid-free paper. For information and catalog write to Jason Aronson Inc., 230 Livingston Street, Northvale, NJ 07647-1726, or visit our website: www.aronson.com

# CONTENTS

| | |
|---|---|
| *Introduction by Rabbi Norman Nass* | *xxi* |
| *A Note to the Readers* | *xxiii* |
| *Preface* | *xxv* |
|    Connections and Importance | xxv |
|    Design of the Present Work | xxvi |
|    Kabbalistic Manuscripts Purchased by Mirandola | xxvi |
|    The Identity of These Manuscripts with the *Sepher Ha-Zohar*—the Chief Text of the Secret Tradition in Israel | xxvii |
|    Sepher Yetzirah and Its Translation by William Postel | xxviii |
|    Christian Students of Kabbalism | xxviii |
|    Vestiges of a Great Spiritual Experiment | xxviii |
|    Records of a Theosophical School in Jewry | xxix |

### Section I. Literature of Kabbalism Historically

| | |
|---|---|
| 1. The Hidden Doctrines in Jewish Literature | 3 |
|    Post-Christian Literature of the Jews | 3 |
|    A Field of Research Probing the Depth of the Human Mind | 4 |

| | |
|---|---:|
| A Secret Religious Tradition Perpetuated from the Past | 4 |
| The Secret Doctrine of Kabbalism and Its Domains | 5 |
| Kabbalistic Philosophy: A Doctrine of Religious Tradition | 5 |
| To the Esoteric Student | 6 |
| No *Scientia Kabbalistica* | 6 |
| Magical and Practical Kabbalah | 6 |
| Of the Secret Doctrine | 7 |
| Of Literal Vesture and the Esoteric | 7 |
| The Ancient of Days | 8 |
| Of the Pentateuch's Stories | 8 |
| Sixty Methods and Seventy Modes of Interpretation | 9 |
| The Supplementary Soul | 9 |
| The Fifty Gates | 10 |
| The Doctrine More Ancient Than the World | 10 |
| Bereshith and the Secret Doctrine | 10 |
| Origin of the Doctrine | 11 |
| Adam's Gift Book | 12 |
| Loss of the Book | 12 |
| Abraham and Moses Recipients | 13 |
| After Moses and David | 13 |
| Days of Rabbi Shimon | 14 |
| Incompleteness of the Doctrine | 14 |
| 2. Kabbalah as Secret Tradition and a Cryptic Philosophy | 16 |
| 3. The Kabbalah and the Talmud | 18 |
| Antiquity of Kabbalah and Talmud | 18 |
| The Materials of the Talmud | 19 |
| Compilation Method | 19 |
| Forms of the Mishnah | 20 |
| Gemara and Talmud | 20 |
| The Two Talmud Versions | 20 |

| | |
|---|---|
| Jurisprudence and Sociology of the Talmud | 21 |
| Metaphysics of the Kabbalah | 22 |
| Some Enigmatic Metaphysics in Talmud | 22 |
| Divisions and Contents of the Mishnah and Gemara in Short | 23 |
| Conclusive Distinctions between Kabbalah and Talmud | 24 |
| Mesorah and Kabbalah | 24 |
| 4. Divisions of the Kabbalah | 25 |
| Kabbalah Confused With Ceremonial Magic | 25 |
| Distinctions Between Ceremonial Ritual and Kabbalah | 25 |
| Theurgy, Talismans, and Kabbalah | 26 |
| Gematria, Notarikon, Temurah | 26 |

## *II. Source and Authority of the Kabbalah*

| | |
|---|---|
| 1. Age of the Chief Texts | 31 |
| Historical Data | 31 |
| Sepher Yetzirah of Abraham the Patriarch | 32 |
| The Tanna Rabbi Akiva, Author of the Sepher Yetzirah | 32 |
| Book of Formation Known to Archbishop Agobard of Lyons, 850 CE | 33 |
| Sepher Yetzirah in the Talmud | 34 |
| Conclusions | 34 |
| 2. Modern Criticism of the Book of Splendor | 36 |
| Attitude and Contrariety of Aristotelians and Their Antagonists | 36 |
| Defense of Zohar by Recent Thinkers | 37 |
| The Hostility of Graetz | 38 |
| Impeachment of the Zohar | 38 |
| Solomon Munk's Convictions | 39 |

| | | |
|---|---|---|
| 3. | **The Date and Authorship of the Book of Splendor** | 40 |
| | Account of the *Sepher Yuhasin* | 41 |
| | Summary of the Case as It Stands | 44 |
| | The Case of the Internal Evidence | 45 |
| | Accusation Number 1 | 45 |
| | Defense Number 1 | 45 |
| | Accusation Number 2 | 46 |
| | Defense Number 2 | 46 |
| | Accusation Number 3 | 47 |
| | Defense Number 3 | 47 |
| | Accusation Number 4 | 47 |
| | Defense Number 4 | 47 |
| | Accusation Number 5 | 48 |
| | Defense Number 5 | 48 |
| | The Arguments Continued | 48 |
| 4. | **The Age of Zoharic Tradition** | 50 |
| | Fantastic Absurdities of Some Critics | 50 |
| | Isaac the Blind | 51 |
| | Evaluation | 51 |
| | Antiquity of Contents of Zohar Do Count | 52 |
| | Mysteries of Rabbi Shimon | 53 |
| 5. | **Kabbalistic Doctrines—Alleged Sources** | 54 |
| | Ten Emanations, Macroprosopus, and Microprosopus | 54 |
| | Philo's Writings and Kabbalistic Doctrine | 55 |
| | Concluding Impression | 56 |
| 6. | **Spain and Southern France—The First Recipients of Kabbalah** | 57 |
| | Spain—A Center of Jewish Learning | 57 |
| | Kabbalism Appeared First in Spain and Southern France | 58 |
| 7. | **Influence of Kabbalah on Jewry** | 59 |
| | The Kabbalah's Sphere of Influence on the Christian Mind | 59 |
| 8. | **Ancient Texts** | 61 |

## Section III. The Written Word of the Kabbalah: First Period–Early Kabbalistic Literature

1. Midrashim, Precursors of the Sepher
   Yetzirah and the Zohar ............................................. 65
   The Chapters of R. Eliezer and the Midrash
     Conen ................................................................. 66
   Other Authorities of These Periods ............................ 67
   Historical Treatises with Kabbalistic-sounding
     Names ................................................................ 69
   Exponents of Speculative Kabbalah ........................... 70
   Opponents of Kabbalah ............................................ 70
   A Short Account of Avicebron as Ibn Gebirol ............ 71
   Gebirol's Life ........................................................... 71
   Kabbalistic Schools of the Period .............................. 72
   Gebirol and the Book of Formation ........................... 72
   Avicebron's System of the Universe .......................... 73

2. The Book of Formation ............................................ 74
   The Transcendental Numerations .............................. 75
   Publications and Versions of Sepher Yetzirah ............ 77
   Connections and Dependencies of the
     Book of Formation ............................................... 77
   Saadya's Commentary ............................................. 78
   The Soul and Reincarnation ..................................... 79
   The Ten Categories: Saadya .................................... 80
   The Commentary Ascribed to Hai Gaon .................... 80
   The Commentary of the Raavad,
     circa 1100–1180, on the Book of
     Formation ........................................................... 81
   Rabbi Azriel's Yetzirah Commentary ......................... 82
   The Character and the Teachings of
     the Commentary .................................................. 82
   The Ramban, Nahmanides ....................................... 83
   The Commentary of R. Eliezer of
     Worms ................................................................ 83

### Section IV. The Written Word of the Kabbalah: Second Period

1. The Book of Splendor: Its Contents
   and Divisions ................................................ 87
      The Zohar and the Sepher Yetzirah ........... 87
      Latin and French Translations .................. 87
      Contents of the Zohar ............................. 88
      Divisions of Zoharic Contents ................... 89
      Book of Genesis and Its Omissions
         and Additions ................................. 89
      Book of Exodus and Its Introductions;
         the Luminous Book; the Faithful Shepherd;
         the Book of Leviticus; Others ............. 89
      Book of Numbers and the Idra Rabbah ......... 90
      Deuteronomy and the Idra Zutra ................. 90
      Rosenroth's Scheme of Tabulation .............. 91
      The External Parts as Understood by
         Rosenroth of More Than Two Centuries Ago ... 92
      Of Zoharic Contents, Continued ................. 94
      Nature of Zohar .................................... 94
      The Wise and the Unwise ........................ 94
      Hidden Meaning of Bible Stories ............... 95
      A Narrative ......................................... 95
      The Mythos of the Rose ......................... 97
      The Voice and the Word ........................ 97
      Power of Faith and Thought .................... 98

2. The Book of Concealment ............................ 99
      Book of Occultation as a Theogony ............ 99

3. The Greater Holy Synod ............................. 104
      The Explanation and Developments of
         the Treatise ................................... 106
      Esoteric Speculation and the Symbolism of
         the Edomite Kings ........................... 106

|     |                                                          |     |
| --- | -------------------------------------------------------- | --- |
|     | Microprosopus: The Lesser Countenance                    | 108 |
|     | Sublime Touches in This Treatise                         | 110 |
| 4.  | The Lesser Holy Synod                                    | 111 |
|     | The Master's Death and Instructions                      | 111 |
|     | The Nuptial Joys of the Soul of the Master Rabbi Shimon  | 112 |
| 5.  | The Discourse of the Aged Man                            | 114 |
| 6.  | The Luminous Book                                        | 117 |
|     | Contents of the Bahir                                    | 118 |
|     | The Holy Living Creatures                                | 119 |
|     | The Significance of the Three Sabbath Meals              | 119 |
| 7.  | The Faithful Shepherd                                    | 121 |
|     | Vicarious Atonement                                      | 122 |
|     | Three Chances for a Repentant Sinner                     | 124 |
|     | The Manifestation of the Shechinah                       | 124 |
|     | Metatron of the Presence Angel Satan and Lilith          | 126 |
| 8.  | Hidden Things of the Law                                 | 127 |
|     | Stages of Mystical Vision                                | 127 |
|     | The Three Angels of Abraham                              | 128 |
|     | Other Intimations and Excerpts                           | 129 |
| 9.  | The Secret Commentary                                    | 131 |
|     | Light of the Supersubstantial Bread                      | 132 |
| 10. | Minor Tracts of the Zohar                                | 134 |
|     | The Omissions                                            | 134 |
|     | Additions                                                | 135 |
|     | Repetitions: *Mathnitin*                                 | 137 |
|     | Secrets of Secrets—Of Human Physiognomy                  | 138 |
|     | Discourse of the Young Man                               | 139 |
|     | The Mansions of Abodes—The Seven Heavens and Seven Earths | 140 |
|     | The Seven Heavens and Seven Earths                       | 141 |

| | |
|---|---|
| Commentary of Ruth—Midrash Ruth and Incongruence by Transcribers | 142 |
| The Ancient and Latter Supplements | 143 |
| The Sublime Prayer of Elijah | 144 |
| God and His Attributes | 145 |

## Section V. The Doctrines of the Kabbalah in Respect of God and the Universe

| | |
|---|---|
| 1. The Majesty of God in Kabbalism | 149 |
|     The Kabbalistic Idea of God and the Evolution of the Universe | 149 |
|     God's Uttermost Transcendence | 150 |
|     Zoharic Teaching of *Ain Soph* | 152 |
|     Moses of Cordoba on *Ain Soph* | 152 |
|     The Raayah Mehemnah on the Notion of God | 153 |
|     Summation | 154 |
| 2. The Ten Sephiroth | 155 |
|     The Mystery of the Operation of the Mysterious Divine Will | 156 |
|     Divine Emanation and Divine Immanence | 157 |
| 3. The Doctrine of the Four Worlds | 160 |
|     The Fountain Text | 160 |
|     The Four Worlds | 161 |
|     The Tree of Life | 164 |
|     A Summary of Correspondences of the Sephiroth | 166 |
|     Conclusion | 168 |
|     Of the Three Hypostases | 169 |
|     The White Head and the Two Countenances | 170 |
|     Male and Female Principles | 171 |
|     Matrona | 171 |
|     The Doctrine Concerning the Sephirotic Tree | 172 |
|     The Theosophy of the Word | 173 |
|     The Word (Logos) | 174 |

4. The Paths of Wisdom and the Gates
   of Understanding                                           176
5. The Doctrine of Cosmology                                  179
   The World Created from Thought                             179
   The Letters of Concealment                                 180
   Discourse on Divine Things: The Doctrine of
      Divine Immanence                                        183
   The Mysterious Stone Shetiah                               185
   Creation and the Instruments Appertaining
      Thereto, Continued                                      186
   Final Intimations in Creation                              188
   Many Worlds Were Made, Arose, and Decayed
      Previously                                              189

### Section VI. Hierarchies of the Spiritual Beings

1. The Soul of Man                                            193
   Introduction                                               193
   The Soul in Kabbalism                                      193
   Belief in the Soul's Immortality—Tenets of Israel          194
   Kabbalistic Pneumatology                                   194
   On Preexistence of Souls                                   199
   The Parts of Division of the Soul                          199
   *Chaya* and *Yechidah*                                     203
   Other Soul Extensions                                      203
   The Supplementary Soul of Sabbath                          204
   The Law Leads the Soul                                     205
   Parable of the Soul                                        206
   The Seven Palaces                                          206
   The Palaces Above                                          207
   The Doctrine of Reincarnation: Metapsychosis or
      Revolutions of Souls                                    208
   Transmigration of Souls of Gentiles                        209
   Resurrection and Reincarnation                             211

| | |
|---|---:|
| 2. Angels and Demons and Metaphysical Doctrine | 213 |
|     Divine Intelligence and Forces | 213 |
|     Choirs of Angels in Yetzirah—Celestial Hierarchies | 214 |
|     Universe Correspondences of the Sephiroth: | |
|         Cortices, Spirits, and Demons | 215 |
|     Samael and Lilith | 217 |

### *Section VII. The Ways of God With Man*

| | |
|---|---:|
| 1. The Narrative of the Earthly Paradise | 221 |
|     Of the Indwelling Glory: Shechinah—Matrona | 222 |
|     Of the Supernal and the Inferior Paradises | 223 |
|     The Making of Man and His Exalted State | |
|         of Radiance | 223 |
|     Formation of Eve | 226 |
|     The Ineffable Nuptials | 227 |
|     The Trees of the Garden | 227 |
|     The Revolt of the Spirits | 228 |
| 2. The Serpent, Son of the Morning, and | |
|    the Fall of the Angels | 230 |
|     God, Also the Author of Certain Evil | 230 |
|     The Spirit of Good and the Spirit of Evil | 231 |
|     Hierarchy of Angels and Hierarchy of Demons | 232 |
|     The Empire of the Demons | 232 |
|     The First Downfall of the Angels | 233 |
|     The Second Downfall of the Angels | 234 |
|     Aza and Azael and Company | 234 |
|     Naamah | 235 |
|     Samael and His Wife, the Serpent | 236 |
|     The Great Dragon | 237 |
|     Other Demons | 238 |
| 3. The Fall of Man | 240 |
|     Man in His Glory and Hereafter | 240 |
|     Samael the Tempter and Rider of the | |
|         Serpent Appeared to Eve | 241 |

| | |
|---|---|
| Contents | xiii |

|  |  |
|---|---|
| Alternative Accounts of the Kinds of Temptation | 242 |
| The Dire Consequences Caused by the Temptation | 242 |
| The Loss of the Celestial Decorations and the Substituted Leaf Coverings | 243 |
| Still Another Account | 244 |
| The Cuirass of Sacred Letters | 244 |
| Of the Beauty of Adam and Eve | 245 |
| Separation Caused by the Trespass and Death | 246 |
| Of the Odors Diffused in Eden for the Vestures of the Soul | 247 |
| Adam and the Serpent | 247 |
| Samael Defiles Eve/Cain | 248 |
| Adam and Eve Both Begot Children From Demons | 249 |
| Another Mysterious Account of a Female Demon | 250 |
| Lilith, the Wife of Leviathan, and the Other Three Demons, Maaman, Ogereth, and Mahaltoth | 251 |
| Finale of the Expulsion from Eden, The Flaming Sword, Conclusion | 252 |
| 4. The Account of the Deluge | 254 |
| Prologue | 254 |
| The Sins Which Brought About the Cataclysm of the Deluge | 255 |
| Noah's Ark and the Meaning of the Ark | 256 |
| The Holocaust | 257 |
| Noah's Experiment | 258 |
| The Confusion of Tongues after the Deluge | 259 |
| 5. The Covenant with Abraham | 262 |
| History of Abraham, the Father of Nations | 263 |
| Abraham and Sarah in Egypt | 264 |
| Melchizedek of Salem | 265 |
| The Token of the Covenant | 265 |
| The Sign of Circumcision | 266 |
| The Covenant of Circumcision | 266 |
| The Metaphysical Principle of the Covenant | 267 |
| Ideas Which Lie Behind the Mark of Circumcision | 268 |

| | | |
|---|---|---|
| 6. | **Moses, the Master of the Law** | 270 |
| | The Marriage of Moses | 272 |
| | Moses, the Faithful Shepherd | 273 |
| | The Promulgation of the Divine Teaching—The Law | 273 |
| | Exaltations of Israel | 274 |
| | The Golden Calf and the Downfall of Israel | 274 |
| | The Original Tables of the Law | 275 |
| | Death of Moses and His Sepulchre | 277 |
| | The Tragedy of the Great Lawgiver | 278 |
| | Moses Will Return | 278 |
| 7. | **The Two Temples in Jerusalem** | 280 |
| | Prologue | 280 |
| | The Glorious First Temple Described by the Zohar | 281 |
| | An Alternative Version Concerning the Sanctuaries | 282 |
| | Lamentations Over the Holy Houses and Places | 283 |
| | Consolation and Hope | 284 |
| 8. | **The Coming of Messiah** | 286 |
| | Messianic Expectation in Israel | 286 |
| | Messianic Expectations, Continued | 287 |
| | Several Messiahs to Precede the Advent of the True King Messiah | 288 |
| | Symbolism Concerning Messiah | 289 |
| | The Intruders | 289 |
| | The Subject of the Messiah in Israel—A Subject of Spiritual Communion | 290 |
| | A Light of Symbolism | 291 |
| | The Advent of the Messiah in Another Version—Calculations | 292 |
| | The Portent of the Messiah's Advent | 292 |
| | The Present Abode of the Messiah and His Suffering | 293 |
| 9. | **The Doctrine concerning Sheol** | 295 |
| | Of Death—The Soul Body Separation and Departure, Its Vision and Accounting | 296 |

| | |
|---|---|
| The Soul of the Departed Meets Adam and Others | 296 |
| The Issue of the Male Issue | 297 |
| The Deathbed Events | 297 |
| The Version of Still Another Account | 298 |
| Of Hell Everlasting or Otherwise | 300 |
| Respecting Canaan | 301 |
| Importance of *Amain* Response | 301 |
| The Zoharic Flux of Eschatology | 302 |
| Other Gleams on the Subject of Retribution | 303 |
| Retribution and Mercy | 303 |
| 10. Concerning Resurrection | 305 |
| Resurrection of the Dead | 305 |
| Tradition of the Thesis of Resurrection | 306 |
| Concealment of the Curative Light, the Dew of Life | 307 |
| The Imperishable Little Bone | 308 |
| Conclusion of Zoharic Eschatology | 309 |

### Section VIII. The Higher Secret Doctrine in Israel

| | |
|---|---|
| 1. The Mystery of Shechinah | 313 |
| The Various Ascriptions and Designations of Shechinah | 314 |
| Shechinah Abides Everywhere | 315 |
| Alternative Allocations of Shechinah | 316 |
| The Task of Lighting Sabbath Candles | 317 |
| Shechinah's Relation to the Letter of Tetragrammaton | 317 |
| The Place of Shechinah in the Sephirotic Tree | 319 |
| Again About the Fifty Gates of Understanding | 321 |
| The Fifty Gates and Man | 322 |
| Integration of the Entire Tree in Shechinah— A Thing To Come | 322 |
| Reminder | 324 |
| Shechinah, the First of Created Beings | 325 |

| | |
|---|---|
| Shechinah, the Architect and Builder | 325 |
| The Doctrine That Shechinah Suffers With Mankind | 326 |
| Shechinah in Exile | 327 |
| The Shechinah of the Supernals and the One Exiled | 328 |
| Shechinah and the Patriarchs | 328 |
| The Shechinah in Egypt | 329 |
| The Allegory of Shechinah and the Three Husbands | 330 |
| A Diversified Version | 331 |
| Shechinah in the Temple of Solomon | 332 |
| Shechinah Did Not Forsake Israel in Exile | 333 |
| Another Version More Despairing | 334 |
| Counterstatements | 335 |
| Summation | 335 |
| Additional Particulars of the Collection about Shechinah | 336 |
| Repetition of the Theosophical Symbolism and Mysticism | 337 |
| Two Alternatives Concerning the Tree of Life | 338 |
| Shechinah and the Holy Spirit Personification | 338 |
| Is the Holy Spirit Synonymous with Shechinah or Not? | 339 |
| The Controversy Continued—The Holy Spirit, the Equivalent or Identical of Shechinah | 341 |
| The Indwelling Glory, Termed Shechinah, in Scripture and in the Text of the Zohar | 343 |
| The Sin Causing the Exile | 345 |
| Still Other Aspects of Shechinah | 345 |
| Shechinah in the Song of Songs | 346 |
| Of Communion | 347 |
| Of Spiritual Communion with Shechinah | 348 |
| 2. The Mystery of Sex and of the Generation of Souls | 350 |
| The Complete Man | 351 |
| The Nuptial State | 352 |

| | |
|---|---|
| The Mystery of Purification and Sanctification in Marriage | 353 |
| The Secret of Matrimonial Union | 354 |
| Communion between Man and Shechinah via Marriage | 359 |
| Holy Souls Which Can Become Incarnate in Jewry | 361 |
| Mystery of Espousals and the Great Mystery of Faith | 362 |
| The Forty-nine Gates of Understanding—the Gates of Compassion and Their Esoteric Metaphysics | 363 |
| The Seven Degrees and the Mystery of Perfect Faith | 365 |
| Other References and Implications of the Mystery of Faith | 366 |
| The Higher Eden River, River of the Life and of Souls | 368 |
| Further Passages on the Production of Souls | 369 |
| Another Aspect of the Mystery of Faith in the Narrative of the Soul Origin | 370 |
| The Universal History of Souls | 371 |
| The Cosmic Soul of the Gentiles | 372 |
| Of the Souls of the Ones Converted From Paganism | 372 |
| The Ten Averse Crowns | 373 |
| Of the Generation of Souls, Continued | 374 |
| Of the Union of Souls in the World to Come | 376 |
| Of the Grand Matrona Herself | 377 |
| Of Enoch/Metatron Also Called Prince of the Inner | 377 |
| The Souls and the Seven Palaces | 379 |
| About the Souls of Gentiles Converted to Judaism, Born of Celestial Mothers | 379 |
| Conclusion | 381 |

## Section IX. The Written Word of Kabbalism: Third Period—

| | |
|---|---|
| 1. Zoharic Treatises and Expositors | 385 |
|     Zoharic Expositors: Moses of Cordova | 386 |
|     Zoharic Schools in Palestine | 386 |
|     Contents of the Garden | 387 |
|     His Tract on the Soul | 387 |
|     The Simulacrum Imago | 388 |
|     Zoharic Expositors: Isaac d'Luria | 388 |
|     Significance of Rabbi Yitzhak Ashkenaazi Luria— | |
|         The Arizal Luria | 389 |
|     The Answer to Why Creation? | 389 |
|     Why Creation at That Given Time or Epoch? | 390 |
|     Emanation of Sephiroth | 391 |
|     The Three Pillars | 391 |
|     The Light of the Sephiroth | 391 |
|     Book of Concealment | 392 |
|     The Balance Principle and the Pillars | 392 |
|     Essence of Prayer | 393 |
|     The Seven Edomite Kings | 393 |
|     Fivefold Division of Souls in the Four Worlds | 394 |
|     The Fivefold Division in the Sephiroth | 394 |
|     The Prototypal Archeplastic Adam | 395 |
|     The Edomite Kings and Adam Elial | 395 |
|     Of the Fall of Man | 395 |
|     Of the Confusion of Good and Evil | 396 |
|     Of Revolution of Souls | 396 |
|     Purpose of the Revolutions of Souls | 397 |
|     Zoharic Expositors: Rabbi Naphtali Hirtz | 397 |
|     The Work: Royal Valley | 397 |
|     Of His Kabbalistic Cosmology | 398 |
|     How Creation Took Place | 398 |
|     The Light Radiation in Compression, | |
|         Expression and Formation of the World | 399 |

Zoharic Expositors: Abraham Cohen Irira 400
Zoharic Expositors: Issachar ben Naphtali 401

2. Expositions of Other Works 402
   Purifying Fire of Alchemy 402
   In Conclusion 404

# INTRODUCTION

Dr. Yisrael (Raoul) B. Nass, my late father, came to this country after the first World War as a teen-age boy. During the twenties, he studied constantly both secular and Torah studies. Basically, he studied alone. After his marriage in 1930, he returned to Switzerland to complete his medical studies.

He returned to the U.S. and began practicing medicine in the East New York section of Brooklyn. He soon began teaching a Talmud class at Congregation Bais Sholom on *Shabbos*. The *shiur* always attracted a couple of *minyanim*. It lasted three to three and a half hours. The class continued for more than four decades. The *shiur* moved from East New York to Yeshivah Rabbi Charm Berlin in Bronxville, and then to Crown Heights and East Flatbush.

During those years, Dr. Nass often added sessions in Saadya Gaon's *Beliefs and Opinions* and the Rambam's *Guide to the Perplexed.* For many years, Dr. Nass answered questions regarding medications for Passover. This was done at the behest of the Gaon Rav Henkin.

The present work is the result of 25 years of study and preparation.

Rabbi Norman Nass<br>
Brooklyn, NY

# A NOTE TO THE READERS

This book contains the very holy teachings of the Midrash Yehi Ohr, meaning, Let There Be Light, by the holy tanna, Rabbi Shimon bar Yochai.

The contents of the book also embody important excerpts of allied books that were often rendered in the form of a story, a narrative, or a parable, to make more sublime contemplation of the subject matter a probability.

Our very holy authors decreed that whosoever reads, rereads, and studies these teachings is assured of salvation and of becoming worthy of resurrection from death even in this world and of eternal life in the world to come.

So read and reread this work, dear friend, in order to leave an impression and a memory of it on your sphere of intelligence and creative spirit.

This is the essence of my appeal to you as the compiler and author of this work. Behold, it is written, "There is found, now and then, one who buys his world even in a single hour."[1]

---

1. Babylonian Talmud, Tractate *Hagigah* 15a.

Thus, invest in these ancient teachings a few hours of reading every week if at all possible.

These holy, divine teachings and writings of the Midrash Yehi Ohr and others were collected and compiled, ordered, translated, and edited with short appropriate comments as was deemed appropriate for an English speaking audience. No attempt was made however, to change the inferences of the holy teachings as they exist in their original form.

The vast majority of Zoharic references in this work refer to the so-called Greater Zohar (the Zohar haGadol), Cremona edition, and not to the presently extant and popular Lesser Zohar (the Zohar haKatan), Mantua edition.

A great many lesser tracts and small fragments embodied in the Cremona edition were entirely omitted or partly left out, or abbreviated later on by the printers of the Lesser Zohar centuries ago. Therefore our choice is the Cremona edition as the primary reference in this book of ours.

Rabbi Raoul B. Nass, M.D.

# PREFACE

The secret tradition in Israel, the kabbalah, is a form of esoteric philosophy. This claim has been admitted from time to time by persons who are entitled to our consideration.

The literature called kabbalistic rose up among the Jews during the Christian centuries immediately succeeding the destruction of the second Holy Temple and the city of Jerusalem and their dispersal from the Land.

## CONNECTIONS AND IMPORTANCE

In contrast to the sacred scriptures of Israel, kabbalism is involved and obscure as regards its outward form, and we must grind our intellectual lenses with exceeding care if we would bring it into perspective. It connects with other literatures (Midrashim), which are included like itself under the general denomination of the mystical, and in a sense, it has been considered to stand at the head of all. It is also part of the history of philosophy, and as such it entered once into the thought of Europe. It is, however, on the theosophical side and it is as a contribution to the thought of the past on problems of life and on mind, that its appeal will be found at the present day.

## DESIGN OF THE PRESENT WORK

The purpose of this manuscript is to provide an account of the kabbalah, expository and historical, and to show forth its contribution to the sacred science of the soul. These are the designs of the present work. Regard has been paid also to the limitations and requirements of those unacquainted with the languages, both ancient and modern, in which kabbalistic literature has been available heretofore (with few exceptions).

## KABBALISTIC MANUSCRIPTS PURCHASED BY MIRANDOLA

There was rumor of a great literature which had existed *ex hypothesi*, from time immemorial in Jewry, heard of historically first in Europe. This was through a single piece of good fortune that befell Picus de Mirandola in the fifteenth century when he purchased from an unknown Israelite, certain strange codices in manuscript. He was himself the pupil in Jewish Theosophy of Elias del Medigo, who filled a chair at Padua and who later wrote two treatises himself at the insistence of de Mirandola. The first of these was "On the Intellect and on Prophecy" in 1481, which was written in Hebrew and remained unprinted, as did its companion, "De Substantia Orbis." This latter manuscript appeared at Basle in 1629. It was edited with a commentary also by Isaac Reggio at Vienna in 1833.

## THE IDENTITY OF THESE MANUSCRIPTS WITH THE *SEPHER HA-ZOHAR*—THE CHIEF TEXT OF THE SECRET TRADITION IN ISRAEL

There came a time not long after this when the treasure of Picus was questioned. People began to distinguish between a false and a true Zohar; the first as the work of one Moses de Leon, belonging to the late thirteenth century, and the second as something undemonstrable in respect to age and value. The distinction remains a speculation, because no one has met with the second. However, it gives us an opportunity to state that these manuscripts purchased by Picus represented the identical work which has been known for six centuries since under the name of *Sepher Ha-Zohar*.

In 1651, the French bibliographer Jacobus Gaffarel published an index of the codices acquired by Picus. The only full translation of the Zohar into a modern language made full use of these later on.[1] There is no question that the treasures of Picus are those which we know under the distinctive name of Zohar, and it seems to have been that authoritative form which was represented later on by the Cremona and Mantua editions. To no historian tracing the bibliography of kabbalism does it appear that there is any earlier codex in manuscript.

De Mirandola must have attained all of this historical recognition in his youth, as he passed away while still in his earlier years.

---

1. *Sepher Ha-Zohar, Le Livre de la Splendor*, Doctrine Esoterique des Israélites, taduit pour la première fois, sur le text chaldaique ... par Jean de Pauly, 6 vol., 1906–1911.

## SEPHER YETZIRAH AND ITS TRANSLATION BY WILLIAM POSTEL

It was after this manner that the work began to be known in Europe. A century later, William Postel translated the Sepher Yetzirah or Book of Formation into Latin. He thus introduced to the learned of Europe the root of kabbalism, the doctrine of the *sephiroth*, the powers and virtues of the twenty-two Hebrew letters of the alef-beth, and the mystery which resides in numbers. The Sepher Yetzirah ranks as the most ancient text of accepted kabbalistic doctrine in Israel.

Picus de Mirandola is also said to have caused the Zohar to be translated into Latin. Alternatively, a Latin version was one of the manuscripts that came into his possession by purchase from the unknown Jew.

## CHRISTIAN STUDENTS OF KABBALISM

Other non-Jewish scholars of that period interested in the kabbalah were Cornelius, Agrippa, Paracelus, and John Reichlin (also known as Cadmion). The names of two Jewish converts to Christianity ought not to be omitted from the epoch of interest in the kabbalah. They were Petrus Galatinus and Paulus Riccius. All of these wrote numerous treatises and exhaustive books on kabbalistic subjects.

## VESTIGES OF A GREAT SPIRITUAL EXPERIMENT

The kabbalah as the secret theosophy of Jewry has been represented to be the channel of and to perpetuate a mystical secret tradition from an early period of mankind. It was initiated with Adam as a secret doctrine. In its depths are found vestiges of a great spiritual experiment that properly should be called the Science of the Soul in God.

The part of us that abides in God and communicates the sense of the Eternal is that which belongs to Atziluth, the most supernal world, and never leaves the supernal realm. The doctrine of *tsur* (Hebrew for "form") and the mystery of *Shechinah* ("the Divine Presence") are also great roots of kabbalism. The best and the mightiest of the older Sons of the Doctrine possessed an inner realization of a great reality. This was expressed outwardly as the Bond of Union.

## RECORDS OF A THEOSOPHICAL SCHOOL IN JEWRY

The age of the records of the antiquity of kabbalistic tradition is of large consequence on the historical side. The message of the texts at their height must be the true essence of our consideration though. Sepher Ha-Zohar belongs in the root-matter, almost certainly to times immemorial; the values and the life and essence which it embodies belong to the great spiritual deep.

# SECTION I
# *Literature of Kabbalism Historically*

CHAPTER ONE

# The Hidden Doctrines in Jewish Literature

## POST-CHRISTIAN LITERATURE OF THE JEWS

Hebrew literature developed in many of the chief centers of Europe and elsewhere following the period of the destruction of Jerusalem by Vespasian and Titus in the first century of the Common Era. Unfortunately, the details of these productive activities are beyond the scope of this reference. This involvement remained largely unknown outside the scattered remnants of the Jews though. Many would be astonished to discover that as far back as the seventeenth century, nearly four thousand Hebrew works existed, for the most part in manuscript, which were known individually and quoted by an authority on rabbinical bibliography, namely, Julius Bartholocci, in his *Bibliotheca Magna Rabbinica, Roma 1678–1692*.[1]

---

1. The work is paged from left to right, but after the Hebrew manner.

## A FIELD OF RESEARCH PROBING THE DEPTH OF THE HUMAN MIND

Almost every conceivable department of human learning and intellectual activity is represented in this literature, which in matters secular just as in things sacred, have the seal of the sanctity of Israel upon all their leaves.

It is an extremely curious and a profound literature which translation has done little to make known, and which is represented incompletely enough even in the great and authoritative textbooks of Jewish history.[2] It is indeed an undiscovered country, still awaiting its Columbus; a land full of wealth and mystery, of strange shrines and sanctuaries shining weirdly far away through the darkness of our ignorance, with a light which reveals a glimpse of the magnificent radiance of Shechinah.

## A SECRET RELIGIOUS TRADITION PERPETUATED FROM THE PAST

Within this literature there is another and stranger literature, the report of which has been among us for several centuries. This storehouse of Hebrew theosophy has exercised peculiar fascination on many great minds. Its gentile students were at one time as keen, if not as numerous, as its Jewish disciples were. In its entirety, it is simply called the kabbalah. The word derives from that which means reception. This title purports that the knowledge embodied in this literature has been transmitted orally from generation to generation. The literature as it exists is the tradition put into writing.

---

2. The work of Dr. Moritz Steinschneider, the bibliographer of rabbinical literature, is perhaps the most important contribution made during recent years.

## THE SECRET DOCTRINE OF KABBALISM AND ITS DOMAINS

The kabbalah claims to be the light of a secret traditional knowledge. One of the titles ascribed to it was *Chokhmat Nistar*—secret wisdom; the initials of these words gave another title, signifying Grace (*chayn*). The recipients of this knowledge were termed *mikubbalim*. The topics of which it is concerned are both sacred and divine. These include the most profound mysteries of God and the emanations of Deity, the celestial economy, the process of creation, the scheme of providence in regard to man, the communication of God in revelation to the just in his church, and the offices and ministries of good and evil angels. Also included are the nature and pre-existence of the soul, its union with matter and its metempsychosis, the mystery of sin and its penalties, the Messiah and his kingdom and his glory to be revealed, the state of the soul after death, and the resurrection of the dead. There are also occasional intimations on the union of the soul and God. Here, if anywhere, is the abiding part, rooted in everlasting values, of the one voice of an old tradition, which bears a message from the past to the modern world.

## KABBALISTIC PHILOSOPHY: A DOCTRINE OF RELIGIOUS TRADITION

The kabbalah is the hidden thought of Israel upon doctrines of Jewish Religion, upon the proper understanding of the Written Word, which is referred to a Divine origin and instruction. Needless to say that by a literature so considerable in its capacity there are many other subjects embraced. But, the kabbalah, in a word, is the hidden thought of Israel upon doctrine of Jewish religion, and upon the proper understanding of that Written Word, which is referred to a Divine origin in Jewry by this esoteric tradition.

I have taken it as it is essentially, namely, a storehouse of affirmed Secret Doctrine; and for the use of students of all Secret Doctrine do I design to present it, so to speak. Its most important aspects here are for the purpose of ascertaining whether it conveys an understanding of things, which when considered in their true light, are merely as of the moment to us here and now as true mystics.

## TO THE ESOTERIC STUDENT

I shall be glad if those whom I address will be content to believe on my testimony, that the Zohar, being the text in chief is one of the greatest books of the world. It is one that stands alone and is comparable to nothing save itself. I am embodying an account of its essence therefore on the great subjects of its concern.

## NO *SCIENTIA KABBALISTICA*

I should wish to exclude from the auditorium those who understand *scientia kabbalistica* as an art of making, consecrating, and using talismans and amulets as a magical mystery concerning the power of divine names, or as source and authentication of grimoirs and ceremonial rituals of evocation.

They will do better to go elsewhere for enlightenment. Here is no *Guide to the Perplexed* in the paths of occult arts. I mention this matter because there is a debased kabbalism, improperly so-called, which deals in these putative mysteries and claims some roots in the past as if it belonged to the authentic tradition of Israel, when it is not even a reflection.

## MAGICAL AND PRACTICAL KABBALAH

The magical kabbalah is not to be confused with what is sometimes called the practical kabbalah, in which are included the artificial methods of gematria, notankon, and temurah, which are principles of exegetical interpretation. These methods are old. About the magical kabbalah, the antiquity must be left unsettled; however, regarding its folly and iniquity, there must be no question.

## OF THE SECRET DOCTRINE

The Secret Doctrine was judged to be inseparable from the literal or written word; it was developed to deepen its meaning and to extend its office. In illustration of this, there is one similitude, which says that the Written Doctrine (the Pentateuch) is the candle or lamp, while the Oral Law is the flame. The thesis was that the written word of Scripture, in every passage and syllable was the word of the Living God.

The Secret Doctrine is of course broadly and generally, a method of interpreting Scripture. It is only as if casually though, that it can be held to apply to Scripture. In any solid sense, the Secret Doctrine is rather the interpretation beneath the sense that is found in the literal word itself.

## OF LITERAL VESTURE AND THE ESOTERIC

There are difficult words used from time to time concerning the simple sense of interpretation, and these should not be taken too seriously. The letters by themselves were always considered precious even as they exist in isolation. However, the difference of that within the word and that which is upon the surface only is well illustrated by a similitude. This states that those who interpret Scripture according to the literal sense set the sacred King and His Bride upon an ass, while those who understand it according to the mystic sense, mount them nobly upon a horse.

The Zohar gives another illustration when it says that the Oral Law enlightens the Written Law. This notwithstanding, the two belong to one another because the Written Law is completed by that which is traditional, and the latter issues from the former, as woman was brought forth from man.

In another place the Written Law is designated under the name of heaven, while the Oral Law is called earth. What is signified may be an obscure counterchange, in virtue of correspondences between things above and below, and this is a recurring Zoharic doctrine (Zohar I, 247b).

Those teachings that are oral are called the voice of the turtledove, and these come from the side of mercy. It is also known as the green wood, in contrast to the literal law, which is dry wood, coming from the side of judgment. A further instance of the unity in both is laid down, that there are three things which are at once hidden and revealed, these being God, the Law, and Israel themselves. The vulgar man sees only the material side, but the initiate discerns also that which is embedded within it.

## THE ANCIENT OF DAYS

To conclude upon these analogies: the manifested part bears no comparison with that which is contained within; that which is essential is called the soul of Scripture; the commandments are its body and the tales are the garments thereof. This is in the World below, while in that which is above, the Ancient of Days is the Soul of Soul in the Law. The soul is that mystery which is called the beauty of Israel; the body is the community of the elect, while the garments are heaven and its regions.

## OF THE PENTATEUCH'S STORIES

"Cursed be he," says the text, "who pretends that the recital of Scripture has no other meaning than that which appears on the surface." If this were the case, Scripture would not be the Law of Truth, the Holy Law, and the Perfect Witness, precious beyond gold and jewels. If it contained only such vulgar elements and simple stories such as of Esau, Hagar, Laban, and of Bilaam's ass, it might be possible to produce something better, apart from all inspiration, in just the same manner as secular books.

## SIXTY METHODS AND SEVENTY MODES OF INTERPRETATION

The truth, however, is that every word of Scripture enshrines a supreme mystery, and upon it, even sixty methods of interpretation exist. Another statement concurs in seventy modes to interpreting Scripture. All of these are true in their results; for the variations of inward meanings are numberless, and all may be true by analogy, though some are brighter jewels, while the pearls of greatest price may be few enough though. For this reason, no doubt, it has been testified that the original Zohar was at least a camel's load.

## THE SUPPLEMENTARY SOUL

It is said that the inner sense of the Law is not less concealed than the world from which it emanates. Those who apply themselves to its study receive as their inheritance the future world (the world to come) as well as that of Jacob, for it is the path of the life beyond. Consecration to the Secret Doctrine brings down what is called the supplementary soul, which is attributed frequently to all pious children of Israel who observe the Sabbath in the plenary sense.

It would seem that true sons of the Doctrine are in permanent enjoyment of this added part though. The soul is brought down by the voices of they who study the Secret Doctrine and it emanates from the land of the living, making him or her whom it overshadows, equal to the angels. When it is said in Psalms, "Bless the Lord, you His angels," the reference is to those who study the Doctrine and are called God's angels on earth. In the world to come, they will have wings like those of the eagle.

Hyperbolically, it is said, however, that the study of the Law succeeds only in the case of him who kills himself for the Law, meaning that it is a path of poverty and a poor man is considered as one who is dead.

## THE FIFTY GATES

Against this, however, he who is dedicated to the study of the Law opens the fifty gates of *Binah,* corresponding to the letter *yod.* This represents the sign of the Covenant and therefore of the male principle, multiplied by the letter *hai,* the letter of Shechinah, which is the letter of the female principle, which produces fruit. The multiplication in question alludes to the generations of the mind as the fruit of study of Divine research.

## THE DOCTRINE MORE ANCIENT THAN THE WORLD

If the next question be how did the Secret Doctrine originate, the answer seems, that it was before the Creation—with God. The sense must be that it was implied in "Elohim," whose image it is. Another explanation is, that it is on the side of mercy, and by mercy the world was made. We find moreover that God created the world by joining thereto the Secret Doctrine. The world was founded thereon.

## BERESHITH AND THE SECRET DOCTRINE

The word *Bereshith* with which Genesis opens, has been rendered sometimes "in wisdom," not "in the beginning," and it is said to signify the Secret Doctrine and its part in the work of creation. The scriptural allusion is "The Lord possessed me in the beginning of His way, before His works of old. I was set up from everlasting from the beginning, or ever the earth was."[3]

It will be observed, that this is personified Wisdom, testifying on her own part. This, it affirms, was the kind of beginning, in which God created the Heaven and earth; the basis of which is His covenant. Hence it is said also: "If the covenant which I have made existed not, there would be neither day nor night, neither heaven nor earth, and I would not have appointed, the ordinances of heaven and earth. . . ."[4] The allusion made to the covenant and the application of the text by the Zohar in this particular connection have been mentioned only to indicate the seemingly eternal pre-existence of the Secret Doctrine.

## ORIGIN OF THE DOCTRINE

After what manner was the Doctrine brought down to earth and to the knowledge of the elect? The thesis of possession and successive custody deepens from a narrative of paradise and this in its turn arises from the scriptural reference to a Book of the Generations of Adam.[5] It is supposed by the Zohar to signify that there was a secret and supreme book, the source of all, including the Hebrew letters. It expounded the Holy Mystery of Wisdom and the efficiency resident in the Divine Name of seventy-two letters. It was sent down from heaven by the hands of the angel Raziel, and Adam was entrusted there-

---

3. Proverbs 8:22–23.
4. Jeremiah 33:25–26.
5. Genesis 1.

with. Raziel is said to be the angel of the secret regions and chief of Supreme Mysteries (Zohar I, 55b).

There is a narrative of an old Midrash called the Book of Raziel, which is said to have been developed by Rabbi Eliezer of Worms. There is also an impostor of ceremonial magic that passes under this same name.

## ADAM'S GIFT BOOK

This gift book placed Adam in a superior position to that of any celestial being. Adam was made acquainted in this manner with supernal Wisdom, and the celestial choirs came down to be present when he read the book. He was cautioned, however, to conceal it and he seems to have studied it in silence (Zohar I, 55b).

The Sacred Name of seventy-two letters was explained in the "Genesis of Man" by means of six-hundred-seventy mysteries which it contains. The mystery of *hochmah* discovered the fifteen hundred keys, which are not entrusted to any celestial being.

## LOSS OF THE BOOK

When Adam, his advantages notwithstanding, fell ultimately into sin and was driven out of the Garden of Eden, the book was still clasped in his hands, but thereafter it vanished, and for long and long he lamented the loss of his treasure. Ultimately it was given back to him, in answer to his tears and prayers, by the angel Raphael.

The variant account (Zohar I, 55b) says that he smote his forehead when the work vanished and plunged to his neck in the river Gichon (Genesis 2:13). The result was that all his body was covered with wrinkles so that he was no more recognizable.

He returned to its study and bequeathed it to his son

Seth, who entrusted it to later messengers, so that the Secret Doctrine might be spread through the world.

It became known as the Book of Enoch after passing through the hands of that patriarch.

There are several Enochian narratives that offer curious points in themselves. According to one account, Enoch became the great archangel Metatron; according to another he was exalted to high heavens and made guardian of their treasures, including the forty-five keys to the combination of graven letters (Zohar I, 56b). An apocalyptic book of Enoch, believed to be a Hebrew text in its original state, has been known in an Ethiopian translation since the year 1778.

## ABRAHAM AND MOSES RECIPIENTS

It is said that Abraham penetrated the glory of his Master by means of the mysteries of this Book of Adam. After Abraham we hear nothing of this secret text. It was a treasure of the patriarchal age.

The external law and the Secret Doctrine were both revealed on Mount Sinai and as Moses transmitted the one to his nation at large, so he communicated the other to certain elders by whom it was handed on.

## AFTER MOSES AND DAVID

The whole secret knowledge came down to the Zoharic period under the darkening of successive clouds. It is said that at the death of Moses the sun was eclipsed and that the written law lost its splendor. At the hours of King David's death, the light of the moon diminished and the Oral Law was tarnished. The consequence was that discussions and controversies began among the sages of the Mishnah, so that joy in the study of the Law ceased for all future generations (Zohar II, 156a). It was pursued previously in clear and full light, and there was that unanimity which comes from certitude among the sons of the Doctrine. Afterward though, it was followed from afar in a state of doubt and separation, amidst wrangling of the schools, who saw only as in a glass and darkly.

Occasionally, new glimpses of light broke forth, as in the days of Ezekiel and others, but those measures were not displayed before doctors who, whatever their zeal and sincerity, were unable to understand them at their proper worth (Zohar II, 5a; III, 19).

## DAYS OF RABBI SHIMON

It was otherwise in the days of Rabbi Shimon, for the glory of the mystic light was at its zenith in him, and he was the revealer in chief of the Zohar's doctrines. The Zohar exalts this master of wisdom above all. It is added, that from the day Rabbi Shimon came out of his cavern, the mysteries were secrets no longer for the colleagues, because the Hidden Doctrine had become no less familiar unto them, than it was to their precursors when it was revealed on Mount Sinai.

## INCOMPLETENESS OF THE DOCTRINE

But when the time came for this great sun to set, in the hours of the master's death and afterward, his disciples and successors sought to produce the words, which they heard from his lips, and the attempt proved a failure; only vestiges remained. But notwithstanding the incompleteness of the Doctrine, it is incorruptible gold, and even its shards are priceless (Zohar I, 216b).[6]

The mystic knowledge of the secret doctrine constitutes the jewels of the Heavenly Bride; its study adorns the Bride

---

6. Note: The reference to the outgoing of the cavern is to be found in the Babylonian Talmud tract *Sabbath*, 33b.

of Heaven with jewels. But it adorns also the souls of its students with all manners of graces and sanctities; their desert is far above anything that follows on mere works. Those who study the Doctrine are set free of all fear, because they are grafted on the Tree of Life and are taught daily thereby. The Divine Doctrine cannot be studied without imparting love for the Divine, so that the fear of God, which is the beginning of Wisdom, is being absorbed by the love of God, which is wisdom in realization, having the awareness of God in the heart. It is also said to lead into the way of truth so that the soul may learn how to return to its master.

It is further added, that he who forsakes the study of the Doctrine is not less guilty than if he separated himself from the Tree of Life, for he is leading the life of separation (Zohar I, 11a).

It seems a counsel to those who would study the secret Doctrine, that there is needed a conscious union by intention, contemplation, and the art of finding in the heart and mind of the student to concur in an ineffable union, which is said to be consummated above.

As to the nature of the ineffable union, we know that the night thereof is the eternal Oneness, in that Divine Darkness, which is otherwise called *Ohr Ain Soph*, the limitless and undifferentiated light. The union there is in a still rest and the changeless simplicity, being infinite and eternal therein.

It will be seen that the sons of the Doctrine were only remotely, and as if by accident, concerned with reserving an arbitrary understanding of this written word in Israel. In short, that there was something which imposed a reasonable and even a zealous reserve, because it was preeminently one of those matters, which the unprepared and sensual mind would wrest to its own destruction. It has furthermore been necessary at this initial stage, to establish the root fact of a Secret Doctrine to justify the long research that follows.

CHAPTER TWO

# Kabbalah as Secret Tradition and a Cryptic Philosophy

The kabbalah claims to be tradition, long-received in secret by one generation from another and reduced at length into writing because of the bad state of affairs of Israel after the destruction of Jerusalem. It is to be expected that its literary methods will offer difficulties to the ordinary student. It has indeed proved unintelligible, upon the surface, in some of its developments. Only a few claimed that they have penetrated to its real sense; they found pleasure in believing, that it is sealed to uninitiated persons, for whom it remains a matter of unrewarded research, though not wanting perhaps in some gleams of unexpected suggestion.

Kabbalah is thus declared to be a cryptic philosophy and its philosophical speculations and metaphysics claim concealment through cryptography. True enough to be sure, kabbalistic theosophy does certainly constitute a methodized ingenuity system, which is curiously inwrought, at least in its later developments as an esoteric philosophy.

Theosophy in its widest meaning denotes the seeking of evidence for the existence of a knowledge, which in effect is hidden science, handed down from remote ages; which knowledge concerns an exposition of the relations between God, man, and the universe.

From this standpoint the true message of the kabbalah is not exegetical or historical. It is of a living and spiritual kind. We shall also see that the kabbalah has been a channel of old tradition.

# CHAPTER THREE

# The Kabbalah and the Talmud

### ANTIQUITY OF KABBALAH AND TALMUD

To understand the place occupied by the kabbalah, it is necessary to say something of that great and authoritative collection, which is known to everyone as the Talmud, a large and an ancient growth. Its starting point has been placed as before the beginning of the Common Era, and its two canons were said to have been less or more fixed in the fourth and sixth centuries.

Some writers ascribe a similar antiquity to the kabbalah. In reality the kabbalah originated among the Jews five centuries before our Common Era, at the epoch of the Babylonian captivity. It was elaborated silently, but it did not attain its definite development until the period of Philo and the Schools of Alexandria. Nevertheless, there are some writers who insist that although there are certain traces in the Talmudic literature of a more esoteric doctrine, it cannot be shown that kabbalistic literature in the form of a Secret Tradition in Jewry had as yet come into existence in writing at these periods. Though some of them do admit a root matter connected with the name of Rabbi Shimon and regarded as his as their source.

## THE MATERIALS OF THE TALMUD

To put it shortly, the sources of the Talmud are said to be the regulations and customs practiced by the authorities in their administration of religious and civil affairs. This source, it is claimed, goes back to the period of Israel's Second Commonwealth. Some of the materials embodied in the literature are of older origin than others. These were certain *Mishnayoth* or repetitions, namely, academically inclined teachings.

In the *Halachoth Olam*, it is said that Jewish teachers had little scrolls of parchment in which they set down all the traditions, sentences, statutes, decisions, and similar, which they learned from their masters; these scrolls were called the volumes of things secret. The work in question is an introduction to Talmudic dialectic and formulae. The author was R. Jescivah ben Joseph HaLevi, a Castillian, who flourished about 1467 and before. It was printed originally at Constantinople in 1510.[1]

## COMPILATION METHOD

Prior to 220 the Common Era, a considerable proportion was engarnered by Rabbi Judah the Prince, the third patriarch of the Western Jews, by whom they were methodized carefully; short comments of his own being added occasionally. He endeavored to suppress all rival Mishnayoth, but some of them were preserved and came to light after his death.[2]

---

1. Metaphorically, this work is alluded to in Habakkuk, iii, 6.

2. For an old account of this labor, see David Ganz, *Germen Davidis*, Leyden, 1644.

A legend says that having converted the Emperor Marcus Aurelius, he compiled the Mishnah at the insistence of that prince. He has been called popularly the Redactor of the Mishnah. He flourished circa 135–220.

## FORMS OF THE MISHNAH

In this way we have:

> a. The Mishnah, or Repetition, the methodized selection of Rabbi Judah the Prince.
>
> b. The Tosephtoth, or Additions, called also Baraithoth, outsiders, or secondary matter, that is, extravagances, in the sense that is of things extraneous; terms applied to the rival Mishnayoth by the followers of Rabbi Judah. These competitive claims were harmonized ultimately by later Rabbis.
>
> c. Thus arose the Gemara, that is, conclusion and completion. It may be noted that the term *gemara* came into use also as a description of the Talmud.

## GEMARA AND TALMUD

The union of the Gemara and of the Mishnah forms the Talmud, from a word signifying "to teach." Strictly speaking, the term Talmud applies only to the Gemara, but it has obtained the wider application, because the Mishnah, the text being essential to the notes, always accompanies the Gemara.

## THE TWO TALMUD VERSIONS

There are two versions of the Talmud, the Mishnah being the same in each.

1. The Gemara collected by Jerusalem Rabbis, representing the school of Tiberias and R. Yochanon ben Eliezer (ob. 279 CE), with the Mishnah forms the Jerusalem Talmud (the Palestinian Talmud). It belongs to the end of the fourth century.

2. The Gemara collected by Babylonian Rabbis, and especially by Rabbina (ob. circa 420 CE), Reb Ashi (353–427 CE), and R. Yosi. These, with the Mishnah, form the Talmud of Babylon, four times larger than that of Jerusalem; the proportion of the Babylonian Gemara to the original Mishnah being about eleven to one. It was begun in the fifth and completed in the sixth century. Additional material was gathered into it subsequently to this period.

## JURISPRUDENCE AND SOCIOLOGY OF THE TALMUD

By the hypothesis of both literatures the Talmud is kabbalah, even as the Zohar is kabbalah, because both are matters of reception by tradition. We see this even from nontraditional sources.

"In older Jewish literature, the name kabbalah is applied to the whole body of received religious doctrine with the exception of the Pentateuch, thus including the Prophets and Hagiographa, as well as the oral traditions ultimately embodied in the Mishnah."[3]

But to say that the Talmud is kabbalistic in the sense of the Zohar is extremely misleading. The two cycles are distinct and indeed divergent. The nature of the tradition is generi-

---

3. *American Encyclopedia*, III, pp. 521, 522.

cally different. The Talmud is not in any sense of the term a theosophical system. The philosophical doctrines of the kabbalah have no place therein. For example, the sephirotic system and the theory of the emanation, which it suggests, are not found in the Talmud.

The Talmud is the construction placed by authority on the jurisprudence, ecclesiastical and political, of old Israel. It is essentially sociology, not metaphysics, even if it has admitted some metaphysics and has some accretions which might be termed mystical. The Talmud became the asylum of some mystical and metaphysical traditions, but it is not mysticism; the way of entrance was the haggadic morality.

## METAPHYSICS OF THE KABBALAH

The literature of the kabbalah discusses the Mysteries of the Supreme Crown, the evolution of withdrawn "Divine Subsistence" into positive being, the emanation or forthcoming of the sephiroth, and the origin of metempsychosis, and destiny of souls and the like. It treats of many philosophical speculations. The Zohar gave to Israel the splendid impulsion of the ideal; it gave philosophy; it communicated the eternal.

## SOME ENIGMATIC METAPHYSICS IN TALMUD

The Talmud contains, however, allegorical interpretations of the Bible. If we find in the Talmud reminiscences of the kabbalah, they concern, so to speak, the exoteric portion or angelology. Existence of the speculative part is shown in the Talmud and the midrashic commentaries on the Bible, solely by the reference to the mysteries contained in Bereshith or the first chapters of Genesis, and in the Merkavah, or vision of Ezekiel.

These are the Talmudic references to the "work" of creation and the work of the chariot. They are referred to, however, only enigmatically. While the Talmud records occasionally that there were conversations between the doctors (sages) of Israel thereon, it does not report the utterances, and the real nature of the tradition does not transpire.

The Talmud is further on traditionally divided into two portions: Halacha, the legislative enactments of the fathers, which alone is law; and Haggada, free interpretation, a collection of miscellaneous utterances, touching on every possible subject. Halacha is rule, the norm. Haggada is legend, saga. Haggadic legends possess an inner meaning; that is, they may be allegorical stories. It is to be noted that the Zohar describes Halacha, Mishnah, and Gemara as heavy and involved. The Mishnah in particular is likened to a hard rock (Zohar I, 276).

## DIVISIONS AND CONTENTS OF THE MISHNAH AND GEMARA IN SHORT

The Mishnah comprises six sections. The first concerns tithes, beasts which it is unlawful to pair, the seeds which must not be sown together in the earth, the threads which must not be interwoven, the fruits which must not be gathered until the trees have passed their third year, and similarly diverse but related matters. It is by no means exclusively agricultural.

The second order (arrangement or section of books) concerns the festivals of Israel; the meats which are prohibited on these, the days of fasting, and myriad other related matters.

The third book deals with marriage and divorce.

The fourth book embodies a consideration of civil contracts, general jurisdiction, civil and criminal actions, penalties, and similar to these.

The fifth section is dedicated to votive offerings.

The sixth order treats matters of purification. In essence the Mishnah is traditional commentary on the legislative part of the Mosaic Torah. The Gemara is completely wanting in the fifth section from the Palestinian Talmud, and it likewise has only fragments of the sixth. Many Mishnaic treatises are wanting in the Babylonian collection, and of many it is the Gemara that is wanting.[4]

## CONCLUSIVE DISTINCTIONS BETWEEN KABBALAH AND TALMUD

The kabbalah and the Zohar are purely speculative thought, metaphysical and theosophical, while the Talmud deals with everyday life and humanity under the Law. Kabbalah starts from a spiritual point of view, contemplating a spiritual finality as regards the Law and its explanation. The Talmud is innately practical, in both its starting point and end. In the face of ignorance, want of perception, and natural waywardness, it has nothing but the strict observance of the Law in all its manifest detail in view.

## MESORAH AND KABBALAH

The term *mesorah* is often confused by some with kabbalah, since mesorah, they say, signifies also tradition. Some claimed that the Jews applied the terms mesorah and kabbalah to one and the same science in ancient times.

These statements are utterly erroneous. Mesorah is rather the criticism of the Hebrew biblical text.

The mesorah is really the converse of the kabbalah. The mesorah is that which was openly delivered by the rabbis; the kabbalah is that which was secretly and mysteriously received by the disciple.

---

4. See the *Jewish Encyclopedia*, vol. xii, s.v. Talmud.

CHAPTER FOUR

# Divisions of the Kabbalah

## KABBALAH CONFUSED WITH CEREMONIAL MAGIC

There are some further false impressions that it is necessary to remove before we can proceed with our subject. For some popular writers and encyclopedias the kabbalistic "art" is simply the use of sacred names in the evocation of spirits. What is termed the kabbalah, they conveyed, is the art of conversing with elementary spirits; or it was to them that, at least above all. Sometimes they united it closely with astrology, and to speak of this occult art was considered equivalent as to speaking of kabbalistic matters.

## DISTINCTIONS BETWEEN CEREMONIAL RITUAL AND KABBALAH

It must be admitted that the term kabbalah was applied early in its history to some forms of medieval magical practice. Thus kabbalah was confused with ceremonial magic. These practices, however, are either late or corrupt derivatives, which are not the esoteric tradition and philosophy. Rather, they are accidents thereof. If we do admit that there were magical practices prevalent among the Hebrews at a remote period and are therefore entitled to be classed in a sense as kabbalah, then these must be distinguished very carefully from the true kabbalah with which we are concerned here. Kabbalah is neither demonology nor theurgy.

## THEURGY, TALISMANS, AND KABBALAH

The tradition of the Sefer Yetzirah, or Book of Formation, and of the Book of Splendor, the Zohar, is not of magic but of theosophy; so, at least until a further stage of our inquiry we shall ignore the kabbalah of magic.

Instead, we shall deal in part with an attempted explanation of the universe and of the origin, nature, and destiny of the human soul. Whereas the theurgic and talismanic use of the Divine Name, and the doctrine of efficacious words belong to a distinct category in Jewish theosophy, they were, however, notions known since antiquity. The essence of Zoharic theosophy must be held distinct therefrom.

## GEMATRIA, NOTARIKON, TEMURAH

The subject matter of the secret tradition is also confused with certain exegetical methods by which a scriptural authority is found for a secret sense of a scriptural letter. These methods must be held distinct from kabbalah. They were, however, matters of reception, and as such are kabbalah; but they are not the doctrinal kabbalah that deals with cosmogony and theology.

These exegetical traditional methods by which a secret sense was extracted from the letter of Holy Scripture comprise three basic traditions. The first is gematria, a cryptographic system by which the letters of a word were converted into numbers and the arithmetical value was used to explain its internal sense. Second is notarikon, which is described as a system of shorthand by which each letter of a word was taken as the initial of another word, thus throwing light on the sentence. Third is the temurah or exchange which is the transposition of letters in a given word or sentence. These devices are met with comparatively seldom in the Zohar.

Their antiquity, however, is well established. The official Aramaic translation, or Targum to the Prophets in the days of King Herod, for example, has recourse occasionally to a variety of transliteration devices when dealing with certain obscure scriptural names. This Targum is known traditionally under the name of its author, Reb Yonathan ben Uziel, a disciple of Hillel the Great.

Thus, in the interest of clearness, the conventional term of kabbalah is applied only in the philosophical traditions as embodied in the Sepher Yetzirah and in the Zohar editions.

The mystics divide the kabbalah, in two ways: the Doctrine of Creation and the Doctrine of the Throne or Chariot, that is, the Chariot of Ezekiel's Vision.

These two divisions are mentioned in the Mishnah by name Maaseh Bereshith and Maaseh Merkavah, and both are said to be secret doctrines. The Zohar identified the Merkavah with the sephiroth or ten emanations, which will be examined at a future stage.

These two divisions are concerned respectively with the natural and the metaphysical world. In a broad sense it may be said that Sepher Yetzirah embodies the doctrine of creation, while Sepher Ha-Zohar embodies that of the chariot. While the Zohar is our chief source of tradition on chariot theosophy, it is also full of mythology about the creation. Both are termed the theoretical kabbalah.

It should be added that outside the cycle of the Zohar, there is a considerable Jewish theosophical and mystical literature.

SECTION II

# Source and Authority of the Kabbalah

CHAPTER ONE

# Age of the Chief Texts

We have to ascertain whether and how far we are warranted by evidence in regarding the texts, which embody the secret tradition in Israel, as authentic memorials and its doctrines as a part of a tradition perpetuated in Israel from early times.

We shall for this purpose conveniently divide the literature into four classes: 1) the Book of Formation, 2) the commentaries on that work preceeding the public appearance of the Zohar, 3) the Zohar itself, 4) the writings subsequent thereto.

## HISTORICAL DATA

The report of an esoteric secret tradition in Israel did not begin to circulate through the countries until the fourteenth century. This is explained by the fact that the chief collection of its archives was generally unknown in Jewry until about 1290 CE. This collection is termed by kabbalists the Work of the Chariot, represented by the Zohar.

The Work of Creation on the other hand, to which the Sepher Yetzirah corresponds, was known as far back as the ninth century and before.

Maimonides in his *Guide of the Perplexed* explains that Maaseh Bereshith corresponds to physical science and Maaseh Merkavah to metaphysical.

## SEPHER YETZIRAH OF ABRAHAM THE PATRIARCH

The Sepher Yetzirah is supposed to embody a tradition handed down from the time of Abraham, and the Patriarch is represented as its author. The fifth chapter of the Book mentions "Abraham our father." R. Judah Ha Levi of the twelfth century speaks of "the Book of the Creation," which "belongs to our father Abraham." It was observed that it is properly a monologue on the part of Abraham, in which, by the contemplation of all that is around him, he ultimately attains the conviction of the unity of God.

## THE TANNA RABBI AKIVA, AUTHOR OF THE SEPHER YETZIRAH

That Abraham received the document and transmitted it was held undoubtedly, but the work itself, it is held, was not reduced to writing until after the destruction of Jerusalem, and tradition ascribes its formal authorship to Rabbi Akiva ben Joseph.

Ben Joseph was the leading tanna of the Period which followed immediately on the destruction of the temple. A tanna was a teacher of the Oral Law.

Rabbi Akiva is said to have perished in the Bar Kochba rebellion 120 CE, but this is wrong. Evidence points to his martyrdom twelve years later for transgressing the edict of Hadrian against the practice of the Jewish religion. He was the head of the Palestinian Jews at the close of the first century and in the beginning years of the second.

Rabbi Akiva was a speculator, with whose notions the scheme of the Sepher Yetzirah seems to be in complete accordance. He is the reputed author of another work as well dealing with the mysteries of the Hebrew alphabet. It is called the *Alphabet of Rabbi Akiva*, being the letters allegorically explained. An early edition of "the Aleph-bait" appeared in Venice 1546 (Bartolocci iv. 274).

In interpreting Holy Scripture, Rabbi Akiva followed the principles of Hillel the Great, a high authority among the scribes in the days of King Herod. Rabbi Akiva promulgated the doctrine that every sentence, word, and particle in the Bible has its use and meaning. To him is also attributed the arrangement and the redaction of the Halacha.

Subsequent generations were so impressed by his marvelous knowledge of divine things that he was asserted to have discovered much of which even Moses was ignorant.

## BOOK OF FORMATION KNOWN TO ARCHBISHOP AGOBARD OF LYONS, 850 CE

The Sepher Yetzirah seems to have been known in France, especially so to St. Agobard, Archbishop of Lyons (see Basnoge: *Histoire de Juifs*, pp. 1493–94 or Tayour's English translation of Basnage: *History of the Jews*, p. 590 et seq, London, 1708).

The evidence is confined to two short passages in the Epistola S. Agobardi "De Judaicis Superstionionibus." In the first, the Jews are branded for their gross notions of the Deity on the ground that they believe Him to be possessed of a bodily form, having distinct members and lineaments, including organs of seeing and hearing, speaking, and similar. Also, that they note only one difference between the body of God and that of man, who is in His image, that the fingers are inflexible, because God effects nothing with His hands. Agobard seems to draw here from the descriptions of the body of God.

In the second passage it is said, "Further, they believe the letters of their alphabet to have existed from everlasting and before the beginning of the World to have received diverse offices, in virtue of which they should preside over created things" (Agobard, opera *Omnia Patrologiae* cursus completus, accurate J. P. Migne, Paris 1851, p. 78). It appears to indicate an acquaintance with Sepher Yetzirah, though deviously misconstruing its meaning, or is alternatively a reference to Akiva's alphabet. It is affirmed that Agobard quotes almost verbatim from the Alphabet. Since literature traveled slowly in those days, it creates a presumption that these were in existence much earlier.

## SEPHER YETZIRAH IN THE TALMUD

The Sepher Yetzirah is mentioned in both Talmuds in connection with the doctrine that heaven and earth were created by a mysterious combination of letters. We must concede that it came into circulation within a measurable distance of the stormy period in which the great Talmudic canons reached their term.

Sepher Yetzirah is also mentioned in the tractate *Sanhedrin* of the Babylonian Talmud, folio 65b and elsewhere.

These references demonstrate the existence of a work reserved to a few. Now then, this work is identical with the Sepher Yetzirah as we now have it. Such is also the unequivocal opinion of the historian Franck in his *La kabbale,* Paris, 1843, p. 75.

## CONCLUSIONS

The Sepher Yetzirah contains the doctrine of an occult power and sanctity inherent in certain divine names, and we know that this belief is very old in humanity and of great antiquity. It may well go back to the Patriarch Abraham in Chaldea as claimed. It is certainly though found at a very early period.

We must allow that this most ancient document of kabbalism does embody something of a tradition of the past from the period of the Babylonian captivity as the Talmud itself indicates.

Phineas Mordell in the *Jewish Quarterly Review, 1913* quotes a tradition that Sepher Yetzirah was written by Joseph ben Uziel. The Hebrew historical works *Chain of Tradition,* and *Order of the Generations* set forth the same claim, the latter adding that there were two Books of Formation and that said Joseph ben Uziel was a disciple of the Prophet Jeremiah.

It should be added that the Sepher Yetzirah is part of a considerable literature of an occult and cryptic complexion, covering the period between the Talmudic age and the first report of the Zohar.

CHAPTER TWO

# Modern Criticism of the Book of Splendor

We shall proceed now to the several problems connected with the Book of Splendor. Chief among these are the questions: 1) Is one modern criticism right in ascribing the Zohar to the thirteenth century and to R. Moses Shem Tob de Leon as its author? 2) Have we evidence that its doctrine was in existence, at a much earlier period, namely at the time of the Roman Emperor Antonius?

### ATTITUDE AND CONTRARIETY OF ARISTOTELIANS AND THEIR ANTAGONISTS

We shall get no help from modern historians in Israel. They possessed no insight.

The Sepher Yetzirah was known and accepted before documentary criticism had been conceived or born. So, when the Zohar was promulgated it was among a mixed audience, who either took or rejected it a priori.

Those who loathed the yoke of Aristotle, these claimed and maintained its integrity. Abraham ben David HaLevi (ob. circa 1126 CE), Abraham ben Meir Ibn Ezra (circa 1092–1167), and Moses Maimonides (1131–1201) would have placed on the neck of Jewry, accorded it a glad welcome. It harmonized with their peculiar aspirations. On the other hand the Aristotelians hated it because it did not consort with their methods.

The following excerpts best show the contrariety of the two factions.

Isaac Meyer writes in his *Philosophy of Ibn Gebirol*, "Its opponents were almost universally Jewish Aristotelians, who opposed the ancient secret learning of the Israelites because it was more in accord with the philosophy of Plato and Pythagoras. Indeed, most likely it emanated from the same sources, the Aryan and Chaldean esoteric doctrine." We must remember that the Patriarch Abraham taught in ancient Chaldea. Also, it is the fact only, which is of value to us, and not Meyer's explanation.

Gould, in his *History of Freemasonry* writes, "When the Saracens became the patrons of philosophy and attention was given to the writings of Aristotle, this excited the emulation of the Jews, who continued in their philosophical course, reading Aristotle in Hebrew translations from the inaccurate Arabic."[1]

## DEFENSE OF ZOHAR BY RECENT THINKERS

It is not until recent times that we have at all any intelligent defense on the part of some Jewish thinkers, for instance, Konitz in 1815 and Frank in 1843 (see Isaac Meyer, op. cit., pp. 20–21 et seq.). Also, see Munk in 1859; and David Luria in 1857 in his Kadmoth HaZohar, which appeared in Johannes-

---

1. London, 1885, ii, pp. 66–70.

burg. Here, the latter work maintains that the completion of the Zohar was much prior to that of the Babylonian Talmud, and that some of its doctrines were cited by Babylonian Gaonim on the authority of a Midrash Yerushalmi, which was in fact the Zohar.

## THE HOSTILITY OF GRAETZ

On the other hand, a strong and informed hostility appeared then too, as that of Graetz in Germany, to cite only one instance. This hostility of Graetz was more strong than well informed. We see no trace in Graetz of any real acquaintance with the kabbalah, about which he writes savagely and with the indiscrimination that we connect with a savage. Thus, he terms the Zohar "a notorious forgery," whereas the chief notoriety concerning it is, that after seven centuries of criticism scarcely two authorities can be found to agree in their estimate. Throughout this part of his history we encounter things uncertain described in the language of certitude, and things for which there is less than little evidence, as if there were overwhelming testimony.

It seems that the prevailing sentiment was that it was intolerable to modern notions, that any cryptic literature should possess a real claim on attention. It is therefore said out of hand that the kabbalah represented by the Zohar is a forgery of the thirteenth century. We must endeavor to comprehend precisely what is involved in this standpoint.

## IMPEACHMENT OF THE ZOHAR

Destructive criticism, in impeaching the kabbalah, has maintained that its foremost work was forged by a single writer, of indifferent claims to any intellect or brilliancy, at the end of the thirteenth century.

There is, as we shall see, no positive evidence worth naming on this point. But the theory of the fabrication of the Zohar by Moses de Leon puts an almost impossible burden on the shoulders of that personage. It is the theory of writers, who have not paid sufficient regard to the most probable and most likely existence of the traditional doctrine which is summarized in the Zohar at a period preceding its appearance by many centuries.

The kabbalah is much too singular in its mechanism and far too piecemeal in its numerous texts to be referable to a solitary author. The evidence on the subject, as far as there is evidence, tends to show that the doctrine was familiar or following from familiar doctrine, the tracts being composed by various disciples.

## SOLOMON MUNK'S CONVICTIONS

This is also the position of Solomon Munk, who maintained that the Zohar and its various tracts and fragments which enter into the compilation are not the inventions of an impostor, but ancient documents used by the editor. These include some Midrashim which are not now extant (*Melanges de Philosophie—Juive et Arab*, Paris 1859, p. 275 et seq.).

These facts are in course of open recognition in academic circles. Of this Dr. Schiller Szinessy offered in his day, the best evidence, when he observed, "almost all that the latest critics have said, concerning the age of the various Targumim and Midrashim, including the Zohar, have to be left unsaid."[2]

---

2. Article on Midrashim in the ninth edition of the *Encyclopedia Britannica*.

CHAPTER THREE

# The Date and Authorship of the Book of Splendor

The chief charges against the Zohar are not a discovery of modern criticism at all. The criticism is based both on external and internal grounds. It is my purpose to show that the indictment breaks down altogether.

It is charged that allusion to late events are found sporadically throughout the work. It is further charged that it had never been heard of previously. It is further charged that the original manuscript, from which R. Moses de Leon claimed to have drawn and transcribed, has never come to light. There is also a presumption arising from an alleged fact that the Spanish Jew, R. Moses, who is suspected of the splendid imposture, lived by transcribing copies of it.

It is alleged that Rabbi Moses made large sums from transcribing the Zohar. This is accepted as fact by all critics who depend on the account of the Zohar as given in the Sepher Yuhasim. The statement, however, has an air of fable. The Zohar is a very large work. Moses de Leon, therefore, must have employed a staff of copyists to transcribe it frequently.

*40*

There is no evidence, however, that he employed anyone. Then he must have worked single-handedly and he could not have made large sums, as alleged, by so slow a process.

As an alternative it has been suggested that he profited much by the patronage of wealthy Jews to whom he dedicated his books; but as to this there is no conclusive evidence. It is merely an inference from the fact that he addressed other works of his own writing to co-religionists, who were, by hypothesis, his patrons.

The last charge is based upon supposed evidence, which claims to be contemporary or thereabouts with the appearance of the Zohar itself.

## ACCOUNT OF THE *SEPHER YUHASIN*

Now let us dispose first of the alleged external evidence. In the year 1566 there appeared in Hebrew at Constantinople a work entitled *Sepher Yuhasin*, or *Book of Genealogies*, by R. Moses Abraham ben Samuel Zakut, who belongs to the second half of the fifteenth century. That is to say, to the reign of Ferdinand and Isabella.

He was a Jew of Salamanca, but he taught at Saragossa. When the edict of expulsion of all Jews was published, he retired to Portugal and was appointed Royal Historiographer by King Emanuel. The *Yuhasin* embraces the entire period, between the creation of the world and the year 1500 CE. It was in great repute among some bibliographers. It is cited continually by Bartolocci.

The point of view of the *Yuhasin* with regard to the Zohar is that it contains deep secrets of the Law and of concealed tradition in Israel. Also, it conforms to the truth as regards both Written and Oral Law, and it embodies the sayings of R. Shimon ben Yochai of the period of the Emperor Antonius, under whose name it appears. It is alleged, though, that the work is that of his disciples, and that finally, it did not become public until after the death of Nahmanides, namely, until the second half of the thirteenth century. Nahmanides is known as R. Moses ben Nachman Gerondi, the famous Spanish Talmudist of Gerona, called also Ramban. He died in Palestine, circa 1270.

It is quite obvious that the author of the *Yuhasin*, R. Moses Abraham, must not be classed among those who opposed the Zohar, as some modern critics have attempted to show.

It will seem almost incredible that in this work which so defends the Zohar, a narrative should be found which appears to represent it as an imposture, devised from mercenary motives by Moses de Leon, otherwise, Moses ben Shem Tov. Yet such at first sight is the case and as such those who impeach the work have accepted it.

The explanation is really simple. The narrative in question is a fragment. Its missing conclusion is really to the credit of the Zohar and it is exculpatory to the transcriber. The proof of all this resides in the fact that the person whose adventures it relates, Isaac de Acco, became assured subsequently that the Zohar was not a splendid forgery, seeing that he embodied some of the Zohar's principles in one of his own treatises. The most biased of modern critics, Dr. H. Graetz, admits the force of this fact.

The narrative of the *Yuhasin* is concerned with the adventures of Isaac de Acco, a disciple of Nahmanides. Acco is Acre, which was besieged by the Sultan of Egypt in 1291. Isaac was one of the Jewish refugees from that city, and he seems to have suffered imprisonment for a time. Isaac laid claim to the performance of miracles by a transposition of Hebrew letters, according to a system that he pretended that he had learned from the angels. He was a visionary. As he was in Novara in Italy, about 1293, he heard that a Spanish Rabbin was in possession of the original Zohar manuscript and being very anxious to see it, he made a journey into Spain.

He heard reports there that the erudite Moses Nahmanides (Ramban) was said to have transmitted the book to his son in Catalonia from Palestine. The ship that bore it, however, was driven by wind to Aragonia or to Catalonia, and the precious volume came into the hands of Moses de Leon.

At Valladolid, Isaac de Acco made the acquaintance of the latter, who declared upon oath, that he was in possession of the manuscript and that it was at his home in Avila, where he would exhibit it to Isaac. They undertook a journey together with this object, but Moses de Leon died at Arevolo on the way.

His companion proceeded to Avila, and there he prosecuted his inquiries among the relatives of the deceased. By one of them, namely, by David Rafon of Corfu, he was informed that Moses de Leon was a spendthrift who derived great profit from his writings, but neglected his wife and daughter, while as for the Zohar, he had made it up out of his own head.

There is, however, evidence to the contrary. When Moses de Leon was elected Rabbi of the Synagogue at Avila, his poverty was such that he could not defray the expenses of the journey. His emoluments in that position did not enable him to support his family. (See *Sephardim, or the History of the Jews in Spain and Portugal*, by James Finn, 1841, pp. 303, 304.)

It does not appear explicitly how far Isaac was impressed by this testimony; but he next had recourse to a wealthy Rabbin of Avila named Joseph, who communicated with the widow and daughter of Moses. He offered for the maiden the hand of his son and a substantial dowry if they would produce the original manuscript of the Zohar. The women had been left in poor circumstances and there was every reason to suppose that they would comply gladly. They concurred however in affirming that there was no such manuscript, that the dead man had composed the work out of his own head, and written it with his own hand.

Hence at any rate, he did not employ transcribers, and whatever price he may have obtained for copies of the work, he could not have multiplied many. Furthermore, if assiduous, he could have had no time for squandering; if idle, he would have no money to spend. Moreover, he must have had at least one copy of his inventions from which to make his transcripts, and there would have been at least that in the house to be shown and seen.

His quest having thus failed, Isaac de Acco left Vila and proceeded to Talavera. There he met with R. Joseph ben Todros and with Jacob, a pupil of Moses, both of whom in reply to his inquiries affirmed that the genuine Zohar was in the hands of Moses de Leon, as they had proved conclusively. The nature of proof does not appear, and the account of Isaac breaks off abruptly in the middle of a sentence describing some testimony, which he received at Toledo, as to an ancient Rabbin named Jacob. This Rabbin had testified by heaven and earth of the "Book Zohar, that R. Shimon ben Yochai was the author." (Epilogue).

Several minor details have been passed over in this account purposely which have awakened suspicion as to the honesty of the narrative.

The point is that it closes with a solemn testimony to the authenticity of the Zohar. Isaac de Acco must have concluded to abide by this testimony, judging from the course, which he took subsequently.

So far, therefore, as the account in the *Sepher Yuhasin* is concerned, assuming that the narrative is authentic, it is not proved that Moses de Leon wrote the Zohar "out of his own head." Outside this document there is, moreover, no proof that he was even connected with it as transcriber.

## SUMMARY OF THE CASE AS IT STANDS

The state of the case of the supposed external evidence against the Zohar, as it stands, is confused. Those who regard Moses de Leon as nothing more than a transcriber from the authentic original manuscripts have had to reckon with certain damaging references to late events, which are found in the Zohar. Those who regarded the transcriber as the concealed author have had to meet the extreme difficulty of supposing that such a collection was the production of one individual, and Moses de Leon at that. Their explanations are assumptions of little value.

## THE CASE OF THE INTERNAL EVIDENCE

The internal evidence against the antiquity of the Zohar may be reduced under the following heads.

### Accusation Number 1

The Zohar refers to the vowel points which are alleged to have been invented in post-Talmudic times.

Elias Levita, a German Jew of the sixteenth century, ascribed the vowel points of the Hebrew language as being the late institution of the Jews of Tiberias, about the beginning of the sixth century. David Levi (in his *Lingua Sacra*, London, 1785) points out in reply to this, that the schools of Judea had been closed already at that period. Furthermore their scholar R. Mocha also introduced the vowels to the Karaites at the end of the sixth century. Levi makes therefore their reception by the Karaite Jews a proof of their antiquity because the Karaites were professed enemies to tradition and innovation.

Unfortunately there are no pointed Hebrew manuscripts prior to the tenth century.

### Defense Number 1

The defenders of the Zohar meet this difficulty in pointing out that the vowel points are mentioned in the Talmud, Tractates *Nedarim*, *Megilah*, *Berachoth* and *Eruvin*, and therefore are not the invention of times posterior to the Talmud. In the Talmud they are said to have been a rule given to Moses the Prophet on Mount Sinai.

In several places of the Babylonian Talmud mention is made of "the distinction of the accents, and in particular, of the accents of the Torah which might be shown and pointed at by the hand." Consequently, they must be visible marks or figures and are to be understood, both of the vowel points and accents. Some dissertation exists which also intends to prove that vowel points existed in the middle of the third century of the Common Era.

### *Accusation Number 2*

The accusers of the Zohar point out further that it quotes or borrows from a book entitled *The Duties of the Heart* written by R. Behai ben Yoseph Ibn Paqudah of Saragossa, about the middle of the eleventh century.

### *Defense Number 2*

The defenders of the Zohar reply that the writer of the *Duties* himself as author has borrowed from the Zohar in one of its earliest forms, the existence of which is traceable from Talmudic references under the name of Midrash of Rabbi Shimon ben Yochai.

According to another summation, the great classic of the kabbalah has passed under three names: a) Midrash of Rabbi Shimon ben Yochai; b) Midrash Yehi Ohr—"Let There Be Light"; and c) Zohar, that is, Splendor or Light, after Daniel 12, 3.[1]

---

1. See "Die kabbalah, oder . . ." Jellineck, Leipsic, 1844.

### Accusation Number 3

The accusers point out that the Zohar mentions two kinds of phylacteries or tefillin, which fact is supposed to prove the late origin of the entire work.

### Defense Number 3

The defenders point out that the existence of two kinds of phylacteries arose through a difference of rabbinical opinion as to the scriptural passages to be used on them. The defenders then go on, setting forth statements and inferences from the Talmud to show that this difference of opinion occurred in early Talmudic times. Though the actual use of two kinds of phylacteries before the tenth century has not been demonstrated.

### Accusation Number 4

The Zohar quotes authorities posterior to its alleged period.

### Defense Number 4

The defenders meet this accusation by pointing out that the bulk of the Zohar is of very early origin, but that in its extant form, it is the growth of later centuries. And that is how late authorities, belonging to the Amoraic school, came to be included and cited in the Zohar. This is true of much early Hebrew literature, canonical or not.

It is further argued that had the Zohar been forged by Moses de Leon, he would have avoided the citation of later authorities.

## Accusation Number 5

The objectors say it is written in Aramaic, whereas at the period to which it is ascribed, meaning that of R. Shimon, Aramaic was the vernacular, while Hebrew was used in religious writings.

## Defense Number 5

The defenders reply that when Isaac de Acco set out on his quest for the original manuscript of the Zohar, he is recorded to have said, "If it be written in the Jerusalem idiom it is genuine, but if in Hebrew, it is not." We thus hear the express statement of a Jewish witness, referred to the thirteenth century, postulating its use of Aramaic.

They further point out that Aramaic is the language of the Targum, which are mystical. The scribe of R. Shimon ben Yochai was undoubtedly the Rabbi Abba whom it mentions, and he, as a Babylonian, must have been thoroughly conversant with Aramaic. Supposing the Zohar to be a forgery produced by Moses de Leon, he was more likely to have written it in Hebrew, which is the language of his other books.

## THE ARGUMENTS CONTINUED

Frank in 1843 raised the pertinent question: How could Moses de Leon, at the beginning of the fourteenth century, treat matters of the most elevated order in an idiom which the most distinguished scholars had been for so long content merely to understand (*La kabbale*, p. 104). Note, the Aramaic dialect of the Zohar is not that of Daniel and Ezra nor of the Chaldaic Paraphrase of Onkelos and Yonathan of the Targum, Talmuds and Midrashim, but it is a mixture of all.

Further note, Dr. Schiller-Szinessy, reader in Talmudic at Cambridge, wrote in the article s.v. Midrashim, in the ninth edition of the *Encyclopedia Britannica,* "The Zohar was begun in Palestine late in the second century CE and finished at the latest in the sixth century. It is impossible that it should have been composed after that time as both language and contents clearly show."

It was also urged that if contemporary with the Talmud, the latter ought to have mentioned it. The reply is, that it does not, however, under the catch word of its late name Zohar, but by the title of *Secret Learning* and by other titles which have been mentioned in this section.

Another argument of the supporters of the Zohar is that Moses de Leon was an unlikely person to have written such a work as the Zohar, because he was intellectually and morally unfit. It seems acknowledged by all sides that his original books are poor in quality. He is termed an inferior kabbalist.

Dr. Schiller-Szinessy shows that Moses was proud of the authorship of his own books, and hence he was unlikely to conceal his hand in the composition of any.

There is no doubt that the Zohar was to some extent sprung upon the Jewish people at the period of its appearance. It received the kind of welcome which would be given to a work which may have been old as regards its material, though unfamiliar in its form. This is sufficient to account for any silence of previous authorities. It may well be that in the shaping of those materials of old and in the impressing of that form, the individual who is supposed to have multiplied copies may have had a hand, while transcribing from the original manuscripts in his possession.

CHAPTER FOUR

# The Age of Zoharic Tradition

For the critics of the Zohar, the most favored delinquent was, of course, Moses de Leon, because he is reported to have circulated the Zohar. But occasionally they make him appear as the tool of other conspirators.

### FANTASTIC ABSURDITIES OF SOME CRITICS

Thus Samuel Cahen in his "Great French Bible" puts up a fantastic, uniquely absurd story, maintaining that the Zoharic writings were composed by a convocation of converted Rabbis, assembled for the purpose in a Spanish monastery, employing Moses as their publisher, and the Church itself figuring as an accomplice. He fails to trace the source of his story.

M. H. Landauer and others argued that the true author was Abraham ben Samuel Abulafia, a prophet and Messiah of his period (1240–1291), who is said to have termed his system "a prophetic kabbalah" (see Orient. Lit. VI. 710–13, 1845–46).

The voice of Heinrich Graetz was raised in favor of the school of Abraham ben David of Posquiere, who belonged to the twelfth century. He has been described as the chief Talmudic authority of his period in Southern France, but most of his works are lost.

## ISAAC THE BLIND

Isaac the Blind of Narbonne (referred also to Posquire, ob. circa 1219) is also a favored name. He has been termed "the father of kabbalah" and is supposedly the one to have conferred names upon the ten sephiroth of the world of emanations, the names by which they are known.

To him, it seems indubitable that kabbalism owes something of development and of impulse.

## EVALUATION

Meanwhile these extreme opinions in all their varieties show that there is a crass criticism, which rules off a great literature and conceptions and teachings reached by all true metaphysics, as we shall see, by a single stroke of the pen into the region of forgery and imposture.

It does not matter that this criticism is always in disgrace, it wrought great harm nonetheless.

It proved Troy town to be a solar mythos, until Troy town was excavated. It undermined, as it believed, the Book of Daniel until fresh archaeological discoveries cast it into the pit, which it had dug. It is truly stupid.

In kabbalistic criticism, its typical representative is Heinreich Graetz, and one can scarcely conjecture by what principle he was guided in his estimate of Moses de Leon. It is the height of exaggeration to which is convoluted the account in the Yuhasin, to the point that it almost exceeds recognition.

The antiquity of the Zohar does not depend so much upon the date of its documents, as on that which belongs to its tradition. Eldershein in his book *Jewish Society* writes: "There existed indubitably, at this late Temple epoch, a mass of doctrines and speculations which was concealed carefully from the multitude" and even, he adds, "from the ordinary scholars." He says also that it bore then the name of kabbalah.

We are, therefore, more concerned to ascertain the state of the content of the Zohar, rather than the form in which it is represented to us.

## ANTIQUITY OF CONTENTS OF ZOHAR DO COUNT

Now, in the history of Zoharic criticism we find that the old students accepted the claim of its tradition back to antiquity. Also, they were disposed to understand the genealogy literally; and further, they regarded that the books contain both of these, just as the printing plates produced by certain writers belong to their works without much suspicion. All this is on the simple authority of the literature itself. Later scholars, however, having found something countenancing the modern origin of the documents, have overlooked the possible antiquity of their tradition. This antiquity is something that calls to be surveyed, apart from the date of its publication. The essential values, in respect of "Theosophy Mystica," surely remain over.

The Zohar is full of elements of old doctrine of remote periods. Its Yetziratic notions concerning the virtue of divine names is found in the Sepher Yetzirah and is found abundantly in the Talmud and Mishnah. Its teaching concerning angels and demons may well be an inheritance from Babylon, as is claimed in Talmud.

With regard to the Zohar's scriptural exegesis, much of it may be an obscure transmission from early Mishnaic and Talmudic times. Here we may follow the learned author of the article on Midrashim in the *Encyclopedia Britannica*. This author states that the nucleus of the work of the Zohar is of Mishnaic times and that Rabbi Shimon ben Yochai was its author, in the same sense that Rabbi Yochanon was the author of the Palestine Talmud. Namely, that he gave the first impulse to its composition.

Add the hints and references found in both Talmuds to the existence of a mystical tradition, and we are led to the conclusion that there was a great body of Secret Doctrine which became revealed gradually; also, which many watered and fostered, with some element of transmutation though, until the growth at length put forth the strange flower of the Zohar.

## MYSTERIES OF RABBI SHIMON

As regards the form, its most ancient part is probably the Book of Concealment. It is advanced by its defenders, that the Zohar is a subject of reference in several texts, both of the Babylonian and the Jerusalem Talmuds, under the name of Midrash of Shimon Ben Yochai. There also existed a text entitled *Mysteries of Shimon Ben Yochai* before the eleventh century. It is reasonable therefore to conclude that early written and oral materials entered into the composition of the Zohar, as we no longer possess it.

CHAPTER FIVE

# Kabbalistic Doctrines— Alleged Sources

## TEN EMANATIONS, MACROPROSOPUS, AND MICROPROSOPUS

Antecedent Jewish influence through Aristobolus and Philo must not be exaggerated. We must, of course, distinguish the fundamental part of the kabbalah from its developments. In the first class are included the Doctrine of the Ten Emanations and of *Ain Soph*, that of Macroprosopus and of Microprosopus. All these will be unfolded and explained later. The subsequent developments in their complexity are referred to in the kabbalistic schools of Moses of Cordoba and of Isaac de Luria.

*Ain Soph* is the final concept of Deity, which is reached by all true metaphysics. It is the ultimate point of theosophical speculation possible to the human mind.

The doctrine of the Ten Emanations or sephiroth is in its turn an intelligible form of device of thought, as it seeks to bridge the gulf between the finite and infinite, between absolute purity and that material world which seems unclean.

The speculations of Macroprosopus and Microprosopus (*arikh* and *zeir anpin*) distinguish between G-d as He is in Himself and in His relation with his children.

The antithesis between G-d and the material world, between the Infinite and the finite is brought nearer our understanding. The absolute transcendence of G-d becomes clearer. Kabbalism denounces those who would attempt to describe G-d as He is in Himself, even by the attributes that He manifests. Philo Judaeus knew and expounded many of these and other kabbalistic preexisting teachings, as we know from his explicit testimony, as to the fact of a Jewish mystical doctrine.

## PHILO'S WRITINGS AND KABBALISTIC DOCTRINE

Both in Philo's writings and in kabbalism the divine nature as in essence is regarded as escaping definition, and ultimately, without characteristics. The descriptions of G-d are all negative, for no name can be given Him. The scriptural anthropomorphism of G-d is allegorized upon in all the descriptions, attributions, and manifestations of G-d in the Holy Scriptures.

The letter of Scripture is regarded as a veil to be interpreted. The visible world is regarded as the gate of the world unseen. In existence, there is an archetypal world which is superior and transcendental. It is the world of superior things and that of phenomena with their archetypes in the normal world. All things seen are both natural and inferior things, and these are all a counterpart of things not seen.

It can be summed up in the axiom; "There is no herb on earth to which a certain star does not correspond in the heavens." The highest culmination, however, is the immediate contemplation of G-d, which is a definite possibility.

All these independent hardy speculations are express points of kabbalistic doctrine, and they are also heads of kabbalistic teaching.

The Zohar affirms a Divine Era, where G-d was alone with His Name, but there was also an antecedent and nameless state. In the Raaya Mehemna, it is put this way: "In this world My Name is written *yod-hai-vav-hai* (implying manifestation of true concept) and is read 'Adon-ai' (Master). But in the World to Come, the same will be read as it is written, so that mercy shall emanate from all sides" (Zohar II, 106a). That is to say, that in the great day of the L-rd, divine love will be manifested, for He is light. All this, in spite of the darkness of our ways, for such are the ways of G-d to man.

## CONCLUDING IMPRESSION

As one goes through kabbalistic doctrines, one feels instinctively, without any necessity of evidence, that these things, composed by the men of the holy Synods, are not and cannot be the unaided creation of Moses de Leon. The Book of Occultation (*Safra d'tzniusa*) bears all the marks of antiquity, for example, no less considerable than that of the Sepher Yetzirah (the Book of Formation, attributed to the Patriarch Avrahom; its compilation to Rabbi Akiva).

## CHAPTER SIX

# Spain and Southern France— The First Recipients of Kabbalah

As we have already stated, Israel possessed a mystical tradition handed down by the oral teachings; thus dating back to comparatively early times.

Now then, the environment of the Jews in the Spanish Peninsula, from say the ninth century and onward, differed considerably from that which surrounded them in other countries of Western Europe.

### SPAIN—A CENTER OF JEWISH LEARNING

Spain was for Israel an oasis in the great wilderness of the exile for the simple reason that much of it was not then under Christian rule. Also, the necessities of the Christian princes in Spain until the thirteenth century led them usually to protect the Jews. The Jews of Spain enjoyed comparative immunity; they possessed even political influence and rose occasionally to high political power. Spain, therefore, became a center of Jewish literature and philosophy. From here, Jewish treatises passed into France and Italy, often under the Arabian equivalents of their Jewish authors' names. Avicebron is a case in point. Many translations were also made. A translation of the Talmud into Arabic is reputed by Rabbi Joseph, a disciple of "Moses, the Sack-Clothed," during the reign of Al-Hakim, Caliph of Cordoba, in the tenth century. The undertaking, however, no longer exists.

## KABBALISM APPEARED FIRST IN SPAIN AND SOUTHERN FRANCE

As mentioned, the Zohar represents a certain aspect of transformation of theosophical thought of many preceding centuries in Israel. There is evidence that this traditional knowledge existed, of course, in Talmudic times as well.

The nucleus is first heard of in Palestine during early Christian times, which follows its connection with Rabbi Shimon Bar Yochai. There is a story of the Zohar being sent from Palestine by Nahmanides. Spain and the south of France are thus pointed to as the chief scenes in which the kabbalistic literature developed. There was a prevailing tone of mystical thought in both these places. This may be also traced more apparently, however, in the post-Zoharic mysticism and in the commentaries of the Zohar which are the work of Spanish Jews.

These writings contain theses concerning the hidden state of Divinity, the operation of Divine Will at the beginning of creation, the emanation of the world, and similar. The Sepher Yetzirah (Book of Formation) and the Zohar came into circulation through the media of print about a century later (1500).

CHAPTER SEVEN

# Influence of Kabbalah on Jewry

The profit that accrued to the mind of Jewry from the promulgation of the Zohar, no one is in a position at the present day to define precisely. It gave, however, most certainly to Israel the splendid propulsion of the ideal. For some it was a path of devotion, a path of life in sanctity, for the attainment of the Good and of the One.

There were also, however, aberrations of enthusiasms and there were those who did their best to wreck Jewry. The History of Sabbatai Tzvi, the spurious Messiah, is a typical point in case.

Numerous indeed are the instances in which kabbalah has been a warrant to direct imposture. Knowledge of kabbalistic mysteries was alleged to have imparted superhuman powers.

## THE KABBALAH'S SPHERE OF INFLUENCE ON THE CHRISTIAN MIND

There were also at the time intellectual kabbalistic influences on Christendom, exercised by a peculiar theosophical claim.

The esoteric tradition of the Jews was supposed to offer the religion behind all religions. Its metaphysics seemed to make a bizarre and strenuous attempt to unravel the mysteries of the universe. The "system mind" appeared excogitated. Strange lights were flashing in the darkness. The mystic Jew seemed to enjoy a certain communication of the Infinite.

Another attraction was to them the mystical side of kabbalism, the return of the soul to G-d, and that path of ecstasy by which it was conceived, that the soul might effect such reunion even in this life. These were "the splendid propulsions of the ideal," and they made for an inquiry at large into the secret tradition in Israel and into the doctrine of the holy kabbalah.

CHAPTER EIGHT

# Ancient Texts

There are various old tracts which connect with the subject matters of kabbalistic literature prior to the appearance of the Zohar. This is the case with the Sepher Yetzirah. All such works laid claim upon oral knowledge, transmitted from the past. The elements of such oral tradition received developments subsequently from the commentators of Sepher Yetzirah, as well as from the Zohar. The attention of early kabbalists was concentrated on the Book of Formation (Sepher Yetzirah) and several elucidations of that work appeared between the eleventh and thirteenth centuries.

SECTION III

# The Written Word of the Kabbalah: First Period—Early Kabbalistic Literature

It appears beyond controversy that there was once a considerable mass of old theosophical doctrine extant in Jewry connected with brilliant and great names; vestiges of which are to be found in the Talmud. The reception of the Bereshith and Merkavah Mysteries often mentioned in the Talmud was the kabbalah.

This somewhat nebulous material contained what was of mysticism in Israel between the period of the Talmud and the period of the promulgation of the Zohar, and which in the course of time became the kabbalah.

CHAPTER ONE

# Midrashim, Precursors of the Sepher Yetzirah and the Zohar

The precursors and antecedents of the Sepher Yetzirah and the Zohar in the world of texts were various Midrashim which are no longer extant. The Sepher Yetzirah was of high authority and was held in high respect in the mystical literature of the Geonic period.

Another such work of great similarity to the Book of Formation goes under the title of the *Alphabet of R. Akiva,* which is dated back to the second century. There are extant two versions of this work. A third Midrash on the ornamentation of the letters is also referred to R. Akiva. Still another old Midrash, connecting with the Book of Occultation, which in its turn is one of the sections of the Zohar, is named Shiur Komah, that is, the Measure of the Height or Measure of Being.

It is a development of the barest scriptural places in which divine members are mentioned. Shiur Komah survived only in two fragments. The date of both these works is conjectural, but there can be no doubt and there is no question of their antiquity in respect of root matter.

Connected with them are the greater and the lesser palace, also known as delineation of the heavenly temples. These Pirke Haichaloth, otherwise Pirke Merkavah, are accounts of seven heavenly temples or palaces, which must be visited in succession by the elect before they can enter the region of the Sacred Chariot. They appear to represent stages of rapture and vision. They connect with the palaces of the Zohar, which are descriptions of the plains of heaven, which descriptions are also given in these haggadic productions.

## THE CHAPTERS OF R. ELIEZER AND THE MIDRASH CONEN

The chief name of this period with which we are concerned is Rabbi Eliezer ben Hyrcanus, whose mystical system as presented in his Pirke Capitula, connects on the one hand with Sepher Yetzirah and on the other one with Zoharic teaching.

In the first place, we have G-d subsisting prior to the creation of the world, alone with His ineffable Name. Next, we have the creation prior to the visible world of the Torah or Law, together with the throne of glory, the Name of the Messiah, Paradise, Hell, and the temple of Jerusalem, that is, the archetype of the earthly temple. Subsequently, the Creation of the world by means of ten words is also discussed.

With this word may be connected the ancient Midrash Conen, which represents the Torah as the foundation of the universe and gauge of it stability.[1]

---

1. The Midrash Conen, "Expositio Stabiliens." See Prov. 3:19. It was the first treatise in a collection entitled "Arze Levanon—Cedri Bibani." See pp. 104, 16. It appeared in Venice in 1601.

## OTHER AUTHORITIES OF THESE PERIODS

The Gaon (Excellency) R. Saadiah ben Joseph (born circa 892, ob. 942), head of the Persian Academy of Sura, was the author of a commentary on the Sepher Yetzirah preserved in the Bodleian Library. It was recently printed in France.

R. Abn-Yussuf Chasdai (Abn Shapruth), a Spanish physician, died at Cordoba between 970 and 990 CE. He was a prince of the exile and temporal head of the Jews in that city. He was also a political minister under two khalifs. He is said to connect the School of Hai Gaon with that of Ibn Gebirol. The dates, however, do not correspond.

The Gaon R. Shereerah ben Chanina was the head of the Academy of Pumbaditha or of Pherruts Schibbur in the neighborhood of Babylon. He was the father of Hai Gaon. He is supposed to have died at the age of one hundred years, circa 1000 CE.

He was distinguished for the violence with which he wrote against the Christians. He was said to possess kabbalistic knowledge. Nahmanides has preserved, in his commentary on the Torah, R. Shereerah's critical observations on the "Delineation of the Heavenly Temples" or more correctly, on the fragments which it embodies under the title of "Proportion of the Height." "G-d Forbid," exclaims he, "that man should speak of the Creator, as if He had bodily members and dimensions." R. Shereerah was despoiled of his wealth and hanged by order of the cruel Cader, khalif of the race of the Abbassides.

The Gaon R. Hai, son and successor of R. Shereerah, was head of the Babylonian School of Schibbur. He is also credited with commentary on the Sepher Yetzirah.

The interpretation of dreams was an occupation of the Jewish academies, and the skill exhibited therein often purchased toleration and respect for the rabbis at the hands of the khalifs. To Rav Hai is attributed a treatise on this art, which was printed at Venice.

His voluminous works have many kabbalistic references, especially that entitled "The Voice of G-d in Its Power." He possessed enormous influence and died as the head of the academy of Pumbaditha (near Baghdad) in 1038.

Solomon ben Yehudah Ibn Gebirol, the scholastic Avicebron, and in all respects kabbalistic as well as otherwise, was a focus of intellectual and literary interest. He was a contemporary of the famous Nagrila.

R. Abraham ben David (or Ben Dior) Halevi (obit. circa 1180) the great orthodox apologist of the twelfth century, has been included in the chain of kabbalism. He is described otherwise as a Spanish astronomer, historian, or philosopher.

Moses Ibn Jacob ben Ezra, one of the greatest Jews of his time, was of Grenada and flourished in the earlier part of the twelfth century. His work entitled the *Garden of Aromatic* shows traces of the doctrine of Gebirol. His commentary of Isaiah, however, is in disagreement with Ibn Gebirol. He wrote on the Divine Name and the mystical attributes of numbers in connection therewith.

There are to be added the names of Judah HaLevi (obit. post 1140), who has some references to the Sepher Yetzirah in his work entitled *Kuzari*; also that of Jacob Nazir, referred to in the second half of the twelfth century; and that of Solomon Jarki and R. Abraham ben David, the Younger. These bring us to the thirteenth century and to the period of Maimonides, who is reported chiefly on the authority of R. Hayyim to have turned kabbalist at an advanced age.

In any case, he connects with the subject and he was acquainted with the existence of the twofold mystical tradition, distinguished as that of Creation and that of the Chariot.

Also of the period were Rabbi Azriel of Valladolid, a famous commentator of the Sepher Yetzirah; Shem Tov Ibn Falaquera, a disciple of Maimonides, and R. Abraham Abulafia, who wrote on the Tetragrammaton, on the mysticism of letters and numbers, and on the mysteries of the law. His works have not been published. He also wrote a book entitled *The Fount of Living Water*, of which there is a Latin version in the Vatican. He was a quixotic adventurer and a messianic enthusiast. These writers and personalities all maintain the authenticity of kabbalistic tradition.

## HISTORICAL TREATISES WITH KABBALISTIC-SOUNDING NAMES

Leading astray on a misconception are such treatises like that of Abraham ben David Ha Levi (ob. circa 1150) by the mere fact of their titles. It is called *Seder Ha kabbalah*, the order of tradition, a historical work. This author is a great orthodox apologist with strong Aristotelian leaven. The occasion of his book was a Sadducean heresy prevalent in Castile and Leon and represented by a work of Abu Alphrag, which maintained that the true synagogue was to be found among the Sadducees. The *Seder Ha kabbalah* vindicated the authority of the orthodox claim.

It embraces the entire history of the Jewish church and the perpetuation of the Mosaic doctrine, which is the tradition named in the title.

This work was the prototype of several later historic productions, some with misleading names such as the *Cohain of the Kabbalah of Gedaliah*.

The author of the *Seder* is still counted as belonging to the Aristotelian groups among the Jews, who adopted Aristotelian principles and possessed culture and enlightenment. There were, however, those groups of Jews who opposed the innovations. All that we connect with the ideal of rabbinical Israel and all the fascination of bizarre thought and of flashes of a great mystical light went into this opposition, which formed the rival school.

## EXPONENTS OF SPECULATIVE KABBALAH

Avicebron represented to some extent this rival school. The writings of this poet and philosopher are said by some to incorporate some Zoharic writings. On the other hand it was also asserted that Maimonides has much to connect him with Avicebron (whose writings he never saw). Yet others asserted that the *Guide of the Perplexed,* the great masterpiece of Maimonides, this great Jew of Cordoba, offers many indications of sympathy with the doctrines of speculative kabbalah. They point out as alleged kabbalistic correspondence of Maimonides, his mentions of a lost tradition, his recognition of a secret sense in Scripture, and his teachings of the inaccessible nature of G-d. Finally also is his conception of the universe as an organic whole. Isaac Meyer maintained even a supposition as well that Maimonides was acquainted with the Zohar.

## OPPONENTS OF KABBALAH

In a general sense, however, those who wished to introduce Aristotelian principles into Jewish philosophy belonged to that school, which subsequently opposed the Zohar, for example, Joseph ben Abraham Ibn Wakkar of Toledo at the beginning of the fourteenth century.

Those who accepted the Zohar, however, belonged to the school which connects with Avicebron, among whom was Rabbi Abraham ben David of Posquiere and Isaac the Blind (ob. circa 1219) with his disciples, Azriel and Ezra. This kabbalistic school produced one of the most important commentaries of the Sepher Yetzirah.

In Avicebron's writings we meet, it is true, kabbalistic connections such as the doctrines of the Inaccessible G-d, of intermediaries between G-d and the Universe, of the emanation of the world, and even of the universal knowledge attributed to the preexistent soul of man. But we do not discover in this theosophist of the eleventh century any distinct trace of typical Zoharic doctrine, let us say, that of Shechinah. However, there remains sufficient to warrant the inclusion of Ibn Gebirol among precursors of Zoharic kabbalism.

## A SHORT ACCOUNT OF AVICEBRON AS IBN GEBIROL

The chief treatise of Solomon ben Yehudah Ibn Gebirol, the once renounced Avicebron, is entitled the *Fountain of Life*, which was extant in a widely diffused Latin version. He wrote philosophy in Arabic and poetry in Hebrew. The Jews valued his poetry but not his speculation, while Christian scholastics debated his metaphysical notions. By both classes of admirers he was celebrated respectively as the greatest philosopher and the greatest poet of his time.

## GEBIROL'S LIFE

Avicebron was born about the year 1021 at Malaga. He was educated in the University of Saragossa and died at Valencia in 1070. He was patronized by Nagdilah (Samuel ha Levi ben Joseph Ibn Nagrelah), a prince of the Exile who was also prime minister of Spain under the khalifate of Habus. Nagdilah was the center and mainspring of Jewish learning in that country.

It seems certain that some of the sacred tradition in Israel and some of its conceptions may be found in the writings of Avicebron, more especially in the *Fountain of Life*, and the *Crown of the Kingdom*. The second one, composed towards the end of his life, is a hymn celebrating the only one and true G-d and the marvels of His creation. The *Fountain of Life* has been affirmed to be the earliest known exhibition of "the secrets of the Absolutely Existing, which is above number" and is "attached to its corporeal Universe." These conceptions are self-evident analogies to sephirotic doctrine. An impartial judgment, however, of the philosophy of Avicebron in *Fons Vitae*, which is a dialogue after the manner of Plato, must pronounce it as tinctured deeply by the Hellenic Greek thought.

Ibn Gebirol's chief treatise the *Fountain of Life* (*Fons Vitae*) became widely diffused in a Latin version ascribed to the middle of the twelfth century. Many scholastics, among them Thomas of Aquinas and Albertus Magnus, cited it. The University of Paris proscribed him though at the period of the publication of the Zohar on the grounds that he favored Aristotle. His book was said to sum the philosophy of the thirteenth century. When the school of Averroes arose, he was unknown among it. At a later period he was unknown to Maimonides.

## KABBALISTIC SCHOOLS OF THE PERIOD

Modern scholars recognize three chief schools which lead up to Zoharic kabbalism: 1) the School of Isaac the Blind, to which belongs Azriel, with his celebrated commentary of the Sepher Yetzirah; 2) the School of Eliezer of Worms, which is largely of the theurgic order; 3) The School of Abulafia, which united to some extent the preceding two and made use of the uric form of the speculative kabbalah.

This affirmation, however, must not cause confusion with regard to the Sepher Yetzirah, which is certainly speculative and is of a much earlier period.

## GEBIROL AND THE BOOK OF FORMATION

Ibn Gebirol seems to have been indubitably acquainted with the Book of Formation. In the second book and twenty-second section of the *Fountain of Life*, this passage occurs: "Hence it has been said, that the construction of the world was accomplished, by the inscription of numbers and letters in the air." This is an obvious analogy with a fundamental notion of the Book of Formation. The table of the thirty-two paths which arises out of the Book of Formation was the theme of one of his poems.

## AVICEBRON'S SYSTEM OF THE UNIVERSE

An impartial examination of the *Fountain of Life* makes apparent Avicebron's kabbalistic correspondences, which are otherwise not sufficiently explicit upon the surface of his book. To bridge the abyss and to make it conceivable that the universe derived being from G-d, he supposes no intermediaries, plus the Divine Will through which the "Absolutely Existing which is above number" is formulae combined with contemplation to achieve union with G-d. This is to say, the exteriorization of mental images for the attainment of an end which is of all things inward and apart from the forms of mind.

CHAPTER TWO

# The Book of Formation

The attribution of Sepher Yetzirah to the patriarch Abraham is imbedded in the text itself, of that minute tract, which is regarded as the chief nucleus of all kabbalism. The rabbinical legend affirms that Abraham transmitted it orally to his sons by whom it was perpetuated in turn until certain "sages of Jerusalem" committed it to writing so that the tradition might not perish, even when the people seemed themselves on the eve of perishing. It then had successive custodians for the transmission.

The Sepher Yetzirah is quoted in the Talmud (*Megilah*, also *Sanhedrin*). It was suggested that an alternative text under the same title was in existence then and is no longer extant. There existed in the Talmudic period a magical work called *Hilchot Yetzirah*. The Talmudic tractate *Sanhedrin* contains the following passage: "By means of combining the letters of the Ineffable names as recorded in Sepher Yetzirah, Rava once created a man and sent him to Rav Zeira. The man, being unable to reply when spoken to, the Rabbi said to him, Thou art a creature of the company [or those initiated in the mysteries of necromancy], return to thy dust."

The work itself is divided into six chapters; the first one concerned with the office of the Sephiroth in Creation, the remaining five termed the instruments, namely, the letters of the Hebrew alphabet. After the revelation of these mysteries to Abraham, he received the manifestation of G-d and the covenant was instituted. "G-d bound the twenty two letters on the tongue of the patriarch and discovered to him His secret" (Sepher Yetzirah, Ch. 6).

There is an absolute distinctness between G-d and His instruments of Creation, whether numbers or letters. G-d, the Faithful King separated from all numbers and transcending all expression, sojourns in eternity and rules the sephiroth forever from His holy throne.

A second point concerns the emanation of the sephiroth, which go forth as the instruments and servants of the king of ages and returning, fall prostrate in adoration before the throne (ch. 1, v. 6 etc.).

It is said that their end is bound to their beginning as the flame is bound to the firebrand, which implies the principle of emanation. G-d is, however, depicted as the active Former Artificer and Maker, Who engraved and sculptured and built and became the Great Architect of the Universe.

## THE TRANSCENDENTAL NUMERATIONS

The first sephirah, classified as One, is described as the spirit of the living Elohim, the living G-d of ages, eternal and forever. It is said otherwise that the spirit of the Holy One is Voice, Spirit, and Word.

Two is the breathing of the spirit, described otherwise as air; the twenty-two letters depend from here, and each one of them is spirit.

Three is the moisture that comes from the breath otherwise, water from air. Herewith G-d sculptured and engraved the first lifeless and void matter. He built "Tohu," the line which circles snakelike about the world, and "Bohu," the concealed rocks imbedded in the abyss, whence the waters issue. This triad of the spirit, the breath, and water corresponds to the conception formed subsequently of the Atzilutic or Archetypal World.

Four is the fire which comes forth from the water; with this G-d sculpted the throne of honor, the seraphim, the ophanim or celestial wheels, the holy animals (four living creatures), and other ministering spirits. Within their dominion He established His habitation.

This numeration combined with numerations Five and Six to form a second triad, which comprises the conception of Briah, the archangelic world of later kabbalism.

The numerations from Five to Nine inclusive are held to represent the Yetziratic world of the four worlds of kabbalism, while Ten the last numeration corresponds to Assiah, the World of Action. It should be remembered that the Book of Formation is concerned chiefly with the sphere of operation, tabulated subsequently of Yetzirah, that is, the Third World of kabbalism.

Five is the seal with which G-d sealed the height when He contemplated it above Him. He sealed it with the name YHV.

Six is the seal with which He sealed the depth when He contemplated it beneath Him. He sealed it with the name HVY.

Seven is the seal with which He sealed the East when He contemplated it before Him. He sealed it with the name HYV.

Eight is the seal with which He sealed the West when he contemplated it behind Him. He sealed it with the name HVY.

Nine is the seal with which He sealed the North when He contemplated it on His right. He sealed it with the name VYH.

Ten is the seal with which He sealed the South when he contemplated it on His left. He sealed it with the name VHY. The ten numerations are finally classed together under the title of Ineffable Spirits of G-d. The sealing names are combinations of three letters, successively transposed, which enter into the name Tetragrammaton.

It should be remembered, however, that just as each sephirah was supposed at a later period to contain all the sephiroth, so also was there a superincession of the Four Worlds, which were all contained in each.

## PUBLICATIONS AND VERSIONS OF SEPHER YETZIRAH

The Sepher Yetzirah was published at Mantua in 1592. A Latin translation by G. Postel preceded it, however, by ten years. The Mantua Hebrew edition was accompanied by five commentaries. It contained two recensions of the text as variants. Another Latin version extant is inscribed to Reuchlinus Riccius. A further edition was published at Amsterdam in 1642 in Hebrew and Latin by Rittangelius. Many other editions followed; some of them with the Hebrew text and German and French translations and notes respectively. Some such translations of it were published quite recently in the United States.

## CONNECTIONS AND DEPENDENCIES OF THE BOOK OF FORMATION

When the Book of Formation came to be printed at Mantua in 1592, five commentaries and connections accompanied it. (Many more can readily be found and might be given by a complete bibliography.) The best known one is the *Sepher Sephiroth*, or Commentary on the Ten Sephiroth by way of questions and answers, which is the work of R. Azriel ben

Menahem. Another commentary by Rabbi Abraham is considered as the most important from an esoteric standpoint; while the earliest in point of time is the work of Saadya Gaon. Gaon is the title, which distinguished the heads of the two academies at Babylon, Sura and Pumbedita, which arose later in the sixth century CE. Next in antiquity would rank another commentary attributed to Hai Gaon in the early part of the eleventh century CE.

There are also commentaries attributed and ascribed to R. Moses Botarel, R. Moses ben Nachman, R. Abraham ben David Ha Levi the younger, and R. Eleazer.

## SAADYA'S COMMENTARY

The commentary of R. Saadya Gaon was published in Hebrew at Mantua, but it was written originally in Arabic; a copy of the original is still preserved. In this commentary, R. Saadya Gaon appears as a theosophist, which is equivalent to saying that this first expository treatise on the Sepher Yetzirah possesses a kabbalistic complexion, though the author has been regarded as a purely rationalistic writer.

The sephiroth of the Sepher Yetzirah show only scarcely a trace of the system of emanations as transcendental numerations. The doctrine of *Ain Soph* has some traces. It is recognized on the one hand that we cannot have an adequate notion of the divinity of his correspondences with the world. On the other hand, it is recognized that some approximate idea may be obtained as to the latter, and that they may be shown forth by means of figures and comparisons.

One illustration tells us that G-d is the life of the world, as the soul is the life of the body; and as in man the soul is all-powerful, so G-d is omnipotent in the world. He is also its supreme reason; and as in man the rational faculty is the guide of life, so the divine power is directed by the divine reason.

## THE SOUL AND REINCARNATION

Saadya Gaon devotes some space to the consideration of the soul in man; connected here with Zoharic kabbalism, but he rejects metempsychosis utterly. He recognizes the soul's five aspects (or divisions) and he calls them by their conventional names, which occur already in the Talmud. Despite Saadya's hostility to reincarnation as understood by the kabbalah, he accepts the preexistence of soul and he teaches that the resurrection of the bodies will take place when all souls destined for earthly life have passed through it. His classifications of the faculties of the soul are a bit defective, however. On account of reason that the souls possess, the soul is called *Neshamah*. On account of concupiscence, it is called *Nephesh*; and on account of anger it is call *Ruach*. The two other names, *Chaya* (living) and *Yechidah* (unique), refer to the vitality of the soul and to the fact that no other creature resembles it.

Saadya Gaon did not ascribe to the divine and angelic names any thaumaturgic virtues. The names of the angels vary according to the events that they are commissioned to accomplish. The divine names are descriptive of G-d's operations. In the work of creation, He terms Himself Elokim. (A *k* sound is substituted for the proper *h* when many divine names are used in a descriptive or philosophical context.) When ordaining the covenant of circumcision, He is called El Shaddai. He is the "I am," in connection with the wonders of the ten plagues; and he is "Kah," when producing the great miracles of the Red Sea.

The Zohar, on the other hand, teaches that the Divine Name AKIK, which signifies "I Am," indicates the unification and concealment of all things in such a manner that no distinction can be established between them. The words *ASHR AKYK*, "That I Am," represents G-d on the point of manifesting all things, including His supreme Name. On the other hand the Name of title *AKYK ASHR AKYK*, "I Am That I Am," is that Name assumed by Him on the occasion of the manifestation of the cosmos; when G-d is called Tetragrammaton (Zohar III, 65b).

## THE TEN CATEGORIES: SAADYA

Saadya explains that the Sepher Yetzirah is concerned with created things and how they came into being. At that point he makes reference to the ten categories, namely, substance, quantity, quality, relation, place, time, powers, position, activity, passivity. They are to be regarded as referring to the numerations to the Sepher Yetzirah. The Ten Commandments are also corresponding to these categories. For example, the commandment against adultery answers to the category of position; for the act itself is a position and a contact.

Lastly in his analysis of the Hebrew *alef-bais*, Saadya Gaon seeks to account for its sequence. *Aleph* is the first sound pronounced, that is, it is vocalized at the back of the tongue. *Shin* is vocalized in the middle of the mouth, and *mem* on the lips.

## THE COMMENTARY ASCRIBED TO HAI GAON

There existed considerable confusion regarding this commentary. Some maintained even that the commentary deals with the Book of Concealment instead of Formation. Furthermore, the authenticity of this tract of Hai Gaon is disputed. It must, however, be admitted that R. Hai had more distinct kabbalistic connections than Saadya. The commentary deals largely with the mysteries of tetragrammaton; it gives us the curious quadrilateral method of writing it by means of letters and circles in a curious diagram.

## THE COMMENTARY OF THE RAAVAD, CIRCA 1100–1180 ON THE BOOK OF FORMATION

The commentary of Abraham ben David Halevi the younger, a contemporary of Maimonides whom he often attacked, is also included in the Mantua edition of the Book of Formation.

R. Abraham, also known as Raavad, was born circa 1110 and is supposed to have suffered the death of a martyr near 1180.

His commentary starts with the thirty-two Paths of Wisdom, referred to at the beginning of the Sepher Yetzirah and goes on through the entire book itself.

Great and uttermost confusion prevails with regard to the personality of the author who is frequently and erroneously identified with the writer of the *Seder Ha-Kabbalah*.

In this work of commentary of R. Abraham there are definite Zoharic elements. There is also the distinction between lower and upper sephiroth which is Zoharic, and it offers a connecting link between R. Abraham and the late kabbalism of R. Isaac de Luria. Moreover, there is the doctrine of the Unknowable God, the "Cause of all Causes," who is not apprehended by anyone outside Himself, being void of all distinction and of all mode of existence. This notion of God appears to be, if possible, more concealed and later than the conception of *Ain Soph*. *Ain Soph* itself is distinguished by R. Abraham from *Kether*, the Crown of Creation, on the remarkable ground that the accident is not made from the essence, nor the *res* from the *non res* or *non ens*. This occasions a difficulty, as to the emanation of the manifest universe it also contrasted with Zoharic theosophy. Otherwise, the commentator describes the *Ain Soph* in terms that are almost identical with Zoharic teaching. Neither unity nor plurality can be attributed to *Ain Soph*, because unity cannot be ascribed to that which is incomprehensible in its essence. The reason is that a number is an accident, belonging to the worlds of extension, time, and place.

## RABBI AZRIEL'S YETZIRAH COMMENTARY

The first place among the dependencies of the Sepher Yetzirah is correctly assigned to the commentary of R. Azriel as a literary and philosophical work. Its author was born in Valladolid about the year 1160. He is said to have been the pupil of R. Isaac the Blind, who was in evidence 1190 to circa 1210 CE. He taught the doctrine of metempsychosis, and a few fragments of his writings are still extant.

Other authors maintain that R. Azriel's teacher was R. Yehuda, son of Raavad. R. Azriel became in turn the instructor of R. Moses Nahmanides, who also belongs to the chain of Yetziratic traditions, and he admittedly brought the influence of his great reputation to bear upon the Sepher's fortunes.

R. Azriel is said to have traveled much in search of Secret Wisdom. He connects with the kabbalistic system, which was expounded by the school of Gerona, and he added the results of his own reflections. Many works have been attributed to him, some which are lost, and some that have remained in manuscript. His explanation of the Ten Sephiroth by way of "Questions and Answers" must have helped to shape the metaphysical speculations of the kabbalah by the logical form of the commentary.

## THE CHARACTER AND THE TEACHINGS OF THE COMMENTARY

R. Aziel's commentary has been the subject of high praise as regards both matter and form. It contains the doctrine of *Ain Soph*, and it has express views on the emanation of the sephiroth, which are said to be contained in *Ain Soph*. Their emanation was possible because it must be within the omnipotence of God to assume a limit. The essence and the real principle of all finite things is the thought of the Supreme Being (compare with Zohar I, 74a). If that were withdrawn, they all would be left as empty shells.

Certain symbolical colors are attributed to the Sephiroth. *Kether* is like the "Concealed Light" or the light, which is veiled in darkness (veiled in luminous mist). *Binah* is sky-blue, because *Binah* is the great sea of kabbalah. *Chokhmah* is yellow, *Chesed* white, and *Gevurah* red. *Tiphereth* is white, red, or pink. *Netzach* is white-red, and *Hod* reddish-white. *Yesod* is a combination of the previous triad, while *Malkuth* is like the light that reflects all colors. According to the Zohar, the color attributions are as follows: *Kether*, black, white, or colorless; *Tiphereth*, purple; *Malkuth*, clear sapphire.

## THE RAMBAN, NAHMANIDES

Moses ben Nachman or Nahmanides was born in 1194 at Gerona. He is said to have had a prejudice against kabbalah at first. Later on, he made acquaintance with the kabbalah and became afterward an enthusiastic student, both of its speculative and of its practical parts. His kabbalistic explanation of the Law (the Torah) was completed in 1268. Among his many other works, *Garden of Delight* and another called the *Secrets of the Torah* are full of theosophical speculations. He left his native land to settle in Palestine, where he died at a great age, circa 1270. His influence was great.

## THE COMMENTARY OF R. ELIEZER OF WORMS

The commentary of Sepher Yetzirah, which passes under the name of R. Eliezer of Worms, seems to have been the work of a German Jew of Germesheim. He was one of the greatest kabbalists of his period. He belonged to a later date than Nahmanides. His works are wholly kabbalistic.

These are first, *The Vestment of the Lord*, quoted by Bartolocci (I. 186); it has never been printed. Second is the *Guide for the Sinner*, exhorting the sinners to repentance and amendment of life (printed in Venice 1543). Third is a treatise on the soul. Fourth is an explanation on Psalm 145. Fifth is a commentary on Sepher Yetzirah. The author flourished around the middle of the fourteenth century.

Other commentaries of the Sepher Yetzirah are referable or ascribed to several others. These include R. Aaron the Great (Bartolocci I. 15) under the title of "Book of Points"; R. Judah Ha Levi, author of "The Kusari"; Sabbatai Donoto, otherwise known as Shabbethai ben Abraham ben Joel, an Italian physician and astrologer, born 913 and died before 982; Judah ben Barzillai, a Spanish talmudist of Barcelona who flourished at the end of the eleventh and early in the twelfth centuries; and to R. Isaac the Blind.

The Bodleian Library has a manuscript entitled "Mishnat," by Josef ben Uziel, which has been classed as a commentary on Sepher Yetzirah; it is also said otherwise to be a supplement to the text itself.

SECTION IV

# The Written Word of the Kabbalah: Second Period

The textbook proper of the Zohar and its numerous connections are here examined to furnish a comprehensive notion of the materials incorporated by this composite work. Its doctrines are studied at a later stage in detail, including their intimations from a mystical or theosophical point of view.

CHAPTER ONE

# The Book of Splendor: Its Contents and Divisions

### THE ZOHAR AND THE SEPHER YETZIRAH

The Sepher Yetzirah text is extant in several languages. It has been available to students and inquirers at large. The *Sepher Ha-Zohar*, on the other hand, is large in itself, and it has considerable supplementary matter and extensive connected literature. Moreover, it is written for the most part in Aramaic, the Jerusalem Idiom (of Isaac de Acco).

### LATIN AND FRENCH TRANSLATIONS

Between the thirteenth and the twentieth centuries it was therefore a sealed book for the great majority of scholars until a full-length version appeared in French within recent years. The other historical collection of Rosenroth, the *Kabbalah Denudata*, by attempting to cover much too wide a field, gives no adequate idea of the work which it is meant to elucidate.

With all its defects, however, the *Kabbalah Denudata* remains of prime value. As it is, it attributes an exaggerated importance to three tracts introduced into the body of the Zohar. It also accepts a little tract called the Book of Concealment, or of Occultation, as the fundamental part of the whole Zohar, that vast theosophical miscellany.

There are, of course, several sources of information, which might have corrected this false impression—the work of Adolf Franc in France and that of C. D. Ginsburg in England, to name two only. The classes of persons who have proved to be most concerned with the subject, however, have been content to follow the lead of Rosenroth.

## CONTENTS OF THE ZOHAR

The Zohar proper purports to be a commentary on the Pentateuch. To summarize an account of Ginsburg: "The Zohar does not (apparently) propound a regular Kabbalistic system, but dilates upon the diverse doctrines of this Theosophy." The long conversations between R. Shimon ben Yochai and Moses record many short and penitential prayers. Of course, the religious anecdotes and the attractive spiritual explanation of scripture passages also appeal to the hearts and wants of men. The description of the Deity and the sephiroth are under the tender forms of human relationship as comprehensible to the finite mind. Examples of father, mother, primeval man, matron, bride, white head, the great and small face, the luminous mirror, the higher heaven, the higher earth, which it gives on every page, made the Zohar a welcome textbook for the students of the kabbalah.

The reader must be dissuaded from supposing that Ginsburg's summary is adequately representative of the work for it contains, for instance, no reference to the doctrine of Shechinah or the Zoharic mystery of sex.

We are, however, placed by this quotation in a position to understand after what manner the literature of kabbalism affected the fervid imagination of the rabbinical Jew, and the kind of influence which it had on him; well illustrated by the fascinating Zoharic theosophy at its highest development.

## DIVISIONS OF ZOHARIC CONTENTS

The Zohar proper, apart from all supplements and interpolations, is divided into five parts corresponding to the five scriptural texts of Genesis, Exodus, Leviticus, Numbers, and Deuteronomy on which it is supposed to be a commentary. The first two are complete, the third and fourth have certain missing portions, while of Deuteronomy there is little more than fragments. The extant work, as printed, is in three parts only; the last comprises all that remains of the commentary on the three later books of the Pentateuch.

Each part is subdivided into various sections, separately entitled: Section Bereshith, Section Toldoth-Noah, and similar.

## BOOK OF GENESIS AND ITS OMISSIONS AND ADDITIONS

Certain appendices follow the commentary of Genesis, being, I-Hashmatoth, Omissions; II-Toseftoth, Additions, and sub voce appendix; III-two important supplements comprising extracts from Midrash HaNealam—Secret Midrash and Sithre Torah—Secrets of the Law.

## BOOK OF EXODUS AND ITS INTRODUCTIONS; THE LUMINOUS BOOK; THE FAITHFUL SHEPHERD; THE BOOK OF LEVITICUS; OTHERS

Independent texts are also introduced between certain sections of the commentary on Exodus and sometimes within the sections themselves, namely, Midrash HaNealam (continued in installments); Raayah Mehemnah, Faithful Shepherd; Sepher HaBahir, Luminous Book; Sithre Torah (all continued in installments), Idra De Maschcanah, Assembly of the Sanctuary; and Siphrah De Zenioutha, Book of Concealment. The commentary on Exodus has also three appendices, two embodying additions and one independent tract on Palaces, Haichaloth. The sections of Exodus have, moreover, certain *mathnisim*, repetitions interpolated. Others follow paragraph 1 of the commentary on Leviticus, while sections vii, viii, and ix of Leviticus are reinforced by continuations of the Faithful Shepherd.

## BOOK OF NUMBERS AND THE IDRA RABBAH

The commentary on Numbers has also independent texts introduced between its sections, namely, Faithful Shepherd in continuations and Idra Rabba Kadisha—Great Holy Assembly—as also certain miscellanies.

## DEUTERONOMY AND THE IDRA ZUTA

Among the fragments of Deuteronomy, paragraph I is followed by a further installment of the Faithful Shepherd. Other portions of this work constitute the extant sections numbered III, V, and VI. To section X is appended Idra Zuta Kadish—Little Holy Assembly.

So far as it is possible to estimate, the Book of Concealment and the Idras are not internal parts of any commentary on the Pentateuch, and in the Zohar they are not combined with the text proper to form one scheme therewith. It may be said that all interpolations are casual, while the appendices to the part of Exodus might change places with those of Genesis, and so of the rest.

## ROSENROTH'S SCHEME OF TABULATION

With this simple unpretentious collation, there may be compared the analytical scheme of Rosenroth of more than two centuries ago. The Zohar is divided thereby into internal and external parts, which are tabulated as follows:

The Internal parts are those which are collected together in one edition. They are:

a. The text of the Zohar properly so called.

b. Sifra De Zenioutha or Book of Concealment, otherwise, that of Modesty.

c. The Idra Rabbah or Greater Synod.

d. The Idra Zuta or Lesser Synod.

e. Sabah De Mishpatim, the discourse of a story of the Ancient One in section Mishpatim.

f. Midrash Ruth or commentary on the scriptural book of that name, existing in fragments only.

g. Sepher HaBahir, the Renowned or Illustrious Book, sometimes called Book of Brightness.

h. Toseftoth, addenda or additions.

i. Raayah Mehemnah or The Faithful Shepherd.

j. Haichaloth, that is, palaces, mansions, or abodes.

k. Sithre Torah or Mysteries of the Torah, that is, the Law.

l. Midrash HaNealam or Secret Commentary

m. The Razai De Razin or Secret of Secrets.

n. The Cremona and Mantua Editions.

The following tracts and fragments are omitted from the Mantua Edition of circa 1558, known as the Little Zohar. They appear in the Greater Zohar, being that of Cremona.

a. Midrash Chatzeis or Commentary on the Song of Solomon.

b. Pekoodah or Explanation of the Torah.

c. Yenookah or Discourse of the Youth.

d. Maamar to Chazei or the discourse beginning "Come and see . . ."

e. Chiburah Kadmaa or Primary Assembly.

f. Mathnitin or Repetitions, traditional receptions.

The sections e, f, g, j, and m of the first tabulation are also wanting in our present day Mantua editions. The Great Zohar, however, the Cremona edition (1558–60) contains all the Treatises enumerated in both lists.

There is preserved in manuscript, it is said, an early Hebrew translation of the Zohar by Barachiel ben Korba, in the Public Library of Oppenheim.

## THE EXTERNAL PARTS AS UNDERSTOOD BY ROSENROTH OF MORE THAN TWO CENTURIES AGO

The external parts are those suppurated to the earlier editions. Those are:

a. *Tikkunei HaZohar*, or supplements of the Book of Splendor, called also the Ancient Supplements, to distinguish them from further, later additions.

b. *Zohar Chadash*—the New Zohar, containing matters omitted in the printed editions. This has four parts.

1. The text of the Zohar itself, through which is scattered the supplement of the tract Midrash HaNealam, part of which appears in the original work.

2. *Tikkunim Chadashim* or *New Supplements*.

3. *Zohar Shir HaShirim* or *Exposition of the Song of Songs*, appertaining to the Zohar.

4. *Zohar Eicha* or *Exposition of Lamentations*, appertaining to the Zohar.

In the previous tabulations are contained everything of the Zohar that has come down to us.

## COMMENTARIES ON THE ZOHAR AND EXPLANATORY BOOKS

1. *Sepher Derech Emeth*, that is, *The Way of Truth*, being various readings in the Zohar arranged according to the Mantua edition.

2. *Binah Amorai* or *Words of Understanding*, being an elucidation of difficulties in Zoharistic vocabulary.

3. *Zohar Chamah* or *Splendor of the Sun*, a short commentary which follows the Mantua edition.

4. *Pardes Rimmonim* or *Garden of Pomegranates* by R. Moses of Cordoba, an explanation of numerous texts in the Zohar and Tikkunim.

5. *Mekor Chokhmah* or *Fount of Wisdom*, forming a continuation or new part of The Way of Truth.

6. *Marah Kohen* or *The Vision of the Priest*, a synoptic work.

7. *Zeir Zahav* or *A Crown of Gold*, largely used in *Kabbalah Denudata* of Rosenroth.

8. *Patach Ainaim* or *Gate of the Eyes*, for the biblical quotations in the Zohar and Tikkunim.

Also recommended and largely reproduced are the manuscript treatises of Isaac de Luria, compiled by R. Hayyim

Vital, and two other imprinted works, a kabbalistic commentary on the whole Torah and a treatise entitled "Chesed Abraham."

## OF ZOHARIC CONTENTS, CONTINUED

In the Zohar proper, there are extravagant speculations and wild exegesis, but it is uncontaminated by monstrous symbolism. It has often a touch of nature to indicate its kinship with humanity. Many rabbinical fables, histories, and apologies are narrated in it, sometimes elucidating a knotty point in Scripture as, for example, whether the destruction of animal life at the deluge indicated that the beasts also sinned. Some of these recount the death of a just man; sometimes they describe visions and are narrating tales of wonder.

## NATURE OF ZOHAR

In a certain manner, the Zohar is a commentary on the Pentateuch, but as such it is only casual and occasional. It has nothing in harmony with the simple sense of Scripture. It often opens abysses where dark clouds hang out and fire flashes and often deeps of meaning which resound with pregnant messages. The governing principle affirmed is the existence of several senses in the written word. They are reducible broadly under three heads, which are compared by the Zohar to the garment: the body, which is within it, and the soul, which is within the body.

## THE WISE AND THE UNWISE

"There are those unwise," says the Zohar, "who behold how a man is vested in comely garments, but see no farther and take the garment for the body; whereas there is something more precious (than either), namely, the soul."

The Law has also its body. Some of the commandments may be called the body of the Law, and the ordinary recitals mingled therein are the garments which clothe this body. Simple folk observe only the garments, that is, the narration of the Law (the Torah), perceiving not that which they hide. Others more instructed do not give heed to the vestment but to the body which it covers. And there are the wise, the servants of the Great King, who dwell on the delights of Sinai and concern themselves only with the soul, which is the foundation of all, and the true Law. These shall be ready in the coming time to contemplate the soul, of that soul, which breathes within the Law (Zohar, Mantua edition Part III, 15b). The higher soul of the Torah is, no doubt, the Divine Sense of the Lord, which gives knowledge of the Word itself. The Word of God issued in a mystery; and the key of this mystery was the reward of the just and wise man in the World to come.

## HIDDEN MEANING OF BIBLE STORIES

Simple recitals and common words suggest only insufficiency of the letter. These are not the sum of the Torah. The manifold sense follows from necessity. Moreover, the sayings of Esau, Hagar, Laban, of Bilaam and of Bilaam's ass cannot be the Law of Truth, the Perfect Law, and the faithful Witness of God (Zohar Mantua Edition; III, 149b).

The Zohar does not unfold in a consecutive form either the allegorical or the mystical meaning. It gives glimpses only in its doctrinal, theosophical, and mystical contents. The purpose of the present survey is, therefore, to offer gleanings and illustrative instances drawn from there and here.

## A NARRATIVE

In the introduction adjoining Genesis and sequelae, a tradition is cited which says that whensoever just men undertake a journey together and discuss on their way subjects belonging to the Secret Doctrine, they are favored by visits of the holy, who dwell in the world beyond (Zohar, Cremona; I, 7a; and I, 37).

When Rabbi Eleazer and Rabbi Abba were travelling to call on Rabbi Yosi, they were accompanied by an unknown porter who carried their baggage. When they began to commune one with another on things appertaining to the mysteries of Law and Doctrine, it came about that he interposed between them, asking pregnant questions and preferring points of debate.

It did not take long to discover that he was one endowed with knowledge. When he spoke of the Sabbath and its keeping, of the day and the night thereof, of the liturgy belonging to the Sabbath, of Divine Hypostases and the Seventy Names of God, they saw also that his science was greater than theirs.

They came down from their saddles to embrace him and would have mounted him on one of their own horses, seeing that he rode upon an ass. He refused them, however, but resumed his discourse otherwise, opining depths and heights in the hidden themes of wisdom, explaining the secret influence exercised by names on the lives of men, telling strange things and new, and concerning the Temples at Jerusalem. Over and above all, these concerned the mystical union between Moses and her who is called Shechinah, throughout the great record.

It is said that they halted again and again and dismounted, but this time it was to fall on their faces before him. When they looked up, however, it was to find that he had vanished from their eyes. Who was this master in Israel and keeper of Hidden Doctrine, to them unknown and clothed in reeds of service?

They had asked many times and he had answered nothing. But it was inferred or assumed at the end that he was Rav

Hamnuna the Ancient, who had returned for their inspiration and enlightenment from the world beyond.

## THE MYTHOS OF THE ROSE

I have cited this gracious story and I might indeed have begun earlier as the Zohar itself begins and told how a conference opens on page one of the mythos concerning the rose of sharon. After that manner, the deeply embedded meanings of the Song of Solomon are unfolded.

The rose is the community of Israel. But the rose is red and white, and in the first of these states the elect people abide under the ministry of judgment, while in the second they are encompassed by thirteen ways of mercy (I, 1a. I, 3). For in another aspect the rose is a cup of blessings as it is also a Chalice of redemption.

## THE VOICE AND THE WORD

Early in the commentary on Exodus we delve again for treasure in the herb-sweet earth of the Song of Songs (4:8), and that which is brought to the surface belongs to the mystery of union between the voice and the Word. There has been intimation much earlier in the Zohar on the same subject, on thought as of the origin of all things, on the inward contemplation of the Holy One before He made the worlds, on the uttering of the voice, which brought forth or manifested the thought, and on creation as the "Word" expressed.

The commentary ends also on the keynote of thought in the Holy One, the mysterious joy thereof and the light which flows out therefrom.

It drew together the forty-two letters comprehended by one of the extended Sacred Names, and out of the relation established in this manner it is affirmed that the world came forth.

In these words, brief and plain as they are, is found at full length the Doctrine of Divine Immanence, the Presence of the Father Almighty—by and within the Word in all that lives and is.

## POWER OF FAITH AND THOUGHT

It is said in the first leaves of the commentary on Leviticus that faith completes the Sacred Name, and little further on, that from the thought of the Holy One come forth those ways and paths which lead to a knowledge of the Name and to perfection thereby and therein (Zohar III, 4b; III, 5b).

We are told also, that it is better for a man never to have been born than to live without uniting the Sacred Name on earth (Zohar III, 7a; V, 18), meaning, of course, by the mode and manner of life which is led here below. The secret of such union belongs to the study of the Law, which is the work of men of faith, the reference being not to the expanded Law, but to that of the Secret Doctrine. It is also understood, that those who study the Law to a real purpose are those who live thereby.

There has been a division brought about between the four sacramental letters comprising the Hebrew Name of God (HaVaYaH); it is the work of man to make an end of this separation. To promote unity in the name of God is the intention, which should occupy the priest when he proceeds to the work of sacrifice. Prayer and good works promote this unity too.

The mystery in the commentary on Leviticus then continues. The complete Name is *HVYH Elokim,* and the work which devolves on all sons of the doctrine is to make evident on earth, that HVYH is indeed Elokim, even as these Divine Hypostases are one in heaven.

CHAPTER TWO

# The Book of Concealment

We are passing now from the commentaries on the Pentateuch to the texts and fragments which are imbedded therein or thereunto added. They differ generically from the corpus of the great text and from the other additions or supplements, because their subject matter is "veiled in allegory and illustrated by symbols." We are now entering a realm of revelation. It happens that two of the tracts in question are expository of the third. I refer to Sifra De Zenutha, with its sequels the Idra Rabba and the Idra Zouta.

## BOOK OF OCCULTATION AS A THEOGONY

The Book of Concealment or of Occultation (the literal translation would be Book of Modesty, in the sense of concealment) was presumed by some to be the root and foundation of the Zohar and also the most ancient portion of that collection. It has been said further that it is a theogony comprised in a few pages, but with developments very numerous. The Book of Concealment and the Book of Formation were the fountainheads of all kabbalism for occult dreamers of the past.

Rabbi Isaac Luria says that Sifra De Zenioutha refers to things which are secret and should be kept secretly and compares Proverbs 25:2: "The glory of God is to conceal the word."

But he supposes also an allusion to the circumstances under which the work is reported to have been composed, namely, during the concealment of R. Shimon for twelve years in a cave.

The work is concerned, however, with the manifestation of the Divine Being as the "term" of His concealment in the eternity that preceded manifestation.

The first chapter deals with the development of what is termed the Vast Countenance, the image of the father of all things, the Macroprosopus, when equilibrium had been established in the universe of unbalanced forces.

This countenance, which is referred to as *Kether*, or the Crown, first of the Ten Sephiroth, is compared to the tongue of a balance, *lingula examinis*. When equilibrium was obtained, the countenance was manifested, the Ancient of Days appeared, God issued from His concealment.

This symbolism of balance depicting the harmony of the universal order is a keynote of the treatise, which in its own words is the book describing the "liberation of the balance." The balance is suspended in the place which is no place, that is to say, in the abyss of Deity, and it is said to be the body of Macroprosopus, referring to the sephiroth Wisdom and Understanding which are the sides of the balance.

"For Wisdom, says one commentator, is on the right, upon the side of Benignity; Understanding is on the left, upon the side of Severity; and the Crown is the tongue in the center which abides above them." The meaning of the symbolism is that equilibrium between Justice and Mercy must be assumed, before the Universe having man for its object could become possible; the source of this notion must be sought in Bereshith Rabbah. Compare also, the teaching of the pre-Zoharic Midrash Conen, according to which the Grace of God prevents the opposing forces out of which the world was created from mutual destruction.

Now then, the countenance, of which no man knows, is secret in secret, and the hair of the head is like fine wool hanging in the equilibrium. The eyes are ever open, and the nostrils of the Ancient of Days (the Ancient One) are as two doors, whence the spirit goes forth over all things.

But the dignity of all dignities is the beard of the countenance, which also is the ornament of all. It covers not only Macroprosopus as with a vestment, but the sephiroth Wisdom and Understanding, called here the father and the mother, descending even unto Microprosopus of whom we shall shortly hear. It is divided into thirteen portions, flowing down as far as the heart but leaving the lips free. Blessed is He, says the text, who receives the kisses. From the thirteen portions there descend as many drops of purest balm, and in the influence of all do all things exist and all are concealed.

In addition to the manifestation of Macroprosopus, the Book of Concealment shows how the Most Ancient One expanded into Microprosopus, to whom is referred the name Tetragrammaton, whereas, "I am" is that of the first Ancient.

The letter *yod*, which is the first of Tetragrammaton, corresponds to the sephirah Wisdom, the supernal He (that is, *hai primal*), to Understanding. The union of these twain brought forth Microprosopus, corresponding to the six sephiroth from Mercy to the Foundation inclusive and referred to the letter *vav*. *Hai* final is referred to the tenth sephirah or *Malkuth*.

It follows, according to this text, that the primal manifestation of Deity, which is connected with the conception of the Crown, has no other name than that which proclaims His self-existence.

Macroprosopus, although manifesting in the Crown, is still regarded as ever hidden and concealed by way of antithesis in respect of Microprosopus, who is both manifest and unmanifest.

When the life-giving influx rushes forth from the Ancient One amid the intolerable refulgence of that great light, the likeness of a head appears.

The distinction between the two countenances (that is, the Vast Countenance and the Lesser Countenance) is the distinction of the profile and the full face. Whereas the God who comes forth is revealed in so doing, the Great Countenance is only declared partially, whence it is obviously inexact to speak of Microprosopus as a reflection. He is rather a second manifestation taking place in the archetypal world.

From the sides of the Lesser Countenance descend black locks, flowing down to the ear. The eyes have a threefold hue, resplendent with shining light, and threefold flame issues from the nostrils.

The beard considered by itself has nine portions, but when that of Macroprosopus sheds down its light and influence, they are found to be thirteen.

Though the ineffable name is referred to the Vast Countenance, it is said also that the ordinary letters of the Tetragrammaton, His occultation, represent the manifestation of Microprosopus by the transposition of the letters.

The Book of Concealment is described in its closing words as the withdrawn and involved mystery of the King. It is added: "Blessed is he who cometh and goeth therein, knowing its paths and ways."

The Book of Concealment is preceded in the Zohar by a fragment entitled Idra De Mashchana, that is, Assembly of the Sanctuary (II, 122b). It is followed by a brief colloquy between R. Eleazer and R. Abba, who affirms that he has recorded its mysteries by command of the sacred lamp, Rabbi Shimon, for the use of the colleagues. Also, that the mysteries will abide henceforth in concealment; that R. Shimon appeared to him in a dream and communicated certain secret teachings concerning the Divine Son or *vav*, begotten from the Father and the Mother, represented by the letter *yod* and *hai.*

The fragment opens with a statement on the authority of an instruction drawn from a treatise entitled, "Mystery of Mysteries." It is concerned more especially with the face and head of the Son, the word that comes from His mouth, and the sound of his voice. It is dealing obviously with symbolism.

CHAPTER THREE

# The Greater Holy Synod

The Book of Concealment is characterized by a multitude of obscurities. The treatise now under consideration is different. It possesses almost a literary aspect. It begins in narrative form, methodizing the ensuing dialogues in a manner which is perfectly explicit.

The Greater Sacred Synod claims R. Shimon bar Yochai as the author of the Book of Concealment, and itself contains the discourses of this master in Israel, delivered in a field beneath trees in the presence of his disciples.

For an account of R. Shimon himself we must have recourse to a narrative of the Tractate *Sabbath* of the Babylonian Talmud, reproduced here in substance.

On a certain occasion R. Yehuda, R. Jose and R. Shimon were sitting together and with them also was Yehuda, the son of proselytes. R. Yehuda opened the conversation saying: "How beautiful are the works of this nation (the Romans). They have established markets; they have built bridges, they have opened bathing houses." Whereupon R. Jose was silent. But R. Shimon ben Yochai answered, saying: "All these things have they instituted for their own sake. Their markets are gathering places for harlots, they have built baths for their own enjoyment and bridges to collect tolls from those who cross them." Yehuda the son of proselytes related this conversation and it came to the ears of Caesar, who proclaimed: "Yehuda who extols us shall be extolled; Jose, who said nothing shall be exiled to Sapphoris [that is, Cyprus]; Shimon who has disparaged us shall be put to death." R. Shimon and his son then went out and hid themselves in the lecture hall, but afterward in a cave where a miracle took place; a date tree and a spring of water being raised up for them.

They laid aside their garments and sat covered with sand up to their necks, studying the whole time, and assuming their vestures only at prayer times, for fear that the same might wear out. In this wise they spent twelve years in the cave, when Elijah came to the opening, and said: "Who will inform the son of Yochai, that Caesar is dead and his decree is annulled?" Thereupon they left the cave.

The secret wisdom embodied in the Zohar is said to have been the fruit of the long seclusion enforced upon R. Shimon by the Roman decree.

According to tradition, the Book of Concealment was the form of Secret Tradition in which it was reduced to writing. The discourses of the Greater Sacred Synod and also that of the Lesser Synod were both recorded by Rabbi Abba. When exposition was about to begin, a voice heard in the air revealed that the supernal assembly had gathered in heaven to hearken. The commentators add that not only the souls of the just were marshaled round the speakers, coming from their rest in paradise, but that the holy Shechinah of the Divine presence descended.

## THE EXPLANATION AND DEVELOPMENTS OF THE TREATISE

The explanations and developments concern the world in its void state, before the manifestation of the Supreme Countenance or Macroprosopus, as also of Microprosopus or the Lesser Countenance, and after what manner the inferior depends upon the superior.

The treatise ends with mysteries of initiation by testifying that he is blessed who has known and beheld the concealed words and does not err therein. The text is hard to approach from the side of its literal sense.

## ESOTERIC SPECULATION AND THE SYMBOLISM OF THE EDOMITE KINGS

The unbalanced forces of the universe (the world in its void state) are considered under the symbolism of the kings who reigned in Edom before a king was raised to rule over the children of Israel, that is to say, before the emanation of Macroprosopus. The kabbalah represents, namely, the present universe as preceded by others which passed away quickly. This notion occurs also in the Talmud where it is said that when God was alone, He diverted Himself by the formation of diverse worlds which He destroyed forthwith, and at last He produced the existing physical order. Compare also the Pirkai of R. Eliezer according to which the basis of the existing universe is the repentance of God over His previous creations. See also other Zoharic references to this subject, Zohar II, 20a, Mantua.

The Idra continues to state that at that time there were neither beginning nor end, and the Edomite kings were without subsistence. The Greater Synod then represents the "Ancient of Ancients" creating and producing the essence of light, which is a reference to the holy Aleph-Beth and the Torah.

The description of Macroprosopus follows in the record of R. Shimon's discourses.

> White are His garments as snow, and His aspect is as a face manifested. He is seated upon a throne of glittering brightness, that He may subdue. The whiteness of His bald head is extended into forty-thousand worlds, and from the light of the whiteness thereof shall the just receive four hundred worlds in the World to come.
>
> The vast Countenance itself is said to extend into three hundred and seventy myriad of worlds. The brain concealed within the skull is the Hidden Wisdom, and the influence of this Wisdom passes through a channel below and issues by two and thirty paths.

It is therefore the influx of *Kether*, descending through the Tree of Life, even to *Malkuth*, which is understood as the kingdom of this world. The hair of Macroprosopus radiates into four hundred and ten worlds, which are known only to the Ancient One. This seems to infer an intimation of Divine Knowledge, which is withdrawn in the hiddenness of divine beings.

The parting of the hair is described as a path shining into two hundred and seventy worlds, and there from another path diffuses its light and in this shall the just shine in the world to come. When the forehead of Macroprosopus, which is the benevolence of all benevolence, is uncovered, the prayers of the Israelites are received; and the time of its uncovering is at the offering of the evening prayer on the Sabbath.

The forehead extends into two hundred and seventy thousand lights of lights, abiding in the supernal Eden. For there is an Eden that shines in Eden: it is withdrawn in concealment and is unknown to all but the Ancient One.

The eyes of the Vast Countenance differ from other eyes having neither lids nor brows, because the Guardian of Supernal Israel knows no sleep. The two eyes shine as a single eye, and were that eye to close even for one moment, the things that are could subsist no longer. Hence it is called the open eye, ever smiling, ever glad.

In the nose of Macroprosopus, one of the nostrils is life and the other is life of life. With regard to the beard of the Vast Countenance called otherwise, the decoration of all decorations, neither superiors nor inferiors, neither prophets nor saints have beheld it, for it is the truth of all truth. Its thirteen forms are represented as powerful to subdue and to soften all stern decrees of judgments.

Thirteen chapters of the Greater Synod are devoted to the consideration of this subject, including the locks in each portion, the number of hairs in each lock, and the number of worlds attributed to them.

## MICROPROSOPUS: THE LESSER COUNTENANCE

After the discourse concerning Macroprosopus the treatise proceeds thence to the consideration of Microprosopus or the Lesser Countenance. The conformations of Microprosopus are disposed from the forms of the Vast Countenance, and His components are expanded on either side under a human form. When the Lesser Countenance gazes on the Greater, all inferiors are restored in order, and the lesser is vaster for the time being.

There is an emanation from the Greater towards the skull of the Lesser, and thence to numberless lower skulls; and all together reflect the brilliance of the whiteness of this emanation towards the Ancient of Days.

From the brain of Macroprosopus an influence descends, from the hair an outpouring of splendor, from the forehead a benevolence, from the cheeks gladness and all these fall upon the Lesser Countenance.

From the brain of Microprosopus there are emanations of wisdom, emanations of understanding, and emanations of knowledge. In each lock of the hair of Microprosopus there are a thousand utterances. His forehead is the inspection of inspection and when it is uncovered, sinners are visited with judgment.

The lesson of the Greater Synod is that wrath may dwell with Microprosopus, but not in the Ancient of Days. So also the eyes of the Lesser Countenance possess lids: when the lids are closed, judgments subdue the Israelites and the Gentiles have dominion over them. But yes, when they are open they are beautiful as those of the dove, for they are then illuminated by the good eye.

Kabbalistic symbolism continues its lines, and states that it is said that two tears dwell in the eyes of the Lesser Countenance, and the Holy of Holies when He wills to have mercy on the Israelites, sends down these two tears. This is for them to grow sweet in the great sea of wisdom, and they issue therefrom in mercy upon the chosen people. The special seat of severity in Microprosopus is the nose, and judgment goes forth therefrom unless the forehead of the Vast Countenance is uncovered, when mercy is found in all things.

The discourse appertaining to the beard of Microprosopus fills many chapters and is full of stories relating to various passages of Scripture. It details minutely the conformations of its nine divisions, what is conceded of the Lesser Countenance, and what it permits to be manifested. It describes the descent of holy and magnificent oil from the beard of Microprosopus.

The body of Microprosopus is androgynous; at this point the symbolism is concerned largely with the sexual organs. For the kabbalist, the body of man was peculiarly sacred; whence for him there could be nothing repellent in dealing exhaustively with its topology.

The sum of the whole treatise can be given in the words of the original. The Ancient of Ancients is in Microprosopus: all things are one; He was all things; He is all things; He will be all things; He shall know no change; He knoweth no change; He has known no change (Idra Rabba, 39, par. 220). Thus, God in manifestation is not separable from God in concealment, and if symbolism depicts Him in the likeness of humanity, it is by way of similitude and analogy.

At the conclusion of the Greater Synod we are told that three of the company died during the deliberations, and that the survivors beheld their souls carried by angels behind the "veil expanded above" (ibid.).

## SUBLIME TOUCHES IN THIS TREATISE

The kabbalah in this treatise recites with no uncertain voice that God is altogether without mutation and vicissitude, that wrath and judgment are of man alone. Thus it places a new construction on the divine warning, "Judge not, lest ye be judged."

The divine other dictum: "I will repay" never meant to the true kabbalist that God would repay to the sinner, in his own spirit, outrage for outrage, hate for hate. God's repayment is the compensation of everlasting justice or the gift of everlasting bounty.

Kabbalah promulgated the real meaning of the forgiveness of sin. Some summarized the position as follows: "Nothing is absolutely evil, nothing is accursed for ever, not even the archangel of evil, for a time will come when his name and angelic nature will be restored to him."

## CHAPTER FOUR

# The Lesser Holy Synod

The Lesser Holy Synod or Idra Zuta is a supplement to the subjects not discussed exhaustively in the Greater Assembly; it is similar to it in its chief characteristics. At the end of the treatise the death of the master R. Shimon ben Yochai is recorded and his instructions are mentioned.

### THE MASTER'S DEATH AND INSTRUCTIONS

The Synod consists of the survivors from the former conclave with the addition of Rabbi Isaac. R. Shimon begins by affirming that it is a time of grace. He is conscious of his approaching end. He desires to enter without confusion into the world to come. He designs to reveal those sacred things in the presence of Shechinah which have been kept secret hitherto.

Rabbi Abba is appointed as scribe and Rabbi Shimon is the sole speaker. The discourse still concerns Macroprosopus and Microprosopus with the correspondences between them. It sketches the subject of Concealed Deity and deals at length with the manifestations of the Lower Countenance.

Concerning the three heads of Macroprosopus, it states that they are "one within the other, and the other above the other." Later on, a considerable extension of symbolism is given regarding the first manifestation of the Ancient One under the form of male and female, which is the emanation or the "forming forth" of the supernal sephiroth *Chokhmah* or Wisdom, and *Binah* or Understanding.

The instruction concerning Microprosopus deals with His androgynous nature and His union with the Bride, who cleaves to the side of the male until she is separated, "et accedat ut cupuletur cum eo," face to face. Out of this comes the kabbalistic doctrine, namely, that male and female separated, are but an incomplete humanity or as the text expresses the idea, are but half the body; that no blessing can rest on what is mutilated and defective, and that no divided being can subsist forever or receive an eternal dowry. "For the beauty of the female is completed by the beauty of the male." This mystic foundation concerning the nuptial state is found and met with often in the Talmud.

The conjunction of the supernal male and female is said to be in the place called Zion and Jerusalem, which further on is explained to signify Mercy and Justice. "When the Bride is united to the King in the excellence of the Sabbath, then are all things made one body." Then the most high Holy God sitteth on His throne, then all things enter and are integrated in the One Undivided Perfect and Holy Name. "When the Mother is united to the King, the worlds receive a blessing and are found in the joy of the Universe" (Zohar Idra Zuta).

## THE NUPTIAL JOYS OF THE SOUL OF THE MASTER RABBI SHIMON

About this point the discourse of R. Shimon ceases and R. Abba the scribe heard nothing. But afterward a voice cried: "Length of days and years of Life." A fire abided in the house the whole day. When it burned no longer, R. Abba saw that the holy light, the holy of holy ones, had been wrapped away from the world. He lay on his right side and a smile shone upon his face. R. Eliezer, the son of R. Shimon, rose up and taking his hands, kissed them. "But I," says R. Abba, "licked the dust under his feet."

It is added that during his obsequies, the bier of the deceased saint was raised in the air, and fire shone about it, while a voice cried, "Enter in unto the nuptial joys of R. Shimon."

CHAPTER FIVE

# The Discourse of the Aged Man

The discourse contained in section Mishpatim and Sabah signifies ancient man (III, 94, Mantua). The section Mishpatim (that is, Judgments) opens with a conference between R. Shimon bar Yochai and a certain aged man. The man is not otherwise identified, on the subject of the ordeals and metempsychosis of the soul, to which there are allusions at some length in the Bereshith division of the Zohar, that is, the first part. It breaks off abruptly, giving place to another conference which takes place at an inn between the same or a second aged man and the sons of the Doctrine, who have met together by accident.

It is described in a colophon as a recital relative to R. Yebba the Ancient, who is moved to reveal at great length the mystery of the soul, its nature, modes or parts, and the law that governs its transmigration. The complex treatise on the Revolutions of the Souls by Isaac de Luria is but a development of the section Mishpatim of the Zohar.

## The Discourse of the Aged Man

In this discourse under consideration, the psychic nature of man is regarded under a sevenfold aspect, whereas other theses reduce it to three, and by one it is extended to ten. Illustrations of such nature cause some writers in the past to speak of a concealed sense in the Zohar and other kabbalistic texts.

It is not to be supposed that when R. Abba and other rabbis divide and subdivide the soul, they mean anything else than to distinguish the successive states and modes which are possible therein and may become actual.

Similarly does modern theosophy affirm that there are seven principles in man. If and when the discrepancy between the variously divided aspects of the soul in man have been harmonized, we shall have reached the concealed sense of the Zohar commentary and its connections as regards our inward nature.

We assume in this case that the "involved" discourse of R. Yebba described the development of mystical experience and the ascent of the soul in sanctity, according to a tabulation of seven stages, ending, as it literally states, in the realization of Divine Union. The text says that a flame of fire comes down from the Supernal World and is joined to the Community of Israel, "that union may be perfect" (Zohar II, 4).

At an early stage of the conference, we hear of a hidden palace that is called the Palace of Love and wherein the souls who arrive there are kissed (Zohar II, 97; III, 389). The text, which alludes thereto is "And Jacob kissed Rachel" (Exodus 29,2). Thereafter, the Holy One, blessed be He, raises them into exalted realms and there rejoices with them, as a father with his beloved daughter. The beautified life in this palace is not the life of union, it is a place of beatitude in the Beloved Presence; it may be called a vestibule. The distinction is vital. Its significance, however, is likely to escape those who are in the Court of the Mystical Temple but not in its holy place, who have conceived the Vision but not the Ineffable Union.

According to R. Abba, the Most Holy had hidden in each word of Scripture a supreme Mystery, which constitutes the soul of that word. Profane man sees, however, only the external body of the word, meaning the literal sense. On the other hand, for those who have eyes, the external word is an envelope through which the soul is seen (Zohar II, 986, II, 987). Another illustration likens the inward meaning to a beautiful virgin shut up in a palace, who contrives a little chink that her lover when he passes, may have a glimpse of her beauty. There are many who go to and fro, but he only who has the eyes of love can see her. It is the same with Holy Scripture, which reveals its hidden secrets only to those who love it. The uninitiated go by on the other side and observe nothing.

There are occasional other intimations and messages. We are told, for example, that penitence cancels everything, loosens all that binds, annuls all decrees and breaks all chains (Zohar II, 99a and III, 399). It is also said that man's conduct here below forms a window in his brain, and if he lives in a state of grace, the glass of that window remains polished and diaphanous, so that his intelligence is a faithful reflection of the Most Holy Intelligence which is above. But the man of evil life clouds his window (Zohar II, 106 and III, 422).

Finally, there is that, for example, which is said concerning the place of children in the "World to Come," namely, that there is a sojourn reserved for them which is higher than that of the just made perfect (Zohar II, 36; III, 439). It is added that children die young to become the defenders in heaven of those who remain on earth.

CHAPTER SIX

# The Luminous Book

Excerpts of considerable length purporting to come from a work entitled *Sepher HaBahir*, or Liber Illustris, are given in the Cremona edition of the Zohar at places which here follow: I—76, 79, 82, 88, 104, 110, 112, 122, 125, 127, 130, 137, 138, 185, 341, 462; II—145, 259; III—151, 176, 301, 333.

These excerpts are omitted in the so-called Little Zohar of Mantua. In 1651 these excerpts were brought together into a volume and published in Amsterdam, which was at that period a great stronghold of Jewry. The *Sepher HaBahir* is alleged to be of higher antiquity than any kabbalistic book. Another view considers the extant extracts authentic, but believes in the existence of an old kabbalistic treatise under the same title, which is now lost.

There is evidence that the *Sepher HaBahir* was in existence prior to the promulgation of the Zohar because it was attacked and denounced by R. Meir ben Simon in the first half of the thirteenth century, thus antedating the period of the public appearance of the Zohar. The extracts that occur in the Zohar represent the original work.

Kabbalistic legend ascribes the *Sepher HaBahir* to R. Nehunya ben HaKanah, the master of R. Ishmael ben Elisha, a high priest who flourished almost a century before the destruction of the sanctuary. Each one was a tanna of the first and second centuries CE. R. Nehunya's name occurs in one of the Bahir fragments. Notable sayings of his are preserved in Talmudic collections.

Other works are also ascribed to R. Nehunya who was a contemporary of Hillel the Elder and of Herod the Great.

The Bahir fragments of the Zohar as mentioned before are absent from the Mantua edition which was simultaneous with the Cremona edition, which contains them. It is possible that they were first added when the Zohar was prepared for press under the supervision of R. Isaac de Lettes, that unknown, but highly learned few, unsurpassable in all the branches of knowledge required, whom the publisher describes.

R. Moses Nahmanides mentions the work sub voce Midrash; R. Nehunya ben HaKanah, in his commentary on the Pentateuch (Genesis I). R. Azriel, born 1160 and teacher of Nahmanides, quotes the Bahir in his commentary on the Song of Songs, which is sometimes ascribed to Nahmanides. R. Menahem Recauatian Ibahian Iow quotes the quotations of R. Azriel and writes that he has afterward discovered them in the Bahir, to which he ascribes Palestinian origin. The treatise proper, however, seems lost.

## CONTENTS OF THE BAHIR

The name Bahir is referred to in Job 38:21. The book is in the form of a dialogue between certain illuminated doctors. It includes the mystery inherent in Divine names. It contains also a very full exposition of the celebrated Shem HaMeforash or Expounded Name of Deity. It contains certain references to the parts or modes of the soul and to the mythos of the fall of Man.

## THE HOLY LIVING CREATURES

A tradition is cited concerning a secret Palace, in which four living creatures are the holiest of all angels and also the most ancient. They are in correspondence with the four letters of the Sacred Name (Zohar II, 826; III, 344). They are also a connecting link between the world above and that which is below (because of their relation to the Divine Name, which unifies height and depth). Mysteries of Scripture are discussed, as well as the Mysteries of God hidden within His own being (Zohar II, 236; III, 346).

## THE SIGNIFICANCE OF THE THREE SABBATH MEALS

R. Abba assures us that three meals must be eaten on the Sabbath Day. The first while it is yet night and this is in honor of Shechinah; the second in honor of Him who is the Ancient of Days; the third to the glory of Him who is begotten of Wisdom and Understanding, according to the doctrine of the Idras. By these meals are the people of Israel set apart from the pagan nations, and those who neglect the three Sabbath meals shall have no part in the sacred palace where dwell the living creatures (Zohar II, 88 or III, 360–361). It is added that Sabbath is the name of the Holy One, which explains why the elect who deserve Sabbath, carry titles of admission to the presence of those angels, who are in its image and likeness.

It is said elsewhere that Sabbath is a day favorable to the study of the Hidden Law, for that which belongs to the name belongs also to the Law. For the Torah is the Name of the Holy One (Zohar III, 366). It is under such auspices that seventy modes of interpreting Holy Writ are revealed to the initiates (Zohar III, 362). Finally, we are told that whosoever observes the Sabbath fulfills the whole Law, from which point of view it might be said its yoke is easy and its burden light.

CHAPTER SEVEN

# The Faithful Shepherd

The Zoharic treatise bearing this title records conversations between R. Shimon Bar Yochai and Moses, who appeared to him, the great light of kabbalah, and gave him many instructions and revelations. Elijah took also part in the conference, and the witnesses included Abraham, Isaac, Jacob, Aaron, David, Solomon, and God Himself. Here are indications that in spite of the exalted doctrine concerning *Ain Soph*, the Zohar recurs occasionally to anthropomorphic conceptions that are found in the Talmud.

The Faithful Shepherd is longest by far of all supplementary texts to be found in the Zohar proper. The various portions are dispersed through the Cremona edition of the Zohar in all three parts. They are more numerous in the third part of the codex. All in all, we find about seventy portions of these excerpts. As in the instance of the Bahir, so also are these excerpts attributable to the period of R. Shimon bar Yochai and his disciples who came after him.

The Discourse of the Faithful Shepherd is important in several aspects. Its views on ichorous atonement and on the Messiah to come teach us the doctrine of profound salvation. Its moral teachings will illustrate its ethical position. Its reference to Shechinah will cast light on this great theosophical doctrine of kabbalah. Its speculations on angels and demons will show the Zoharistic foundation for the system of pneumatology.

## VICARIOUS ATONEMENT

The discourse introduces two phases of ichorous atonement. The first one is effected through the suffering of just men in a general sense, or in the aggregate.

"When the righteous are afflicted by disease or other suffering, in atonement for the sins of the world, it is so ordered, that all the sinners of their generation may obtain redemption." Every member of the physical body demonstrates this. When all these are suffering through some evil disease, one of them is afflicted (that is, by the instrument of the leech), so that the others may recover. Which member? The arm. It is chastised by the blood being drawn from it, which ensures healing in all other members of the body. It is in like manner with the children of the world; the members are in relation with each other, even as those of the body. When the Holy Blessed One willeth the health of the world, he afflicts a just man therein with pain and sickness and heals the rest through him. How is this shown? It is written: "But he was wounded for our transgressions, he was bruised for iniquities; the chastisement of our peace was upon him, and with his stripes we are healed" (Isaiah 53,5). By his stripes, as by the bruises (incisions) made in bleeding the arm, are we healed, that is; recovery is insured to us as members of one body (Cremona ed. III, 101).

Here is expressed the great idea of the solidarity of humanity. An instance of illustration follows in the text immediately. It reads:

> This is also exemplified in the history of Job. For the Holy Blessed One, seeing that the entire foundation was sinful, and how Satan appeared to accuse them, said unto him: "Hast thou considered my servant Job, that there is none like him in the earth (Job 1:8), to save his generation through him?" This may be illustrated, by the parable of a shepherd, who beheld a wolf approaching to rend his sheep and destroy them. What did the shepherd? Being wise, he gave unto the wolf the strongest and stoutest bellweather, even that which the flock was accustomed to follow, and while the wolf was bearing it away, the Shepherd hurried with his sheep to a place of safety and then returning rescued the bellweather from the wolf. So does the Holy Blessed One deal with a generation. He surrenders a righteous man into the power of the accuser, for the salvation of the generation through him. But when such a one is strong like Jacob, it is said: "A man wrestled with him" (Genesis 32:24). But he, Satan, will be unable to prevail, and in the end he will supplicate the righteous man to release him (ibid. 26). The righteous man chosen by the Holy Blessed One is too strong for the evil one and bears the cruelest afflictions willingly for the redemption of his generation. Whence also he is held as their savior, and the Holy Blessed One constitutes him shepherd over all the flock, to feed them in this world, and to rule over them in the world to come. (Cremona II, 106)

It is evident from the Zoharic commentary on Job that Satan too is God's minister, and the Almighty has recourse to a stratagem in order to save his people. The problem of evil remains obscure.

"The ancient pillars of the world [i.e., the intellectual luminaries of Israel] differ," says the same disquisition, as to the nationality of Job. One affirms that he was a righteous Gentile who was chastised for the atonement of the world. At a certain time R. Hammarumnah met the prophet Elijah and said to him: "How is it to be understood, that the righteous man suffers while the wicked one has joy of life?" He answered saying: "The just man of few sins receives his punishments for these in this world, and hence it is, that he suffers here. The man whose sins are many, while his good deeds are few, he receives recompense for the latter in this world, and hence has the joy of life."

## THREE CHANCES FOR A REPENTANT SINNER

Occasionally the Zohar illustrates an elementary spiritual truth by a happy reference to scripture, as for example concerning the change necessary to repentant sinners.

"Those who are oppressed with sin need a change of place, a change of name and a change in their actions, even as it was said unto Abraham: Get thee out of thy country" (Genesis 12:1). Here is a change of place. Also, "Neither shall thy name any more be called Abram, but thy name shall be Abraham" (Genesis 17:5). Here is a change of name. A change of deeds: he changed from his former evil actions to good actions (Cremona II, 186).

## THE MANIFESTATION OF THE SHECHINAH

The Zoharic speculations on Shechinah are a great treasury and their study at full length belongs to a much later section. Here be mentioned that it is said in the Faithful Shepherd that the relation of Shechinah to other lights of creation is like that of the soul to the body. But she, for this Divine Manifestation is presented under a feminine aspect, "stands to the Holy Blessed One, as the body stands to the soul." The Shechinah is the vestment of the Almighty. But it is added that

God is One with his manifestations, for He is complete perfect Oneness.

It is otherwise in man, says the Faithful Shepherd. "His body is earth, but the soul is called reason. The one is death, the other is life." But the Holy Blessed One is life, and Shechinah also is life. Whence it is written: "She [meaning the Shechinah, but the scriptural reference is to Wisdom], is a Tree of Life to them that lay hold upon her" (Proverbs 3:18).

The Faithful Shepherd affirms, that the Holy Blessed One is concealed in the mysteries of the Torah and is known or manifested by the commandments, for these are His Shechinah and this is His image. Thus, Shechinah is not merely the visible splendor which shone in the Holy of Holies as a manifestation in the Temple. The Torah is that something of the divine.

The passage continues:

> As He is humble so is Shechinah humility. As He is benevolent, so is she benevolence. As He is strong, so is she the strength of all the nations of the world. As He is truth, so the truth is she. As He is the prophet, so she is the prophetess. As He is righteous, so is she righteousness. As He is King, so is she Queen. As He is wise, so is she wisdom. As is He intelligent, so is she His intelligence. As He is Crown, so is she His diadem, the diadem of glory."

Therefore the masters have decided, that all whose inward part is not like unto the outward semblance shall have no admission to the House of Doctrine. As the image of the Holy Blessed One, whose interior His is, whose outward splendor is Shechinah. He, His interior internally, she His exterior externally, so that no difference subsists between her the outward and Him the inward, as she is an outflow from Him, and hence, all difference is removed between external and internal. Further, the inner nature of HVYH is concealed, therefore is He only named with the name of Shechinah, that is to say, Adonai. Hence the Masters tell us on the part of the Holy One: "Not as I am written [YHVH], am I read" (Cremona II, 118b, III, 456).

The connection instituted between Shechinah and *Malkuth*, in the light of alleged unity of God and the vestment which conceals Him suggests the sense of immanence of the divine in the universe.

## METATRON OF THE PRESENCE ANGEL SATAN AND LILITH

We shall close the quotations with two references to angels and demons in the Faithful Shepherd. The first concerns the great Angel of Presence, Metatron, who, in this text, is the sole occupant of the Briah world as the supernal Adam or is of that world of *Atziluth*. He is the garment of Shaddai. According to some, his form is that of a boy; while others ascribe to this angel a female aspect. This shows a connection with Shechinah and indeed, Metatron; with the difference of an added letter, signifies the Cohabiting Glory (Zohar III, 106).

There are secondly certain references concerning Samael, or Satan, and his wife Lilith. Satan was once a servant of the Holy Blessed One, and Lilith was a maid of "Matronetha" (Cremona III, 134). Their ultimate destruction is limited. But meanwhile, Lilith is the devastation of the world and the lash in the hands of the Holy Blessed One to strike the guilty. So she too is God's minister.

CHAPTER EIGHT

# Hidden Things of the Law

The extant fragments of this tract occur in the Cremona edition of the Zohar as follows: II, 250. Still others occur in the Amsterdam Codex. The words *Sithre Torah* signify Secret Doctrine; otherwise mysteries of the Divine Teachings (that is, Torah) and its hidden things.

The tract itself occurs only in the Zohar and not a line of it is extant elsewhere. It contains scriptural exegesis. It also contains much on the evolution of the sephiroth, which we shall discuss in another section. There is in it one passage, however, which has been thought to distinguish certain stages of mystical vision.

## STAGES OF MYSTICAL VISION

It is said that the glory of the King is discovered in three colors (Zohar I, Appendix III; II, 720, 721). The first is above and so far away that no eye can perceive it in its clearness; but it is distinguished dimly by contracting the range of vision (that is, by half opening the eye). It is of this Divine manifestation that Scripture says God appeared to me far off (Jeremiah 31:3). The second color is seen when the eye is hardly opened at all. Of this it is written: "What seest thou?" (Jeremiah 1:3). The third color is that bright luminous flash which cannot be suffered at all, except between the rolling of the eyes when the lids are closed altogether, and the eyes move in their sockets. There can be seen then in that rolling, the light as of a luminous mirror. But the color thereof can be comprehended only by him who beholds the shining with eyes shut and as if in recollection. Whence it is written: "The hand of the Lord was upon me" (Ezekiel 37:1), and, "The Hand of the Lord was upon me in the evening" (Ezekiel 33:2).

It is added on the authority of another sacred text that all prophets stood in need of an explanation to make their visions intelligible, save Moses only, who could on highest Divinity (see Numbers 12:7, 8). No doubt the kabbalists had visions and means of inducing visions, as well as modes of contemplation and occasional deeper states which pass under this name.

## THE THREE ANGELS OF ABRAHAM

The discourse proceeds then to another illustration of color symbolism in the case of the three angels who appeared to Abraham.

It is written: "And lo, three men stood by him" (Genesis 8:2). These are the three angelic emissaries clothed in human forms, which came down to this world and showed themselves to the children of men. They correspond to three colors of the rainbow: white, red, and green. The white is Michael, because he is the right side; the red is Gabriel, because he is the left side; and the green is Raphael. And these three colors are those of the rainbow, because it is never seen otherwise than with them. Thereby also was the Shechinah revealed to Abraham. It is written also:

And they that be wise, shall shine as the brightness of the firmament (Daniel 12:3). They shall shine with a light, which is enkindled by igniting a splendor. That brilliant light which is hidden, the spark of all sparks, of all lights, is therein invisible and hidden, concealed and made known, seen and not beheld. This shining light came out from the Supreme Fountain of enlightenment, which is shown in the day and hidden at night. It illuminates the ordinances of the Torah and all colors are concealed therein. . . . Those three colors, which are beheld below, are in the likeness of colors that are above and are unseen by eyes of flesh. The light is called by the name YHVH. (I, Appendix 3; II, 722, 723)

It follows that the three men are three angels clothed in the light of Shechinah. The color symbolism in Sithre Torah leads to a disquisition of Divine Names and Titles. The tale of the three angels teaches us furthermore that when God manifests on earth He appears in the form of Shechinah.

## OTHER INTIMATIONS AND EXCERPTS

In another intimation on color symbolism we are told that even as white is the foundation of colors, while all return therein, there is also a white light of the spirit. Even a light of mercy from which other lights emanate (meaning, sacred qualities and virtues), this also belongs to the Divine Order. It is mysterious and concealed. No one who depends on bodily vision perceives it; it is reserved for the just alone (Zohar II, 78b). Those who seek to know it should meditate on the precepts of the Law by day and by night (Joshua 1:18).

We are reminded of another Zoharic passage which affirms that the world was made by Mercy, derived from the Supernal Loving Kindness abiding in the world above. That is to say, that Mercy is greater than Judgment and is that which moves therein and rules in all.

We are told elsewhere the Scriptural ordinance to sanctify the Sabbath day is not merely the synthesis of all other Scriptural commandments and earns the same merit as the observance of all, but that it lifts up those who do so into a realm of everlasting memory (Zohar II, 91a, III, 370). That is to say, that forgetfulness is found only below; but in the world above, that which we are is known, that which we were is with us, and the future stands revealed.

It is finally affirmed that the letter *aleph* calls upon us to proclaim the unity of God (the numerical value of *aleph* is one). The text goes on to tell us that *aleph* is a letter of prohibition as well as of command, since it forbids us to acknowledge the identity of the true God with any pagan divinities. It is added that the same letter forbids us to be seduced by magic and the art of evoking the dead (Zohar II, 91a, III, 368–369).

CHAPTER NINE

# The Secret Commentary

The fragments of the Midrash HaNealam are found in the Cremona edition at the following places: I—257, 260, 261, 264, 265, 268, 269, 270, 273, 286, 296. They discuss chiefly the destiny of souls, future punishment and rewards, the resurrection of the body, the paradise above and its relation to the paradise below, and doctrine concerning angels and demons. The consideration of these subjects is reserved for another section subsequently.

A few of the intimations, however, concerning the soul and its destiny may be offered here and now.

At the beginning of this Midrash, we hear of the soul in glory because it ascends thus into heaven and also, that its splendor is called a spirit of the Holy One; meaning therefore, that the soul is encompassed by the Divine Presence. But it is only a light which is reflected thereupon by an event to come; for it is said presently that the Holy One comes to the soul, accompanied by Abraham, Isaac, and Jacob. We are told by the assurance of R. Eleazer that the souls of the just desire after that moment, when they will leave the vanities of this world and enjoy the life to come.

## LIGHT OF THE SUPERSUBSTANTIAL BREAD

It is said a little later that the souls' joy in heaven is in the contemplation of the glory of God and in the nutriment of higher lights (super-substantial bread). The suggestion that light in the celestial world becomes the nourishment of those who have been admitted therein becomes a subject of discussion by various masters in Israel. The epoch under discussion is that which follows the resurrection, a time when the Holy One will be in union with His creatures; the just will be conscious of His inward Presence, and they shall know Him as if they saw Him with their eyes (loc. cit. Toldoth, II, 713–715).

It has been handed down, that at this time, He Who is Holy and Blessed will prepare a feast for the righteous, that is, a spiritual nourishment defined as the splendor of Shechinah between the cherubim on the Mercy Seat. A later intimation says that this will be a food of joy, experienced by contact with the Holy One otherwise rejoicing in His joy. Reference is then made to Psalms 33:4.

There is also a wine reserved for the righteous from the creation of the world, and it is said to signify hidden and immemorial mysteries which will be revealed in the age to come. The summing-up sentence affirms that it has not entered into the heart of man to conceive what God prepared for those who love Him (Isaiah 64:4).

The Midrash goes on with pregnant explanation, according to which, the Leviathan of Isaiah and the Talmud, the "behemoth" of Job, analogous rabbinical legends are things written for the crowd, which understands only material rewards and punishments. We know, however, what is the faith of the just, and whither their aspirations tend, namely "to rejoice with God, with a joy which shall be wholly spiritual."

For the rest the Secret Commentary tells us that the study of the Holy Doctrine (Torah) and the study of the Secret Law was the consolation in chief which was sought by sons of the Doctrine through the exile of the Gentile centuries. The Temple was destroyed and it was not possible to offer sacrifice. But always the Torah remained; and the reward of dedication thereto was that of the world to come, understood as the Mountain of the Lord, the Mountain of Delight and Felicity (Zohar I, Appendix III; II, 680).

CHAPTER TEN

# Minor Tracts of the Zohar

Up to now we passed in review the more important Midrashim and fragments to be found in the Zohar proper. The Cremona edition contains many more texts and pieces, and a great many supplements and additions make up the contents of Zohar Chadash. A few items, however, shall be noticed here briefly for the sake of comparative completeness.

## THE OMISSIONS

Hashmatoth—Omissions—are comprised in the first Appendix to Part I of the Zohar, which is the commentary on Genesis. Some of them form part of the Sithre Torah or Hidden Law of the Luminous Book and of the Faithful Shepherd.

Some other notes thereof concern a few other subjects of consideration.

a. The White Head in the Book of Concealed Mystery to which the Divine Name Tetragrammaton YHVH is allocated.

b. The Glory of the Lord, that is to say, Shechinah, which was revealed in the Tabernacle, is identified with what is termed the Sea of Wisdom in the Supernal World, meaning the sephirah *Chokhmah*—Wisdom. We shall see, however, that the Shechinah in transcendence is referable to *Binah*—the Sea of Understanding.

c. It is said that the Sun and Moon are placed under the presidency of two powerful angels; that Esau was under solar dominion, while Jacob was under lunar influence. For this reason, the one would rule over nations here on earth, but the other in the world to come.

d. It is affirmed once more that the true sacrifice of Expiation is the study of the Torah, that is, the Secret Doctrine (Zohar I, 251–253a; II, 591–597).

## ADDITIONS

The various adjunctions called tosephtoth or additions which occupy the second appendix of Part I, are also extracts from the same Midrashim already enumerated. The only excepted paragraph under the title of Additions is found also in Appendix I, so that these two are left for our consideration (Zohar I, 283, 284a; II, 657–658).

In one of them the Great Sea is again identified with "Wisdom, instead of Understanding." Wisdom is also referred to Shechinah throughout the Zohar. It follows there the second and third sephiroth: "Wisdom and Understanding." Otherwise, *Chokhmah* and *Binah* in the "Tree of Life" are one in a state of union, and it is shown elsewhere in the Zohar that this union produces Divine Knowledge, which is obvious by the nature of things.

By the second one we learn that two spirits are provided for just men: one which animates them in this world and one in the world to come, both now being in joint activity. Later on we shall learn that the highest part of the human soul never leaves the supernal.

There are also additions that constitute the first and third appendices to the commentary on Exodus (Zohar II, 235–244, and 296–296a; IV, 261–273, 307–318).

Appendix I is a conference on the Celestial Tabernacle. The subject matter is derived, it is said, from a book entitled *Supreme Mysteries*. The Tabernacle above is built upon twelve thousand worlds, while the Tabernacle below corresponds by its material images to the Celestial Chariot. But it is in the likeness also of the Tabernacle of Adonai, even as this is in analogy with the higher Tabernacle of YHVH. In this connection it is affirmed that the Divine Name YHVH, designates the male principle in deity, while the Divine Name Adonai signifies the female principle. It is then added that these two are one.

Later on it affirms that the holocaust ascends to the infinite or to that which is without end or beginning; a Supreme Will more mysterious than all other mysteries—its name is Nothing.

This also should be noted, awaiting that time when we shall be called to consider the majesty of God in kabbalah.

The subject of the holocaust reoccurs and it is then said that man was intended originally as an offering to the Supreme Spirit, but man fell and animals were substituted in consequence.

The additions of Appendix III are drawn in part from Zohar Chadash and in part from *Sepher HaBahir*. Among subjects of consideration in those which remain over, we shall make mention of: 1) express prohibitions in respects of magic, sorcery, the evocation of the dead, and the practice of astrology; 2) a discourse on the creation of Paradise, the pillar which is based thereon, and goes up to the Throne of Glory or the sapphire firmament which is above, and the splendor which fills the Blessed Place when the Holy One comes down to visit the just therein; 3) an affirmation that the tradition of the Law, delivered to Moses on the Mount Sinai, alludes to the Oral Law (that is, Oral Torah), and this was transmitted by him to Joshua and by the latter to certain Elders. Whereas, Deuteronomy 31:9, concerning transmission by the sons of Levi, refers to the Written Law. (There are also Additamenta or Accessions scattered through the entire Zohar Cremona edition in all its parts in close to forty places.)

## REPETITIONS: *MATHNITIN*

Two of these may be of special interests of notice. One of them has reference to the Mystery of Faith.

It is said in the first *mathnitin*, or else rendered Traditional Reception, that "those who would penetrate the Mystery must hearken concerning the well by which Moses sat, and helped the daughters of Yithro to water their father's sheep" (Exodus 2:15–19). On the side of external things it is the well of Jacob (Genesis 29:2–10). But on the inward side it is Adonai, even Adonai YHVH the Lord God. As it says, "O Lord God, Thou has begun to show thy servant thy Greatness and thy mighty hand, for what God is there in heaven or in earth, that can do according to thy might?" (Deuteronomy 3:24). The text goes on to quote Daniel (9:17), "A cause thy face to shine upon Thy Sanctuary that is desolate, for the Lord's sake."

It is certified that this figurative well conceals a sacred spring, the name of which is *YHVH Tzivaoth*. The well in fact is the Ark of the Covenant which belongs to the Lord of all (Exodus 2:16). We shall also find that Adonai is a name of Shechinah, that Shechinah is described emblematically as a well and is also the Ark of Covenant. In this case Shechinah is the Mystery of Faith which is revealed only in God (Zohar II, 12b-13a; III, 56–57).

The second of the *mathnitin* describes a hierarchic order in the empire of the demon (Zohar III, 73b-74a; V, 200–201).

It also introduces Metatron, the Great Angel of the Presence. He is said to bear a sword, its foreboding characteristics particularly change every instant from male to female. We shall find that Metatron himself transforms in the same manner. He belongs to the Zoharic Mystery of Sex and so also does *Shechinah* (who is called Adonai). The two revealing Mathnitin are concerned with the subject Mystery of Faith, as we shall find in future references.

## SECRETS OF SECRETS— OF HUMAN PHYSIOGNOMY

The single fragment extant of Raze de Razin is found in Part II of the Cremona edition of the Zohar beginning at column 134. (See also Zohar Chadash 56a, Venice edition.)

It treats first of the connection between the soul and the body; and second of physiognomy, which we shall study in future references. In the present connection, however, we shall say that kabbalistic physiognomy has nothing to do and no connection at all with the accepted principles of this art.

Four general types of the human countenance are distinguished by the text in chief, and these are referred to as the faces of the four living creatures in Ezekiel's vision (Compare Zohar II, 73b, 75a Yethro). We have thus the leonine, the bovine, and the aquiline types, and another, less easy to characterize, by corresponding to the "living creature" which "had the likeness to a man."

The approximation of any individual to a given type depends upon his intellectual and moral rank. Physiognomy, however, according to the Zoharic Secret of Secrets, does not consist in the external lineaments but in the features which are drawn mysteriously within us. The features of the face vary following the form which is impressed on the inward face of the spirit. The spirit only produces all those physiognomic peculiarities which are known to the wise; and it is through the spirit only that the features exhibit meaning.

When spirits and souls pass out of Eden, they possess a certain form which is afterwards reflected in the face. The Secret of Secrets tells us also that every feature in a given countenance indicates to those who can read therein, whether it is possible or not for the possessor to be initiated into Divine Mysteries. In the writings of the Gaon, R. Sherirah, and in other literatures preceding the appearance of the Zohar, we meet with notions of physiognomy and chiromancy of a parallel kind. They also reoccur in the supplements to the Zohar.

## DISCOURSE OF THE YOUNG MAN

The little history that has passed under this name will be found in the Cremona edition of the Zohar, Part II, and comprises a few columns (91 et seq.) which follow after the "Book of Concealment." In some editions it appears in section Balak.

It is the account of a rabbinical prodigy, the son of R. Hamnuna, living with his widowed mother in a certain village. One day two disciples of R. Shimon Bar Yochai, namely, R. Isaac and R. Judah, passed through this village on a journey and paid a visit to the widow. When her son returned from school, she wished to present him to the rabbis to receive their blessing, but he declined to approach them, after the unamiable manner of prodigies. The reason assigned in the narrative is that he discerned by the odor of their garments that they had not recited the requisite "Hear O Israel" in honor of the unity of God.

He did not disdain, however, to converse at the table delivering sundry discourse. Some of these subjects pertained to the symbolism of washing the hands, a function of mystery, in part because it is written: "So they shall wash their hands that they die not" (Exodus 33:21), that is, Aaron and his sons, when entering the tabernacle of the congregation. Similarly, others pertained to grace on meals, and to the Shechinah. Also, on the utterances of Jacob; particularly regarding the verse of Genesis 48:16; "The angel who redeemed me from all evil, bless the lads." He conversed also on other matters.

The discourses impressed the disciples of R. Shimon bar Yochai, to whom they gave an account of the adventure. They paid subsequently a second visit to the lad, who unfolded to them further secrets of the Torah concerning the heave offering (Numbers 15:19), the mystery of bread and wine, and on grace after meals. When again the facts were reported to the "Lamp of Knowledge" (R. Shimon), he pinioned, that the lad would not continue on earth, for the Holy One would call him to Himself.

## THE MANSIONS OF ABODES—THE SEVEN HEAVENS AND SEVEN EARTHS

The methodical treatise, under the title that is termed in the original "Haichaloth"—Palaces, gives an account of the structure of Paradise and the infernal region as an appendix to the commentary of Exodus. In the text of the Cremona edition and in its supplement, many "Palaces" and several "Series of Palaces" are found; we shall deal with them later on.

According to one tabulation, the mansions are seven in number and were the original habitations of the earthly Adam. After the Fall of Man, they were reconstituted and became the abode of the saints. R. Shimon testified otherwise to nine Celestial Palaces, which are of no definable form, being the Thought of the Holy One (Zohar II, 269a; IV, 302).

The term which signifies mansion, temple, or palace is applied by later kabbalists to *Malkuth*, in which Tiphereth is said to be concealed as in a palace. So also, the name Adonai or Lord is the palace of Tetragrammaton, because it is the same number, sixty-five, as heichal—palace. This name is attributed to *Binah* and in a special manner to *Kether* on the authority of the Zohar, for heichal is restructured to *hai chol*—Here is All, that is, "All" is contained; seeming that *Kether* includes the whole world of *Atziluth*, because the supernals are in unity. In another sense the term is applied to the sephiroth generally. In the plural haichaloth—palaces—are the branches of the sephiroth in the inferior worlds. The Palace of the Holy of Holies corresponds to the Three Supernals *Kether, Chokhmah,* and *Binah.*

## THE SEVEN HEAVENS AND SEVEN EARTHS

The Zohar tells us also of the seven heavens, one above the other like the layers of an onion. "Each heaven trembles with fear of its Lord, through Whom they all exist and all are taken away." Over all the Holy Blessed One holds all in His power. There are further seven earths below, arranged after the same manner. "These earths are disposed according to their names and between them is the Garden of Eden and Gehennah." They are inhabited by creatures of whom some have four faces, some have two, while others are single-visaged, like humanity.

They are not the children of Adam. Some of them are clothed in skins and others in shells, like the worms that are found in the earth.

Mention is also made that the *ADNI* is God in manifestation, while *YHVH* stands for God in concealment. It emerges then that the Immanent and Transcendent are One in God. Also accordingly God and Shechinah are One; for *ADNI* equals *ELHM* with the Shechinah, which is the deeper sense of this doctrine of theosophy.

## COMMENTARY OF RUTH—MIDRASH RUTH AND INCONGRUENCE BY TRANSCRIBERS

These Zoharic extracts are also found in Sithre Torah, Sepher HaBahir, and Midrash HaNealam and in the Mathnitin and others. The subject matter of the extracts may be tabulated briefly thus: The libations of water made at the Feast of Tabernacles signify the grace and favor the Holy One will pour upon the world, when impurity has passed from earth (Zohar, Appendix I, 656; II, 627). Wine is an emblem of Severity or Fear and milk of Mercy (Zohar, Appendix I, 270a; II, 637, 638). Their point of meeting is Peace (ibid.). The world was created by means of ten words and among these are *lover* and *beloved, joy* and *mirth*. These are words of irreparable optimism, ever recurring in the Zohar, and which words mean that the good things of the Lord are ever in the Land of the Living (ibid. 275a; II, 643). The word *sacred* belongs to all books of Scripture, but to the Song of Solomon in a peculiar manner, the most beautiful book, even as the citron is the fairest of all trees (ibid. 282; II, 653). Its versicles are subject to two hundred and sixteen interpretations, and R. Eliezer to R. Abba communicated them on one occasion (ibid., Appendix III, 46; II, 678). There is a paradise on earth, as well as a paradise on high, and there is a celestial Gehenna, even as there is a Gehenna below. The hell that is above is the abode of Jews who have neither kept the Law nor repented of their sins; the earthly hell is the place of the shadow of death, an eternal terror (Zohar 26; II, 686–687. Cremona ed. Midrash Ruth, III, cols. 114, 124, 130, 174, 181, 184, 323, 530. The Mantua edition, though, is regarded as Codex Correctus).

It must be remembered that a space of time approaching three centuries elapsed between the time of the first promulgation of the Zohar and the date when it was first printed. Many hands of transcribers were active in it. The persecutions of the Jews inaugurated by the atrocious edict of Ferdinand

and Isabella in Spain may have contributed much to the incongruencies of the transcribed manuscripts during that fiery epoch.

## THE ANCIENT AND LATTER SUPPLEMENTS

Subsequent to the Book of Splendor, we have two series of Zoharic writings, distinguished as its ancient and later supplements.

There should be added, however, that considerable importance and authority have been ascribed always by kabbalists to the Ancient Supplements. They contain explanations of the term *Bereshith* by R. Shimon bar Yochai, after seventy different ways; and hence the work is divided into seventy chapters with eleven further chapters added at the end. It was printed by Jacob ben Naphtha at Mantua in 1557, and it appeared again at Cracovia.

We find in these Ancient Supplements the attribution of the members of the human body to the sephiroth. According to the Zohar itself, the erect figure of humanity exhibits the letters of the Tetragram, superposed one upon the other (Zohar II, 42a Mantua).

The apex of the head and brain is referred to *Kether*, the brain as a whole to *Chokhmah*, the heart to *Binah*. The back and breast are attributed to *Tiphereth*, the arms to *Chesed* and *Geburah*, the legs to *Netzach* and *Hod*, the generative organs to *Yesod*, the feet to *Malkuth*.

Some out of the seventy ways of interpreting the much-debated word *Bereshith*, which is rendered "beginning" in Genesis, are suggestive and curious. Here is one instance thereof. "In the beginning God created." This is the soul when it emerges from the bosom of its mother and is taught thereof. "And the earth was without form, and void, and darkness was upon the face of the deep" (Genesis 1,2), because the eyes of the soul were closed. Hath it opened its eyes? "And God said.

'Let there be light.'" Hereafter man is gathered in from this world and this then is written about the soul. "And God said, 'Let the waters under the heaven be gathered unto one place, and let the dry land appear.'" When the soul is removed from a man, his body remains even as "dry land."

A most celebrated quotation from the Ancient Supplements is the Prayer of Elijah, though it belongs only to the prefatory part, the beginning of the second preface.

## THE SUBLIME PRAYER OF ELIJAH

Lord of the Universe, One alone art Thou, but not according to number. Thou art the most sublime of all that is sublime, the most withdrawn of all things concealed; and conception cannot attain Thee. Thou hast produced ten forms, which we call sephiroth, and Thou guidest by means of these, the unknown and invisible, as well as the visible worlds. By them Thou doest veil Thyself and permeated by Thy Presence, their harmony knows not change. Whosoever shall regard them, as divided one from another, it shall be accounted unto him, as if he dismembered Thy unity.

These ten sephiroth are developed in successive gradations; so that one is long, another short, and the third intermediated between them; and whether from above or below, art guided Thyself by none.

Thou hast provided the sephiroth with garments which serve human souls as intermediate phases. Thou hast veiled them with bodies, so-called in comparison with encompassing vestures; and taken together they correspond to the members of "the human form." Thou art the Lord of worlds, Foundation of all foundations, the Cause of all causes. Thou dost water the tree, from that source which spreads life—everywhere, as the soul spreads it through the body. But Thou hast Thyself neither image nor form, in all that is within or without. Thou didst create heaven and earth, that which is above and that, which is below; with the celestial and terrestrial hosts.

All this didst Thou do, that the worlds might know Thee. Yet no one can conceive Thee in Thy reality. We confess, only that apart from Thee, whether above or below, there can be no unity, and that Thou art Lord of all. Each sephirah possesses its allotted name, after which angels are also called, but none describes Thyself, the One alone, Who doest, all names inform, to all impart their force and their reality. Didst Thou withdraw therefrom, they would be left like bodies devoid of souls.

Thou art wise, yet not with positive wisdom; Thou art intelligent, but not with a definitive intelligence, nor hast Thou a fixed place. Though all these things are attributed to Thee, so that man may conceive Thine Omnipotence and may be shown, how the universe is guided by means of severity and mercy. If, therefore, a right or left side, or if any center be named, it is only to exhibit Thy government of the entire universe by comparison with human actions; but not because any attribute can be really imputed to Thee corresponding either to mercy or severity.

# GOD AND HIS ATTRIBUTES

The distinction between God and His attributes and hence between God and the sephiroth, which in a manner are His attributes emanated, is insisted on elsewhere in the Supplements by the help of a striking illustration.

> Woe unto those whose hearts are so hardened, whose eyes so blinded, that they regard God as the totality of His Attributes. They are like unto a man who should describe the King as the totality of his insignia. Behold, a king wears his insignia only that he may be known through them. And verily, the King of kings, the Concealed of all hidden, the Cause of all causes, is

disguised in a splendid garment, so only that He may be known thereby and thereby may impart to the dwellers on this earth a conception of his sacred nature. (Supplements, 21)

The Ancient Supplements are identical in their teachings with the Zohar itself and are in semblance throughout. Some affirm that the originals existed from time immemorial at Fez in Africa. There is a statement in the Supplements that the revelation in full of the Zohar is reserved for the end of time. It will be the work of Moses.

Some suppose that the tracts were brought to Fez by disciples of Rav Hai, the Gaon of the Sages of Chirvan on the Caspian Sea.

The Zohar Chadash—the new Zohar—is broadly embracing: a sequel to the Hidden Commentary, certain additional supplements, a commentary on the Song of Solomon, and another commentary on the Book of Lamentations. It was published in Crakow in 1703 by Isaac ben Abraham of Neustadt. It may be noted that later still, a certain Isaac ben Moses of Satanow is said to have produced a false Zohar, but it was unmasked speedily.

SECTION V

# The Doctrines of the Kabbalah in Respect of God and the Universe

CHAPTER ONE

# The Majesty of God in Kabbalism

The fundamental doctrines of the kabbalah are the following: 1) a philosophy of the absolute, 2) the evolution of the universe in part by way of emanation and in part by creative acts. A further distinction of the evolution is correlated upon four worlds, the last of which only was brought into being by a process of creative action as we know it.

Subsidiary theosophics connected with these subjects are: (1) the contrast between God in Himself and God as revealed to His people, that is, to finite intelligences; 2) the sacramental nature of the conventional symbols; 3) the way of attainment, in respect of human knowledge and wisdom, in divine things.

## THE KABBALISTIC IDEA OF GOD AND THE EVOLUTION OF THE UNIVERSE

There has been proposed a conventional division of kabbalistic doctrines into metaphysics and into transcendental physics of the kabbalah. However, the science which explains the doctrines concerning God, man, and nature admits of nothing but a permanent mystic communication between them; the best manner of studying it is therefore to follow its view as to the eternal order.

It begins in that Absolute, which it is the purpose of all fundamental wisdom to communicate and make known to man. It attempts to exhibit the transition from the Absolute to the Related, from the nominal to the phenomenal, and to establish a chain of correspondence between the infinite and the finite. It is, however, more than a philosophical attempt to bridge over the gulf which separates the timeless from the temporal. Moreover, the intermediaries of the transition are the ladders of ascent by which man returns to the Divine. Hence it is more than an explanation of the universe. It is a sum of the peculiar revelation of God and a sum of true religion founded on recognized Scriptures. It is described most adequately as a system of theosophy, of the Wisdom of Israel, applied to the Mystery of God. It begins with a confession that it is unsearchable and that beyond our highest conception of all that is most divine, there is the unknown and knowable God. Even in the mystical communication possible between the divine and man, the essence escapes our apprehension.

We can indeed know God, but not as He is in Himself; our knowledge being made possible through the manifestation of His Deity. This takes place after two manners: a) by meditation of the law of nature in the physical universe; and b) by the Law of Grace, which is the manifestation of God in His relation with the souls of His elect.

## GOD'S UTTERMOST TRANSCENDENCE

In the eternity that preceeded either of the manifestations mentioned, God's Deity was withdrawn into Himself or subsisted after a manner which transcends entirely the conception of human faculties. In the tract of the Zohar entitled the Faithful Shepherd, it says, on the authority of R. Shimon Bar Yohai, that before God created the archetypal idea which underlies the form of the world, He was alone, without form or similitude, and hence there could be no cognition of Him (Cremona ed., Raayah Mehemnah, II, col. 73). God in the uttermost transcendence is eternally in this state, which is postulated here as prior to creation; that is, God's transcendence is beyond realization by the human mind.

It is said that the Glory of the Holy One is so sublime and so highly exalted that it remains eternally secret; no man can penetrate the deeps of the Divine Wisdom. The place of His exaltation is unknown to man and angels (Zohar I, 103a; II, 18; Ezek. 3, 12). This is held to be intimated by the Prophet when he said: "Blessed be the Glory of the Lord from His place." The names that are ascribed to God's Deity in this abyssal condition are not Names which present the condition or the Divine Nature. They are conventions of the philosophical hypothesis; they are terms which serve to indicate that God, prior to manifestation, is nameless, even as He is beyond reach. The kabbalah speaks of God being alone with His Name, that is, the Divine Tetragram. This state of the Supreme preceded the whole creation, according to Maimonides.

The Zohar continues saying, God is the Ancient One; the most ancient of all the ancients, but this describes only the eternity of His subsistence. He is the Hidden of all the Hidden Ones, but this concerns only His concealment. This leads us into the Zoharic doctrine of the infinite, expressed in the mystery of *Ain Soph* or the Divine Essence, abiding in the simplicity and undifferentiating of perfect unity without end. The separate abstract significance of the word *ain*, and abstract conception of nothingness includes an attempt to register the ineffable nature of an infinite mode.

## ZOHARIC TEACHING OF *AIN SOPH*

We have just seen, according to the Faithful Shepherd, that prior to the creation of the world, God was alone, formless and resembling nothing. It is added that in this state it is forbidden to represent Him by any image, even by His Holy Name, or by any letter or by any point (vowel) (Mantua, II, 423). *Ain Soph* is understood moreover as the limitless mystery of Divine thought, the center of all and the secret of all secrets (Zohar I, 21a). References to this state of Deity are comparatively few in the Zohar. *Ain Soph* is met with frequently, however, in the commentaries on the Zohar and in the writings of the students of R. Isaac the Blind.

According to the Book of Concealment, God's dwelling is in a place which is not a place, "locus qui non est." Here we come into subtle metaphysics as the "non-ens" dwells in the "non-est," which involves metaphysically stripping away every attribute pertaining to manifest existence. This is necessary to attain some idea of unmanifest abstract being; unconditioned. Such are the levels of obstruction discussed therein.

## MOSES OF CORDOBA ON *AIN SOPH*

The Zoharic commentator, R. Moses of Cordoba, in his Pardes Rimonim (that is, Paradise of Pomegranates), Tract 3, affirms that the cause of causes is called *Ain Soph* because His excellence is without bound and there is nothing which can comprehend Him.

*Ain Soph* was located above the sephira (root of sphere or numeration), which is regarded as the Throne of Ineffable Deity. It is added that *Ain Soph* dwells in the hiddenness thereof. Here we find symbolized our intellectual recognition of that which exceeds our intelligence, that which symbolizes that "Absolute," in which resides the essence or potentiality of all. According to the Zohar, God is immanent in all that has been created or emanated and yet is transcendent to all.

*Ain Soph* is the subsistent state of Deity Itself; whence it follows that there is a manifested state of the Divine Nature, but it is certainly not the visible world. How this manifestation occurs will be indicated later on.

The notion of God is absolutely simple unity, without any multiplication above all number, above Wisdom, although Wisdom is one of its first emanations.

The angels are according to Moses of Cordoba neither simple nor without multiplication, in comparison with the notion of God.

## THE RAAYAH MEHEMNAH ON THE NOTION OF GOD

The book entitled *Faithful Shepherd*, quoted in *Beth Elohim* (The House of God) says:

> Woe unto him, who makes God to be like unto any mode or attribute whatsoever, even if it be one of His own. Woe still more if he make Him like unto the sons of men, whose elements are earthly, and so are consumed and perish. There can be no conception attained of Him, except in so far as He manifests Himself, when exercising dominion by and through some attribute. Abstracted from this there can be no attribute, conception or ideal of Him. He is comparable only to the sea, filling some great reservoir, as for example, its bed in the earth, wherein it fashions for itself a certain concavity, though that thereby we may begin to compute the dimensions of the sea itself.

We see that it affirms that the forms under which God is manifest are merely subjective.

## SUMMATION

To sum up the subject, the Zohar testifies that God is essentially without form, but in His manifestations, He is seen or discerned under different aspects according to a scale of degrees, which will be unfolded in the study of the paths of wisdom (Zohar I, 275a; II, 644).

The Zohar also testifies that the most secret of all Mysteries is that which is called "Nothing," being the Most Holy Ancient from whom the Light flows forth (Zohar I, 64b; III, 283; I, 43b; III, 194).

This notwithstanding, it is affirmed that in the essence of the infinite there are neither intentions nor lights nor brightness. The explanation is that although every light emanates therefrom, they are not in that state of shining which would enable man to grasp the nature of the infinite: it is a Supreme Will (Zohar II, 239a; IV, 267). The unity of God contains no distinctions whether manifest or unmanifest.

The union effected with the Holy of Holies ascends to *Ain Soph* (the foregoing not withstanding) because all perfection must tend to fusion with the "Mysterious Unknown," which is the object of all desires, though in *Ain-Soph* there are no desires, even while they subsist only by reason thereof (Zohar II, 26b; V, 74–75).

*Ain Soph* is symbolized by the letter *aleph* (Zohar 257a; V, 597). The later kabbalists posited *Ain Soph* as a Hidden Light, above *Kether*, at the head of the sephirotic tree.

CHAPTER TWO

# The Ten Sephiroth

Having postulated the existence of the "unconditioned Absolute," the next concern of the kabbalah is the mode of manifestation of that withdrawn inconceivable nature. The process of elimination to which reference has been made already attained the ultimate and fundamental conception of deity. The attribution of absolute reality to that which has been stripped of all realism, however, has resulted in something which was outside intellectual comprehension. The antithesis of anthropomorphism was merely a convention of the human mind. The intellectual difficulty became a ground for exaltation of the conception. The Zohar says that it is called *Ain* not on the ground of nonentity, but so it may be inferred—because that which is wholly outside our knowledge is for us as nothingness.

As regards that latent deity of *Ain Soph*, there remained to account for the bond of connection between this abyss of the Godhead and the visible universe. There remained further to establish another bond of connection between the absolute transcendency of *Ain Soph*, apart from all limitation outside all human measurement and the conception of the Lord of Israel which has anthropomorphic stature and measurements.

The kabbalah therefore is concerned with the problem and the difficulty of conceiving why the abyssal state in which God unmanifest had been sufficient to Himself from eternity should at any period have had another mode suppurated to it. The answer of the kabbalah is, of course, in a word: the movement of the Divine Will. In this, the Unknown Absolute, above all number, manifested itself through an emanation in which it was immanent, yet as to which it was transcendental.

## THE MYSTERY OF THE OPERATION OF THE MYSTERIOUS DIVINE WILL

The kabbalah supposes an eternity antecedent to this initial operation of the Divine Will. The Zohar says expressly that in the beginning was the Will of the King. At the same time there is the already quoted warning of the Zohar: "Woe unto him, who shall compare Him with any mode or attribute, even with one of His own" (II, Raayah Mehemnah, col. 73 Cremona, Mantua, II, 42b).

Later commentators of the Zohar however took for themselves more freedom of expression. Thus we find Rabbi Naphtali Hirtz in his treatise entitled "The Royal Valley," saying: "Blessed be the Holy Name. Before anything was; He, by His simple Will, proposed to Himself, to fashion the worlds. The King is not given without the people, as it is written in Proverbs (14:28). In the multitude of the people is the King's honor. And it is the nature of the supreme Goodness to dispense good. Now, if the world were not, on whom could He bestow it?"

The exegetical treatise "Gates of Light" intimates that the exertion of Divine Will in the production of the emanations is a path so secret, that no being, not even Moses, could understand it. At the same time, this Divine Will is good and pleasurable—without end or limit. Hence, according to the characteristic optimism of the Zohar and the kabbalah, this world is in some respects the best of all possible worlds.

## DIVINE EMANATION AND DIVINE IMMANENCE

To ascertain something of the nature of the process of transition of the Divinity from the state of the "non-ens" and of how it was accomplished, we are brought back to the word, which was already cited, namely, the word *emanation*. The kabbalah repudiates implicitly the axiom: "ex nihils nihil fit" (nothing from nothing). For the "non-ens," dwelling in the unconditional state, wherein is neither time nor place, is the fullness which contains the all. In this Divine Plentitude, pre-existing eternally was the substance of all the worlds, which therefore came forth from, that is, emanated from, God. (Note: the term "non-ens," that is, no thing, is not, however, an absolute negative or void, but some Thing unknown to man.)

The system of emanations of the kabbalah is not, however, its only foundation, for it rests also on the identity of thought and existence or otherwise the Doctrine of Divine Immanence. On Zoharic authority, however, we have it that the idea of emanation belongs more especially to the Divine Nature unfolding from within itself, that it may be revealed ultimately to and within an external universe. God is the inward power of this cosmos and God is the abiding Grace of this universe. For the rest, at this moment, it is enough to say that after the world of emanation, there is a world of creation, a world of formation, and a world of manifestation or action.

The first consequence following the operation of Divine Will was the manifestation or unfolding of the Divine Attributes, that is, the transition of Deity from the latent to the active mode. This is so far as such terms can be used in respect to a state where there was no universe in which manifestation could take place, no created intelligence to cognize it, and no objective for action. God, Who was above all number, now produced a decade of numbers in this subsequent activity. This decade of numbers in the sense of the sephiroth is brought forth from *Ain Soph*. The decade of numbers must not be taken crudely to signify mere arithmetical numerals. It was powers, forces, vitalities, virtues, attributes, and principles that were thus produced or unfolded. These are the Ten Sephiroth which are tabulated as follows with their conventional titles. They appear in the Zohar as divine emanated essences.

1. *Kether*, the Supreme Crown
2. *Chokhmah*, Wisdom
3. *Binah*, Intelligence or Understanding
4. *Chesed*, Mercy; otherwise *Gedulah* or Magnificence, Benignity or Greatness
5. *Geburah*, Severity, Judgment, Awe, or Power
6. *Tiphereth*, or Beauty
7. *Netzach*, corresponding to Victory
8. *Hod*, or Glory
9. *Yesod*, or the Foundation
10. *Malkuth*, or the Sovereign Kingdom

Note: The conjunction of *Chokhmah* and *Binah* produced a quasi-emanation *Daath*, or Knowledge, but it is not one of the sephiroth proper.

The sephiroth, that is, emanations, are regarded as vessels, receptacles of Divine power and attributed as they developed. These receptacles were usually considered spherical.

The treatise "Beth Elohim" in its descriptions concerning the sephirah *Kether* involves the idea of circularity. The author of the book *Gates of Light,* refers the term *sephira* to the Hebrew word signifying sapphire, a stone which on account of its brightness and purity is a symbol of the sephiroth. (Compare, Ex. 24:10: "And they saw the God of Israel and there was under His feet as it were, a paved work of brilliant sapphire, and as it were, the body of heaven in its clearness.")

We now see that various profound meanings are attached to these ten emanations. The study of the system of the sephiroth constitutes by itself, a research full of complexity for the benefit of the circle of initiates. But we are only concerned with what it was intended to explain simply.

The initial purpose of the sephirotic system, as a doctrine of emanation, was to explain intermediaries between the Deity and the material world and similarly, to bridge the gulf between the finite and the infinite and to effect a correspondence by stages between the inconceivable purity of the Divine Nature and the uncleanness of matter. The ten numerations of the Sepher Yetzirah are, in fact, as we have seen, the scheme of the Ten Sephiroth.

CHAPTER THREE

# The Doctrine of the Four Worlds

The fundamental doctrines of the kabbalah were shown to be a philosophy of the Absolute, and the evolution of the universe in part by emanation and in part by creative acts. Now we will see the distinction of this evolution into four worlds; the last of which was brought into being by a process of making.

The sephirotic system is concerned first of all with the mystery of the Divine Evolution, that is, with God evolving the universe. The uncreated Will of God moved forward by a mysterious operation and certain manifestations or relations of the Deity became established. By a kind of flowing forth or emanation, four worlds were produced in succession.

An early description of these worlds is found in a treatise on emanation: "Masseket Atziluth of the Speculative Kabbalah."

## THE FOUNTAIN TEXT

The references of what is said upon the subject in the fountain text are as follows. There is a sephirotic degree entitled

*Malkuth*. It seems clear, that to what world soever this name is allocated, one sephirah alone is signified, being that which is tenth in numeration and is actually called *Malkuth*, signifying the Kingdom (Zohar I, 18a; I, 112). *Malkuth* is supposed to be designated by the word *bow* when it is said: "I do set my bow in the cloud" (Genesis). It is testified that Scripture makes use of three expressions, to create, to form, and to make, in allusion to the three worlds which are below the World of Emanation (Zohar II, 298).

Divinity in the world of *Atziluth* is God in the Hiddenness, yet moving toward manifestation.

Beyond is the unknowable mode of *Ain Soph*, from which it emanates. But in *Atziluth* there is a state of emanation, although it is a world of unity; for God and His Shechinah in *Kether* are brought forth, so to speak, into *Chokhmah* and *Binah* as Abba and Eimma, the Father in Supernal Wisdom and the Mother in Supernal Understanding.

## THE FOUR WORLDS

It follows that the four worlds are those of Emanation, Creation, Formation, and Manifestation, otherwise action or the material universe. The Hebrew equivalents are: *Atziluth, Briah, Yetzirah*, and *Assiah*.

The union of God and His Shechinah takes place in *Atziluth*, the World of Emanation where there is no separateness (Zohar III, 109b; V, 276). Also, the Angels of Briah are from the body of Shechinah (Zohar V, 275).

It is said that the princes of Israel, the wise, the intelligent, the zealous, heroes, men of truth, prophets, just men, and kings are all from the World of Emanation. Yet there are others from the World of Creation and the Shechinah is sacrificed for them.

There is also a reference to the Worlds of Divine Hiddenness. The first can be neither seen nor discerned and is known only to Him Who is concealed therein. It alludes to *Ain Soph*. The second is attached to the first and the Holy One is manifest therein. It is presumably *Atziluth*. The third is the beginning of division, signifying created intelligence and is the world of superior angels, Briah (Zohar III, 159a).

For the sons of the Doctrine, the Four Worlds are symbolized by the Hebrew word *pardes*, signifying a garden or orchard and understood as that of Paradise. The four consonants of the word are the initial letters of four words signifying the literal sense of the word of Scripture, the symbolical sense, the allegorical sense, and the mystical or kabbalistic sense. It went to show in the eloquent manner of symbolism that the Divine World is truly divine in all its stages, and that its study is an ascent from the world of manifested things to that of Deity and to the exalted notion of deity. It is also an ascent to the exalted notion of things unseen, and of Him Who reigns not alone in the world to come, but in this one which we see with our eyes, and who fills them both and by Whom the soul is replenished on all the places of being.

Each of the Four Worlds is subdivided into those ten spheres, which are called sephiroth or numerations and which have already been tabulated.

The first three sephiroth are allocated as the three Supernal Degrees of Divine Hypostases and the first one of them is called *Kether* (Zohar I, 22b; 139). It is also said that when the world of manifest things was in the state of Tohu, God revealed Himself therein under the hypostasis Shaddai. When it had proceeded to the condition called Bohu, He manifested as the hypostasis Tzabaoth. But when the darkness had disappeared from the face of things, He appeared as Elohim. Thereto appertain the words: "And the spirit of God moved upon the face of the water" (Genesis 1,2). This is understood as a reference to the sweet and harmonious voice heard by Elijah and termed, "The voice of the Lord is upon the water" (Psalms 29, 3). This signifies completion of the Sacred Name

(HVYH). Hence, in the vision of Elijah, it is said that "the Lord (HVYH) was not in the earthquake"—it was Shaddai. He was not in the fire—this was Tzabaoth; but He was in the still small voice, being that of the Spirit of Elohim, and the Name of HVYH was complete (I Kings 19, 11–13) (Zohar, ibid.).

The Name is composed of four letters, the relation of which to the Divine Essence is like that of limbs to the human body (Zohar I, 16a). But this notwithstanding, the hypostases are three only; *Kether* is the first, *Chokhmah* and *Binah* are the other two. The three bars of the Hebrew letter *shin* symbolize these, which also exhibits their essential unity (Zohar III, 194; V, 503). According to a further statement the crown symbolizes the first light, and the second light or hypostasis forms the sephira. These lights appeared to Abraham (Genesis 18:1). The third light which was seen by Jacob (Genesis 32:31), proceeds from the two first (Zohar I, 130–131).

The following sephirotic division represents the original text. *Kether, Chokhmah,* and *Binah* are referred to the world of *Atziluth*. To the second world of Briah are allocated *Chesed, Geburah,* and *Tiphereth. Yetzirah* comprises *Netzach, Hod,* and *Yesod. Assiah* is *Malkuth.* The Ten Sephiroth are contained, therefore, within the four worlds.

According to the Zohar, the sephiroth are comparable to chariots for the degrees of the Divine Essence. The word *degrees*, which is used very frequently in the text, illustrates the idea of gradations in the nature of the Presence, as the spheres of manifestation proceed further from the head of the tree. The supernal world contains the highest degrees of which the human mind can conceive by the intellect of faith, and *Kether, Chokhmah,* and *Binah* form one unity therein.

Briah is the world of created intelligence; its content flows over into *Yetzirah.* The third world and the fourth are implied in the Zohar, that as in Briah God created the forms of consciousness to which He would manifest Himself by Divine Modes, so in Yetzirah he produced the pattern, idea, or archetype of the visible and material cosmos, referred to as *Assiah*.

As for the names allocated to the Ten Sephiroth, *Kether* is the crown or summit of the entire sephirotic system. *Malkuth* is appropriate in respect of the visible world. Mercy and severity will be explained when we arrange the sephiroth in what is called the Tree of Life in the kabbalah. *Yesod* has a deep significance, which we shall understand later. *Netzach* and *Hod*, victory and splendor, we will also leave for another occasion.

The source of the Zoharic Ten Sephiroth or Numberings is the Sepher Yetzirah or Book of Formation, which is twice mentioned in the Zohar (Zohar II, 389a; IV, 315).

## THE TREE OF LIFE

The Sephiroth are also represented as arrangements in diagrams of the Tree of Life, as already mentioned. There is first the Middle Pillar, and there are the right and left sides corresponding to Mercy and Severity. *Chokhmah* is on the right of *Kether* and *Geburah* on the left (Zohar I, 164–165). *Chesed* is the right and *Geburah* the left arms. *Netzach* and *Hod* are the right and left hips, for the tree in this case has become a human figure. The right side is life and the left is death (Zohar I, 139). The Pillars of Mercy and Severity are thus completed, according to the scheme of the tree. The Middle Pillar is called the perfect pillar and is one of the hypostases in the Divine Essence (Zohar I, 101). The active light of the right side enters therein and so too does the passive light on the left. The Word issues from this union and according to another text, Abba and Eimma—the Holy Father and the Holy Mother—beget it in the world of the supernals. Elohim forms the Middle Pillar and therein are the union and fecundity of the waters above and below, meaning sephirotic degrees (Zohar I, 17; I, 103). It is "Mine eldest son Israel" (Exodus 4:22). Therefrom is to be understood that Israel is in the likeness of the Highest. The four rivers of Eden seem to be *Chesed, Geburah, Netzach,* and *Hod* (Zohar I, 28a; I, 165). The Middle Pillar is the Tree of Life and the two other pillars are perhaps together the Tree of Knowledge of Good and Evil. There is no evil when these are united with the Central Pillar, which process is also called the tent of peace and the seventh day, the Sabbath (Zohar I, 276; I, 28a, I, 165). The Central Pillar is Shechinah. It is the peace in particular between the light of the right side and that which in another place is called the darkness of the left (Zohar I, 254a; II, 599).

The Talmud and the Mishnah come from the Middle Pillar (Zohar 255a; II, 601). In an alternative allocation, the Middle Pillar is called the son of *yod,* but also the *hai* which is *Binah* (Zohar II, 115b; III, 445). The Middle Pillar is otherwise the Master of the House (Zohar III, 272a; IV, 37).

It is said of the right arm that it draws the immensity of space in love, like the arm of the male drawing the female (Zohar I, 64a; I, 375). The law of faith is on the right side (Zohar II, 82a; III, 342). The left arm draws the immensity of space in rigor (Zohar I, 64a; I, 375). The serpent constitutes the left arm; thence emanates the impure spirit. It is that of water and the side of sadness. These engender darkness, and the way of escape is by the harmony that can be instituted between the mercy and grace of *Chesed* and the severity of *Geburah* (Zohar II, 103b). The left side is without pity in the state of separation (Zohar II, 198b, 387). Yet according to another allocation, she who is Matrona is the left side as well as the Middle Pillar. She is the latter apparently, because she is the ground and state of union, and it is known that she is the Mother of Mercy. Shechinah, who is a divine hypostasis, dwells in each sephirah (Zohar III, 109b; V, 276; II, 250a; 584).

A day will come when the left side shall disappear and good will obtain only (Zohar II, 190a; IV, 174). It is further said the mercy and severity of *Chesed* and *Geburah* are united in *Tiphereth* (Zohar III, 233a; V, 563).

The holy degrees are declared to emanate from the holy side and the impure degrees from the impure side (Zohar I, 203b; II, 409). So does the Sepher Yetzirah describe the sephiroth as the abyss of good and evil. The Zohar speaks, however, in one place of the union between good and evil (Zohar II, 34a; IV, 166). It is mentioned there as a secret or mystery, and it is indicated in another place that there is a sense in which the left side is on the way of attainment (Zohar IV, 60b; IV, 268; III, 443).

We also learn that the Shechinah who is a divine hypostasis dwells in each sephirah (Zohar V, 276). The difficulties arising from allocation of evil of spheres in which God was present everywhere are mitigated when we remember the words of the text. The Middle Pillar draws the right and left sides, the good and the evil together in which union evil dissolves as such and then obtains entirely under the name of benignity, which is that of the Middle Pillar. It is therefore to be understood as a transmutation. Later on we will also learn that the Ten Sephiroth were repeated in all of the Four Worlds.

The conventional Tree of Life connects the sephiroth together by means of lines which are called paths, twenty-two in number, and these in connection with the sephiroth themselves constitute the thirty-two paths of the Sepher Yetzirah.

## A SUMMARY OF CORRESPONDENCES OF THE SEPHIROTH

The following summarizes the correspondences of the Ten Sephiroth in succession. *Kether* is the crown or head of the tree. It is the first hypostasis, but not the first Cause of Causes (Zohar I, 216; I, 131–226; I, 138). The First Cause contains within itself two hypostases, understood as male and female (Zohar I, 226; I, 139). God manifests with *Shechinah* in the degree of *Kether*. It is also said, however, that the first and third sephiroth are united as male and female. It is also said the *Kether* and *Chokhmah* are never in separation (Zohar III, 242b–243a; V, 581). This is true, however, of the whole supernal triad or the first three sephiroth.

Regarding *Chokhmah* it is said that it is by the sublime and impenetrable mystery of this sephirah that the world exists and all other mysteries depend therefrom. It is the second sephirah or the second hypostasis and it is called "man." Otherwise it is Abba, the Father (Zohar II, 3b). *Chokhmah* builds the house. It was concealed like the Supreme Point before creation, and it is called *yod.* It is eternal wisdom and therein is concealed the eternal thoughts, which is the great voice, meaning the still small voice, which is the house of eternal wisdom (Zohar II, 29a). In contradiction to these it is said to be the sister, meaning thereby the Shechinah. It is also daughter and mother; it is the beginning of all (Zohar Appendices III, Secrets of the Law, II, 50–51).

*Binah* is intelligence or understanding, and its number is said to be fifty, because of the fifty gates of understanding (Zohar I, 71a; 106a; II, 34). It is the concealed world and motherhood is its image. It is also penitence, the degree of the moon, the mystery of the Supreme World and the community of Israel (Zohar II, 206, 220).

The letter *hai* is allocated to *Binah,* and is then described as the only daughter, or alternatively Eimma, the Mother. It is the Throne of Mercy; and the celestial fire, which descends as *Malkuth,* is the Throne of Justice and the fire that goes up (Zohar III, 6a, 27b; V, 76). It is the sweetness of God and it constitutes the mystery of the Levite. The house is built by *Chokhmah* and is established by *Binah* (Zohar I, 161b).

*Chesed* is the male side and the Patriarch Abraham is referred thereto (Zohar I, 94a). The Divine Name of the Tetragrammaton is attributed to *Chesed,* and it is even called in one place the first degree of Divine Essence (Zohar I, 173b). It is merit, as demerit is *Geburah.* It is the place of revelation and it is the twin sister who came into the world with *Vav*. Otherwise it is said that *vav* is the son of *yod* and *hai*. It unites to the *hai*, symbolizing *Chokhmah*, and itself represents *Binah*. What, however, it represents really is the six lower sephiroth (Zohar V, 210–211).

*Geburah* or *pachad* is sometimes used in a good and sometimes in an evil sense. The world is based thereon in the sense that severity is indispensable; but it could not subsist without mercy. It is said also to be the repentance of God, and it seems even to connect with Samael. It was by *Geburah* that Jerusalem was destroyed (Zohar I, 160).

*Tiphereth* is beauty. It is the heart of the sephirotic tree and it is called Heaven. It is also glory (Zohar I, 34a).

*Netzach* and *Hod* come from the Celestial River. *Netzach* is in correspondence with the covenant according to one attribution. *Netzach* and *Hod* represent also the messiahs mentioned by the Talmud. In the macrocosmic human figure, *Yesod* is the organ of generation and it receives light from the Supreme Sephiroth. It is said to issue from the right and left sides, meaning that it draws from both, as *Malkuth* issues from *Yesod*. *Malkuth* is connected with Israel, regarded as son of the King. It is the rainbow or at least the arch thereof. It is also the lower firmament (Zohar III, 68a).

## CONCLUSION

In conclusion the following point may be drawn. All supreme degrees and all sephiroth are one, and God embraces all sephiroth. The law is *Chesed*. *Binah* is repentance, and *Malkuth* is confession. God and the ten crowns are one (Zohar I, 268). To ascend to Paradise above it is necessary, that souls should cleave to the Middle Pillar. There is a unity of the Ten Sephiroth and there is joy in the world, when order reigns among them. Finally, the Holy One manifests in the sephiroth for those who comprehend them (Zohar II, 211a).

## OF THE THREE HYPOSTASES

Concerning the three Divine Hypostases, there are three that bear testimony in *Atziluth*. There are three lights that form a single light, and so these three are one (Zohar I, 17b). The scriptural reference is "Let there be light" (Genesis 1:3), which is in Hebrew. The first word is the verb in the imperative. This word is *yod, hai, yod*. Yod is regarded as a symbol of the three Divine Hypostases and designed to show that the three are one (Zohar I, 166).

The chief symbolism, however, is drawn from the sacred name of the Tetragrammaton, being *yod, hai, vav,* and *hai*. Their symbols are called one on account of the unity of God. *Yod* and *hai* are the supreme mystery forever impenetrable. On the *yod* are all things based, and it is never in separation from the *hai*. As the prototypical male principle, it has man for another symbol. *Hai* is the female principle and it has woman as its emblem. It signifies many mysteries and its true name is the Shechinah. The letter *hai* is duplicated in the Sacred Name. It is said to terminate both the first and second parts thereof. The world was created by the *hai* or alternately by the *yod* and *hai* in the perfection of their concurrence. The *vav* is the free son and it is this that diffuses all blessings. The *yod* unites with *hai* as male with female and gives birth to the *vav* as son. The three dwell together in unity. *Vav* is the eternal world (Zohar I, 159a).

So far of the three Divine Hypostases, there is also the final *hai* which completes the Sacred Name and this is called the Daughter (Zohar I, 159a). It is said of this daughter that the *hai* came down to earth. The first *hai* is liberty above and the second is liberty below. The high priest depends upon the *hai* which is above, but the ordinary priest from the *hai* which is below (Zohar I, 354b).

Another type of symbolism of these letters is found in Part III 10b, V, 31. We shall not bring it here at length.

It follows that the two letters *yod* and *vav* of the Name belong to the male principle, and that *hai* primal and final belong to the female principle. The second *hai* will rise from the earth, meaning that it will be united with the Divine Hypostasis in the world of transcendence. The *vav* will be united to the *hai* as a bridegroom to a bride, and then there will be union everywhere—between the *yod* and the *hai* above, between the *vav* and the *hai* final (Zohar II, 228a).

It is said that *yod* is *Chokhmah* and *hai* is *Binah* and it is added that they sustain *vav*. The second *hai* is represented as in union therewith. For fuller information on these points, we must transfer our attention to the additional books: The Assembly of the Sanctuary, The Book of Concealment, The Great and Holy Assembly, and The Lesser Holy Assembly (Zohar II, 122b).

## THE WHITE HEAD AND THE TWO COUNTENANCES

The Secret Book comprises a discourse concerning the "White Head"—the ancient or Great Countenance. The same subject is continued in the Great and Holy Assembly. We find symbolized therein the Master with the white mantle and resplendent visage called the Holy of Holies (Zohar III, 128a). The White Head is without beginning and without end, before its reign was established and the Crown, that is, *Kether*, was assumed. This is a reference to *Ain Soph Ohr*, which pours down into *Kether*. The White Head is called *Ain Soph*, but is the first procession therefrom, connected by means of a white thread or bond of union with the Great Countenance. There is that which is called the Lesser Countenance, which presents, however, a complete aspect of humanity and is extended through many symbolical worlds. The distinction between the two heads is that in this case the hair and beard are black (Zohar III, 128b). The authorities are Daniel (7, 7), "The hair of his head like pure wool." The Zohar rendition is "whitest and purest wool." The other verse is from the Song of Solomon, 7, "The locks are bushy and black as a raven." When serenity operates, however, the hair of the White Head becomes black.

The Lesser Countenance has eyelids, because it has periods of sleep. It has a complete visage in manifestation. Because severity is one of its attributes, it has a distinctive name, being Lord; whereas the Great Countenance is called *Ain* because it draws and is emanated from *Ain Soph*, though it is located in *Kether* (Zohar III, 136b).

## MALE AND FEMALE PRINCIPLES

Notwithstanding these points it is laid down that the Lesser Countenance emanates from the Greater, and that the Greater Countenance metamorphoses into the Lesser. The latter is actually the former, as if seen through a curtain, and that they are one and the same. The body of this Sacred Form is described fully and is that of the male, perfect in all its members (Zohar III, 131b).

## MATRONA

Of this form there is a counterpart of perfect womanhood. These two were primordially side by side until the Ancient of Days put the Lesser Form to sleep and detached the female principle, whose name is Matrona; allegorically called Bride, Daughter, Betrothed, and Twin Sisters. The object of separation was, that the Bride might come to the Bridegroom in the great sacrament of matrimonial union, that they might become one body and as if one flesh (Zohar III, 142b).

All is mercy in this union. It constitutes the Law of the Sabbath and it is this that God blessed and sanctified. The sacred organ of intercourse is called Yesod on the male side, and it has access to the concealed and mysterious region on the female side which is called Zion. It is a holy place and all the holiness of the male enters therein. It is said that Matrona dwells in the supernal sanctuary, that is to say, in *Binah* and the Jerusalem, which is manifested on earth, that is to say, in *Malkuth*. It is because she is united to the male in the unseen world that she is joined in manifestation with man in faith (Zohar III, 143a).

The reference to Yesod shows that the Lesser Form is extended through the lower Sephiroth. It is the begotten son of *vav* in the tree of the sephiroth. Its name is *Daath*, or Knowledge; being a semi-sephirah, representing the junction point of influences flowing from *Chokhmah* and *Binah*. The inference is that the Lesser Countenance or Head is located there, while the feet are established on *Malkuth* (Zohar III, 291a). The Daughter or the Bride is the *hai* final of the Divine Name and we shall learn that her present dwelling is in *Malkuth*.

## THE DOCTRINE CONCERNING THE SEPHIROTIC TREE

According to the symbolism of the Idras, the Great Countenance is in *Atziluth* and it encompasses therefore, the three Supreme Sephiroth: *Kether, Chokhmah*, and *Binah*. It is located in *Kether*, where it is at once male and female. These principles being brought forth subsequently: the male principle into *Chokhmah* and the female into *Binah*, who produced between them *Daath*, which is the Divine Son.

We have therefore in the sephirotic tree the first Divine Manifestation proceeding from *Ain Soph* and interpenetrated thereby that it bears sometimes the same name. Insofar as it is postulated in *Kether*, it is not differentiated into male and female, but these are implied and according to other testimony the Shechinah is certainly there. When the Sacred

Ancient One wished to establish all things, He constituted male and female in His supreme region, namely, the Father and Mother, owing to whom all is made male and female. These are the second Divine manifestations in *Chokhmah* and *Binah* (Zohar III, 290a). The third Divine manifestation is in the lower sephiroth as son and daughter, brother and sister, king and queen.

The Great Countenance is Macroprosopus, the soul of the greater world, while the Lesser Countenance or Figure is Microprosopus, the soul of the lesser world and Adam the First, his Bride being the archetypal Eve. They form together the *habitaculum* of all created intelligences, the hierarchies of consciousness.

We can sum up by saying that the Book of Mystery and the Idras are a great allegory of man and his analogues coming forth from God. Male and female they were implied and conceived in Him. Male and female He manifested Himself on account of them. Male and female they came forth in Him and from Him. Male and female they abide above and below. Male and female they return too in refinement to Him; as we shall see clearly and fully later on.

## THE THEOSOPHY OF THE WORD

The full consideration of the Four Worlds and the Ten Sephiroth belong essentially to the chapter of the majesty of God in kabbalism. It shall be added, however, that here is Zoharic theosophy of the Word, and how the term should be referred in respect of the Divine Hypostasis. Again it is said that the Word was manifested in the sanctuary because it was indispensable to the existence of the latter on earth, that the Divine should be present therein. But what appeared between the cherubim on the mercy seat was the presence in the form of the Shechinah (Zohar I, 16b).

## THE WORD (LOGOS)

Onkelos in his paraphrase substituted the term Meimron for God Who is thus identified with the Word. In the Zohar it is held that the Word in Scripture is designated under the term *Bereshith*, because in order to fulfill the work of creation, this term was engraved "under the form of a turnstile." This is representing the six great celestial directions, the four cardinal points together with height and depth. The Word seems also to be specified under the name Sabbath. It had birth by the union of the active and the passive light, the latter being called darkness, and it discovers to us the Supreme Mysteries (Zohar I, 3b).

It is said: "While the King sitteth at his table, my spikenard sendeth forth the smell thereof." It is to be understood that the King means the Supreme Principle, while the spikenard signifies the Word, which is king below. He has formed the world below, on the model of the world above. Thought and the Word are held to be of the same essence. Seen through the medium of one region, this essence appears as thought, but through another as the Word (Zohar I, 74a).

The Doctrine of Israel is placed between two voices, one of which constitutes the Supreme Mystery, but the other is more accessible. The first is the Great Voice, "the voice out of the midst of the darkness." It is interior, imperceptible without cessation or interruption. Thence cometh the Secret Doctrine, which in its manifestation is called the Voice of Jacob, and this voice is heard. The Voice of Jacob is placed between the interior imperceptible voice and that Word which resounds abroad and is identical with the Written Law.

The Great Voice is the House of Eternal Wisdom and is female, as a house should always be. The Word is the House of the Voice of Jacob, that being the literal and this is the esoteric doctrine. When the Song of Solomon testifies "the voice of the turtle is heard in our land," the reference is to that voice which emanates from Him Who is the inward essence of all. It is the Voice that utters the Word, as for example, the Word that ordained circumcision for Abraham so that he might be made perfect. The Voice is added and joined to the Word, meaning that what is conceived in thought passes into expression, whether of speech or of action (Zohar I, 50b).

The reader is asked to observe that the root matter of the Secret Doctrine of the relation and union of male and female as enshrined in the Secret Tradition of Israel is as such the root matter of a metaphysical foundation. Thus, it is far removed from anything that belongs in public ways of life to the idea of sex.

CHAPTER FOUR

# The Paths of Wisdom and the Gates of Understanding

The ways of eternity are thirty-two. These are the paths of the Sepher Yetzirah, namely, the Ten Sephiroth and the twenty-two letters of the Hebrew *Aleph-Beth*. The Doctrine concerning them is a dependency of the Sepher Yetzirah. The paths are referred to as the Sephira Chokhmah and are termed channels, at once hidden and revealed. In the Faithful Shepherd, *Chokhmah* is called the highest of all paths, embracing and including all that are beneath it, and the influx of all that is derived therefrom. It also connects with *Chokhmah* the words in Job 28:7: "The bird has not known the path, neither has the eye of the vulture beheld it."

The first path is called the Admirable Mystical Intelligence, the Supreme Crown. It is the light that imparts understanding of the beginning which is without beginning. It is also the First Splendor. No created being can attain to its essence.

The second path is called the Illuminating Intelligence. It is the Crown of Creation and the splendor of the Supreme

Unity, to which it is most in proximity. It is called the Second Splendor.

The third path is called the Sanctifying Intelligence and is the foundation of Primordial Wisdom, termed the creation of faith. Faith emanates therefrom.

The fourth path is called the Receiving Intelligence because it receives the emanations of the higher Intelligences, which are sent down to it. Herefrom all spiritual virtues emanate, by way of subtlety, which itself emanates from *Kether*, the Supreme Crown. It is also mentioned that the Divine Name Elohim is mentioned thirty-two times in the first chapter of Genesis.

Some words must be added concerning the fifty Gates of Understanding referable to *Binah*, the third sephirah. It sketches all universal science and embraces all possible departments of knowledge. Its exalted themes concern only intellectual (theoretical) knowledge.

The principle of the enumeration is to be sought in the symbolism of the Hebrew word *col*, which signifies all and the consonants of which are equivalent to the number fifty. They are called Gates of Understanding because no one can attain to the Paths of Wisdom unless he enters by these.

We shall not enumerate them all categorically. They begin with the first matter, proceed through the varying elements of science to the theory of composite substances. They proceed to organic life and the physical, intellectual, and psychic nature of man and afterward to the heavens, planets, and fixed stars and the *primam mobile*. Then they proceed to the orders of the angelic world and finally to the supermundane and the archetypal world and that of *Ain Soph*, transcending human intelligence.

It is said that Moses did not attain to this, the fiftieth gate.

The scheme in full of the Gates of Understanding is found in the treatise entitled: "The Gates of Light" by

R. Joseph Gikatalia ben Abraham, which contains a full reference to the mystery of the word *col*—all.

All created things, it explains, have come out of these gates, so that in a sense their knowledge connects with the mystery of universal generation. It may be observed, it says, that the addition of the feminine indicator (the suffix *hai*, which has a numerical value of 5), to the word *KL* which itself is equal to fifty, gives *KLH* or bride—the Bride of Microprosopus, the Lesser Countenance, whence follows the whole mystery of spiritual generation in man. For *KLH* connects *KNST*—Congregation (of Israel). It brings us back to that place called mystically Zion and Jerusalem, in which the Divine is communicated to man.

Thus, the waters of Secret Doctrine fructify the art of Gematrioth. We shall return later on to the Gates of Understanding in the light of another Mystery and shall enumerate the intimations of the Zohar thereon.

CHAPTER FIVE

# The Doctrine of Cosmology

For the theory of creation, I shall draw from many quarters of Zoharic texts, simplifying at every point. We shall speak of the cosmos in a general sense as created by the Holy One. When the Holy One, Who is the mystery of all mysteries, willed to manifest Himself, He constituted in the first place a point of light which became the Divine Thought (Zohar I, 2a). In the Zohar (Zohar III, 28b), a passage is found where it is said that the words: "Lord my God" (Psalm 4, 1) are the foundation of the mystery concerning the unity and the indivisibility of the world at the moment when it was conceived in the Supreme Thought.

## THE WORLD CREATED FROM THOUGHT

Within this point of light, God designed and engraved all things, but especially that which is termed the Sacred and Mysterious Lamp, being an image representing the Most Holy Mystery. The Most Holy Mystery is identical with what is called the Mystery of Faith. (The Sacred Mysterious Lamp must not be confused with what is called the lamp of God, being simply the general notion of merit [Zohar I, 74a].) It follows in the meantime that the universe was created by and from thought. It must be noted that thought and the word by which it is formulated are of the same essence. Seen under one aspect this essence appears as thought and under another aspect it appears as the word. For the processes of the human mind, they are inseparable. (It is the transition from conception to expression [Zohar I, 439b].)

The authority for this revelation is the prophet Elijah, in an excursus on the words: "Behold Who has created these things" (Isaiah 40:26). In the beginning, however, that is to say in the point of Divine thought, the creation was only in the subject of the Divine Mind, as the text says. It existed not. It was hidden in the Divine Name, and this was also hidden. The symbolism of this thesis is very deep herein. The Sacred Name of God presupposes those who can pronounce or at least conceive it. The Name exists for man and its letters are images of the Word, as antecedent of necessity, for manifestation can be only to consciousness.

Now the world is said to have been created by the help of the Hebrew letters, whence it follows that their archetypes were produced first. They are said to have emanated from one another (Zohar I, 204a).

## THE LETTERS OF CONCEALMENT

After their emanation, the Sacred letters, the Great Letters, the letters that are above, of which those on earth are a reflection, remained in concealment for a period of two thousand years before the Holy One proceeded further in His work (Zohar I, 2b). When He willed so to do, the letters came successively before Him to show cause why each one of them should be utilized as an instrument in the task. The letter *beth* was chosen; but not because it is the initial of the word *barah*, meaning "to create," nor yet because it is that of *bereshith*, meaning "In the beginning," with which the Book of Genesis opens. Rather, it is because it is the initial letter of the word *barach*, which signifies "to bless." Also in the Talmudic treatise of Hagiga, Chapter 2, we find an affirmation that the world was created by the letter *beth*; but there is also a counter affirmation there by another authority substituting the letter *hai*. It shows that in the root sense, all is right with the world, that the letter *beth* was used in creation. The Zohar, like the Hebrew Scriptures, is canonical and subcanonical. It is sealed with sanctity. The writers had passed that sacred initiatory degree in which the soul looks for: "Good things of the Lord in the land of the living" (Psalm 27:13). Another story of the letters and their pleadings is mentioned elsewhere with variation respecting the letters *raish* and *teth* (Zohar I, 204a).

The Divine intention to make use of the letter *beth* for the reason stated delineated the motive of the worlds, showing that the instrument of creation was the power to bless all things. The intention was further to manifest the Divine Name therein as an indwelling presence of the universe and as a glory standing above the four quarters thereof. The procedure is symbolized by reciting that the Holy One engraved in the ineffable word those letters which represent the Mystery of Faith, being *yod, hai, vav,* and *hai*—the synthesis of all worlds above and below. (The mystery of faith is, as mentioned before, the hidden doctrine, that there is male and female above, as there is male and female below.) God represents the central point and the cause of all things, concealed and known forever, being the Supreme Mystery of the Infinite (Zohar II, 126b).

It is that point of Divine Thought which has been mentioned previously, and from it there issues a slender thread of light, which is itself concealed but which contains all light receiving vibrations from Him Who does not vibrate and reflecting light from Him Who does not diffuse light. He is the mysterious point of God centralized in thought on the world about to be produced. The slender light gives birth to a world of light that enlightens the other worlds. When the central point—the thread of light—and the light itself, being the world, are united, then union is perfect. This is the office of the Great Name shadowed forth in part but the primordial elements, which were produced at the beginning of Creation, were without feature, as it is said: "The earth was without form, and void" (Genesis 1, 2). This is like the sign drawn by a pen overdrawn with ink, and it was by the grace of the Sacred Name of forty-two letters that the world assumed shape (Zohar II, 30a). Note: The Name of forty-two letters is an expansion of the Tetragrammaton, for if the consonants of the Name are written at length thus: *yod, hai, vav,* and *hai,* their sum in numbers is forty-two. After that manner the letters themselves are extracted to make up the expanded Name.

All forms emanate from these letters, which in manner are the crown of the Tetragrammaton, that is to say, the Sacred Name of the enumerated four letters. By their combination and superposition and by the figures thus obtained, above and below, the four cardinal points had birth with all other images. The letters of the Sacred Name were the molds of the work of formation and as such they were arranged in a reverse order to that which is indicated here.

Many things, however, were united or drawn together in the mind of the Holy One for the perfect purpose of His providence, in respect of all that which was to come into being. He contemplated in His foresight the Mystery of the Law and because it was impossible for the world to subsist without it, He created the Law to rule in all things above and below and to sustain them. Because of the Law in which the possibility of transgression is implied, He created also repentance as a path of refuge in Himself, of return at need to Him (Zohar I, 207a). But the Law is said to be contained in the Sacred Name and to be summarized by the Decalogue, the ten sections which correspond to ten other Names. These appear to be described alternatively as ten creative words, which are reducible to three. For it is said, "With the Spirit of God in wisdom and understanding" (Exodus 31:3). The end in view was that God might manifest Himself and be called by His Divine Name. It is said, however, elsewhere that the words by the help of which the world was made were not established until it pleased God to create man. The intention was that he should be dedicated to the study of the Law by which the world subsists. In this study, man is said to sustain creation (Zohar II, 14b). It is also to be noted in this connection, that this Name was not revealed to the angels, which is an instance of showing that man was in a position of superiority to all other hierarchies of beings (Zohar I, 2a).

## DISCOURSE ON DIVINE THINGS: THE DOCTRINE OF DIVINE IMMANENCE

The discourses on divine things are rung after many manners by the great bells of tradition, when they offer forth the work of creation. The truth that emerges is the operating efficacy of the Divine Will in the entire manifest universe.

Nature, according to the Zohar, is the garment of God (Zohar I, 2a). It is that in which He appears and wherein He is veiled, so that we can look upon Him and know Him in His vestured aspect. But it is not of God and is still less God (when) manifest. It is that which He took upon Himself for the purpose of appearing.

Prior to the period when the Divine Name was formulated for the ends of creation, He was apart from the kind of definition implied therein, and this one definite state is termed "Who" by the Zohar, as in the words: "Behold Who has created that" (Isaiah 40:26). So we see (also) that the product of Creation is called "that" or "what." The Hebrew words are respectively *mi* and *eleh*. The product specified by the Zohar for creation was Elohim below, who thus came into being when the letters emanated from each other. (In the transcendence God and Elohim are inseparable; and the first movement toward the production of a manifest universe was to send forth their living images below as male and female. That which was of the nature of God became of the nature of the cosmos.) The explanation of *mi* and *eleh* is that by the pairing of *eleh* and *mi* is obtained the word Elohim. *Mi* or "Who," the Unnamed remains always attached to *eleh* or "that." In God these two descriptions are inseparable and it is thanks to this mystery that the world exists. This is the doctrine of Divine Immanence in the cosmos of manifested things.

Apart from this there could be neither the things themselves nor the harmony which produces music, the accord, the grace, the beauty of creation. It was to make known this doctrine that Elijah once showed himself to R. Shimon on the seashore, after which he took flight, as the text says: "and R. Shimon saw him no more"—at least, not at that time (Zohar I, 2a).

The same passage in Isaiah is expressed also elsewhere to affirm the whole work of creation. By who above and by that below has all been made (Zohar I, 29b). When we read in yet another place that Scripture was the architect under God, the reference is also to Elohim—either in the vesture of the Written Law or in that of the Secret Tradition (Zohar II, 161a).

We also saw that the word *bereshith* is rendered sometimes in "wisdom" which is so recognized by the Zohar on the authority of the Chaldaic paraphrase of Onkelos. It is therefore added that the world exists owing to the sublime and impenetrable mystery of *Chokhmah*. For creation is a work of wisdom, operating by means of benediction (Zohar I, 3b).

God said: "Let there be Light," and it is affirmed that all celestial legions and powers emanate therefrom. When first manifested, its brilliance filled the world from end to end; but where God foresaw the number of the guilty, He concealed and rendered it inaccessible (Zohar I, 30b).

## THE MYSTERIOUS STONE SHETIAH

We shall add here as an appendix, the symbolism of the stone called Shetiah, which occurs also in the Talmud in the tracts called *Yoma* and *Sanhedrin*. G-d cast the mysterious stone Shetiah, which was originally a precious stone in His Throne, into the abyss, so to form the basis of the world and give birth thereto (Zohar II, 222a). Its extremity was conceded in the depth, while its summit rose above the chaos. It was the central point in the immensity of the world, the cornerstone, the tried stone, the sure foundation. However, this is also that stone which the builder rejected (Zohar I, 231a). This last allocation is inscrutable at the surface since by hypothesis of the narrative, it was used in the building from the beginning. Finally, it is said that it was that stone which served Jacob as a pillow, and thereafter for an altar, which allocation is not less inscrutable (Zohar I, 72b).

It was the good stone, the precious stone, and the foundation of Zion. The tables of the Torah were made from it and it is destined for the salvation of the world. Jacob called it the House of Elohim (Genesis 28, 22), meaning that the hypostasis to which this name is attributed transfers her residence from the world above to that which is below. It has been carried by Aaron when he entered the Holy Palace (Leviticus 14:3), and it was held in the hands of David when he desired to contemplate close at hand the glory of his Master (Zohar I, 231a).

The stone was overturned by the iniquity of man until Jacob restored it to an upright position. Solomon was also one of those who restored it and thereon he built the Sanctuary. This stone was inscribed with the Divine Name before it was cast into the abyss (Zohar I, 91b). We may not know how to harmonize these references to the mysterious stone and how Jacob, Aaron, David, Solomon, and others obtained parts of it. Its secret mystery remains for the elect ones.

For the rest, it is said that the world did not obtain stability until Israel received the Law on Mount Sinai. Also, that God created the world after He delivered the Law. He ended His work in the Levitical Law with it, which is the basis of the world. This legendary Tablet or stone with which we have been dealing, it is a level of Sabbath also, concerning the Secret Doctrine, of which Abraham is also the foundation thereof. Abraham was the one just being on whom it rests, because it was he who made it permanent, and he who first nourished all creatures (Zohar I, 89a).

These lines of thought, though appearing unrelated one to another, serve to turn the students' attention to understand how the mystic stone is the central point of the world and how at this point is the Holy of Holies (Zohar I, 231a).

There is also the stone "cut without hands" of Daniel 2:35, and it is said in the Zohar to represent Him Who is the Shepherd, the stone of Israel (Genesis 49:24). It is the community of Israel which shall be called the House of God (Genesis 28:22). According to the Faithful Shepherd (Zohar III, 279b), the stone of Daniel was engraved with the letters of the Tetragrammaton, and it is not to be identified with the stone of Moses, being that rock which he smote twice (Numbers 20:8–11).

## CREATION AND THE INSTRUMENTS APPERTAINING THERETO, CONTINUED

Now, to continue with the doctrine of cosmology and of the relation of the Word to the Divine Transcendence. It is said that the six days were created thereby, being lights emanating from the Word and illuminating the world. It is also Divine Seed from which manifest things come forth. It is specifically affirmed that the world was created by the Word united to the Spirit which operated at that time, being the sound of the Word as a voice, which spoke and it was done. The authority for it is Psalm 33:6: "By the word of the Lord were the heavens made and all the host of them by the breath of His mouth," for one is not without the other (the Word is not without the Spirit) (Zohar I, 156a).

For dispensation of the light, this Word was joined with the Father; the light itself proceeding from the Father and being as such incompatible with matter (Zohar I, 16b). In the union of the Father and the Word, it became accessible thereto, seeing that henceforth it proceeded from both. Before the manifestation of the Word, the light proceeding from the Father formed seven letters, which were without body and for this reason were inaccessible to matter. When the sacred, nebulous clouded fire, which is called "darkness upon the face of the deep," appeared for the transmutation of matter, seven other letters were formed also from pure light and hence inaccessible to matter like the first seven. When the Word manifested, the remaining eight letters were formed and then the whole alphabet was rendered accessible by the casting down of that barrier which separated matter from the celestial rays. It is for this reason that according to Scripture Elohim said: "Let there be light" (Genesis 1:3). The firmament was made likewise and the waters were separated from the waters, or, the light above from the light below. It was subject to this separation, that matter became susceptible of light (Zohar I, 16b).

Now the Word is said to be designated by the name Elohim. The firmament constituted the line of division. Thereunto could the light come down. But the firmament is also at the same time a bond of union between the one and the other, so that both are united. It is said also that the Word assumed the form of the alphabetical signs and it is in this form presumably that thought passes into written expression (Zohar I, 21a).

The greater light which God made to rule the day is a symbol of God Himself, while the lesser one which rules the night is the Word, regarded as the end of thought. It is also said elsewhere that if this world has been the work of the Lord Himself—meaning through the name of the Tetragrammaton—everything would have been everlasting therein, but being that it is the work of that Divine Essence called Elohim, it is all subject to destruction (compare also Psalm 44:9).

The six days of creation are light emanating from the Word for the illumination of the world. Their corresponding six nights God holds in concealment for a good purpose of His own. And it is thanks to the Word that the waters of the celestial river flow forever to irrigate the worlds that are below.

## FINAL INTIMATIONS IN CREATION

When the Holy One created the world, He engraved the mystery of faith in letters of sparkling light. He engraved it above and below, because it is the same mystery and because the world below is the mirror of that which is above. By means of the mystery of faith, He created the worlds. It is then asked in another place, What worlds? The answer is matrimonial union. These are the worlds which God does not cease from creating. It follows that the sex mystery is also a veil of creation. Another intimation is given in these words, "The union of the male and female principle engendered the world." So also in the emanation of the letters *aleph* and *beth* are postulated, from which two come forth the rest of the aleph-bet; and hence it is said that these two are male and female. It is said elsewhere that the letters expressing the male principle are not susceptible of transformation, while those expressing the female principle can be counter changed by means of certain combination. *Beth* is a female letter; and it was already explained that *beth* was the instrument of creation. *Hai* is considered a female letter in the Zohar, while *vav* is masculine.

## MANY WORLDS WERE MADE, AROSE, AND DECAYED PREVIOUSLY

Another intimation is that God took the heap of letters in His Hands and began to make worlds therewith over and over, but they had no consistence; the reason being that the covenant had not yet been made. This present world is under the law of circumcision within the manifest order and the destroyed worlds arose and decayed previously unceasingly. It is said that their destruction was because those who dwelt therein did not accept the commandments of the doctrine. It is not that God undoes His works, but the works undo themselves by refusing salvation. Why, it is asked, should God put an end to those children whom according to tradition He created by the Second Hypostasis called *hai*.

It is only under the Law and the Doctrine and in virtue of the Inward Covenant of circumcision that man is hereby made male and female by Elohim (establishing in him cosmic harmony). Man was created prototypically in the likeness of the world below and in that of the world above. He was also so made, that he represents the Celestial Lover and Beloved Who are symbolized by the letters *yod* and *hai* and are united by *vav*. So proceeds there the mystery.

SECTION VI

# Hierarchies of the Spiritual Beings

CHAPTER ONE

# The Soul of Man

## INTRODUCTION

The doctrine concerning the soul of man is of great importance in the kabbalah, for man in reality is the center about which the whole tradition revolves. The great text of the Zohar contains all vital intimations on the parts, divisions, or states of the human soul, its preexistence, and its destiny. Mention is also made of the choirs of angels, and kabbalistic demonology. The fall of the angels, however, will be considered in another section. The Talmud contains both materials of celestial and infernal hierarchies.

## THE SOUL IN KABBALISM

In the previous section, we described shortly the kabbalistic instruction as to the essential Nature of God. Also, the transition from the Divine Unmanifest to the manifestation of Divinity, the extension of the powers and attributes thus developed through the archetypal creative, formative, and material worlds; the kabbalistic hypothesis of creation and the doctrine of transcendental and natural science.

Now it remains for us to present in brief outline the doctrine of spiritual essences according to Jewish theosophy.

Preexistence of the spiritual nature in man and its subdivisions are found in the Talmud. The distinction between a holy intelligence and an animal soul in man is found in the Book of Concealment. We read there that "when inferior man descends [namely, into this world], there are found in him according to the supernal form. Man therefore, is constituted from the two sides, the right and the left. As from the right side he has a holy mind, as from the left side he has an animal soul. The extension of the left side was the consequence of the fall."[1]

## BELIEF IN THE SOUL'S IMMORTALITY— TENETS OF ISRAEL

Israel holds belief in the soul's immortality in connection with that of resurrection of the body as our tenets. The thirteenth and last article in the profession of faith of Maimonides reads: "I firmly believe, that there will be a resurrection of the dead, at the time when it shall please the Creator, blessed be His Name." The Talmud teaches the doctrine of the soul and its five divisions, giving them names familiar to kabbalism.

## KABBALISTIC PNEUMATOLOGY

The doctrine of the soul in kabbalism is in close connection with that central doctrine which the Zohar calls the Mystery of Faith, or even a part of it. "There is that which must be done

---

1. *Siphra D'Tzniutha*, ch. IV, par. 7–9.

in heaven, brought down amongst the similitudes of earthly things, and finally restored to heaven." We shall consider the doctrine of the soul under four heads: 1) preexistence, 2) the parts of the soul, 3) the soul in the world to come in respect of the blessed state only, 4) reincarnation. We shall yet separately treat the doctrine concerning Sheol.

The general thesis regards preexistence and that which belongs thereto. When the Holy One willed to create the universe, He formed in the first instance those souls which were intended subsequently to dwell in human bodies. The method of expression is "He formed," but the more adequate Zoharic expression is not one of formation, but one of begetting. The point is that souls are affirmed to have a father and mother and they are produced in virtue of their union. The basis for it is "let the earth bring forth the living creature" (Genesis 1:24). This creature being held to mean the soul of the first celestial man (Zohar II, 12a). The Zohar teaches also the foreknowledge of the soul.

The place of the tarrying of the souls is said in many places to be the Paradise below, which means the lower Eden or the earthly Paradise. It is also an abode of disincarnate souls who have entered that path which leads to the blessed life; but it is not their final home (Zohar II, 96b). It is also said that each soul has its form like that of the body which it is destined to animate.

Before the souls left the presence of their Maker, all those souls destined to incarnate under the obedience and election of Israel were conjured to keep the precepts of the Torah. The soul is also pledged to the study of the Law and the attainment of the mystery of Faith (Zohar I, 223b). Compare also Talmud, tractate *Niddah*, 31.

While they wait incarnation in Paradise, they are clothed with bodies and have countenances like those that they are destined to possess hereafter, but these vestures are of course of a spiritual psychic kind. There is no real joy for the soul, save in the body of Paradise; in that of earth, it is shut out from communication with the supreme mysteries (Zohar II, 50a).

When the time arrives for embodiment, each soul in its turn is called before the Holy One and is told which physical envelope to inhabit. Paradise is a place of blessing and it may be that from the gold bar, thereof it has leaned out and seen no reason to descend of its own accord or to quit present happiness "for bondage and temptation." It is assured, however, that from the day of its creation, it had no other mission than to come into this world. It submits therefore and is stripped of the paradisiacal body that it may be clothed with veils of earth. It takes the road of earth sorrowing and proceeds into the exile of human life (Zohar II, 96b).

It is declared that what is learned by man as a consequence of his habitation here below was known previously by him in the world above. This apparently is the case with those who love the truth and are righteous in the unearthly life. God has already set aside those who are wicked below. The incarnation of these is being delayed through frequent enforced visits to the abyss. Those who are headstrong here were headstrong prior to their incarnations. This was said in the presence of R. Shimon and was accepted by him showing that it was compatible with the doctrine of free will (Zohar III, 16b).

Seeing that the earthly Paradise is the house of preexisting souls and the place to which they return after death, it might seem that the fall which took place therein was in the prototypical man, or "Adam Primordial" in whom all souls fell. R. Menahem Rekanati maintained this. He also maintained that the man of Eden was in a sense Adam Primordial—as the first human being. But the prototypical Adam Primordial of the Zohar is the divine son conceived in *Daath* and so extended through the lower sephiroth, that he stands on *Malkuth*.

Souls descend in a preestablished order of succession. Precedence is taken by Palestine, and descent to earth reaches its term therein. After this the souls are thence distributed to the whole world (Zohar I, 101a). There are exceptions to the order of succession. These correspond to the idea of those who are born out of due time. It is said that male souls come from the "Tree of Wisdom and female souls from an inferior tree!" It is explained in another place that just souls attached to the sacred King by true love, are longer than others do in coming to this earth (Zohar II, 101a).

All souls awaiting incarnation are arranged in pairs. The one which is destined to animate a male is by the side of one who is to animate a female, so that those who are united below have been united previously above. The references are always to the souls of Israel (Zohar I, 91b). They descend together, but they pass into the charge of an angel who presides over the pregnancy of women and they are then separated. Sometimes the male soul animates a man first, sometimes the reverse (ibid.). It is not said that a mistake ever occurs, and it is not meant to account for certain sex aberrations.

When the time of marriage comes, the Holy One unites them as before and proclaims their union. After the spouses and apparently intercourse, they become mystically speaking one body and one soul.

Another variant of this notion says that prior to their descent on earth, all souls form a unity and are part of the same mystery. Separation into male and female takes place by reason of incarnation, but they are again made one in marriage. At one place it is also stated that whether or not a man shall meet in this life with the soul predestined to himself in union, even from the beginning, depends on his own desert. There are also Zoharic considerations on the subject of sister souls who have been so to speak, miscarried (Zohar III, 43b).

A counter thesis locates the souls prior to incarnation in the superior Eden, instead of the Paradise below, and according to one account the descent for a period into the earthly garden takes place just prior to incarnation; the time being thirty days. Here it says that when the soul is in the act of descending towards this world, it visits the earthly Paradise, where it sees the souls of the just who have left this life. It goes also to Sheol and sees the souls of the wicked. Again it is said in another place, that the soul is from the sanctuary on high. It is that temple which is mentioned in Exodus 15:17 as the "Sanctuary of the Lord, which Thy hands have established" (Zohar I, 7a). There the account is that they pay only a flying visit for the purpose of inspection and to serve as object lessons to act as a guide in earthly life.

Another alternative affirms that from an epoch which preceded the creation of this world, all souls have been in the presence of the Holy One, and there they remain until they are called to go down on earth (Zohar II, 282a). It was especially the union of male and female souls, which existed before creation. The time of union in intercourse corresponds to midnight on earth. It is a union in the contemplation of God, and the joy thereof brings forth other souls which are those of gentiles who become converts to Jewry (ibid.).

All emanate from the same region and during their sojourn in heaven they share in the government of things above and below (Zohar III, 68a). There are also certain souls which are kept in the hiddenness and are guarded in a particular manner. When these enter into earthly bodies, they have the power to remand into heaven without dying. Of such were Enoch and Elijah (Zohar III, 68b).

There is some trouble in effecting a harmonious junction between the soul and its earthly envelope. It is said to be attached to the body by one end only. It is not definitely established therein until after thirty-three days and for the first seven it goes in and out continuously. The soul and its envelope develop simultaneously, meaning that their union becomes more perfect. But care of the soul is needed for this purpose, just as the body needs care. The soul, however, is in the care of heaven (Zohar I, 197a). One of the reasons that heavenly circumcision does not take place until the thirtieth day, and that for three days thereafter the body is in a state of suffering, two texts are quoted viz.: Leviticus 12:4 and Exodus 23:30 (Zohar III, 43b).

## ON PREEXISTENCE OF SOULS

Another reference on preexistence is that it is said that the souls of the patriarchs preexisted in the thought of God before the creation and were connected in the other world, whence they came forth in their due day. The text opposite thereto is "the flowers appear on the earth" (Song of Solomon 2:12) meaning that the souls of the patriarchs appear in this world (Zohar I, 10a). The Zoharic hypothesis, therefore, is that the soul world is a world of thought in God; that the thought precedes the Word as it is shown to have done, in respect of Creation generally; and that souls are uttered forth continuously, passing ultimately into expression in flesh.

## THE PARTS OF DIVISION OF THE SOUL

Connected with preexistence is the mode of generation or creation of souls, but of this later on. Here we shall proceed to discuss the parts or divisions of the soul. In a summary way the teaching is that man is composed of three things: life or *Nefesh*; spirit, which is *Ruach*; and soul, that is, *Neshamah*. By these he becomes a living spirit, a term however, which is applied more especially to *Neshamah*. They are also called three degrees, or vital spirit, intellectual spirit, and soul proper. *Nefesh* is the fallible part, for sin is suggested neither by *Ruach* nor by *Neshamah*. It is said elsewhere plainly that the vital spirit sins, but not the soul. It is also said elsewhere, however, that the defilement of *Nefesh* defiles *Ruach* and *Neshamah*. The three degrees are superposed one upon another in the order already given, and Neshamah is attached to God. All these parts are not, however, the imprescriptible possession of every person in life. The higher parts are earned by serving the master (Zohar I, 27a).

The Living Spirit is also said to proceed from the mouth of Shechinah, who is called "Living Soul." Here is another aspect of souls being uttered forth by the Divine (Zohar I, 27a). Seeing that this is the Shechinah in transcends, who is the third hypostasis and the Mother—Eimma—in the supernal sephirah *Binah*, we understand the kind of union which subsists between here and the Father—Abba in *Chokhmah*. There is the Divine Thought in *Kether*—it is formulated mentally in *Chokhmah* and it is uttered in *Binah*, producing the living intelligences, which are therefore begotten in the Supernal Paradise. More complex is understanding the thesis as to understand which thought processes preexisted and which constitute man in manifestation as a living being.

It is further said that some persons are judged worthy to possess a *Neshamah*, others a *Ruach* only, while yet others have a *Nefesh* and nothing more. These last ones, by reason of their deficiency, are attached to the impure spirit. The *Nefesh* alone is imprescriptible or necessary to the man's existence (Zohar I, 25a).

Other statements are the following. Man is endowed with a *Nefesh* in the first place, and it is given him as a preparation for leading a holy life. The three degrees constitute one soul and are attached on to another (Zohar I, 206a). A contradistinction hereto is another ruling, which suggests that the possession of *Nefesh* and *Ruach* leaves man useless for the purpose of the *Shechinah* in captivity, and of Moses who abides within here. The reason being is that they seem to be unskilled in the Secret Doctrine (Zohar I, 28a). To continue, a man who possesses only *Nefesh*, if he comports himself worthily with this gift another spirit is poured into him, which is like a crown of

*Nefesh* and this is *Ruach*. The man is then illuminated by light from a superior region and is in a position to discern the Laws of the Secret King. If he still continues worthy, he receives the crown of *Ruach*, the name of which is *Neshamah*. It is also called Soul of God. It seems obvious that it is this only, of which preexistence, paradisiacal life, and the Divine Vision can be predicated. The point is that according to this version and contrary to the doctrine of descent of souls, *Neshamah* does not come down and incarnate at birth in the human being (Zohar III, 70b).

The addition of *Neshamah* to the higher parts of the soul is to be understood according to an alternative statement as a gift of grace. Then a state of sanctity is attained in which a lapse into sin is very unlikely. It has become not less difficult to sin, than before it was to abstain from sin, ergo it is said elsewhere that *Neshamah* cannot sin.

Elsewhere again we find a harmonization of the disparities arising from the doctrine concerning the descent of souls, the preexistence, and the statement of the successive additions of higher parts of the soul. For it is said that when the soul, meaning *Neshamah*, leaves the celestial region and comes down towards earth, it is joined to the intellectual spirit. Afterward, both are joined to the spirit of light, that is, *Nefesh* (Zohar I, 62a). The spirit of light and the intellectual spirit dwell together and depend one upon the other; but the soul's spirit is independent of both.

Another thesis is that when man proposes to live in purity, heaven comes to his aid, granting him the holy soul by which he is purified and sanctified. But if he is unworthy and will not live in purity, he is animated only by *Nefesh* and *Ruach*.

Another classification we meet in the Zohar considers *Nefesh* as the soul which forms the body and presides over the propagation of beings. *Ruach* is the soul which causes *Nefesh* to act and determines its kind of action. *Neshamah* is the supreme force issuing from the Tree of Life. These three degrees separate after death, each returning to the place from which it was brought. *Nefesh* is presumably of the earth, or earthy; for it is said to remain in the tomb. *Ruach* passes to the earthly Paradise, where the high priest Michael offers it as a holocaust to the Holy One and it remains in the joy of Paradise. (Note: It is qualified that it remains in Paradise for a period and then returns whence it came, because the spirit *Ruach* goes back to God, Who gave it.)

*Neshamah* ascends on high. It returns to the Tree of Life, because it came therefrom. This version of the tripartite personality of the soul postulates survival in three separate directions, for *Nefesh* is alive in the tomb whence it later on ascends (Zohar I, 287b).

In late kabbalism, we find sometimes *Ruach*, termed spirit, meaning the human soul itself. It was held to extend through the body to be rational and self-subsisting, but its mode of comprehension was by intermediaries and not direct. It was also the seat of good and evil and hence of the moral attributes. *Neshamah* is understanding in late kabbalism; the individual intellect communicated by the Divine Intellect.

One Zoharic intimation says that man acquires the soul of soul by fear of the Lord and by wisdom. He acquires the soul by penitence. Abraham represents the soul of soul. Sarah is the soul. Isaac is the intellectual spirit; and Rebecca's is the vital spirit (Zohar I, 287b).

Another speculation designates *Nefesh* as the soul in a state of sleep. *Ruach* is the soul in a waking state, that is, the stage of becoming alive to things above. It is also said that these two do not differ in essence. Above these is Neshamah, which is the soul proper. These grades of the spirit of man are the image of the mystery of Wisdom, and to fathom them is to discover that Wisdom. When *Neshamah* is preeminent in man he is called holy (Zohar I, 265a).

## *CHAYA* AND *YECHIDAH*

The parts of the spiritual personality were enumerated as triadic until now. But an extension more elaborate than followed here is given elsewhere, where it is said that the soul has five names, being *Nefesh, Ruach, Neshamah, Chayah,* and *Yechidah* (Zohar I, 83a). This is an extract from the Faithful Shepherd. But as we mentioned before, *Chayah* is sometimes a synonym for *Ruach*. Late kabbalism explains that *Yechidah* is individuality, the unique unity or correspondence by which man becomes like unto the First Cause. *Chayah* is a condition of ecstasy and of unity between the particular and the universal intellect, that is, the union of our life with that life which is Divine.

## OTHER SOUL EXTENSIONS

Other utterances of the Zohar teach us the following. Ascent in the grades of sanctity can provide additionally to these tragic parts of the spiritual personality, and in succession: 1) a soul from the world of emanation on the side of the daughter of the King (Zohar II, 94b); 2) a soul from the world of emanation on the side of the Son of the King, authority for this being the verse of Deuteronomy 14:1, "Ye are children of the Lord your God" (ibid.); 3) a soul which is from the side of the Father and the Mother. The verse appertaining to this being Genesis 2:7, "And He breathed into his nostrils the breath of life; and man became a living soul"; (4) a soul which reflects the four letters of the Sacred Name Tetragrammaton (ibid.). A man in possession of this soul is the image of the Heavenly Master. Of him it is said, Genesis 1:28: "And have dominion over the fish of the sea. . . ." There are still other fragment extensions of the soul, as we shall see elsewhere.

## THE SUPPLEMENTARY SOUL OF SABBATH

We shall add here, however, that there is a casual supplementary soul added to the students of the Divine Doctrine on the Sabbath day, after which it returns whence it came. It appears to be a sacred soul issuing from the Tree of Life, and is adapted to the work of the recipient. An alternative account attaches it to all good Israelites who fulfill the Law of the Torah, whether they are students of the Sacred Doctrine in the deeper mystical sense or not.

The state of the soul in the world to come and that concerning the blessed life of the departed is described in several ways. When the good soul is preparing to leave this world, and while it is suspended from the body only at the larynx, it beholds three angels to whom the dying man confesses his sins. These spirits engender the souls of the just and they accompany the glorious Shechinah, for no man leaves this world without seeing the Shechinah at the last moment of life. The soul prostrates itself before Shechinah and praises God. It seems then to enter a cavern, wherein is a door leading to the earthly paradise. There it encounters Adam, the Patriarchs, and all the just, who rejoice with her and she is admitted within the Garden. Either then or previously, she has been furnished with an envelope other than the fleshy body but still having the form thereof. It is said, as to this, that the days of life are a vesture and the days of man's life on earth are his vesture in the world to come, insofar as he has lived them worthily. The odors given forth daily in the Garden of Eden perfume the precious vestments woven out of the days of man.

It is said elsewhere that the soul cannot have two vestures at the same time, even as the spirit of good and the spirit of evil cannot dwell together. The heavenly envelope is assumed, or the soul is clothed therewith, when that of earth is decomposed as well as laid aside. This rests on the authority of R. Shimon. The object of Samael is to hinder man from receiving the garment of heaven, and this he can do until the fleshy body has dissolved. But this reference is to *Nefesh*. The *Ruach* is itself not at rest. It is only after the complete return of the earthly part to earth, that it is drawn back to the Holy Spirit that gave it.

It is stated that there is one vesture for *Neshamah*, another for *Ruach*, and one finally, of an external and scarcely perceptible kind, for *Nefesh*. All are formed from the days of life. But at the same time the commandments of the Law are the vesture of *Neshamah*. We must remember that *Neshamah* is clothed in righteousness, because it cannot sin. It is admitted that the wise in doctrine have not reached a full agreement on the subject, yet the number of vestures is three.

Notwithstanding the previous testimony, *Nefesh* is bound up with the body in the tomb for twelve months only, after which it goes wandering and enters into communication with those who are still incarnate, to inquire respecting their sufferings and to pray at need for them.

## THE LAW LEADS THE SOUL

Then we are taken to another point of spiritual progression which states that when the soul of a man, who has been consecrated to the study of the Law during life, quits this world, it goes up by the roads and pathways of the Law. This is so that his knowledge is a getaway in attainment; while the souls of those who have neglected such study go astray in the paths which lead to the region of *Geburah*, where they suffer punishment. In another manner of symbolism, the Law goes before the soul when it rises into the celestial regions, and it opens to him all the teachings (Zohar I, 175b).

The Law remains with the soul until the day of resurrection, when it will take up the defense of the soul. This again is in deference of the students of the Law; and it is said that after their resurrection they will preserve intact all knowledge which they had during their antecedent life. Their knowledge will be extended further so that they will be able to penetrate mysteries which were concealed from them previously (Zohar I, 185a). Those who are dedicated to the study of the Law on earth will be so occupied also in the world to come. After the period of resurrection is life (Zohar I, 185a). For the pursuit and union hereafter is a penetration of the divine mystery in which the soul progresses forever.

## PARABLE OF THE SOUL

There are seven palaces on high containing the Mystery of Faith. It is said that six of them are accessible to the understanding of man, but the seventh is secret and forms part of the Supreme Mysteries. These are seven stages of union, like a tower going up to God. The secret of the seventh, "the eye has not seen." In this state the union is ineffable, and we have no title to term it and not any word which is within the measures of things expressible.

## THE SEVEN PALACES

There are also seven palaces below, and among these one is superior to the rest as it holds both from heaven and earth. They are postulated in relation to certain grades of advancement in the world to come. When the souls of the just leave material life, they enter the first palace and are occupied with preparation for the next stage of their experience (Zohar I, 38a).

The second palace is the sojourn of those who have suffered morally and physically in the present world, but notwithstanding this, have given daily thanks to their Master and have not neglected prayer. The Messiah descends into this abode and thence he draws souls into the third palace, which in turn is the place of those who have suffered extremely in earthly life as the result of serious disease. It contains also the souls of young children, and of such as have shed tears over the destruction of the Temple. They are consoled by Messiah, who brings them into the fourth Palace, where the souls are of all who have shared the sorrows of Zion, and those also who have been slain by heathens. The fifth palace is the sojourn of true penitents who have restored their souls to a state of purity and of those who have sanctified the Name of their Master by going to meet death for His glory. There also are the souls of those who have repented on their deathbeds (for the great fatality of life resides in final impenitence). The sixth palace is the sojourn of the souls of Zelatores, who have proclaimed the Master's unity and have loved Him with a true love. The seventh palace is the one called superior in respect to the rest. It is also more secret and mysterious. The soul on its departure from earth enters this palace for a moment. The beatific vision which it beholds is not mentioned. It is then immediately relegated to that place of sojourn which corresponds to its state at death. So the Zohar develops the idea of ascent in the scale hereafter. Above the seven palaces there is the other ineffable order of supernal palaces and beyond the present epoch in created things there is the messianic age to come (Zohar I, 38b).

## THE PALACES ABOVE

It is said: "That I may dwell in the House of the Lord all the days of my life, to behold the beauty of the Lord and to inquire in His Temple" (Psalms 27:4). The "beauty" is held to designate the palaces above. The Temple means the palaces below (Zohar I, 41b).

The seven superior palaces are: 1) the basis and beginning of the mystery of Faith; 2) the abode of Faith; 3) the place in which worthy souls are offered in sacrifice; 4) the palace of judgment, whether propitious or otherwise; 5) the palace of Love; 6) the palace of Mercy; and 7) the Holy of Holies and the final end of souls (Zohar II, 186b).

There are several systems of palaces described by the Zohar of variant accounts. There are those in which speech prevails, but in others, intention or thoughts prevail. The latter are more exalted in order, because silence is better than speech, seeing that it stands for the contemplation of God in the heart. The object of all palaces above is to preserve the Shechinah in the world below. It is not invariably easy to see, whether the subject of discourse is the palaces which are above or those which are below (Zohar II, 187b). There are also seven of prayer provided with doors by which the prayers of man ascend to the Great Master. The first corresponds to the "paved work of a sapphire stone" (Exodus 24:10). It leads to the Heaven of Heavens. The second "is like the body of heaven in its clearness" (ibid.). The third is a palace of pure untinctured light having a point of golden splendor. The fourth is a palace of seventy lights, while the splendor of the fifth is like that of the lightning and thunderbolt, combining purple with many colors. The sixth is the palace of Will, and it diffuses twelve lights. Its mystery is expressed by the words: "Thy lips are like a thread of scarlet" (Song of Solomon 4:3). It is also the palace of Mysteries; and it is separated from the other habitations by a veil. Herein sojourns the Infinite Will (Zohar II, 141a).

## THE DOCTRINE OF REINCARNATION: METAPSYCHOSIS OR REVOLUTIONS OF SOULS

There is a clear system of reincarnation in the Zohar scattered throughout. A doctrine of paternity states that when a man has failed to have children in this world, the Holy One will send him back as many times as needed to fulfill what has been neglected. Therefore, he is compared to a plant that is removed continually from the ground and located elsewhere in the hope that it will do better (Zohar II, 186b).

Those who have accomplished their mission during a single sojourn on earth rest near the Holy One. Those who return are those who have not finished their work, whether it be that of parentage or otherwise (Zohar II, 187b). Here is the inference of reincarnation for the doing of that which had been previously left undone, and for the undoing of that which was amiss formerly. Hence it is said in one place that the words "seeing that he also is flesh" (Genesis 4:3) signify, that the spirit of man, meaning his soul, will be many times reclothed with flesh until the time comes that the soul shall be susceptible of receiving the spirit of God. It is added that the Holy One will someday ransom the world and will grant the spirit in question, to men generally, so that they may live eternally. This alludes apparently to the permanence of the resurrection state. This is said to be shown by the words: "For as the days of a tree, are the days of My people" (Isaiah 65:22); and also: "He will swallow up death forever in victory" and "The Lord will wipe away all tears from off all the faces" and "The rebuke of His people shall He take away from off all the earth, for the Lord hath spoken it."[2]

## TRANSMIGRATION OF SOULS OF GENTILES

Reincarnation or transmigration would seem also to be the invariable fate of the Gentiles. The souls of pagans who deliver up their bodies in the Holy Land are not received in heaven. They wander about in the universe and transmigrate many times and finally return to the unclean place whence they came (Zohar II, 141a).

---

2. Isaiah 25:8.

The souls of Israel which leave the body outside Palestine have also transmigration and wanderings before reaching the region assigned them (ibid.). Spaces of time intervening between death and rebirth are not mentioned by the Zohar. The new event is sometimes immediate. Sheth, for example, was animated by the soul of Abel, which thus returned to earth. Adam is said to have called his son Seth, to mark the end of a situation; the consonants of his name being the two last letters of the Hebrew alphabet.

In contrast at the birth of Benjamin, he left the body of his mother, which his soul had previously animated (Zohar I, 55a). At the death of Rachel, her soul now animated the soul of Benjamin (ibid.). It seems to follow that in each case, there were two souls at one time in the same body. It is said further, that Phineas received the soul of Nadab and Abihu who were alive at the time. It is added that when Phineas slew Zimri and Cozbi, the tribe of Shimon was keen on avenging the death of their chief. The soul of Phineas fled, and the two wandering souls took possession of its vacant place (Zohar III, 216b).

R. Shimon testifies that this is a mystery, meaning that their souls did not find refuge under the wings of the Shechinah because they left no children and had thus diminished the figure of the King (Zohar III, 216b).

We shall speak again briefly of the place described variously, in which souls are reserved, waiting the period of their primary embodiment in flesh. The notion is mentioned that at the Messianic period, the "fount of souls" will be exhausted, leading to the creation of entirely new cohorts (Zohar I, 28b). The Talmud calls this place Gooph. But it is also said that there will come a time when old souls, meaning souls in migration, will be renewed for the renewal of the world (Zohar I, 119a). Each of these souls who have been incarnated previously will be united to a newly created soul. This is as written: "And it shall come to pass, that he that is left in Zion, and he that remains in Jerusalem, shall be called holy; even every one that is written among the living in Jerusalem" (Isaiah 4:3) (Zohar I, 119a).

We see by these Zoharic extracts that reincarnation is complicated by several considerations. In certain cases we see that impingement or overshadowing occurred. R. Isaac de Luria put down the full systems of the development of reincarnation in his book *Revolutions of Souls*.

## RESURRECTION AND REINCARNATION

It was alleged that in case of souls who take flesh several times, the body which shall rise will be that in which the soul has succeeded in taking root, meaning, that in which it has fulfilled the Law in perfection (Zohar I, 131a). Those bodies in which the soul fails to reach its ends are like dried up trees, which fall to dust, and they will rise no more (Zohar I, 131a). So much for resurrection in connection with the idea of rebirth.

As for those who have been rotted only in wickedness, it may be added that the Zoharic doctrine of the world to come, and the recompenses and punishments therein, is quite independent of any reincarnation hypothesis. They are two notions. As regards resurrection, there is a variant of the above view, according to which the soul will return into the last body that was animated. But the previous bodies will rise also and will be animated with new souls. If these bodies have fulfilled meritorious work, they will continue, but if not, they will return again to dust (Zohar I, 131a).

A summary of some incidental points may follow here. In Ecclesiastes 1:4 we read: "One generation passes away and another generation cometh." It is said that the generation that comes is that also which has passed. Reincarnation is sometimes despite the soul and sometimes apparently otherwise (Zohar I, 268b). In one place we read plainly those souls are sent for a second time on earth, that they may repair faults committed on the first occasion (Zohar II, 109a). They come back also through the workings of grace, as for example, when husband and wife have been sterile through no fault of theirs in a previous lifetime (Zohar II, 109a). On the next occasion, they will be enabled to fulfill the Law. Every Israelite is reborn an Israelite.

Reincarnation is good, because good reasons are behind it. But as it is not good in itself, it is well to be spared therefrom. In conclusion, we shall say that rebirth befalls those who do not study the Law (Zohar II, 109a). This text further bears testimony, that incarnation may take place thrice because of the words: "Lo, all these things worketh God oftentimes with man" (Job 33:29). The Zohar renders the passage to mean even the third time.

CHAPTER TWO

# Angels and Demons and Metaphysical Doctrine

In the previous chapters, we learned that the world of Briah is that of Creation, that is, of emanation of creative forces. These forces are B'nai Elokim. Briah is therefore the Elokim world, that is, the world of archangels, as it is described in later kabbalism. Archangels therefore, Michael, Raphael, Gabriel, Uriel, and similar are B'nai Elokim. Metatron however is described as a sort of demiorgas and as a Divine Hypostasis, following Talmudic opinions. (See Tractate *Sanhedrin* and elsewhere.) Otherwise, it is assumed that the divine intelligences and forces of the Briah world are archangels or B'nai Elokim, also called in short Elokim.

Thus the three men who appeared to Abraham in the vale of Mamre to announce the destruction impending over the cities of the plain were three archangels.

## DIVINE INTELLIGENCE AND FORCES

Of the hierarchy of spiritual beings outside humanity, we meet with various classifications by different rabbinical writers in

Talmudic times. The following descending scale depends from Zoharic expositors. They are tabulated on the Tree of Life and the four kabbalistic worlds with an evolution of the Ten Sephiroth in each world.

The archangels of Briah, corresponding to the evolution of the Ten Sephiroth through that world, are usually enumerated as follows.

1. Metatron is the Angel of the Presence, or World Prince, corresponding to *Kether*. When written with a *yod* (Mittrun) the name Metatron signifies Shechinah; without that letter, it signifies the angel who is "legate of Shechinah." He is also called Naar or Boy (Tractate *Chulin* 60a, Tosephot; *Yebamoth* 16b, Tosephot). We shall later see that he has other and more pregnant titles.

2. Raziel, the Herald of Deity, corresponding to *Chokhmah*.

3. Tzaphkiel, contemplation of God, corresponding to *Binah*.

4. Tzadkiel, Justice of God, corresponding to *Chesed*.

5. Samael, Severity of God, corresponding to *Geburah*.

6. Michael, Like unto God, corresponding to *Tiphereth*.

7. Haniel, Grace of God, corresponding to *Netzach*.

8. Raphael, Divine Physician, corresponding to *Hod*.

9. Gabriel, Man of God, corresponding to *Malkuth*.

## CHOIRS OF ANGELS IN YETZIRAH—CELESTIAL HIERARCHIES

The world of Yetzirah or Formation is said to be that of the angels, who are divided into ten choirs.

According to the most usual attribution, the choirs of Yetzirah are as follows:

1. Chayoth HaKodesh, the holy living creatures, or the animals of Ezekiel, correspond to *Kether* of Yetzirah.
2. Ophanim, or Wheels, also mentioned in Ezekiel, corresponding to *Chokhmah*.
3. Arelim, or Mighty Ones, correspond to *Binah*.
4. Chashmalim, or Brilliant Ones, correspond to *Chesed* (of the world Yetzirah).
5. Seraphim, Flaming Serpents, corresponding to *Geburah*.
6. Malachim, or Kings or Messengers, correspond to *Tiphereth*.
7. Elohim, or of God, corresponding to *Netzach*.
8. B'nai Elokim, or Sons of God, correspond to *Hod*.
9. Cherubim, the Seat of the Sons, corresponding to *Yesod*, the foundation.
10. Ishim, or Beautified Souls of Just Men, correspond to *Malkuth* of the sephiroth of Yetzirah world.

These ten orders are also summarized in the notion of a third Adam, Yetzirah; represented by the *Malkuth* of the Yetziratic world, man in the likeness of the angels, the Adam Microprosopus of the Idras. As we have the corresponding notions of the second Adam of *Binah*, and the first Adam of *Atziluth*.

## UNIVERSE CORRESPONDENCES OF THE SEPHIROTH: CORTICES, SPIRITS, AND DEMONS

The world of Assiah, or of matter, is that into which Adam descended at the fall, and beneath it is the abode of evil spirits; the shells, envelopes, and cortices mentioned in kabbalah. This abode contains the order of retrograde spirits, corresponding by inversion to the angels of Yetzirah, and the archfiends, corresponding after the same manner, to the archangels of the Briah world. But there are also many material correspondences which are not of shells and demons.

The Infernal Hierarchies are usually enumerated as follows:

1. Thaumiel, or doubles of God, said to be two-headed, so named because they pretend to be equal to *Kether*. This is properly the title of the averse Sephirah corresponding to *Kether*. The cortex is Cathariel according to the Zohar supplements. Satan and Moloch are said to be the archdemons.

2. Chaigideiel, a term signifying "placenta" or else "obstruction," in the sense of an impediment to heavenly influx. This averse sephirah corresponds to *Chokhmah*. Its cortices are the Oghiel or Ghogiel, which leave to illusory or material appearances, in opposition to those of reality and wisdom. The archdemon is said to be Adam Balial and so again is Belzebuth. The Dukes of Esau are connected with this number.

3. Sathariel, the concealment of God, meaning that this averse sephirah, unlike *Binah* or Intelligence, hides the face of mercy. In the Zohar supplements it is termed Sheireil, from the hirsute body of Esau. The Dukes of Esau are referred alternatively to this number before they were referred to the averse correspondence of *Chokhmah*.

4. Gamchieoth or Gooph of Sheklah, disturber of all things, is the averse correspondence of *Chesed*. The cortex seems to be Azariel according to the Zoharic supplements. The archdemon is Ashtaroth.

5. Goheb, or burning in the sense of incendiarism. This is the averse sephirah correspondence of *Geburah*, and

the antithesis of Seraphim or Fiery Serpents. The cortex is Uziel. The archdemon is Asmadens.

6. Togarin, wranglers (according to Isaac de Luria), because this averse correspondence of *Tiphereth* strives with the supernal *Geburah*. The cortices are called Zamiel, and the archdemon is Belphegor.

7. Harab Scrap, dispersing raven, referring to the idea that this bird drives out its young. This is the averse correspondence of *Netzach*. The cortices are Thaumiel and the archdemon is Baal Chanan.

8. Samael, or embroilment, corresponds to *Hod* (the Supernal Glory). The cortices are the Thaumiel according to the supplements of the Zohar. The archdemon is Adarmelek.

9. Gamaliel, the obscene in averse correspondence to *Yesod*, which signifies generation of the higher order. Oghiel, which another classification attributes to the averse correspondence of *Chesed*, is mentioned in the Zoharic supplements as the cortex or Galmiel and the arch-fiend is Lilith.

10. Lilith, who according to the Zohar, is a stryge who slays infants. According to another tabulation, the averse correspondence of *Malkuth* with whom, however, later kabbalah connects Nahema, the demon of impurity. Note: Nahema is a succubus who brings forth spirits and demons after intercourse with men, says the Zohar in various places.

## SAMAEL AND LILITH

According to Zoharistic doctrine, however, the chief personalities of Assiah are Samael, who is to some extent the averse Adam Kadmon, and his bride Lilith. In a general way, it is said that as in the holy Kingdom so is it in that of iniquity, as in the circumcision so also in the lack thereof. Samael, also called Satan, is said to be the uncircumcised and his bride is the prepuce, which, it is added, is the serpent (R. Shimon bar Yochai in Tikkunim, or Supplement No. 18. See also Beth Elohim; most of this metaphysical doctrine is post-Zoharic in origin. It must be added, that both Talmuds abound with histories and teachings on this subject.)

SECTION VII

# The Ways of God with Man

It is shown that the biblical account of the earthly Paradise, is a mystery of sex. The fall of the Angels, which connects indirectly with this obscure subject, is said to be responsible for all uncleanness subsequently on earth and in man. It comes about in this manner that the Fall of Man belongs to the same mystery and is developed as such in numerous variations. "The wickedness which was great upon the earth," and "which broke up the fountains of the deep," and "opened the windows of heaven" in the Deluge narrative, was an iniquity of sex aberration. Even the subsequent sacrifice of Noah, "a sweet savoir to the Lord," was sanctified and acceptable because of its high intent respecting this Supreme Mystery. The covenant with Abraham was made in this connection and its whole foundation and subject is said to abide therein. The Divine Teaching (Torah) promulgated on Sinai was not apart therefrom. The history of Moses is itself a history of spiritual espousals.

When the time came for a house of the Lord to be built in Zion, this great mystery in its transcendence was illustrated by the presence of the Shechinah in the Holy of Holies, as a bride in the abode of her spouse. Finally, the advent of Messiah, the divine Son, in the sense of secret tradition the letter *vav* in the Sacred Name of Four Letters (the Tetragrammaton), is to raise up her, who is his Bride in exile, and to prepare for the Sabbath of Creation, which is a period of true bridals.

CHAPTER ONE

# The Narrative of the Earthly Paradise

It must be remembered that there are two Gardens of Eden which are in communication one with another, while one leads to the other. The one is the Mystery of Sex as it was formulated originally on this lower earth by the Secret Doctrine; but this Garden was ravished. The Mystery of Sex is called in the Zohar Mystery of Faith and Supreme Mystery. The other Garden is a Mystery in Transcendence, as it subsists in the Eternal World, the world of the supernals.

According to later kabbalah, the Superior Paradise is referable to Briah in respect to souls and to Yetzirah in respect to angels. The Zoharic teaching, however, allocates it to Briah and it is, therefore, in the supernal world of *Atziluth*. The Inferior Paradise is in Assiah. We have seen also that the Higher Eden is the abode of souls, awaiting incarnation and, that the Lower Eden is, so to speak, the threshold of entrance into the life of earth. So also on the return journey through the gate of death, the Lower Paradise is a tarrying place for the souls of the just before they ascend higher, that is to say, into the supernal Eden, where perfect liberation is enjoyed (Zohar III, 196b). Gan Eden is applied in the Zohar both to *Binah* and *Malkuth*, as the Sephirotic locations respectively of the Superior and Inferior Eden.

## OF THE INDWELLING GLORY: SHECHINAH—MATRONA

The subject of the Mystery of Faith, called Supreme Mystery in the Zohar (and which is also the Mystery of Sex), is a matter of some difficulty to disassociate it from that Divine Personality—the Indwelling Glory (Shechinah)—which is the central figure of the Aramaic text of the Zohar. (See the Book of Creeds and Opinions, Section II, by R. Saadiah Gaon, concerning Shechinah; the full discussion thereof later on.)

In the symbolism of this subject, womanhood is the Garden in transcendence. She is also the Garden below or alternatively their mystery. Their image amidst the exile and penitence of this present order is also woman: woman in her betrothals; woman in her espousals; woman as wife, mother, daughter, and sister. We shall see later on that all these designations are also titles of Shechinah the Indwelling Glory and Divine Personality. Shechinah can be regarded from two points of view: as woman in the archetype, and as the Mystery of Sex. Essentially those two are educible to one. But the male is not without the female, nor is the woman apart from man in respect of this mystery, which includes all. It is the concealment of God, being however the concealment of *Kether* and not the *Ain Soph*, of God also as He is manifested in the Secret Doctrine and of prototypical Humanity.

It is also the mystery of the traditional Fall of Man and of all the banishment which the elect are postulated as having suffered. It is owing to this mystery that each one of us is incarnate here, and it is also through this that we return homeward into the refuge of the Wings of Her, whose name is

Shechinah. Shechinah is with us at this day in the bondage of our mortality, but she is also the law of our liberation.

## OF THE SUPERNAL AND THE INFERIOR PARADISES

The Paradise above is called "the Sanctuary O Lord, which Thy Hands have established."[1] The Paradise below has the Holy of Holies for its image and both are at the center of the earth called Zion and Jerusalem, the place and house of peace. For it is said the Matrona dwells in the supernal sanctuary; that is to say, in *Binah* and in Jerusalem, which is manifested on earth, in *Malkuth*. And it is because she is united to the male in the unseen world, that she is joined in manifestation with man. This is defined as the quintessence of all faith; for all faith is comprised in this mystery(Zohar II, 127a).

The Paradise or palace below is modelled on the pattern of that which is above; for the Divine presence in *Malkuth* as the kingdom of this world does not differ from the Divine Hypostasis in *Binah*, which is the world to come. The Lower Garden was formed and planted by the Holy One, that He might have joy with the souls of the just, who dwell therein. But the Garden, which is placed in the transcendence under the Wings of Shechinah, is the place of contemplation for souls in the sweetness of the Lord, and herein is the Blessed Vision (Zohar III, 143b).

## THE MAKING OF MAN AND HIS EXULTED STATE OF RADIANCE

There are two accounts in Genesis of the making of man, one dovetailed into the other. According to the text, man was

---

1. Exodus 5; Zohar I, 7a.

made in the likeness of Elokim, that is to say, male and female; for which reason we shall see that Shechinah, whose title is Elokim, is presented as male on a few rare occasions. Invariably otherwise though as female, that the alternative has the aspect of a willful confusion of issues.

In the narrative of the earthly Paradise, Adam being the male and having the female latent within him, was made in the first place. Now, it is said that when the Holy One created Adam, He exhorted him to walk in the way of goodness and revealed to him the Mystery of Wisdom, by aid of which he could attain even to the supreme degree (Zohar I, 140b). He gave him also the Law, and taught him His ways (Zohar I, 199a). Man was crowned with celestial crowns and was so formed, that he could rule over six directions of space. He was perfect in all things and wore the seal of the heights on his countenance. The angels encompassed him and honored him, revealing mysteries relating to the knowledge of their Master. He on his part beheld all Supreme Mysteries and all Wisdom, exceeding the science of the angels, and he knew the Glory of God. The intention was that he should remain united in heart and mind to Him Who was his model, thus being preserved unchanged like God Who is the synthesis of all things and in Whom all is unified. It is also said that God encompassed Adam with glory from on high, meaning the resplendent vehicle or vesture in which Adam was manifested before he was clothed with skins, as one consequence of his fall (Zohar I, 240a).

We are told in Genesis 2:15, that "the Lord God took this man and put him into the Garden of Eden, to dress it and to keep it." The Zohar explains that Adam in his original state of radiance was set to offer sacrifices in the Garden on an altar there, which altar he profaned by his fall and so became a tiller of the ground (Zohar I, 57b). In another place it is said that he was set to grow roses. Blood offerings were not instituted as yet; the offerings of Adam were therefore offerings of inspiration. The roses were children of Shechinah because she is the Rose of the World (Zohar II, 109a).

In respect of the Garden itself, we learn that the whole world is watered by that mysterious river which went forth out of Eden, meaning the Paradise that is above. It came from a secret place on high and brought life to things below (Zohar I, 30b). It brought celestial waters and thus gave birth to the plants and fruits, which flourished in the Garden (Zohar I, 59b). The river vivifies all things else. The river brings sanctity from on high, and when the Kingdom of heaven shall have come under the form of first fruits of the earth, the latter will be raised and made equal with heaven. Life is, therefore, holiness, and the world subsists on holiness.

As regards the formation of Eve from the side of Adam, the narrative of the Zohar tells us that Adam and Eve were joined side by side originally. They were not face to face, because as yet: "the Lord God had not caused it to rain upon the earth" (Genesis 2:5). This is given on the authority of R. Shimon (Zohar I, 35a). The same verse, however, adds, "and there was not a man to till the ground." Our master R. Shimon explains the fact that there was no man, because Eve had not yet been created, and man was as if nonexistent, seeing that he was incomplete in her absence—a doctrine which is obtained everywhere regarding our human nature (Zohar I, 35a).

The point of the doctrine of the Zohar in this case is man, being superior to all the works of creation, must model the union of man and woman on that of the arch-nature, that is above. But the union face to face could not be accomplished until after that of heaven and earth, which was manifested by rain. The basis is that sex-union of humanity takes place in an opposite position to that of all the animals, namely, face to face. This symbolizes the spiritual mystery of the intercourse which constitutes the transcendental unions. It is further intimated that in their original state, not only was Adam made male and female, but so also was the woman attached to his side (Zohar III, 117a). For it is written: "Male and female created He them" (Genesis 1:27). This is part of the Supreme Mystery. It is said to constitute the glory of God and to be the object of faith. In the root nature, it is regarded as inaccessible to human reason. By this mystery was man created as well as the heaven and the earth. It is inferred that every figure which does not represent male and female has no likeness to the heavenly figure of the Great Adam the Cosmic. The Holy One does not make one His dwelling except where male and female are united, and there only His benedictions are disposed. This is why Scripture says, "And God blessed them and called their name 'Adam' on the day when they were created."[2]

The Zohar tells us that the condition of side to side was an imperfect union, because it was not a true union in the likeness of heaven. The latter is eye to eye, and beyond it there is another state. Eve was joined to Adam until he was put to sleep. The place of his enchantment was that place where the Temple was built subsequently (Zohar I, 34a).

## FORMATION OF EVE

It is said, "*He* took one of *his* ribs . . . and filled in flesh in its place." (Genesis 2:21–). The Zohar infers the subtlety, that the second pronoun *his*, alludes like the first pronoun He to the Lord God. The plural *ribs*, says further the Zohar, signifies the virgins, meaning the maidens of honor of Matrona; one of whom was taken to be the helpmate for Adam. It is further said, "bone of my bones, and flesh of my flesh" (Genesis 2:23) to signify Shechinah, the Indwelling Glory, who is the guide of man on earth, which is in close connection with womanhood (Zohar I, 28a). However, other versions of the narrative then follow there.

---

2. Genesis 5:2.

## THE INEFFABLE NUPTIALS

When the time came for man and woman to be joined face to face, the text of the Zohar applies this to intercourse. "They stand fast for ever and ever, and are done in truth and uprightness" (Psalms 111:8). The reference is to the state of true nuptials, ineffable in the holy transcendence, when between the male and the female, as between the wings of the cherubim, the glory of Shechinah manifests. When within and without are over and there is neither marrying nor giving in marriage, because those which were once in separation have entered into the heaven of union. The words, they "stand fast" are said to designate male and female, whose union here below will subsist through all eternity in the world that is above (Zohar I, 35a). The words of Genesis 2:6: "There went up a mist from the earth and watered the whole face of the ground," signifying the desire of the female for the male. It is added, that man was taken from his place and was transplanted and changed about, that man and woman might attain perfection and it is claimed in one place, that the sleep of Adam signifies this captivity.

## THE TREES OF THE GARDEN

Now, concerning the trees of the garden. The Tree of Life is identified with the Secret Doctrine in its inward form. It is the Holy Law, which offers aspects of truth in all its interpretations. The fruits of this tree subsist forever and give life to all. It gave life in particular to the twelve tribes, who issued therefrom. It covers with its wings those vessels that are pure souls. These fruits are sweeter than honey. At the end of time, the purified Israel will depend from this tree only. It is Knowledge in the true sense, which is supernal, that Knowledge is above reason. Those who are attached thereto possess life in the world to come as well as life in this world (Zohar I, 106b). The tree is the center of all life (Zohar II, 2a).

The Tree of Knowledge of Good and Evil is reputed to have been a vine and the forbidden fruit was the grape (Zohar III, 158b). It is said also to be the female principle when unsanctified and in a state of separation. It is also intimated there that the Tree of Knowledge is that evil woman who is the wife of Samael, and intercourse with her is incest, idolatry, and murder. It is the averse side of the sex-mystery. Wine, therefore, and fermented drink were interdicted to the priests in the Sanctuary (Zohar I, 36a).

## THE REVOLT OF THE SPIRITS

Among the narratives concerning the Tree of Knowledge of Good and Evil is one which relates how this tree invited many spirits to revolt before they were furnished with bodies, meaning in the state of preexistence, which we discussed previously. Eden so furnished, these spirits conceived a plan to descend on earth and assume possession thereof. God classed therefore the spirits in two categories, the good being placed on the side of the Tree of Life and the evil on the side of the tree of mixed knowledge (good and evil). He provided the first with bodies; but when the time had come to do likewise in respect of the second, the Sabbath interrupted the work of creation. Otherwise, there would have been wreck and ruin from end to end of the world. By this intervention, the Holy One provided the remedy before the evil, that is to say, in advancing the hour of the Sabbath. The evil spirits had the mortification of seeing good spirits invested with desirable bodies, while they in their deprivation were impotent (Zohar I, 14a). It seems to follow that the desire of the evil side is sex debased in iniquity. The infernal hosts are therefore in a state of inhibition, arrestation, and unsatisfied longing.

In general, as regards both trees, the Secret of Holy Doctrine of the Zohar looks forward with gladness in all its aspects towards that time when the elect will depend no longer on the Tree of Good and Evil. Then they will not be subject longer to a Law, which legislates on things permitted and forbidden, on clean and unclean things. Our entire natures will be drawn that day from the Tree of Life, and there will be no further debates about the evil and impure. For, concerning this time to come, it is written: "I will cause . . . the impure spirit to pass out of the land" (Zechariah 13:2). Herein is the rest which remains for the people of God, and the fruition is herein of those good things of the Lord, which are gathered into the Land of the Living. The Tree of Knowledge is the Tree of Death, in contrast to the Tree of life (Zohar III, 124b).

Thus proceeds the Mystery of Faith. Between the spirit of good and the spirit of evil she stands who is called woman. It is said in another place, and they shall then abide in harmony, in the turning of the evil, to account on the part of goodness, and by the help of woman the spirit of good preponderates over that of evil. The Tree of Life preserves all who are attached to it from death forever. And, it is said of the other tree, that those who are attached to it cleave also to death. The text quoted is: "Her feet go down to death. Her steps take hold on hell" (Proverbs 5:5) which also means, womanhood is on the side of evil.

CHAPTER TWO

# The Serpent, Son of the Morning, and the Fall of the Angels

A study of angelology, the fall of the angels and the hierarchy of demons which came about as consequence, has to begin in Talmudic literature and would be itself an undertaking of considerable magnitude. We shall confine our remarks to a few general heads, to elucidate things which led up to the Fall of Man, and some which followed therefrom. But first a few words on the subject of evil, and how it is regarded in the text of the Zohar.

## GOD, ALSO THE AUTHOR OF CERTAIN EVIL

It seems to follow by implication from several statements, some of which have been previously cited, that there is a certain sense in which God is the Author of evil. But the evil, which is created by God, is to be distinguished, however, from that which man works on his own part: "It is woe to those who make themselves wicked" (Isaiah 3:11). It is ruled, however, that "He has made everything beautiful in His time"

(Ecclesiastes 3:11); because He is glorified by the works of the just and the occasional good acts of wicked (Zohar II, 11a).

Now then, the Zohar's system being given, in which not only do all things come from God, but He is present immanently in all. It is not unnatural to accept evil as a direct consequence without debate; though there is a very keen sense of the burdens.

## THE SPIRIT OF GOOD AND THE SPIRIT OF EVIL

Thus we find the notion implied in several places, that the Holy One has created both the just and the unjust (Zohar II, 11a); or that he formed man of a spirit of good and a spirit of evil. The exoneration resides in the fact that evil is a service to good, because good turns evil to its place (Zohar I, 49a). Moreover, God created a certain tree, the eating of which meant that the full understanding of the evil side of things entered into the life of humanity but is imparted also the knowledge of good. From this point of view the Tree of Trespass is the prohibition which defines evil and separates that which is so imputed from what is recognized as good, as does the Written Law.

The exoneration in chief, however, we find in a discourse of R. Shimon who says that merit and demerit would have been equally impossible for man if God had not created the Spirit of Good and the Spirit of Evil, and if He had not composed our nature of both (Zohar I, 23a). The Spirit of Good and the Spirit of Evil are on the right and on the left of man. If the last lives in purity, the first acquires an ascendancy over the second, so that both combine to protect him in all his ways (Zohar I, 165b). The Spirit of Evil is in a state of incompleteness unless man nourishes him by sin (Zohar I, 201a).

Those who thus nourish this master of theirs are maintained in turn by him; when the happiness and prosperity of the Gentiles is a fruit of the union of Samael and his prostituted wife. It is admitted that evil is stronger than good. But even the demon contains a particle of sanctity without which he could not exist.

## HIERARCHY OF ANGELS AND HIERARCHY OF DEMONS

About the hierarchy of the blessed angels in the Zohar we hear generically of great hosts and cohorts, battalions of guardian, usually for purpose of honor, as when angels accompany Shechinah on some of her missions. It is mentioned, for example, that forty-two sacred angels, commissioned for the service of Shechinah, came down with Shechinah when she accompanied Israel (Jacob) into Egypt. Each bore a letter of the Divine Name of forty-two letters.

There are also clouds of messengers. It is specified that Metatron is the leader of the invisible hosts and that his place is immediately beneath the throne of God. It is also said here that Metatron is the name assumed by Enoch when he was raised to heaven. We have mentioned already choirs of angels as the order of cherubim, seraphim, chashmalim, arabim, tarshishim, ophanim, ishim, melachim, elohim.

As regards the infernal hierarchy, there are various categories consisting of angels who kept not their first estate and of demons generated in several ways. Generally speaking, the empire of demons is under the presidency of three chiefs or princes, who are described as three impure branches from which depend seventy minor branches and these are the leaders or angels of the seventy Gentile nations.

## THE EMPIRE OF THE DEMONS

Then again, the infernal hierarchies are specified as comprising ten degrees or ten crowns below and corresponding as such to numerous hierarchic grades, separated in appearance yet communicating one with another—being ramifications of a single tree. There are ten crowns to the right and ten crowns to the left, for there is a right and there is a left side in the empire of the demons; this being modelled throughout on that of God.

There is even an infernal triad, in correspondence as such with the sacred triad that is above and the observance of the Paschal Lamb was instituted to break its bonds. There are averse seraphim in the form of serpents emanating from the evil serpent. There are finally seven averse palaces, corresponding, on the one hand, to the palaces that are above and on the other, to the seven names which are attributed to the tempting spirit: Satan, Impure, Enemy, Stumbling Block, the Uncircumcised, Wicked, Crafty.

Now for the metaphysical account thereof. When the passive light designated in Scripture as darkness was joined to the active light on the right side, following the ordinary arrangement of the sephirotic tree, many celestial legions made ready to revolt against the other in place of equilibrium and harmony. They declared this by virtue of the Middle Pillar—declared themselves for the light of the left. There was apparently antagonism between the modes. When the Middle Pillar manifested the perfect unity of God, the good legions renounced the struggle and submitted. Those which were evil persisted and gave birth as a consequence of hell. It seems to infer that the potentiality for evil of those belonging to the passive side was greater than that of the active side. It is said elsewhere, that the "Sons of God" (Genesis 4:2) were angels of the evil side who were in a state of perversity from the beginning.

## THE FIRST DOWNFALL OF THE ANGELS

In this manner discord was introduced into the world on both sides, and some of its vibrations remained on that of the good powers. The scriptural allusion is: "And God made the firmament and divided the waters which were under the firmament, from the waters which were above the firmament" (Genesis 1:7). This text signifies in this sense of interpretation, the *hai* separated the discord, which had its source in the angels who kept not their first estate from that which was introduced into the world by those who were cast into the abyss. Both disruptions had, however, their result below. But that which belonged to the first class redounded to the glory of heaven.

## THE SECOND DOWNFALL OF THE ANGELS

This is so far concerning one category of souls, rejected from heaven and enchained below.

There was another class, however, the downfall of which was consequently on the Holy One assembling several legions of superior angels and advising them, that He intended to create man. They replied by quoting the Psalmist, when he said: "Nevertheless, man being in honor abideth not. He is like the beasts that perish" (Psalms 49:12). Thereupon the Holy One stretched forth a finger and burned these blessed legions, after which He called others into His presence and made the same statement. Their answer to this was, "What is man that Thou art mindful of him, and the son of man, that Thou visitest him" (Psalms 8:4). The Lord explained that man should be made in His image and would be superior to those whom He addressed.

## AZA AND AZAEL AND COMPANY

There were moreover those "Sons of God" who saw "the daughters of man that they were fair," and they include Aza and Azael, who entered into a dispute with Shechinah on the advisability of creating Adam, seeing that he would end by sinning with his wife. The Shechinah replied that before they made accusations of this kind, it must be postulated that they would prove more chaste in their own persons. In some codices of the Zohar is added that Shechinah intimated at this point that Adam will indeed end by sinning with a single woman, but it will prove also with her that he will be able to repair the fault. This while the lost angels will sin with many women and will be deprived of all reparation. This was the conclusion for the moment. But the children of God had recourse to the daughters of men and "took them wives of all that they chose." The result was that Shechinah stripped them of their sanctity and of all parts in eternal beatitude, which had been the case also with the rebellious angels belonging to the first category: these are burnt eternally in Sheol.

According to one version, Aza and Azael became enamored of the daughter of Cain. One text also says that the aforementioned sons of Elokim were actually sons of Cain.

When Aza and Azael were cast down, they assumed bodies on earth and were imprisoned therein. It was subsequently, according to this version, that woman seduced them and they are alive at this day, still instructing men in the art of magic, which they had begun to teach soon after their descent. Aza and Azael belonged to that class of angels who appeared under the form of men and it was possible, therefore, for them to exist on earth. "They assumed bodies to come down and because of the revolt they could not unclothe to reascend." By their union with women they engendered giants, the "mighty men of old," and "men of renown" mentioned in Genesis 6:4. Aza and Azael were finally chained on certain black mountains, which Laban and Bilaam frequented for instruction in the forbidden art.

## NAAMAH

According to another version, Naamah, the sister of Tubal Cain, was from the side of Cain the murderer. She was a seducer of men and spirits including Aza and Azael, who again were the children of God mentioned in Genesis. She became the mother of demons and is still abroad in the world, exciting the desires of men, more especially in dreams of the night. She is associated with Lilith, of whom we shall soon hear more. It is testified by this tradition that demons are subject to death in the same way as human beings. This obviously applies to the progeny and not to first parents, this as Samael, Lilith, and Naamah are still in activity.

There were, in all, five orders of intelligence which seem to have been cast out of heaven, and some of them were incarnated as men. These were the giants of Genesis: the Nephilim, the descendants of Amalek, the Intruders of the Talmud, and so forth. It is on record that they caused the destruction of the Temple.

## SAMAEL AND HIS WIFE, THE SERPENT

There is a distinction made in Zohar between the Serpent mentioned in Genesis and him who rode thereon. It is said that the serpent was the female and was she who is called the Prostituted Woman. It is she whose "feet go down to death" (Proverbs 5:5). She was the wife of him who rode on her back, and this was Samael the death angel. It comes about in this manner that there is male and female on the evil side, even as there is on the sacred side; though in a rough and general sense, the right side is sometimes said to be masculine and the left feminine. It is said, also, that the adulterous woman by whom the world is seduced is the sword of the destroying angels.

Samael and his wife the Prostituted Woman are impurity taking shape as such, and from their union issue powerful spiritual leaders, who are spread abroad in the world and defile it. Samael mounted on the serpent's back is a symbol of the evil side of sexual intercourse, that is to say, after the manner of the beasts. Samael is the tempter spirit whose purpose is to put man to the test, and his other name is the End of Darkness, which is equivalent to "end of all flesh." But, when the Zohar speaks of the spirit of evil generically, it affirms that this is an old and insensate thing. The reference is then to the "old and foolish king" (Ecclesiastes 4:13).

The serpent was condemned to go upon her belly; this means that God took away those feet which are the support of the body. Here the text intimates profoundly and says Israel would not be supported by the Law, which was built to encompass it as the hills stand around Jerusalem.

As there is a serpent below which is still at work in the world, so there is a sacred serpent above which watches over mankind in all the roads and pathways and restrains the power of the impure serpent. This one is one of the adornments of the heavenly throne.

## THE GREAT DRAGON

From the union which is predicated concerning Samael and the evil serpent, we hear of the great serpent or dragon, which came to pass and which was cast into the abyss with his legions when the Sacred Name of forty-two letters was first graven upon the seal of God. But the abyss subsequently gave up the demons and the surface of the earth was covered with darkness until celestial light illuminated the world. This spirit of evil has chiefs and messengers under his orders, intervening in all acts of man. Yet the serpent can only defile the soul by special authorization therefrom.

Hence, Israel still suffers on account of the impurities which came from the side of the first serpent, from the impurities of ill-doing spirits and from those of demons, but especially from the impurities of that particular reptile which is called "the other god," and is identified with Amalek. He is said to be the cause of all uncleanness in the world in all the degrees thereof. He is apparently on the male side and as such is an assassin, while his wife is a mortal poison because she incites to idolatry. This is curious in this connection, because the name Samael is held to signify the "venom of God." Samael is also the angel of death, who destroys man with a single drop of poison. Amalek might be his synonym. There are said, however, to be two demons: sub voce Amalek and the Divine malediction of the first serpent applies to both.

## OTHER DEMONS

For the rest, demons are the excrement of the earth and are designated by the word *Tohu* while *Bohu* signifies that part of the world which is free from demons. Tohu, the first state, is that of the infernal cohorts, so confused with matter that they formed one body therewith. A separation was accomplished by the fire which is referred to under the name of darkness, when it is said the "darkness was upon the face of the deep" (Genesis 1:2). For there is a light of the world below which is in separation from the world above and this is said to generate demons without number.

But to make the clarification complete, "the Holy Spirit brooded upon the face of the waters" (Genesis 1:2). It is added that so long as the purification was unfinished, the spirit of the demon still interposed between heaven and matter to deprive man of the pure vision of God.

For the rest, we shall meet with the serpent and Samael again in the next section and shall see after what manner they enter into the Mystery of Sex. As a conclusion to this part, it is desirable to say that the world will not be set free from the serpent and this prince of demons Samael until the coming of Messiah the King, who will cast down death forever. This applies also to Samael the death angel and the serpent on which he rides in union. The Holy One, blessed be He, created the tempter spirit so that He might put man to the test.

In a sense, he is also God's minister. There is a counsel not to affront the demon, since in virtue of such imposed office, he would be saved like the executioner. One text of the Zohar affirms therefore, that even the evil spirit will be restored at the end of days. The inference is extracted out of the words: "He brought back all the goods, and also brought again his brother Lot" (Genesis 14:16).

Moreover, as the infernal male and female principles symbolize the sex mystery in the deeps of corruption, we have to remember that even in these deeps it is a reflection of the Mystery that is on high, and it may not be without an element of redemption. Also, it connects with the truth of things, working towards a justification of the Divine Ways in all the quarters of the universe.

Furthermore, the meditating and reconciling principle between good and evil is held to be womanhood, and hence it is said that the Spirit of Good and the Spirit of Evil can only abide in harmony so far as the female is between them, she having part in both. It is then only that the Spirit of Good, which constitutes pure joy, attracts the female and thus preponderates over the Spirit of Evil.

## CHAPTER THREE
# The Fall of Man

Adam fell on the very day of his creation and his sojourn in the Paradise, a life of glory and divinity, was followed by a life of shame. The Zohar tells of a gradual degeneration of Adam, because the workings of the beast "more subtle than any," were in process prior to the manifest temptation of Eve. The first Sabbath followed the decree of expulsion, which took place in the very day of his creation, the notion being drawn from this text of Isaiah 17:2: "In the day shalt thou make thy plant to grow and in the morning shalt thou make thy seed to flourish." The Zohar renders it thus: "The day that thou have planted, your seed shall produce only wild fruits."

### MAN IN HIS GLORY AND HEREAFTER

It appears that the original union of man, male and female, was apart from fleshly sensations and it was therefore a union in modesty. There is a suggestion that children were born to

Adam in the Garden of Eden, that is to say, souls. And if they had come with him out of the garden, man would have had eternal life. He was expelled, however, to engender children outside. Later on when Adam said: "This is now bone of my bones and flesh of my flesh" (Genesis 2:23), he was seeking to dispose Eve in favor of such intercourse, because they were one only of each gender. It was out of this temptation, arisen immediately after these words of tenderness, that the spirit of evil awoke to substitute carnal pleasure for its own profit in place of pure affection. The object was also to sully the sanctity above by defiling man below in the first place. After the Fall of Man, it is said that the Tree of the Trespass was banished from Paradise. The apple and the tree are also understood allegorically. It is also called sometimes the fruit of the vine, that is to say, grapes. The meaning is veiled and its explanation is to be understood as a certain mystery of knowledge belonging to the dominion of sex. These grapes are the fruits that are said to be agreeable (on the authority of Genesis), but they trouble the spirits of those who make bad use of them. This is as Noah did in the case of his own vine, and as Deuteronomy has it in chapter 32, verse 32: "Their grapes are grapes of gall, their clusters are bitter." The tree is also allegorical and moves with man through the places of his exile.

## SAMAEL THE TEMPTER AND RIDER OF THE SERPENT APPEARED TO EVE

He who rode upon the serpent, the Tempter Spirit or Samael, appeared and all creatures took fright when he appeared. He is said also to have descended from heaven so mounted, as if he were an accredited messenger. He approached Eve and testified that the Holy One created the world by help of the Tree of Knowledge, that by eating thereof and so only was He able to create the world. If the woman ate of it on her own part, she would attain the same power. The allusion was to the mysteries of Faith and Sex, intimating that the universe was a work of generation. The sense to which this testimony was a preface proved a lying travesty of the true practice.

## ALTERNATIVE ACCOUNTS OF THE KINDS OF TEMPTATION

There are also alternative accounts as to the kind of temptation. In another case it is said that the peculiar atmosphere of the demon, which encompassed the mystical fruit as if lying in a hot bed, seduced Eve. Again in a third alternative, it is an intimation of a seduction which the text reads into the temptation mystery, arising from the betrayal of love which had not appeared in the world until Adam and Eve were set toward one another face to face. It was also an outcome of the blind turning toward conception and generation, so that in this sense Eve was made victim as a result of her own womanhood. It is suggested again in this place, that Adam and Eve began to engender children from the moment that they were put face to face.

## THE DIRE CONSEQUENCES CAUSED BY THE TEMPTATION

By reason of one or another cause, Eve decided to taste the fruit which had the faculty to open the eyes of those who approached it, meaning in things concerning the Tree of Life itself. The result was a division between life and death, as if the peace-ensuring Middle Pillar had been removed from the sephirotic tree, and Shechinah had ascended to *Kether*, leaving the sephirah *Malkuth* without God in the world. The threatened death seems to have been understood spiritually. It is said elsewhere that the serpent takes away the higher souls—*Neshamoth*, of all flesh.

There was division also between the Voice and the Word, so that the Voice spoke, yet the Word was not uttered. It all was the consequence of separating life from death. The analogy of which is the separation between man and woman by the chastisement of the menses, so that she is in hiding like the moon, which is taken away from the heaven of stars for a week, from month to month.

It also reminds the sons of the Holy Doctrine how it fares with them in the actual present. And so it is added that since Israel has been in captivity, the Voice has been divided from it, whence the Word is audible no longer. The suggestion comes from Psalms 39:2: "I was dumb with silence. I held my peace even from good but my pain was greatly excited. The word remains in the heart, but the lips which should speak are paralyzed."

## THE LOSS OF THE CELESTIAL DECORATIONS AND THE SUBSTITUTED LEAF COVERINGS

Another tradition substitutes a mystical vine for the apple tree. Eve pressed grapes and gave the juice to her husband. The opening of their eyes was to behold all the ills of the world. At that period neither he nor his wife had as yet been clothed with skins, which are sometimes understood as material bodies. They discerned their nakedness. The explanation of this will be cited in the following. In the act which constituted their trespass, they lost that celestial lustre and decoration of sacred letters which had covered them previously. They clothed themselves therefore, with leaves of the same Tree of which they had eaten, with leaves of the vine or fig. These leaves are said in more than one place to signify demons, meaning the evil side of fleshly desires. They knew now all secrets of the lower world and seeing that the leaves of the Tree were the most pleasurable of that region, they sought to acquire force therein by that means.

## STILL ANOTHER ACCOUNT

Another account of the Zohar states that the verses which read: "And when the woman saw that the tree was good for food and pleasant to the eyes, she took of the fruit thereof and did eat" (Genesis 3:6) designate the first union of Adam and Eve. She consented originally to the union as a result of her reflections on the values of conjugal relations and by reason of that pure affection and tenderness, which united her to Adam. But the intervention of the serpent had as its result that Eve: "gave also to her husband with her" (ibid.), which means that their conjugal relations changed, and that she filled him with carnal desires.

Henceforth, desire was first on the part of the woman, she alluring the man. This evil notwithstanding, the acts performed between them subsequently were in correspondence with those which obtain above. For the Spirit of Evil imitates the Spirit of Good, and that which it occasions below in malice, the Spirit of Good fulfills in holiness above. This implies "a sublime mystery," which is said to exceed the capacity of most men.

## THE CUIRASS OF SACRED LETTERS

When Adam and Eve had sinned, the Holy One stripped off the cuirass formed by the light of the sacred letters with which they had been invested. It was then that they saw that they were naked. Previously, the cuirass had shielded them from all attacks whilst they were free therein. "And they sewed fig leaves together and made themselves aprons" (Genesis 2:7). This means that they betook themselves to the delights of the lower and material world: leaves of the Tree of Good and Evil, fleshly pleasures and the consequences thereof. It is however to be observed that the evil is not without the good in the Tree of

Knowledge. It was the profanation of a Great Mystery, but the seeds of redemption remained. For that reason the Zohar discerns a promise of salvation hidden in the words: "And the Lord God commanded the man, saying; 'Of every tree of the Garden thou mayest freely eat, but of the Tree of Knowledge of Good and Evil, thou shalt not eat of it. For in the day that thou eatest thereof, thou shalt surely die'" (Genesis 2:16–17). This was prior to the creation of Eve, according to the literal account of Genesis; therefore, it is to be noticed that he alone was commanded and he alone was forbidden.

Another version affirms that the forbidden fruit signifies woman herself, and the verse appertaining thereto is "Her feet go down to death; her steps take hold on hell" (Proverbs 5:5). The Tree is said, moreover, to signify man. This sense of the woman being the forbidden fruit postulates the kind of relations between the woman and the serpent, between the man and Lilith, of which we hear otherwise. Woman is also signified by the garden when it is said: "And a river went out of Eden to water the Garden" (Genesis 2:10). Prior to the trespass, this river penetrated into the woman and irrigated her waters. It is added that when men are in such a degree of sanctity, there is perfect unity and of this unity it is said: "In that day there shall be one Lord and His Name One" (Zechariah 14:9). Subsequent to the sin, the Holy One clothed Adam and Eve with vestments belonging to flesh alone.

## OF THE BEAUTY OF ADAM AND EVE

It appears that previously the flesh was glorified by light of the spirit. It is stated otherwise that they had garments of light, thanks to which they were raised above the higher angels, who had recourse to them in order to enjoy light.

Towards the close of the Zohar, R. Eliezer, in the course of a discussion with another master of the Secret Law, allows that Adam and Eve were clothed with garments of skin before the Fall, but they were then glorious vestments, which became gross subsequently. He adds that their eyes were opened by the trespass to the material form of the world, whereas previously they had beheld in all things only the celestial side.

A later tradition declares that the beauty of Adam was reflected from the glorious Throne, while the beauty of Eve was such that no creature could look on her. Even Adam could not do so until after the trespass, when both lost their supernatural loveliness. The physical beauty only was theirs afterwards.

## SEPARATION CAUSED BY THE TRESPASS AND DEATH

According to yet another account, the sin of Eve was one of separation that, according to the Zohar, designates death. On the correlative side it is said elsewhere that when Adam ate of the Tree of Good and Evil, he provoked the separation of woman from man.

On the day of transgression both heaven and earth sought to flee away, because they were established only on the covenant of God, with man. This is as it is written: "If My covenant be not with day and night, and if I have not appointed the ordinances of heaven and earth" (Jeremiah 33:35).

When Adam forsook the way of faith and the tree, which is the synthesis of all trees, he lapsed from a region of stability into one susceptible of variation, exchanging life for death. The Tree of Life preserves all who are attached to it from death forever. Humanity was made originally in the likeness of Elokim, which likeness was obscured by the Fall so that the faces of men were transformed, with the result that they began to fear the beasts who had been afraid previously of them.

## OF THE ODORS DIFFUSED IN EDEN FOR THE VESTURES OF THE SOUL

I will put forth here another intimation which belongs to a variant order and symbolism and is distinct from these. It is a moral consideration as well as Secret Doctrine. It states that numerable pleasant odors are diffused forever throughout the Garden of Eden to prepare the precious vestments of the soul, which are formed from the good days spent by man on earth. For the earthly Paradise is also a place of sojourn for the departed on the return, whence they came.

"And they knew, that they were naked" (Genesis 3:7). This means, according to tradition, that they were aware of being without the precious vestures which are formed of stainless days. As a result of the trespass, no such day was left to Adam, and it is in this sense that he was naked. According to another intimation, that which was stripped from him was a robe of glory, wherein he had no need for the vesture of stainless days; his need arose only afterward.

When Adam repented, the Holy One clothed him with other garments, but they were not garments of days. There are two places in which the garments of skin are said to be robes of glory with which they were clothed by God, in which they left Paradise, in virtue of which they resembled those who are on high, and wherein they were ultimately buried. They were also permeated with the odors of Paradise.

## ADAM AND THE SERPENT

It is further said that when Adam sinned the evil serpent cleaved to him and defiled him as well as all future generations. As regards the serpent, it is further said in the Cremona edition that Samael descended upon the earth with all his hosts, and he sought upon the earth a companion like unto himself. It had an appearance even as a camel, the Hebrew letters of which mean also "reward" or "recompense."

The serpent was ultimately able to penetrate secretly into man's interior and Adam submitted to this so that he might know the mysteries of things below. The serpent showed him all the pleasures of the world. It is testified by the "colleagues" that the Fall of Man was one of sin with a woman in the normal sense, which attaches to this expression. It is also sometimes added that with woman man will repair his fault, which involves the reintegration of nuptial union in the order of divine things.

## SAMAEL DEFILES EVE/CAIN

It is then added that sexual desires have caused all evils; but as the debate continues, a modification follows in its course with the correction that in themselves they are good or evil, according to the spirit that inspires them. Now, seeing that it is to Eve that sin of a sexual order was first imputed, the question is who instructed or initiated her? The answer is that the serpent—meaning Samael—had "criminal relations" with her and injected his defilement into her; Adam was not affected until she communicated in turn to him. She cohabited with Samael who corrupted her and by him she became with child, bringing forth Cain.

The story of this cohabitation is also of Talmudic origin and it will be found among other places, in the Tractate *Sabbath*. The Midrash Ruth affirms that the serpent defiled both Adam and Eve. The paraphrase of Jonathan ben Uziel states furthermore categorically that when Adam knew Eve his wife, she had conceived already of the angel Samael (Genesis 4:1). Apparently as a result of the dual intercourse, she brought forth Cain who is said to have resembled the beings that are above, not those who are below. Eve is also recorded there to have said: "I have gotten a man, an angel of God" (ibid.). Our text reads that she said, "I have gotten a man from the Lord" (Genesis 4:1). Our text, of course, also reads in Scripture: "And Adam knew his wife Eve; and she conceived and bore Cain" (Genesis 4:1).

The sexual nature of the fall of man is thus further developed in the Zohar in another place where it is affirmed that Adam was defiled by the impure spirit before his union with Eve. Also, that the son, whom he begot in this state of impurity, was from the left side: so was Cain born. But when Adam repented, he engendered a son from the right side: so was Abel born.

Another account (ibid.) on the authority of R. Eliezer, recurs to the earlier thesis specifying that Cain was begotten from the serpent, but that after intercourse with Adam, Eve conceived again and so brought two sons into the world: one of the works of the serpent and one of the works of Adam. The image of Abel was from on high and that of Cain from below (ibid.). This statement is at issue with the quoted paraphrase of Jonathan ben Uziel. Furthermore, we find in the Zohar Chadash, Yithro, that the seduction of Adam by Lilith and of Eve by her companion Samael caused our mortal condition. This is the sense in which death was brought into the world, "and all our woe"; the springs of generation were tainted.

## ADAM AND EVE BOTH BEGOT CHILDREN FROM DEMONS

Another story recited that the relations of Samael continued for a long time with Eve, who bore him many children. They were not in human likeness. The time episode, of course, was after the expulsion from Paradise.

So also after the death of Abel, Adam separated from his wife and he began to receive visits from two female demons with which he had relations, and he engendered those evil spirits and demons which infest the world. It is pointed out that there is no need for surprise at this, because every man in his dreams sees such women occasionally, observes them smiling at him and if they excite his concupiscence, they conceive and bear demons. These demons most likely were the Lilith and Naamah mentioned elsewhere in the Zohar.

Adam remained separated from his true wife for one hundred and thirty years, continuing to engender; and so long as he was defiled by the infection of the impure spirit, he had no desire for union with Eve. It returned, however, when he purified himself "and he begot a son in his own likeness, after his image," Seth.

It is further taught that if Adam had never sinned, man would never have tasted death as the condition of his entrance into the world beyond. In another place, it is maintained that in the unfallen state, Adam and Eve would have engendered children emanating from the Holy Spirit.

Still dwelling upon the mystery behind sex, the Zohar generalizes on this matter saying that so long as man follows the path which leads to the left side, his desire is towards the impure only; but the just, who walk in the right way, have children worthy of themselves. It seems, therefore, that the Fall of Man was not the result of human intercourse per se, taking place between Adam and Eve, but of some aberration in sex, variously described.

## ANOTHER MYSTERIOUS ACCOUNT OF A FEMALE DEMON

There is an alternative account not mentioned previously which balances the copulation of Eve and Samael by the relations subsisting for a long period of time between Adam and Lilith amidst all the splendors and perfection of Paradise, prior to the creation of the helpmate, Eve. Creation of Eve was to substitute human for impure pleasures and so she was taken ultimately from the side of Adam. So we discern another sense in which it was "not good that the man should be alone," as well as in Adam's saying: "This time she is bone of my bones and flesh of my flesh." It would seem apparently that this one was another Lilith who was Adam's wife in Paradise and identical with the black Lilith there was another one. . . .

## LILITH, THE WIFE OF LEVIATHAN, AND THE OTHER THREE DEMONS, MAAMAN, OGERETH, AND MAHALTOTH

There are many scattered references to this female demon Lilith, who in one of her forms appears to have been of the mermaid type. For when it is said that God created great whales, the reference is to leviathan and his wife Lilith (Genesis 1:24). She goes abroad in the night. She is the instigator of punishments clamoring daily for their infliction. She is said to preside over all fish that are charged with missions to this world. The Zohar says that these demon fish are called: "the first born in the land of Egypt" (Genesis 12:20). These are the sacred angels of waters that are above separated by God from the emissaries of Lilith in the waters below. It must be noted here that this Lilith is distinct from the "adulterous woman," who was the wife of Samael.

She is termed, in one place, servant, in opposition to that servant who is Shechinah, who presides over the birth of children, but Lilith devours them. Lilith is the mother of demons. She is the most terrible of all evil spirits, but she took refuge in the deep when God created and adorned Eve.

A Talmudic version relates that Lilith was created from the same earth as Adam and she refused in the end to serve him, through pride, respecting her origin. Lilith is rendered screech owl, and the word *Lilith* occurs in the original Hebrew in Isaiah 34:14. The root in Hebrew signifies *night*. R. Elias recognized four mothers of demons: Lilith, Naamah,

Ogereth, and Mahalath. These are also mentioned in the last chapter of the Talmudic tractate *Pesachim*, and elsewhere in the Talmud in the same and in similar capacities.

It is further stated that when the tables of the law were broken, it was then man perceived that he was naked. It is said further that the words: "They heard the voice of the Lord God" alludes to the voice of God on Mount Sinai. And furthermore, it is stated that since the day that Adam fell, the world was in a condition of poverty until the arrival of Noah, who, having offered a sacrifice, restored the world to its normal state.

It is obvious that there have been sacrifices before; that is, the acceptable offering of Abel previously. But there was something particular about the offering of Noah as we shall see in the next chapter. So also was there something particular about his drunkenness, which was in reality an exploration of Divine Mysteries. We know of the indignity which befell him in punishment thereof. We shall discuss it when we discuss the sin which led to the Deluge.

## FINALE OF THE EXPULSION FROM EDEN, THE FLAMING SWORD, CONCLUSION

At the time of Adam's expulsion from Eden it is said that Adam had expelled the Lord from his own heart and also as a manifest Presence from that world, which man had ravaged by his trespass.

Adam is said to have chanted the ninety-second Psalm in his flight and the Sabbath intervened to protect him, so that he was not entirely driven out until the end of the Sabbath day. The way of the return to the Garden was barred by the Flaming Sword lest worse evils be brought upon the world. The Flaming Sword which turned every way (Genesis 3:25) signifies angels set over the chastisement of man in this world. It is said also to have symbolized the trials with which God overwhelms man that he may be restored to the way of goodness.

We have seen that the temptation and the Fall of Man signified, among other things, an aberration of sex, a declension and a materialization therein from the perfect way of nuptial. We also say that the ascent of the sephirotic Tree of Life is a return into union (according to the secret school). We shall find it to be a journey in the graces and glories of the sacred Shechinah, who presides over perfect nuptial, which if begun on earth is completed in the world of the supernals. It was said also that a day shall come when the world will be avenged of the serpent. The world will remain in the toils of the serpent until that day shall come, when a man corresponding to Adam and a woman who is comparable to Eve, shall vanquish not only the serpent but the angel of death and destruction who rides thereon. This will be the day of the coming of the tree of Life, which will obtain the remission of sins and will enchain the serpent. The male and female will be united in the Garden of Eden, as they were before the fall. The nakedness of the natural Adam is the nakedness of good works and of obedience to the commandments of the Law, which is understood as that Secret Doctrine which is concerned with the Mystery of Faith.

It may be added here that Adam and Eve were interred together in a cave having a door that opened on the Garden of Eden; and there also some of the Patriarchs were buried.

CHAPTER FOUR

# The Account of the Deluge

**PROLOGUE**

We have seen that the mystery of the earthly Paradise connects with the Mystery of Sex. The fall of the angels connects also with this mysterious subject. It is said to have been responsible for all uncleanness subsequently on earth and in man and having helped to bring about the Fall of Man and his aberration in the Mystery of Sex. Finally, the wickedness which was "great upon the earth," which broke up "the fountains of the great deep and opened the windows of heaven" in the great Deluge, was an iniquity of sex aberration. It is a mystery which cannot be revealed in its entirety to the world.

The way of human generation and that of humanity belongs also to this great mystery by virtue of its correspondence with things above, when it came forth resplendent at its first birth. The Zohar namely postulates a mystery of spiritual intercourse belonging to the state of paradise, and in the body of our present life, a natural intercourse, which can be raised into the sacredness of things Divine. Between these there was a sexual iniquity described in the language of earthly lust and constituting the Fall of Man. But the Fall was not merely a sin of natural intercourse.

Had this holy correspondence of human generation with things above been maintained, there would have been no path of human regeneration. For men would have walked in union, even as "Enoch walked with God." It is furthermore implied that in the birth of Seth, human generation was uplifted into the sacred world because only he, says the Zohar, was in the image and likeness of his father, who was in the likeness and image of God. The path of nuptials was therefore followed by the saints of old in accordance with a practice of wisdom, which will be indicated hereafter. But this was not the way of the world. We shall now consider those stages of the downward path, which led up to the Deluge, in accordance with Zoharic theosophy. We shall find that the mystery of sex was here on the averse side.

## THE SINS WHICH BROUGHT ABOUT THE CATACLYSM OF THE DELUGE

In explanation of the cataclysm of the Deluge, the text of the Zohar dwells on the wickedness of man, that it was very great over the whole world as recorded in the Holy Scripture. The patience of God was extended until the evil began to take that form which is described as the spilling of blood vainly on the earth.

The sex aberration here designated is the crime attributed to Onan (Genesis 38:9) and the Zoharic Doctrine affirms that no man who is sullied in this manner shall enter the Heavenly Palace or behold the face of the Shechinah. The offense of this aberration being very grave, the Shechinah is driven away.

Because of its prevalence, the world fell into corruption; in part through the sin itself and for the rest by the absence of Shechinah. It was as if the principle of life had been withdrawn or that the loss of the head caused the body to decay. The world had become like an unclean woman who has to hide in the presence of her husband.

Yet, this was not the last state. For a time came when corruption reached such a point that there was neither shame nor concealment any longer. The sin of Onan had corrupted the earth as well as man. The semen literally seeped into the earth. Also the earth is called corrupt when man is in a state of decadence.

Now then, the waters above represent the male principle, while the female principle answers to the waters below, as is their posture in the act of intercourse. The sin postulated was concerned with the waters of the male principle and it was necessary therefore that the whole contaminated earth should be purified by the waters of the Deluge. But the waters above, which are spiritual, and the spiritual waters below concurred therein for the floodgates of heaven were opened and the fountains of the great deep were broken up.

The vicious state of the world at the time period occurred because at the Deluge period, the world had as yet not been purified fully from the infection of the serpent. The complete purification took place for a moment at the foot of Mount Sinai. The generation then was also without faith—more especially concerning the secret subject matter of that which is called the Mystery of Faith. Men were attached, at that period, to the leaves of the Tree of Good and Evil, meaning the spirit of the demon.

## NOAH'S ARK AND THE MEANING OF THE ARK

The Ark of Noah is said to be a symbol of the Ark of the Covenant. Noah had to be shut up in such a vessel here below, because this comes to pass also in respect of the mystery, which is on high. He could not be so enclosed until God entered into a covenant with him. He was then able to save the world and this corresponds with the Supreme Mystery. It is said that Noah walked with Elokim, who is the covenant of peace in the world. He was predestined from the day of creation to be shut up in the ark. Noah's ark was feminine, because it was a house for those who were saved from the waters of the Deluge. But it is unbecoming for a wife to receive anyone as a guest at her house without the consent of her husband, so when Noah proposed to enter the ark, it was necessary that God the Spouse or Master of the house should authorize his union therewith. It was therefore at the invitation of God that he so entered. So too is it written: "For thee have I seen righteous before Me in this generation (Genesis 8:1).

Now, Elokim is Shechinah, the Celestial Bride, and it was by the permission of Shechinah the Bride and the Mistress of the house that Noah had a permit to leave the ark when the Deluge was over within whose precincts he had dwelt (ibid.).

After leaving those hospitable quarters, Noah made a present to Shechinah and he erected an altar to God and offered sacrifices thereon. Noah, however, received his reward directly from Shechinah, who is called Elokim, because it is said, Elokim blessed Noah and his children saying: "Increase and multiply and fill the earth" (Genesis 9:1). For Shechinah presides over nuptials and the fruit of nuptials.

## THE HOLOCAUST

As regards the altar itself we must remember that Adam made an offering. The Deluge, however, overturned Adam's altar. And when the time came for Noah to sacrifice on his part, he raised up for this purpose the overthrown altar of Adam.

The allusion throughout of Noah's sacrifices is its connection with the Mystery of Sex. It should be pointed out that this is the case with every kind of burnt offering. The verse in Leviticus 1:17: "A burnt sacrifice, an offering made by fire, of a sweet savour unto the Lord" is alluded to in the Zohar on that passage to read *woman* instead. Such translation would read or signify that the holocaust is a woman and as such an agreeable odor to God. The holocaust, of course, is male as is written in the text: "a male without blemish," but the allusion is to its connection with Shechinah, who is often termed in the Zohar, the sacrifice of the Holy One.

The real purpose of Noah's holocaust was the union of the male and the female principles, as these should never be in separation. Noah offered a sacrifice because he represented the male principle, which the Holy One united to the ark, which latter represented the female principle.

The Zohar tells us that the Holy Land was not covered by the waters of the Deluge, as it is said in Ezekiel 22:24: "Thou art the land that is not cleansed, nor rained upon in the day of indignation." Furthermore, the Deluge came to be called: "the waters of Noah" for he prayed for himself only and not for the world. It seems that had he chosen to, he could have prevailed with God to spare the whole creation.

## NOAH'S EXPERIMENT

Now Noah planted a vineyard, as it is narrated in Genesis. But according to one Zoharic opinion, he transplanted the vine which had grown in the Garden of Eden. It transpires, however, only by inference that this signifies the Tree of Knowledge. According to another view, he merely moved an ordinary vine of earth to a more favorable place. The fact that Noah pressed the grapes, even as Eve is said also to have done, and partook of the juice and so became drunken is affirmed to contain a mystery of wisdom. We have seen that the lady of all our race, that is, Eve, was making an experiment of knowledge, and so we shall understand further that which followed in Noah's case was an intoxication after its own kind. Noah was concerned with an experiment, having set himself to fathom that sin which had caused the fall of the first man. His intention was to find a cure for the world in place of Eve and her poison, derived from the serpent.

But Noah became drunken by laying bare the Divine Essence without having the intellectual strength to fathom it. This is why Scripture says that he was drunken and was uncovered within his tent. The meaning is that he raised a corner of the veil concerning that breach of the world which ought always to remain secret. The tent of Noah was really the tent of the vine. The ark was the means of transmitting the true knowledge concerning the mystery of sex from one epoch of the world to the other.

The experiment made by Noah was for the purpose of restoring the Mystery of Sex to its proper place in the spiritual life of man, after his lapse and degradation from the perfect union signified by the state of Paradise.

## THE CONFUSION OF TONGUES AFTER THE DELUGE

The builders of Babel are said to have found a book containing certain Mysteries of Wisdom, which had belonged to the generation destroyed by the Deluge. It might seem that the book was the primeval memorial of secret knowledge which, as we have seen previously, was transmitted to Adam and thence to the chiefs of the people, leaders of sanctity in the early generations. According to another version, however, the book was rather a record of magical art, as this was attained by Enoch (20. I, 56a, 323).

Enoch's knowledge and ability in occult science, it is said, exceeded that of his predecessors from Adam downward. This also is the sense in which we are to understand the scriptural statement that he, Enoch, began to "call upon the name of the Lord." This is to say he used the Divine Name to compel spirits in accordance with recognized procedures of magical operation (ibid.). For the Zohar always recognizes the claim of magic as the art of a secret power, but it is condemned in all its branches and in all its modes.

The progress of this science assumed then such proportions that the wicked generation of the Deluge expected to escape Divine chastisement by recourse thereto. With the help of its mysteries, they prepared even to make war on the Holy One, which was also the intention of those who planned the tower of Babel.

Like their predecessors, they had great trust in magic. It was enough for them to pronounce words and things were accomplished. But the project had its source in a limited knowledge concerning the Mystery of Ancient Wisdom. We find also a statement where it is said that Adam transmitted the celestial book containing the Mystery of Wisdom to other men who penetrated this mystery and seem to have imitated God thereby. The succession of the keepers of the treasure has already been enumerated elsewhere in this book (20. I 767a; 446). It appears likely, therefore, that there were two primeval books recognized by the Zohar: one of Adam and the other one of knowledge which was either evil in itself or could be converted readily into evil.

At the dispersion which arrested the building of the tower, those concerned therein lost even their partial knowledge. The confusion of tongues was, of course, a punishment adjudged instead of the original existence of only one language (ibid.).

We have already spoken of the union between thought and the word. This was symbolized by the original existence of only one language. When men became separated from God, unity was no longer possible among them. The plan of Babel was elaborated with ingenious perversity, as the builders desired to quit the celestial domain for that of Satan and so substituted a strange glory for the glory of God.

But, finishes the Zohar, the apocryphal prophecy of Sohphonia assures us that at the end of days the Lord will change the tongues of all the people into a pure tongue, so that all may invoke His Name and all pass under his yoke in one spirit. "Because then I will restore to all people a chosen lip and a unity of words, that all may call on the name of the Lord and may serve Him with one shoulder" (Zephaniah 3:9).

CHAPTER FIVE

# The Covenant with Abraham

The call came to the patriarch Abraham; in answer, he left "the land of his nativity in Ur of the Chaldees, and entered into the land of Canaan" (Genesis 11:31; 15:7). The journey was literal no doubt and stood as such at its value. But it was also a mystical travelling and in this respect it belongs to a higher currency.

Abraham had been endowed with a spirit of wisdom, and by the use of its talents had attained knowledge of the celestial chiefs who govern the various divisions of the habitable world. He had gone further also than this, having discovered that Palestine was the center of the earth as well as the point of departure in its creation. He had not as yet ascertained what chief ruled it, but he concluded that such a president must be head over the entire cohort. The study of the Holy Land was therefore the intent of his journey, and he drew for that purpose on all his stores of astrological knowledge. Still he was unable to penetrate the essence and importance of that Supreme power which ruled the worlds

262

innumerable, and which was postulated in his mind as the spiritual chief of Palestine.

When at the end of his resources, however, the Holy One manifested on His own part, counseling that he should enter into himself, learn how to know himself, and forsake all the false occult science to which he had recourse previously. This is another sense in which he was to come out of his own country.

## HISTORY OF ABRAHAM, THE FATHER OF NATIONS

All this could be constructed to imply that Abraham was addicted to a kind of magic, an art of dealing with spirits (ceremonial magic), which follows a ritual and prescribed verbal formula. The sequel shows, however, that he was exonerated in virtue of his intention.

The words, in Genesis 13:1: "Go into a land that I will show thee" mean that Abraham was to be occupied henceforth only by those things which God would make known to him. The essential nature of the Supreme Power which rules the world could not be included in the revelation, being above human understanding (ibid.). The direction to leave his country signified that he should abandon his studies of the moral influences connected with different regions; to leave his kindred was to abandon the science of astrology; to leave the house of his father was to cease from the manner of life observed therein.

It was therefore, a journey into Divine obedience rather than a journey of the soul in the Divine. But this path of conformity is itself a ladder of sanctity by which man can be united to the Holy One and is indeed the one way of our ascent. Abraham went up this ladder stage by stage until he attained that point, which was designed in his case. As it is written: "And Abraham journeyed going on still toward the South" (Genesis 12:9); this being the Holy Land, wherein he was to reach the highest degree of holiness.

## ABRAHAM AND SARAH IN EGYPT

But it is written that there was famine in the Land, which means that the country was not as yet consecrated and Abraham proceeded, therefore, which is assimilated to the spiritual garden of the Lord: "As the Garden of the Lord, as the Land of Egypt" (Genesis 13:10). The consequence of Abraham's absolute faith in God was Abraham's great knowledge. Abraham knew the mystery of the spiritual Garden of the Lord, the degrees of which are in correspondence with those that are below, that is to say, with Egypt, which is therefore said to be assimilated. But the nearer that he drew to Egypt, the more he cleaved unto God. This notwithstanding, as the journey had not been authorized divinely, he was destined to suffer therein in respect of Sarah (Genesis 12:14–20). It is said that the Holy One was seeking to prove Abraham, and for this reason allowed him to act on his own initiative in visiting Egypt.

Now Abraham had lived so modestly with his wife and in such holiness that he had never looked upon her face previously. Only as they drew near to Egypt did she raise a corner of her veil, and he saw that she was fair. Now, Sarah was under the protection of Shechinah and during the night that passed in the palace of Avimelech, she was accompanied by angels belonging to the superior degrees, who gave thanks to God. The beauty of Sarah was a reflection of the Divine presence. It is affirmed that the description of Sarah as Abraham's sister, made by Abraham in a verbal economy as recourse to subterfuge, was a description of Shechinah, who was with her.

In Egypt, Abraham found a great center of occult arts and again betook himself to their study. But this time he penetrated the secret of evil without being led away thereby. He returned thence to his own grade or degree, which is indicated by the words: "And Abram went up out of Egypt... into the South" (Genesis 13:1), meaning the inward height of his sanctity. From this time forward, he knew the Mystery of Supreme Wisdom and became the right hand of the world. This is indicated by the words in Genesis 13:3, "From the South even to Beth-El," which is the integral stone, the stone of the world and Jacob. But he was yet to proceed further, "going on still toward the South" (Genesis 12:9), rising from grade to grade as one experiencing the infinite and winning his aureole.

So did the Holy One become his patrimony and after Abraham was parted from Lot (Genesis 13:12), he dwelled in the land of Canaan which is the place of faith (ibid.).

## MELCHIZEDEK OF SALEM

Of Melchizedek, king of Salem, the Zohar says that his offering of bread and wine symbolized the world above and world below. The bread and wine of Melchizedek were symbols of nutriment and blessings for the world. The sense in which he was "priest of the Most High God" is that in the sanctification of himself, he raised the world below to the height of that which is above. Concerning the mission of priesthood, the Zohar says that this conjoins the world the world below to that which is above by an indissoluble bond.

## THE TOKEN OF THE COVENANT

The second section of the history of Abraham opens with the making of the covenant between God and the Patriarch and the whole of his later history, and it deals with the "token" or signing of the Covenant and the mystery foreshown thereby.

The Patriarch was originally named Abram. By the addition of the letter *hai*, Abram was transformed to Abraham. But the *hai* was not added to his name until he had suffered circumcision and it was thereafter that the Shechinah became attached to him. The letter *hai* was added also to the name of Sarah as a symbol of the female principle (Zohar I, 93a).

## THE SIGN OF CIRCUMCISION

The characteristic physical sign of all Israel on the male side, says the Zohar, is not an arbitrary ordinance or a hygienic observance or an aid to continence, but rather a secret seal of purity. The text implies further that indubitably it had reference also to the purity of womanhood, because her protection was therein. According to the Zohar, the male side of humanity, in its separation from the female, had no true title to the name and prerogative of man. This implies that while the masculine shares in humanity, it is true man only in union with womanhood. The covenant implies therefore, the union of the male and female principles (Zohar II, 26a).

## THE COVENANT OF CIRCUMCISION

When Abraham was circumcised, he separated himself from the impure world and entered into the Sacred Covenant, into that Covenant on which the world is based; and it follows that the world is founded on him. Expanding this, the Zohar affirms that by Abraham God created and therefore the Covenant of circumcision is the origin of heaven and earth (Zohar II, 91b).

The *hai* added to the name of Abram, after he had fulfilled the ordinance, is said to symbolize the five books of the Divine Teaching (the Torah, the Law), which are the records at length of the five books of the Covenant. But that which begins on earth is raised gloriously into heaven and is prolonged through all the worlds. The sign of the Covenant constitutes the foundation of the Sacred Name and of the Mystery of Faith. It is said further that the Sacred Sign of the Covenant is fixed at the base of the throne, between the two thighs and the trunk which is a reference to the sephira Yesod, when this is placed on the tree. When it is said in Genesis 23: "And the Lord visited Sarah," it was that degree of the Divine Essence, says the Zohar, which was symbolized by the *vav*. It is added that all is contained in the mystery of *vav*, and thereby all is revealed.

As the sun enlightens the world, so the sacred sign enlightens the body; as a buckler protects man, so does this. No evil spirit can approach him who preserves it in purity. By the fact of circumcision, man enters under the wings of Shechinah. He who preserved the sign of the Covenant and fulfills the commandments of the Law is righteous from head to foot, and his life in continence is his title to a part in the world to come (Zohar I, 8a). The text for it being "Blessings are upon the head of the just" (Proverbs 10:6) The head of the just signifies the sign of the covenant (Zohar I, 8a).

## THE METAPHYSICAL PRINCIPLE OF THE COVENANT

It is said also that so long as a man is uncircumcised he cannot unite himself to the Name of the Holy One; but after circumcision, he enters that name and is joined therewith. Those who do not preserve the sign in purity make separation in a manner between Israel and the Holy Father. All the forces of nature center in the organ of the covenant. Also, in the metaphysical principle of the Covenant it is said that there was subsequently hidden and enclosed that light, created when God said "Let there be light." The reason being that light symbolizes the fructifying principle of the semen. It is this which is called in scripture "the fruit of a tree yielding seed" (Genesis 1:3) (Zohar I, 89a).

It is counseled: "suffer not thy mouth to cause thy flesh to sin" (Ecclesiastes 5:6). The exhortation is understood as a restraint place upon speech, lest this should generate evil thoughts calculated to soil the consecrated flesh which is marked with the seal of the Holy Covenant. When the Psalmist says: "The firmament shows His handiwork" (Psalms 19:1), it is to the mark of the Covenant that reference is made, that is, "the work of His hands." So also those other words: "Wherefore should God be angry at thy voice, and destroy the work of thine hands" (Ecclesiastes 5:6). They are an allusion to those who keep the seal in purity.

In yet other terms, the firmament publishes the names of those holy men who have lived in chastity, and our part is to plead for their intercession with God Who hears them always. Their names are written in the Book of God, which is the great firmament of stars; they are the company which follow the Heavenly Spouse (Zohar I, 8b).

It is further said concerning the Sign of Covenant that the holy flesh, which is the "organ of sanctity" is marked with the letter *yod* when circumcision has been performed upon it. The letter *yod* symbolizes also the configuration of the Celestial River that is the source of souls. The words "Sanctify unto me all the firstborn, whatsoever opens the womb, among the children of Israel" (Exodus 13:2) is a commentary on the letter *yod*, which is the firstborn of all the heavenly sanctities (Zohar I, 13a).

## IDEAS WHICH LIE BEHIND THE MARK OF CIRCUMCISION

Various verses in Scripture and especially in Psalms chapter 115 enumerate three enclosures, one within the other. These are the courts, house, and tabernacle, and, says the Zohar, whosoever subjects his son to the holocaust of circumcision may be assured that the Holy One will draw the child to Himself and make his abode in the innermost of those enclosures. The father too will earn no less merit than if he had offered all other sacrifices in the world and had raised up the most perfect altar. The understanding of these things is based in the most profound Mystery of Sex, and the place of that mystery is indicated by the correspondence, mentioned in another part, between the sign of the Covenant and the Sacred Crown (Zohar I, 94b).

The mark of the Covenant is imprinted above as well as on man below. The Kingdom was removed for a period from David because he had not preserved the sign with perfect purity. He who keeps it has nothing to fear from Severity, that is, judgment, being united thereby to the Name of the Holy One. He who defiles it cannot aspire to the marks of God, which are royalty and Jerusalem. The sign is the gate of the body, therefore when this sign is held in sanctity, the gates of heaven are always open (Zohar I, 94a).

The history of Abraham, the father of nations, theosophically lies in the way of its understanding as an inward text of election, applicable to every soul in Israel.

CHAPTER SIX

# Moses, the Master of the Law

The biblical story of Moses issues in a mystery. It was he "whom the Lord knew face to face" (Deuteronomy 34:10). Having died in the Lord on Mount Nebo, he was also buried by Him and "no man knoweth of his sepulchre unto this day" (ibid. 6).

In the Zohar, the story of Moses is intensified in mystery. For about him it is said, "there arose not a prophet since, in Israel like unto Moses" (Deuteronomy 35:10). Moses was not in his conception after the manner of man who had preceded or of those who came after him. His parents were the "man of the house of Levi" (Exodus 2:1) and she who was "a daughter of Levi" (ibid.). These had their hearts uplifted unto Her who is called Shechinah, second of the Divine Hypostases, at the time of that union, when it is said that "the woman conceived and bore a son" (ibid. v. 2).

The consequence of this was that Shechinah reposed on the nuptial bed of his parents (Zohar II, 11a). He was therefore born "not of blood, nor of the will of the flesh, nor of the will of man" merely but of God. And even from the day of his birth, the Shechinah never quitted him.

It is further said in the most cryptic manner of the text, that the "man of the house of Levi" was the angel Gabriel, who is called man, as it is written: "Even the man Gabriel, whom I had seen in the vision at the beginning" (Daniel 9:21). The house of Levi signifies the Community of Israel (which signifies also the School of Sanctity above in the sephira *Binah*). The daughter of Levi is the soul, meaning that the parents of Moses stood for these symbolically (ibid.).

The father of Moses is said to have been espoused to Shechinah, apparently in the sense which she overshadowed him and was attached to him. Otherwise he would have been unworthy to beget the Lawgiver. But it is also added that the daughter of Levi, whom he espoused, was the Shechinah in the sense of being her symbol below (Zohar II, 19a).

Moses ascended into that region where Shechinah is said to extend her wings, as it is written: "He did fly upon the wings of the wind" (Psalms 18:9). The Lawgiver is affirmed, moreover, to have been the first man who attained perfection, even as Messiah will be the last (Zohar II, 78a). Elsewhere, however, it is said that he was not perfect in all things, the reason being that he was separated from his wife (Zohar I, 234b).

The explanation is that in order to attain perfection there must be union not alone with that which is above, but also with that which is below. A Talmudic statement regarding this issue in the tract *Sabbath* (chapter 8) reckons, however, the fact of his separation among his titles of honor. The Pentateuch does not mention clearly this separation, but there is a Talmudic tradition which says that they ceased to cohabit. So it is also said elsewhere that Moses the Lawgiver attained the degree of *Binah*, but not that of *Chokhmah*. This may mean that he did not open the fiftieth gate of Understanding, which gives upon the path of *Dalath*, leading from *Binah* to *Chokhmah* in the sephirotic tree (Zohar III, 223a).

## THE MARRIAGE OF MOSES

The difficulties as regards the earthly espousals of Moses increase when we learn elsewhere that he separated himself from Zipporah, his wife, by the ordinance of God, that he might be joined to the heavenly light of Shechinah (Zohar III, 180a). It is also intimated elsewhere by Rabbi Shimon that to attribute children to Moses (Gershon and Eliezer) was in some sense beneath his dignity, as he had entered into spiritual espousals; the Scripture, therefore, attributes the children of Moses to the mother only in Exodus 18:5 (Zohar II, 69b). The whole is a question of the Mystery of Sex.

To conclude as to the marriage of Moses, there was a moment when God said to the Lawgiver: "Let it suffice thee" (Deuteronomy 3:23). That which was sufficient, says the Zohar, was the prophet's union with Shechinah to whom he was nearer in truth than hands and feet; for as we have seen, they were not in separation prior to his birth in this life. So also, he was under the guidance of no messenger from heaven, but under that of God Himself because God and His Shechinah are one. This is held to follow from the words: "And he said unto Him, if the Presence go not with me, carry us not up hence" (Exodus 33:15). In his union with Shechinah, Moses represented the male principle. In virtue of this union, Moses was the light of the moon. For Shechinah in her manifestation below or in the work of her providence concerning the children of men does shine in the light of the Eternal Sun of Justice; the man then being Moses' symbol.

It is by Moses that the men of this world are held to have found salvation, for he communicated the vital spirit of the Tree of Life. If Israel had not sinned, this spirit would have been preserved forever in Israel by virtue of the gracious Law contained in the first Tables (Zohar III, 260b).

## MOSES, THE FAITHFUL SHEPHERD

There was no servant so faithful as Moses the Faithful Shepherd. He knew all the celestial degrees and he was never tempted to join himself otherwise than to the highest. His fidelity was greater than that of Ezekiel for the latter is said to have divulged all the treasures of the King (referring to the Work of the Chariot in Ezekiel's vision). The title of Moses was that he kept the Secret Law secretly, transmitting it only to the elect, and that he made public the Exoteric Law, which does not contain the Mystery of Faith. In this sense, he is called the elder son of Adam and the reason is the keeping of the mystery (Zohar I, 28b).

## THE PROMULGATION OF THE DIVINE TEACHING—THE LAW

Moses ascended Mount Sinai clothed in the vesture of Shechinah, being that cloud which he entered and in virtue of which it was possible for him to go up. The intention of the Law was to place man under the domination of the Tree of Life which means that there would have been no mysteries, the Torah in this aspect being the Spouse of God, and therefore, it is the Shechinah herself or the Mystery of Faith expounded. It is that mystery which is beheld in contemplating the face of Shechinah in the state which is eye to eye.

If this intention had been fulfilled, there would have been no distinction of an Oral and Written Law. But what intervened on the foot of Mount Sinai was causative that another order followed contrary to the design of Providence. Now, it is affirmed in the Zohar persistently that a change took place in Israel at the foot of Mount Sinai (Zohar I, 63b). The whole seems to be some unstated matter of Secret Doctrine.

## EXALTATIONS OF ISRAEL

It is testified that Israel was joined anew to the Tree of Life, so that it had the heavenly splendor and realized their lights. It experienced the ineffable joy which fills the hearts of those who desire to know and to understand the Supreme Mysteries. The Holy One with that cuirass, formed from the letters of His Sacred Name which was the protection of Adam and Eve before their fall, reclothed the nation. The serpent could cleave no longer to Israel, and it is affirmed to have disappeared from the world. We must understand all this as a reflection rather of the Divine Intention in its union with the covenant made by the people on their part, "All that the Lord hath spoken we will do" (Exodus 19:8). They were washed also and sanctified (Zohar I, 28b).

## THE GOLDEN CALF AND THE DOWNFALL OF ISRAEL

Alas, right afterward all this exaltation of Israel, in the absence of Moses and in the uncertainty as to what had become of him but in the absence otherwise of all temptation, Israel adored the golden calf. The old evil order was thus reinstated and the serpent returned. All this being reputed to have taken place after Israel was able to contemplate the celestial splendor and enjoy the vision of supernal lights. Even as it is written in Scripture, "And Israel saw that great work which the Lord did" (Exodus 19:31).

The riot of the feast which followed the idol worship signifies also a sexual orgy, so that she, who presides over the Mystery of Sex in sanctity, was driven from the people, and her secret was taken from them. When Moses came down from the mountain carrying the Table of the Law, he broke them in the presence of the people. For the original Tables constituted the liberation of all, meaning the separation from that serpent, who is called "the end of all flesh." One of the consequences of this separation from the serpent would have been no more death. The children of Israel then lost the power of contemplation and celestial splendor and that of vision of supernal lights, even as the contrast of another passage of Scripture shows clearly. For it is said in Exodus 34:30, "And when Aaron and the children of Israel saw Moses, behold, the skin of his face shone and they were afraid to come near him" (Zohar I, 63b).

## THE ORIGINAL TABLES OF THE LAW

The original Tables of the Law were formed originally from a single block of sapphire, but God breathed upon them and the precious stone was divided into two parts. They were created prior to the world by coagulation of the sacred dew, which is said to fall in the Garden of Apples. They were written before and behind and were symbolized by the loaves of the countenance. The writing thereon was like black fire on white fire. Yet the stones were transparent. The writing on the obverse side was read from behind and that on the reverse was read from the front. This alludes to the interconnection of the Written and Oral Law.

The tables were given to Moses on the Sabbath day. The Tables were cast from the hands of Moses and were broken (Exodus 32:19). This was because the letters took flight and they fell of themselves from his hands. No writing remained upon them that could possibly be seen by Israel in contemplating the fragments. The tables were broken because Israel was not worthy to profit by them; and that which was shattered is said to have been not only the Written but also the inward and Oral Law. Even as Scripture says, "And the Lord said unto Moses . . . I will give thee tables of stone, and a law, and commandments which I have written" (Exodus 24:12). The word law, says the Zohar, signifies that which is written, while the word *commandments* refers to the Oral Law (Zohar III, 26b).

Thus, the higher order of liberation and mercy and that of the revelation of the secret union were taken henceforth into concealment. The malediction brought upon the world by trespass and removed for a moment as the people passed under the shadow of Mount Sinai descended again upon them. The tables came out of that region from which all liberties issue and on which they all depend. Over the mystical mountain they diffused a sweet odor, because the sanctities of the world of sanctity inhered therein. But this passed away when the golden calf was set up for the worship of the nation (Zohar III, 26b).

The second tables embodied another record, says the Zohar, which was the law of opportunism, the law of thine, of prohibition and denial, and mine being that of bondage. It was sacred after its own manner because it was a shadow of the first intention, but it reflects at a very far distance. It follows and is intimated that it is a work of the Tree of Knowledge. But the Secret Doctrine with all the Oral Law by which the Secret Doctrine is encompassed is the Tree of Life. The art of its mastery is long. Of all the sons of the Secret Doctrine since the days of the Patriarchs and prophets, only Rabbi Shimon could have been said to possess it in its fullness. The sons of the Secret Doctrine raised only a corner of the veil. After Rabbi Shimon, the reign of certitudes was over, and the great quest in the hiddenness was pursued by groping, not erect as before with the light of sure enlightenment shining from a meridian sun on the heads of the initiates.

But to sum up, we must say that Moses gave other tables to Israel and these were from the side of the Tree of Knowledge of Good and Evil from which the Law emanates. The other tables emanated from the Tree of Life (ibid.).

This Written Law is represented by the word *Daoath* or "knowing"; it is completed by that which is tradition (Zohar

I, 48b). The doctrine is sometimes called *Chokhmah* or Wisdom and sometimes *Binah* or Understanding. The reason for this is that it had been formed by the complete Name, that is, HVYH ELOKIM, being the Divine symbol for male and female.

The traditional Law came out of the Written Law, as woman was brought forth from man according to the Mystery of the Garden. The Traditional Law can exist only in unison with the Written Law. The Oral Traditional Law, although it is a balm of life for the just, it is a mortal poison for the unjust (Zohar I, 268a).

## DEATH OF MOSES AND HIS SEPULCHRE

We have seen already that Moses was interred outside the Holy Land and "No man knoweth of his sepulchre unto this day" (Deuteronomy 34:6). This sepulchre, says the Zohar, signifies the Mishnah. The Secret Doctrine, that end of all revelations, was interned in the written word. The Mishnah is the maidservant who takes the place of the mistress. But the tradition says that the inner meaning, like the spirit of Moses, remained with the elders and was handed on secretly (Zohar I, 27a).

The Scripture mentions "the children of Israel wept for Moses in the plains of Moab thirty days" (Deuteronomy 34:8). They might have mourned him had they known, though the triumphs and exiles continued henceforward for they lost the Secret Doctrine of which he was the personification. It was withdrawn when he left as if into a secret sanctuary, and no voice issued therefrom until the days of Rabbi Shimon. He was even as a rose of sharon which blossomed on the ruins of Jerusalem in the days of Vespasian. Moses was the life of the Doctrine, and hence it is affirmed that when he ascended to the height of Pisgah, "his eye was not dim, nor his natural force abated" (Deuteronomy 34:7). It is recorded also of his figure in its prime, that it resembled the sun in its splendor; so perfectly did his moon reflect that glory (Zohar I, 28a).

We find, however, other statements in the Zohar telling us that Moses did not die. The text repeats it rather on an authority which is not its own and adds that no man does die who is graced by faith. The authority mentioned is the Midrash Rabbah on Deuteronomy 34. The Zohar quotes the Midrash again in still another place (Zohar I, 28a).

## THE TRAGEDY OF THE GREAT LAWGIVER

We gain the impression from the Zohar, which transpires and adds up to the sad fact perhaps, that there is an aspect of failure about the great Lawgiver. His stiff-necked generation prevailed against him to the extent that he could fulfill only the shadow of what he proposed. His intention was to deliver the truth which makes men free; but they were fit only for a substitute. This is set forth in a single passage of the text where it is affirmed that Moses sought to bring the Shechinah out of exile, but he failed (Zohar I, 28a). We gather therefrom that Shechinah implies the Secret Doctrine and it signifies that the first tables were written to clarify the Secret Doctrine, but the context was destined to remain in exile so long as Israel was incorporated as a people in its own place and land. So long as the Shechinah is in captivity and not brought into liberation, Moses never leaves her (Zohar I, 28a). What Moses did on earth was, however, to attract Shechinah to Israel (Zohar I, 68a).

## MOSES WILL RETURN

It is said therefore in another place that Moses will return to earth at the end of time to complete his mission by revealing the true name of Shechinah, which is also in the hiddenness.

Those whom he brought out of Egypt he will then lead into knowledge. This is why it is exclaimed by Job: "The Lord hath given and the Lord hath taken away. Blessed is the name of the Lord" (Job 1:21). What it is that will take place is what was to have been fulfilled at first. The elect will be set free from the death angel by the true tables of the Law.

Meanwhile, Moses obtained the degree of *Binah* as we have seen, but not that of *Chokhmah*. His death was, says the Zohar, from the other side, which means the right side; the left one being the side of the serpent (Zohar I, 58a).

The death of Moses was not caused by the sin of Adam, but by the operation of a Supreme Mystery.

Of Joshua his disciple it is also recorded that he did not die through his own sinning, but through the serpent's counsel to Eve. This is said to be expressed in the words "his servant Joshua, the son of Nun, a young man departed not out of the Tabernacle" (Exodus 33:11). The history of Moses, therefore, is in reality a history of spiritual espousals.

CHAPTER SEVEN

# The Two Temples in Jerusalem

**PROLOGUE**

When we look in retrospect upon the checkered history of our nation and on the purport of its life, we do not fail to discern the uplifting of strange portents in our spiritual sky. The full significance of these was not rightly to be recognized beforehand; only after the event. In retrospect, the portents were everywhere; the world's creation, the story of the Garden of Eden, the judgment of the Flood, and the rest of the Divine Providence were like trumpet voices concerning all that was to follow. It was Israel delineated throughout.

Abraham might turn to the south and again he might turn therefrom, but the reason in either case was of that to come in respect of the twelve tribes. The stories of old look weird in a light which suggests that they were recorded before the events with which they are supposed to deal. The occurrences of the past were also fateful in respect of later things. For example, when the tables of the Law were broken by Moses, this is said to have occasioned the ultimate destruction of the First and Second Temples (Zohar I, 26b).

## THE GLORIOUS FIRST TEMPLE DESCRIBED BY THE ZOHAR

There are two aspects of the Temples in the Zoharic texts and they do not harmonize. I will collate them under the motives attaching to each. There is first that aspect where there is no shadow of vicissitude as to the glory and the plenary grace, which inhered in the design and execution of Solomon's Holy House. The Inner Sanctuary constituted the heart of the world. The Shechinah dwelt there after the manner of a virtuous and faithful wife, who never leaves the abode of her husband. It was therefore well with Israel during this period (Zohar I, 84b).

The building plan was sketched by a supernatural hand and was delivered to David by whom it was shown to Solomon. The Temple was erected on seven pillars, the craftsmen following the design point by point until the work was finished. There was a sense in which they followed blindly; but there was also another sense in which the work was self-executed. It was guarded by the archangel Metatron. The work as self-executed is suggested by the silent nature of the building. We hear of this in Scripture: "And the house, when it was in building, was built of stone, made ready before it was brought thither; so that there was neither hammer nor ax nor any tool of iron heard in the house while it was building" (I Kings 6:7).

The analogy is that of creation, for the world evolved of itself with God as the beginner of the work. Hence David said: "Except the Lord build the house, they labor in vain that build it" (Psalms 137:1). The meaning is that the Lord designed the Temple and the work went on of itself (Zohar II, 164a).

It is also said, "Except the Lord watch the city the watchman waketh in vain" (Psalms 137:1). This is Jerusalem in its building. The moon is symbolized as shining at the full during the whole period. The Temple was built for the union of the King and the Matrona—God and His congregation in Israel.

We are told of the structure in its completeness, that the earth inhabited by the Gentiles encompassed the Holy City, which was the center of the inhabitable world. The town encircled the Holy Mountain. The mountain surrounded the session-house of the Sanhedrin. This in its turn stood about the Temple. The Temple encompassed the Holy of Holies where the Shechinah dwells, and where these are: the propitiatory, cherubim, and the Ark of the Covenant. The Holy of Holies itself was built on that foundation stone, which as we know already is held to form the central point of the world. It is identified with the celestial throne of Ezekiel and in appearance it was like a sapphire. For we read in Ezekiel 1:26: "And above the firmament, that was over their heads, was the likeness of a throne, as the appearance of a sapphire stone."

The stone, says the Zohar, signified the celestial throne, and the throne of the vision signified the Traditional Law, while the appearance of a man, "who sat thereon, was the Written Law." Solomon is said to have united Matrona to the Supreme King by the building of the Temple and there was joy everywhere, both above and below. The Temple itself is understood as the spiritual union of male and female, apart from any fleshy union. It symbolizes, therefore, the Mystery of Sex at its highest (Zohar I, 150a).

## AN ALTERNATIVE VERSION CONCERNING THE SANCTUARIES

The second or alternative aspect of the Temples, as collated from the Faithful Shepherd, follows here and is drawn from the Faithful Shepherd exclusively.

The First and Second Temples were transitory things in their nature. They should have been the work of God Himself, but because of Israel's sin in the wilderness, the First temple was built by Solomon and hence it did not subsist. So also at the Epoch of Ezra, again on account of sin, the Second Temple was erected by men, and there was no ground of subsistence. It follows by inference that so far no truly real holy house has been built as yet, nor has even the real true city of Jerusalem been constructed in reality as yet. The world is still awaiting that promise of the Lord: (Zechariah 2:5) "I, says the Lord, will be unto her a wall of fire round about, and will be the glory in the midst of her" (Zohar III, 221a).

There are even further suggestions. It is said that from the day when the Holy One raised the Supreme Sanctuary, the celestial favors were never manifested in the terrestrial Temple built of stones and mortar. The inference is that there is a house not made with hands, which is termed elsewhere a place of spiritual nourishment. The kingdom of heaven accords it to those in need of it, and that sanctuary brings all the poor under the shadow of Shechinah (Zohar II, 108b).

## LAMENTATIONS OVER THE HOLY HOUSES AND PLACES

The temple of Solomon was a symbol of penitence as well as a house of prayer, and its destruction signifies an impenitent state. The cause of its destruction is said otherwise to have been the separation of the *hai* and *vav* in the Divine Name as the result of sin. The people were sent into exile and the Shechinah was driven out. The *vav* went in search of the *hai* but she was in a distant place. It looked toward the sanctuary, but it was burnt. It looked for the chosen people, but they were in exile. It turned toward the source of benedictions, but it was dried up. The reason was that the male principle was no longer united to the female principle (Zohar III, 75a).

It is said otherwise that the destruction of the First Temple dried up the sources of Shechinah above, and the Second Temple, those of the Shechinah below. All light was clouded so that the saints of this world were no longer enlightened. During the exile in Babylon, the wings of the Mother in Transcendence (that is, the Shechinah) did not cover her children. There was therefore a separation between the *yod* and the first *hai* of the Divine Name. The reference is made, of course, to the spiritual state of Israel, and it shows a strange spiritual understanding of the fall of man.

During this present and greater exile, the Divine Name is divided now as it was divided then, albeit that which it signifies is one eternally above.

In another form of symbolism it is said that the First Temple was destroyed because it wanted light, which was absent also from the Second Temple. In a still greater degree, the Second Temple signified the fleshly union of male and female. Shechinah was reigning on the Mercy Seat. The priests of the First Temple ascended the walls of the Sanctuary holding their keys in their hands and said to God: "Hereunto we have been Thine administrators; henceforth take back Thy possessions." The sun turned away from the moon and enlightened it no longer; there was no day without maledictions and sufferings. This is the burden of the "valley of visions" in Isaiah 22:1 (Zohar I, 255a).

## CONSOLATION AND HOPE

After the lamentations of the Zohar over the Holy Houses and Places, the Zohar continues to tell us that another day will come when the moon shall resume its primal light. It will be that period mentioned in Scripture: "Behold, my servant shall deal prudently, he shall be exulted and extolled and be very high" (Isaiah 42:13). The reference is to the Messianic epoch when the world will be restored, impurity will disappear therefrom, and death shall be cast out forever. The Holy One will remember his people Israel and the Temple shall be rebuilt. Formerly, it was based on severity and wrath, but it will be restored in charity and it will be founded thereon. Meanwhile, since the destruction of the Sanctuary here below, the Holy One swore never to enter the Jerusalem above until Israel returned in the Jerusalem below. No blessings have gone forth either in the world above or in that which is below, for these worlds depend on one another. The consolation of the elect is, however, that in the absence of a place of a sacrifice, devotion to the study of the law will bring the forgiveness of sin more readily, than the burnt offerings of old (Zohar I, 181b).

The great mystery in transcendence of the House of the Lord, built in Zion, was the presence of Shechinah in the Holy of Holies as a bride in the abode of her spouse.

CHAPTER EIGHT

# The Coming of Messiah

## MESSIANIC EXPECTATION IN ISRAEL

Amongst the kabbalistic teachings concerning a deliverer to come to Israel is the teaching of expectation stating that the elect and more especially the sons of the Divine Doctrine must hope always for the coming of the man of holiness. For it is said: "I will wait upon the Lord, that hideth His face from the house of Israel, and I will look to Him" (Isaiah 8:17). Messiah is the man in transcendence, the man who is allocated in one place to the sephirah *Chokhmah* (Supplements of the Zohar).

It is further said: "He is the man more precious than fine gold" who is mentioned by Isaiah 8:12. It is also on record that he shall be raised above all the inhabitants of the world, who will adore him, prostrated in his presence (Zohar I, 204a).

The Spirit of Elohim which brooded over the surface of the waters is sometimes regarded as the Spirit of Messiah, who washed his robes in heavenly wine from the creation of the world; a statement which bears witness to the aspect of His eternal generation. He is also the sacred moon on high, having no other light than that which it receives from the sun above. It must, however, be noticed that the Shechinah is also symbolized by the moon at times. Of course, we find that Moses and Solomon both had the moon as a symbol (Zohar I, 240a).

## MESSIANIC EXPECTATIONS, CONTINUED

According to Midrash Talpiyoth, the Messiah will bring eternal peace for Israel and all those who will enter by conversion into the House of Jacob. It is said in the Zohar that, according to tradition, wherever the words *King Solomon* are mentioned in the Song of Solomon, this King of Peace is designated. Conversion at the Messianic period will be on a great scale, because all the nations of the world will gather about the King Messiah when he shall be manifested. Seeing that the words of the Scripture must be fulfilled: "And in that day there shall be a root of Jesse, which shall stand for an ensign of the people; to it shall the gentiles seek, and his rest shall be glorious" (Isaiah 40:10). It will be time for the revaluation of mysteries which the will of God has concealed through the ages, but as the day of the King Messiah approaches, even little children shall know the Mysteries of Wisdom. It will also be a time of union, for in the "Sabbatical epoch" the Holy One will accomplish union between souls. All the blessings of Israel will be realized in Israel, which will form one people only on earth, as is written in Ezekiel 37:22: "and I will make them one nation in the Lord." The meaning is that all nations shall become one nation of the Holy One. There will be, though, a great war of the world preceding this (Zohar I, 29a).

## SEVERAL MESSIAHS TO PRECEDE THE ADVENT OF THE TRUE KING MESSIAH

Before the advent of the King Messiah, however, there are several other Messiahs to come. There is he who is to be the son of Yishai. Eternal life is possible through the Messiah the Son of Yishai, as is cited in I Samuel 20:31, "the son of Yishai lives upon the earth" (Zohar I, 29b). The Messiah son of Yishai is said to be master of all, by whom the earth is nourished (ibid.).

There is second, Messiah the son of Ephraim, of whom it is testified that he will be driven back from Rome (Zohar III, 120a).

A third personality mentioned is Messiah merely the son of Joseph. It was suggested that the third Messiah is identical with the second Messiah. The fourth Messiah is the son of David. The son of David is said to be the Sephira *Netzach*, while the son of Ephraim is Sephira *Hod* (Zohar III, 243a). Messiah the son of Joseph and Messiah the son of David are both mentioned in the Talmud.[1] One of the "Omissions" in the first appendix to the first part of the Zohar affirms that the last two are one.

There are certain Midrashim which agree with these Zoharic accounts. According to Talmudic references, however, the son of Joseph will suffer a violent death and will be succeeded by the son of David. The Zohar agrees with that in one place, but adds that he will rise again. Mention is also made that there is one Messiah who will suffer death. But in another place a distinction is made between Messiah son of David and the son of Joseph who will be slain.

Again we find a passage elsewhere in the Zohar where it is denied that the Messiah son of Joseph will be killed, because he is compared to an ox, and evil has no hold over him. It is

---

1. Tractates *Avoda Zora*, *Succah*, *Yebamoth*, and *Sanhedrin*.

of this Messiah that it is said in Scripture: "He was wounded for our transgressions ... and with his stripes we are healed" (Isaiah 53:5). However, the fact that he will die is reaffirmed a few folios later.

## SYMBOLISM CONCERNING MESSIAH

It is said, alas, that one of these alternative deliverers is poor and mounted on an ass, while the other is the firstborn of a bull. They are the symbols of the two cherubim stationed before the Garden of Eden. Metatron is the symbol of the Flaming Sword. It is further said that the Messiah, who is the son of Joseph, will be united in his mission to the Messiah the son of David, but he will be slain. The one is the conqueror of the great Rome, and the other one of the "little Rome." The number sixty is fixed for the manifestation of the first and the number six for the manifestation of the second. Now then, the number six is represented by *vav*, and the letter *vav* is said to symbolize the Eternal World. The son of David is connected with this number.

It should be added here that the words in Zechariah 9:9: "Lowly and riding upon an ass, and upon a colt, the foal of a she-ass," which are referred to the Messiah are not understood literally, for the ass represents that demon which shall be curbed by the "King" to come. The explanation given is that the demon, who is called the ass, can be made subject with the Sacred Name "Shaddai." It follows, that Messiah, who connects with the ox symbolically, will overcome the demon or ass; and hence it is forbidden in Deuteronomy 22:10 to yoke an ox and ass together.

## THE INTRUDERS

The time of the coming of Messiah will be when all souls who are kept in the treasury of souls against the day of their incarnation shall actually come hither in flesh. Thereafter, it would seem that new souls would be incarnated in Israel. Then shall the chosen ones deserve to find (they shall not fail herein) their beloved and sister soul, predestined to each from the beginning of creation. In allusion to this, Scripture says in Ezekiel 36:26: "A new heart also will I give you and a new spirit will I put within you." And again, in Joel 2:28: "It shall come to pass that I will pour out my spirit upon all flesh, and your sons and your daughters shall prophesy, your old men shall dream dreams, your young men shall see visions." The intruders shall be exterminated at the time when this shall be accomplished, which is said to be of old tradition as we shall see in the next section.

To this period there is referable also that text of Genesis which says that Adam and Eve were "naked and not ashamed" (Genesis 2:25). The reason was that the intruders are the cause of luxury and when they disappear, all leaning toward incontinence will vanish likewise. The reference to the intruders is primarily to the mixed crowd that followed Israel during the Exodus from Egypt, and who were not afterwards separated from the chosen people. In one place, it is said, these aliens were souls in transmigration from antecedent destroyed worlds. It will seem also that the alien people are understood spiritually as the prompters towards evil which is within us.

## THE SUBJECT OF THE MESSIAH IN ISRAEL— A SUBJECT OF SPIRITUAL COMMUNION

One cannot help feel this Secret Doctrine is sealing and veiling the grace to come. It means the change that is to come over the dream of Israel, which is to enter into its own on all the places and in all the worlds by the help of the right spirit renewed within them. This is the Spirit of Messiah, as it is written: "Renew a right spirit within me" (Psalms 2:10). It is also the Spirit of God "which moved upon the face of the waters" (Genesis 1:2). It is to this spirit that David aspired.

That rectified period is the one when all portals shall open. Out of the heart and the mind shall the intruders be cast, once and for all, and the soul shall find the Spouse.

The subject of the time of Messiah in Israel is a forecast of that time when the mystery of Union, which is now a Mystery of Faith, shall have entered into realization in experience on this earth of ours. As in the world above, there is communion between Shechinah and the Holy One, so in that which is below there will be such a spiritual communion between the Lover and the Beloved that the voice of the turtle, which is the Song of Solomon, shall be heard everywhere.

## A LIGHT OF SYMBOLISM

We have mentioned in Section IV the testimony of the Zohar that the second *hai* of the Divine Name Tetragrammaton fell. We have also seen that the second *hai* has the symbolism of daughter, and that, whereby she will be raised, is the *vav* which has the symbolism of son. So we read in the Zohar that in the time of the letter *hai*, that is, when the *hai* shall rise from the earth, God will fulfill that which is mentioned in Isaiah 60:22: "I, the lord will hasten it in its time." But the Zohar renders it thus: "I am the Lord; and it is I, who will hasten these marvels, when the time thereof shall have come." When Israel was driven from its abode, the letters of the Sacred Name were separated one from another, if it be permissible to so speak; the *hai* was separated from the *vav*. Hence the psalmist said, "I am dumb with silence" (Psalms 39:3). When the *vav* is separated from the *hai*, the world is stilled. The day of the letter *hai* is the fifth millennium—the period of Israel in exile. When the sixth millennium comes, the *vav* shall raise up the *hai*, and Israel shall be lifted also from the dust. After six hundred years of the sixth millennium, the Gates of Supreme Wisdom shall open and the springs of Wisdom shall begin to pour upon the world, which will make it ready to enter worthily into the seventh millennium and this latter will constitute the Sabbath of Creation (1840–1939). Compare also Babylonian Talmud, Tract *Sanhedrin*, 97; 99; 111.

## THE ADVENT OF THE MESSIAH IN ANOTHER VERSION—CALCULATIONS

The account of another version in other passages gives us even the exact year of the Messiah's advent, assuming that we could have a proper point of departure for calculation. There we read that when sixty years have elapsed after the seventh century of the sixth millennium, it is said that heaven shall then visit the daughter of Jacob. In the seventieth year the King Messiah shall be revealed in the province of Galilee.

## THE PORTENT OF THE MESSIAH'S ADVENT

The portents of the King Messiah's advent shall be the following:

1. The rainbow, which is now tarnished because it serves only as a memorial that the world will be destroyed no more by a deluge, will shine very brilliant dyes like a betrothed lady, adorning herself to enter the presence of her spouse.

2. A star will rise in the East, and swallow up seven stars in the North (20. III; 212b, V, 536).

3. After a period, a fixed star will appear in the middle of the firmament and will be visible for seventy days. It will have seventy rays and will be surrounded by seventy other stars.

4. The city of Rome will fall to pieces (Zohar ibid.).

5. A great King will rise up and will conquer the world. There will be war against Israel but the chosen people shall be delivered. According to one account, the seventy celestial chiefs, who rule the seventy nations of the earth, will marshal all the legions of the world to make war on the sacred city of Jerusalem, but they will be exterminated by the power of the Holy One.

It is written in Obadiah 5:18: "And the house of Jacob shall be a fire and the house of Joseph a flame, and the house of Esau for stubble." As such stubble, by such fire and flame shall the nations perish. Thereafter the King Messiah will cause Jerusalem to be rebuilt. The Holy One will remember that covenant which He made with Israel; and in such day will David also be raised up. The Messiah will draw to him the whole world; it shall be so to the end of the century and then the *vav* shall be united with the *hai*. It will be the period of true bridals; the Messiah will bring about union between the palaces above and below, as also between El and Shaddai.

## THE PRESENT ABODE OF THE MESSIAH AND HIS SUFFERING

The soul of Messiah is preexistent in common with all souls, and its present place is the Garden of Eden according to prevailing opinion; but the testimony is not in full accord whether this is the Eden above or the Eden that is below. Wheresoever it be, there is a most secret place in the hiddenness which is called the "Bird's Nest," and therein he abides. But he visits various palaces and the "School of Doctrine."

In the Paradise there is also a certain place which is called the Palace of the Sick. The Messiah enters therein and calls upon all the diseases and sorrows and troubles of Israel in exile to assail him; and this comes to pass accordingly. Were it otherwise, there is no one who could suffer the penalty due to his misdeeds. Hence it is said in Isaiah 53:4: "Surely he has borne our grief, and carried our sorrows." So long as Israel dwelled in the Holy Land and sacrifices were offered therein Israel was preserved from all maladies and penalties. Now it is the Messiah who bears them, as it is affirmed, for the whole world, that is to say, the world of Israel.

One more statement on the subject matter which may stand by itself was left until the last. It is said, almost at the beginning of the Zohar in that part which is called Preliminaries, God created man with the object of preparing for the advent of the Messiah who is God's son. This is in connection with the "Lesser Countenance," and also in correspondence to the letter *vav*, about which we have heard in several previous sections. This intimation, however, is not in undiversified agreement with a few other intimations about which we have also heard and which stand in contrast. The advent of Messiah, in connection with the raising of the letter *vav* in the Sacred Name of four letters, is to raise up her who is His Bride and to prepare for the Sabbath of Creation, the period of true bridals.

CHAPTER NINE

# The Doctrine Concerning Sheol

The question of reward and punishment in the world to come is by no means a subject of unanimity in the Secret Tradition of kabbalah. It concerns also the question of the temporal or eternal punishment reserved for disincarnate souls. I will speak first of that which is held to occur at the time of death, and then of punishment in Sheol, with special reference to its duration.

Many things which are hidden from the mind and the heart of man, so long as the body is in health, are beheld by the soul when it is hovering between life and death. This is held to be the spiritual interpretation of the verse in Job 37:7 which reads: "He sealeth up the hand of every man, that all men, whom He has made, may know His work." The Zohar reads it thus: "He causes every man to sign with his own hand, that each may know His Acts."

## OF DEATH—THE SOUL BODY SEPARATION AND DEPARTURE, ITS VISION AND ACCOUNTING

Three messengers descend who begin to count up the days that a man has lived, the sins that he has committed, and all the works which he has accomplished here below. The dying man confesses with his lips to the facts so related and he signs the verbal process psychically with his own hand. Inasmuch as sins are committed while spirit is united to body, the account must be taken before their separation is completed. Thereon is he judged now, for there is a particular judgment as well as a general judgment at the end of time.

Zoharic pneumatology is sometimes inextricably abstract, but we may remember some testimony related once before that *Neshamah* cannot sin, whence it cannot be under the judgment. *Nephesh* remains with the body for twelve months; and it would seem, therefore, that it is *Ruach* which enters into reward and punishment as a result of this particular judgment. In contrast hereto we must further remember that all parts of the inward personality are but one by another account of the Zohar, which recognizes fundamentally only body and soul.

## THE SOUL OF THE DEPARTED MEETS ADAM AND OTHERS

On quitting this lower world, the man gives account to his Master on the basis of the record which has been mentioned. Having crossed the threshold, he recognizes many persons whom he knew on earth. As mentioned in the previous, he beholds also Adam seated before the Garden of Eden, so that he may rejoice with those who have observed the commands of their Master. Adam is ever encompassed with a multitude of the just, who have learned how to avoid the path going down to hell, and who have been gathered into the abode of Paradise.

## THE ISSUE OF THE MALE ISSUE

Another account says that when the soul leaves this world, it is stopped by a number of angels who preside over the offices of severity, and it is prevented from passing through that door by which it would attain a place on high if the person has left no pledge on earth, meaning no son. Those who would enjoy the inheritance of God and be united with Him forever in the land of life must have produced male issue, so that the Divine Law may continue to have its servants through all generations.

Thus, we see expressed the higher desire that prevailed in Israel towards the increase and predominance of the people. It was not alone that they might inherit the earth, but that the Divine teachings of the Torah might prevail therein for the Glory of God. The production of children was, therefore, a continuous building of a house not made with hands, which might become fit for God's habitation. The holy Mystery of Sex was therefore a Great Mystery of Sanctity and a Divine Work in the world.

## THE DEATHBED EVENTS

It is also said elsewhere that the day of death is the day of the Lord. When the Holy One desires that the soul should return to Him, it does so return if worthy. There is first purgation by fire for those who are imperfect and yet not deserving of entire condemnation. In the case of a just man, his approach by the gate of death is proclaimed in the Garden of Eden throughout the thirty days which go immediately before the event. During these days the soul is separated nightly from the body and ascends to heaven for the purpose of inspecting the place reserved for it in the world to come.

Another tradition mentioned by the Zohar tells us that at the actual hour of death man is allowed to see his departed relations and friends. He recognizes these and they appear to him with the same countenances which they wore here below. Many deathbed visions are narrated in this context. If the man is worthy, his relations and friends salute him full of joy. In the contrary case, he beholds only the guilty whom he has known and who are expiating their offenses in hell. They are all plunged into sadness. Relations and friends accompany the soul into the other world and show him the place of his reward or punishment.

It is also said that the highest place in the "world to come" is kept in reservation for those who have penetrated the mysteries of their Master and learned how to cleave to Him during life. For the illumination of the mind by "Divine Things" has a very great reward; but works and good deeds are also very necessary.

## THE VERSION OF STILL ANOTHER ACCOUNT

Another side of the story is that when the souls of those who have studied the Holy Doctrine relinquish the body which is composed of the four compound elements, they ascend into heaven or into that part and region which is allocated to the four living creatures (compare Ezekiel, ch. 1).

More generally, the spirit which man attracts during life will draw his soul after death. Should it have been the Holy Spirit which he attracted, he will be raised thereby into the higher realm and there, incorporated in the legion of sacred angels, he will become a servant of the Holy One. The authority for it is: "And I will give thee places to walk among these that stand by" (Zechariah 3:7). The Zoharic version is: "I will give thee access among those who stand before me." He enjoys that light in the world above which he has desired here on earth. It is called "the Splendor of light in reverberation," reflected by that light which is in the region above all regions. Souls are clothed in what is characterized as the Mantle of the Master, in the absence of which they would be incapable of approaching the light and of contemplating it. This mantle or these vestments as they are called in another place are said to be stored in a certain Palace, each being adopted to that soul for which it is reserved. The vestments are the soul's clothing, corresponding in things above to that worn by the high priest in the ceremonies of the sanctuary. It is further said that in the earthly Paradise souls are clothed with good works, but in the Paradise above they are clothed more gloriously, namely, with purity of intention, rightness of heart, and prayers.

All the good works that have been performed by him or her are so to speak embroidered thereon. The soul is not clothed, however, until the thirtieth day after death, because the sins committed on earth have to be expiated during this period by the bad and by the good indifferently. It is expiation by fire and a passage through a river of fire. There is moreover a punishment of the body in the grave for a period of twelve months, during which the so-called animal spirit or *Nephesh* is attracted thereto and suffers therewith; but the just are not subject to this. The *Nephesh* knows also the suffering of the bereaved survivors, but cannot go to their aid. After the twelve months, it is clothed with that envelope referred to previously and passes on wings through the world, learning from the *Ruach* the misfortunes which befall men and seeking to communicate with these, so that they may pray for the evil to be averted.

## OF HELL EVERLASTING OR OTHERWISE

And now with regard to those who go down into hell. There is a distinction and a counter-distinction of statements, tabulating and predicating the nature of their torments everlasting or otherwise.

It is laid down that the Holy One forgives every man who repents of his sins. But it is woe to those who will not repent and who persist in their evil conduct. They will be precipitated after death into hell and will not issue therefrom through all eternity.

The same idea is expressed analogically in another place as follows: "The souls of those who defile their bodies, and of the evil generally, go down into hell and never come forth therefrom." Of those it is said: "As the cloud is consumed and vanishes away, so he that goeth down to the grave shall come up no more" (Job 7:9). Sheol the Zohar interprets here as hell in this verse. Again, to fall into the hands of him who is called "the Angel of Vindication" is defined by the Zohar to be "death in eternity." The Angel of Vindication is Doma. For the most part the Gentiles are said to be his victims, while that which protects the Israelites against him and his consequences is the Sign of the Covenant, if it is preserved in purity. Respecting punishment in the other world, however, man was not considered to have attained his majority—as being capable of punishment—until he has reached the age of thirty years. So much for the everlasting category.

As for the opposite category, first there is an unqualified statement that the guilty are chastised in the fires of hell, but they are not damned for all eternity. Indeed the period has been fixed by tradition at twelve months, being that of the suffering of Job and also of *Nephesh* with the body. (Compare all that with the Babylonian Talmud, Tractate *Rosh Hashanah*, 17a.) This assurance and its consolation are drawn from Isaiah

33:12 where we read: "And the people shall be as the burning of lime; as thorns cut up shall they be burned in the fire." The Zohar version renders it "thorn-bush" thus instituting a comparison with the burning but unconsumed bush on Mount Sinai.

## RESPECTING CANAAN

Another extract of the Zohar states that at the "end of time" all the guilty will be saved with the single exception of Canaan. It is said that this mystery is not unknown to those who are familiar with the high roads and bypaths of the Secret Doctrine. In another place we find arguments in the Zohar to the effect that all men will be acquitted at the celestial judgment.

As for Canaan, we all are acquainted with the biblical tradition of the wrongdoings of Ham, the father of Canaan, and of the curses Noah bestowed on him respecting Canaan; the whole being a part of a sex mystery. It belongs to the realm of sex mysteries, as those prevailing over the marriage of Batsheva and Uriah, before she was espoused to David. It is further added that those who know this mystery will be in a position to see why the Holy Land was given as a patrimony to Canaan before the coming of the Israelites.

## IMPORTANCE OF *AMAIN* RESPONSE

The authority of yet another tradition affirms that there are various compartments in hell, one beneath another and corresponding to the different degrees of culpability found among men. The lowest of all bears the name of Abaddon, and the man who is cast therein is lost through all eternity because it has no door through which he can go out. It is about this place that it is said: "As the cloud is consumed and vanishes away; so he that goes down to the grave ["Sheol"] shall come up no more" (Job 7:9). This not withstanding, says the Zohar, we learn otherwise from Scripture that: "He sends down into hell and again He brings forth therefrom" (Samuel I 2:6). The first of these verses refers to the lowermost pit, and the second refers to one of those places from which escape is possible. Abysmal hell is also reserved for punishment of acts of irreverence. The denizens of this region of the "deep below the deep" are also those who, prompted by disdain, have always omitted the word *Amain*, which completes the forms of prayer.

## THE ZOHARIC FLUX OF ESCHATOLOGY

Two eschatological points shall be mentioned here in this connection. Once it is said that the impure soul which is cast into Sheol is sometimes drawn out therefrom and carried through celestial realms with this cry going before it. "Such is the lot of those who transgress the commandment of their master" (compare Job 20:29). It is then returned to its place. This is mentioned in that part of the text which limits the period of damnation to twelve months, after which the soul is remitted to a suitable region.

Another text gives a brief picture of souls located in Paradise proceeding to view ceremonially the chastisement of the guilty. The last statement is given to us on the authority of Rabbi Shimon and it occurs in one of his discourses.

It is further imputed that there are three chiefs in hell acting as overseers of those who are doomed for murder, incest, and idolatry. The chastisement is by fire and ice. An elucidation in another place explains that the waters which fall from above are cold as ice, while the fire which comes up from below is water which burns. It also states that the souls of the heathen will never come out of hell.

## OTHER GLEAMS ON THE SUBJECT OF RETRIBUTION

It is recorded that those who were guilty on earth but were also punished on earth will not suffer in eternity if they have shown resignation here. We find also another statement of mercy to the effect that all men, including heathen in general, will be acquitted at the general judgment. There is one place from which it seems to follow that even Satan himself will become again an angel of light. It is even added that while we are to be on our guard against the attack of the demon, we are not authorized to treat him with contempt.

## RETRIBUTION AND MERCY

Alternative supplements on the subject of eschatology occur and will be briefly recorded. The souls of those who die impenitent go forth naked and find no envelope. Yet it is set forth elsewhere pretty plainly that some kind of vesture is essential to personal existence. These souls suffer punishment in hell, but many of them are saved at the end of time, being those souls who intended to repent but did not get to the work. They take up their task in Sheol, and its gates are opened subsequently in their respect. There is nothing more agreeable than this to the Sacred King. It is laid down furthermore that even those who are just and nearly approach perfection go down into hell. This happens because all have been guilty of some offenses at least; but also because it is theirs to bring forth with them, those very sinners who had proposed to repent in this life and have succeeded only on the other side of the grave.

We have learned already elsewhere in the Zohar that good intentions in the right direction of heart and mind rate greatly, and uttermost sacredness is ascribed to them. Such intentions are even greater than works if they pass continually into work. Mercy is therefore theirs. The Zohar holds out, however, little hope for persons who have planned no atonement; they remain in the place of perdition forever. This is the case especially with those who have led a life of debauchery; they do not have respite on the Sabbath like the rest of the damned. There is, however, another thesis there showing that the flames of hell are stilled of necessity on the day of Sabbath.

We find, therefore, ample suggestions that all Jews will ultimately enter into some kind of salvation. Also, Divine mercy will prevail and make hell give up all its prey at the end of days, whether Gentile or prince of demons, whether men or demons, including Canaan.

The great rabbis of the Zohar also countenanced prayers for the dead; one of them asking another to visit his tomb for seven days following his burial, there to plead for his soul. It is also testified that the faithful departed pray for those who are alive, without which the latter would be unable to subsist for a single day or even part of a day, which means the intercession of the just above for those who need help below. Compare also Babylonian Talmud, Tractate *Sabbath*, 89b.

# CHAPTER TEN
# Concerning Resurrection

## RESURRECTION OF THE DEAD

Here we shall record that which is advanced by Zoharic theosophy on the subject of the doctrine of physical resurrection. We are concerned here in reality with the root matter of the tradition, which is not one of metaphysical speculation merely or dogmatic teaching. The physical resurrection, we shall find, is physical above all things. We shall get acquainted with the modus operandi of the whole process.

Are the Gentiles included in the scheme of resurrection? This must be left as an open question. We know for certain from several sources that the very just and pious ones from among the Gentiles have definitely a share in the world to come. As for the rest we find this negative categorically in one place. The words there are, that God will command his servant who is charged with the work of resurrection not to restore the souls to the Gentile peoples. In another place it is added by way of reexpression, that only the circumcised will subsist at that dreadful day. Again we find that it is said, without qualifying the statement, that the guilty will rise with the just, will do penance, and will enjoy thereafter the light of God. There can be no question, however, that the reference is to Israel alone. But even here there are reservations. For certain persons belonging to the past of Israel, persons conspicuous for their ill-doings, are regarded as blotted out completely so that for them there is neither judgment nor rising. The allusion there is to the sin of Onan, the enormity of which is ever present in the Secret Holy Doctrine. Once it is even said that resurrection is by the merit of chastity.

The vesture of holy days, about which we have heard, is a particular aid of the just. Another account tells us that when a man has maintained his soul in its pristine purity, on leaving this world many lights are poured upon him, and he is preserved against the day of resurrection in a hidden Palace of Love, where the King of Heaven kisses the holy souls. The scriptural authority is Exodus 21:9: "He shall deal with her after the manner of daughters." It follows that all souls in respect of God are held to be His daughters.

## TRADITION OF THE THESIS OF RESURRECTION

The thesis of resurrection in general is put forth as follows. When circumstances required it, a simple morsel of wood, the reference being to Aaron's rod, was transformed by the Holy One into a thing having body and life. With how much more reason will He change into new creatures those forms that previously possessed a vital spirit and a holy soul, fulfilling the commandments of the Holy Torah and consecrated to its duty. It is the same bodies that have existed heretofore which will be resuscitated, as it is written: "Thy dead men shall live" (Isaiah 26:19), and they will be animated by the same souls. There is a sense, however, in which they will be formed anew, but they will have the aspects of old and will be therefore recognizable. The new formation is more especially a Divine Act of healing, so that the lame and the blind will be disqualified thus no longer. This will be effected by the rays of that primitive sun which shone at the beginning, embracing the whole world from one extremity to the other. The robes of glory or psychic vestures and vehicles with which the embodied soul is clothed in the state of beatitude, being psychic garments, will serve in the transfiguration of the risen physical body. The fire of that primitive sun will consume the Gentile nations. The light of this concealed sun encompassed Moses as an infant among the bulrushes. It surrounded him on Mount Sinai, whence the children of Israel could not look upon his countenance; and in some sense, it remained with him for the rest of his life.

## CONCEALMENT OF THE CURATIVE LIGHT, THE DEW OF LIFE

After God had beheld the generation of Enoch with those of the deluge and confusion of tongues, He concealed this light which had curative properties. Its future restoration, as stated, signifies the restoration and enlightenment of Israel. It is said: "In that day shall there be one Lord and His Name one" (Zechariah 14:9).

The resurrection of the dead will take place in the order of their internment: if a wife was the first to be buried, it is she who will rise first. This rule will prevail through the ages with one exception in favor of those who died in the desert; the trumpet will sound for these sooner than for the earliest of humanity. When the great day approaches, it will be the task of Metatron to embellish and glorify the bodies in the sepulchers and to prepare them for rising, but it is Matrona who preserves souls until the resurrection. When the hour sounds, however, the Holy One will cause a dew to fall, and it is thanks to this dew that the event of resurrection itself will be accomplished. It will be a dew of light and it will emanate from the tree of Life.

It is said elsewhere that at the time of resurrection, the waters of that heavenly fountain, which is represented by the letter *yod*, will flow forth afresh. The thirty-two paths of communication between things above and below will be open freely and all letters of the Sacred Name will be complete, which has not been the case in the world heretofore.

There is a special dispensation in respect of students of the Secret Holy Doctrine. Without prejudice to those who died in the desert, it is those students who will be raised first and they will bear witness in favor of the rest. The instrument in their case will be a wind which shall be the synthesis of all winds. The risen bodies of these will subsist always, because the Torah will be their protection.

## THE IMPERISHABLE LITTLE BONE

Each man who is born into the world is provided with an imperishable bone in his present physical body. It is from or on this bone that his organization will be built up anew at the time of resurrection. It is like the rib taken from the side of Adam. The bone in question will be to the risen body that which the leaven is to the dough. The poetry of the subject is expressed in one place in the saying that by virtue of the dew of light already mentioned, the resurrection of bodies will be as the springing up of flowers.

The miraculous raising of the natural body during the event of resurrection will take place only in Palestine. The great majority of Israel, however, will be dying outside the precincts of the sacred land. The holy tradition teaches us that after their reconstitution, the bodies of such persons will be transported underground to the Holy Land, and then only will they receive their souls. The complete resurrection will begin in Galilee. Souls will come down through the gates of heaven and rejoin their bodies. At first it will be a day of severity, for the Holy One will demand an account of all actions prior to the separation of soul and body. The books of record will be opened and the chiefs of severity will stand ready to act. But Israel is a nation of the elect; the guilty that rise with the just will do penance and thereafter will enjoy the Divine Splendor.

Cryptic passages tell us also by intimation that the "serpent will rise up to bite, and man shall tremble in all his members." It is also testified that the tempter spirit and his two daughters will be transformed. Formerly he was called Lot, meaning malediction, but hereafter he will be called Laban, meaning white. But again in another passage, extermination is meted out to him. And again in another passage, it is merely said that he will disappear.

The Holy One will bless the bodies of the just and will render them like the body of Adam in the state of Paradise. Such souls will bring with them the higher lights which nourish them during their sojourn in heaven, between the death and the rising, and those lights will make their bodies radiant. Soul and body shall know their Master. A great festival will follow; the Talmud mentions the salted Leviathan promised to the elect. The Zohar reflects that for the truly just it will be spiritual, because those who are truly just have no need to eat or drink, but are nourished by the Splendor of Shechinah.

## CONCLUSION OF ZOHARIC ESCHATOLOGY

It seems that subject to the distinction on the question of duration of punishment, all souls at death go to the place prepared for them, and the judgment connected with the resurrection determines, once and for all, the state of humanity forever. There is neither change nor vicissitude thereafter. The just in their risen bodies will behold the Divine so that the earth shall be filled with the knowledge of God. It is also affirmed that those bodies shall be unto them as a lasting habitation. The body shall be made wholly, even as it was formerly (meaning the body of Adam in Paradise, unfallen) that it may be like unto the holy angels. Their bodies will be like the splendor of the firmament or like silver that has no alloy. So will the earth be renewed.

SECTION VIII

*The Higher
Secret Doctrine
in Israel*

CHAPTER ONE

# The Mystery of Shechinah

The Secret Doctrine of the Zohar concerning the Holy Shechinah is the mystery of sex at its highest. Shechinah herself is the Mystery of the Oral Law. There is a very true sense in which the Secret Doctrine of the Zohar must be said to center in that mystery, which lies behind the wonder and glory of Shechinah, a recurring, incessant subject throughout the text of the Zohar. We must, however, proceed carefully not only on account of the difficulties but also because the keys of the Mystery of Shechinah open into a region about which there are great motives for speaking with considerable reserve, when it is possible to speak at all. The vast body of cryptic writing in this matter of Jewish theosophy and the practice concealed behind it arose out of that one verse in Scripture which says, "So God" (that is to say Elokim) created man in his own image. "In the image of God created he them, male and female" (Genesis 1:27).

The sole object with which the Holy One, blessed be He, sends man into this world, is to know that HVYH is Elokim.

Herein is also all true joy of heart. There is also a grafting of the two Holy Names in kabbalism producing the Sacred Name of nine letters; the consonants succeeding one another alternately, thus: *yod, aleph, hai, lamed, vav, hai, hai, yod, mem.* It is also said: "And the Lord God formed man" (Genesis 2:7); HVYH Elokim, the male principle united to the female according to the Zohar. Man is said to be grafted on Elokim as the latter is grafted on HVYH.

Thus we shall open the high conference respecting the Mystery of Shechinah, which is a mystery of man and God. It is the mystery of man in the likeness of Elohim, of the relation between things above and things below, of intercourse for union upon earth performed in the spirit of celestial union and transmutation of one by the other for the work of God in the world. In this union abides the mystery of Faith, which is the synthesis of the whole Law (Torah). This is the Written and Oral Law and of all that exists whatsoever.

## THE VARIOUS ASCRIPTIONS AND DESIGNATIONS OF SHECHINAH

Now, union is not identity, whence it is said further that HVYH and Elokim are distinct and not synonymous, though together they form a unity. This is as it is written: "Unto thee it was showed, that thou mightest know, that the Lord is God" (Deuteronomy 4:35) (that is, HVYH is Elokim, quotes the Zohar). We must remember too that Elokim is also a title of Shechinah and so also is Adonai, in which sense, when in manifestation, she is called the Mirror of HVYH.

Shechinah is myriadfold in respect of her designations, but the ascriptions are always feminine. Now she is the Daughter of the King, now she is the Betrothed, the Bride, and the Mother, and again she is sister in another synonym in relation to the world of man at large. There is also a sense in which this Daughter of God is or becomes the Mother of man.

In respect of the manifest universe, she is the architect of worlds acting in virtue of the "Word" uttered by God in creation. In respect of the account of Paradise, the Shechinah is the Eden which is above, whence the river of life flows forth that waters the Garden below. This is also Shechinah, as she is conceived in external things or Shechinah in the symbolism and synonyms of Bride, Daughter, and Sister in the world below.

Considered in her Divine Womanhood in the world of transcendence, Shechinah is the Beloved who ascends towards the Heavenly Spouse and she is Matrona, who unites with the King, for the perfection of the Divine Male is the Divine Female. Hence it is said that the perfection joy HVYH is in Elokim. In respect of the title of Shechinah as Elokim there is an Elokim in transcendence concealed and mysterious, an Elokim that judges above and one who judges below; but all three are one.

## SHECHINAH ABIDES EVERYWHERE

As such, the Oral Law is the image of Shechinah, while the image of HVYH is the Written Law (Zohar IV, 102). So also Shechinah is the waters that are above the firmament in respect of her title as Elokim, but she is the waters below the firmament when she manifests as Adonai (Zohar I, 17b; 18a; I, 108). As Elokim she is the Middle Pillar (Zohar I, 278a; Faithful Shepherd II, 647, and 241a; and II, 552). All the various aspects are collocated to show that Shechinah abides in all; she is at once above and below; she is without even as within. She is that Divine Presence which walked in the Garden of Eden in the cool of the evening, and which went before Israel in the desert. She protects the just man, who has fulfilled the precepts, dwelling in his house and going forth with him in his journeys (Zohar I, 76a; I, 448). In relation with Elokim, Shechinah is the middle degree of the Divine Essence, corresponding to the Pillar of Benignity in the Tree of Life (Zohar I, 150b; II, 194).

## ALTERNATIVE ALLOCATIONS OF SHECHINAH

The Zohar affirms and reaffirms that the Shechinah is female in essential aspect, whether in symbolism as the Bride of God, in the transcendent state, or whether as the tutelary guide of humanity (Zohar II, 118b; III, 456; II, 207a; IV, 210). There are, however, certain alternative allocations which appear in the Zohar, namely, these that follow.

Shechinah is the Liberating Angel who delivers the world in all ages, who is ever near to man and never separated from the just. Of her it is said, "Behold I send an Angel before thee to keep thee in the way, and to bring thee into the place which I have prepared" (Exodus 23:20). It is stated, though, that this Liberating Angel manifests as male and female. He is male when he dispenses the celestial benedictions on the world below, because he then resembles a male nourishing the female; but when charged with offices of judgment, she is called female, as a woman who carries her child in the womb. The Flaming Sword, which turned every way to keep the way of the "Tree of Life," is a symbol of this Angel and of Shechinah in the dual sex of both (Gen. 3:24). Mercy is always counted as masculine and severity or judgment as feminine (Zohar I, 228b; II, 502; I, 230a; II, 508; I, 232a; II, 516).

Elsewhere, it is said that those who understand these male and female attributions know the great wisdom. The exposition to this wisdom is given later on when it is stated that Matrona is feminine insofar as she is identified with the male principle and this is how interchange of sex in divine things must be understood throughout. It is then said distinctly that in this respect, whether the feminine or masculine form is used by Scripture the same degree is always and only designated (Zohar II, 100b; III, 406; III, 31a; V, 84). So also Metatron, who is an aspect of Shechinah, is indifferently male and female, changing incessantly according to the vibrations of the union. Now, it is also said that Shechinah is to Metatron what the Sabbath is to the weekdays. We are to understand that she is rest and the rapture of rest; yet in that rest is the intercourse of spiritual union (Zohar III, 73b; V, 201; III, 243b; V, 581).

## THE TASK OF LIGHTING SABBATH CANDLES

Now then, the union is to be understood only in a spiritual sense, and at the apex of this union sex distinction has ceased. And only from this point of view can it be that Shechinah is mentioned sometimes, as if she were on the male side. But in characteristics and in mission, Shechinah is always typically female. It is she who comprises all women in her mystery (Zohar I, 228b; II, 501), and this is why Shechinah does not abide except with him who is united to a woman. The task of lighting the Sabbath candles devolved on the matrons because they are in the service of Matrona. This act was regarded as an "earnest" of long life for the husband, of a holy posterity for both, and a great personal reward for themselves (Zohar I, 48b; I, 281).

## SHECHINAH'S RELATION TO THE LETTER OF TETRAGRAMMATON

The relations of Shechinah to the letters of Tetragrammaton are as follows. The *hai* which is above, meaning the first *hai* of the Sacred Name, is the symbol of Shechinah in transcendence, while the *hai* final represents the Shechinah below or in manifestation, connected with the idea of *Malkuth*. (It is said also that the *hai* final is the child of the first *hai*.) *Malkuth* here is understood as the world of Assiah. According to one account Shechinah has been in manifestation so long as the world was created. She is, however, above and below at one and the same time, there encompassed by twelve sacred legions and the supreme Chayoth or Living Ones, hereby the twelve sacred tribes of Israel (Zohar I, 27b; I, 174; I, 85a; I, 489; I, 159b; II, 227).

The *yod* and the *hai* constitute the Father and the Mother (HVYH-Elokim) in *Chokhmah* and in *Binah*. Shechinah is the Mother, Matrona, above and Matrona or Mother below. From the constant and ardent love of 'hai' for *yod*, there issues *vav*, conceived and born of *hai*, who also nourishes *vav*. But *vav* came into the world with a twin sister, bearing the name of Grace. The two took root on earth and constituted the *hai* final. This is a reference to the metaphysical conception of their affirmed union. Then and thus was *vav* united to the *hai*, meaning the second *hai* of the Divine Name (Zohar I, 28a; I, 177; III, 10b; V, 31; III, 77b; V, 210–211).

It follows that there is a descent of *vav* into manifestation; but this notwithstanding the *vav* has its place in the Supernal World and so also has the final *hai*. For it is obvious that the Divine Name must be perfect above before it can manifest below. (In the scheme of Divine Names allocated to the ten sephiroth by late kabbalism, the name HVYH is referred to *Chokhmah*).

As the *hai* in manifestation, the Shechinah is the repose of beings below and in transcendence of beings above, referring more especially to souls who have attained beatitude, which is defined as the vision of Shechinah. The *vav* is the male child or the son. The *yod* of the Sacred Name is ever united to the primal *hai*, and when the *vav* is also joined thereto, it is union everywhere, including that which should obtain between the *vav* and the *hai* final (Zohar III, 108a–b; V, 274; II, 40b; The Faithful Shepherd III, 189–190; Zohar III, 118b; V, 305; III, 267b; VI, 23).

Owing to the present state of the world, however, this union has been broken. In a withdrawn sense, the *yod* of the Sacred Name designates the Supreme Thought, while the *hai* designated Shechinah as the heart of Love in that Thought (Zohar III, 230a, V, 570).

To conclude as to the Divine Name, its consonants bear the vowel points of the name Elokim. Otherwise this divine Name has the pointing of Adonai. From these two things seem to follow: 1) that the intimate union between HVYH and Elokim is here indicated by silent eloquence; 2) that the degree of hypostasis (that is, that part of the Divine Nature with which man is in communion on earth) is that which the Secret Tradition understands as Shechinah. It is she who enables the name to be expressed on earth. She enables that God be realized in the hearts of men.

It leads to the conclusion that in the perfect state, the manifestation of the *hai* final on earth would be in espousal with *vav*. But there is separation in the present order until that which now hinders shall be taken out of the way; my reference is to the period foretold in the Zohar when the *vav* shall raise up the *hai* (Zohar I, 90a, I, 511–512).

## THE PLACE OF SHECHINAH IN THE SEPHIROTIC TREE

The next point posed for our consideration is the place of Shechinah in the sephirotic tree. We shall state right at the inception that the attributions throughout the kabbalah are almost as many as the references. Only one, however, is predominant. Shechinah is the Middle Pillar as we have seen, the Pillar of Benignity, extending from *Kether* to *Malkuth*; and she takes up the sephiroth to God or to the place which is no place, beyond the infinite height and depth, the infinite of all directions embraced by the tree. This is the place of *Ain Soph*. To avoid mental confusion, we shall add that according to the

Idras, the son of *vav* is extended through the three worlds, which are below the world of *Atziluth*, and he is called also the Middle Pillar. But he is in union with *hai* final, or Bride, therein. This was really only during the perfection of the manifest world. They are in separation now, for the *hai* is fallen to earth, that is, to *Malkuth* and has to be raised by *vav*. The notion is that the *vav* is also involved, though the *vav* has not also fallen. Similarly is Adam involved in the calamity of Eve. The account is also an allegory of man and woman, involved by a fatal construction, respecting the Mystery of Sex, but it intended to redeem the trespass with the life belonging thereto.

With reference to Shechinah raking up the sephiroth to the place of *Ain Soph*, this is a matter of inference from one isolated statement. This statement says that Shechinah in her ascent draws up the Ten Sephiroth. It is logical that where she draws them is beyond *Kether*. Now beyond *Kether* is *Ain Soph* by the tree hypothesis. It is said that when Shechinah rises toward God, she causes all the Ten Sephiroth to go up with her (Zohar I, 24a; I, 149).

The Middle Pillar is also described otherwise as the trunk of the tree, it being understood, that the root is in *Kether*, so far as the genesis and the narrative of the soul is concerned. But the Middle Pillar is in *Malkuth*, in respect of the return journey to God which is a journey through the Shechinah or under her glorious leading (Zohar I, 241a; II, 552).

In another form of symbolism Shechinah is the body of the Tree, and the elect of Israel are the clouds of witnesses forming the branches. But it is also said that Shechinah is the crown of the Middle Pillar, the synthesis of all the sephiroth, the synthesis of every Sacred Name expressed or implied in the wisdom of the Sacred Doctrine (Zohar I, 242b; II, 555; II, 158a; IV, 94).

Shechinah is to God that which the vowel point is to the letter; a thing not distinct therefrom, but the means of its utterance. Shechinah is further the crown of the seven lower sephiroth. This brings nearer to our understanding the allocation of the semi-sephirah *Daath* or Supernal Knowledge to the center of the influence, coming from *Chokhmah* and *Binah* as tabulated later on in kabbalism (Zohar II, 158a; IV, 94).

## AGAIN ABOUT THE FIFTY GATES OF UNDERSTANDING

We mentioned already the appendix to the Sepher Yetzirah, concerning fifty Gates of Understanding referred to *Binah*. The same reference is also made by later kabbalists. But this ascription is countenanced by the Zohar when it is said that these Gates are in the region of the Supreme Mother (Shechinah in transcendence) who gives power to the Mother below (Shechinah in manifestation). This determines that the Shechinah is in *Binah* and that the first *hai* of the Divine Name is also therein (we find also a statement saying that the head of *vav*, the son, is in *Daath*, as we have seen previously).

As regards the number fifty which is otherwise allocated to Shechinah, we should note that the Jubilee year occurring once after every forty-nine years is allocated to the Divine Mother in *Binah* just as the Sabbatical Year occurring every seven years. The Sabbatical Year is referred to the Mother below, that is, to the Shechinah in manifestation, so that her number on earth is seven, whereas the number of Shechinah in transcendence is fifty (Zohar III, 262a; VI, 12; III, 108b; The Faithful Shepherd; V, 274).

It is said further that the side of severity emanates from Shechinah though she is not herself Severity. We know that the Pillar of Severity is on the left side of the diagram of the sephirotic tree, at the head of which is *Binah*. Shechinah emanates from the left side, states the Zohar (Zohar III, 275b; VI, 44).

## THE FIFTY GATES AND MAN

The Fifty Gates are also a symbolism concerning the return of man to the heights, by the operation of Shechinah, as by a journey through the great distance, for the first Gate is in matter and the last one in God Himself. According to tradition, this Gate was not opened by Moses—presumably as we have seen—because he ceased to cohabit with his wife on earth (the Mystery of Sex). The Gate in question is a gate in *Binah*, so that God is attained by man in and because of Shechinah, for which reason her number is said to be fifty, though from another point of view she is not contained in number (Zohar III, 108b; The Faithful Shepherd; V, 274; Zohar II, 164b; IV, 108).

## INTEGRATION OF THE ENTIRE TREE IN SHECHINAH—A THING TO COME

There are, however, various allocations. Two supernals, namely *Chokhmah* and *Binah*, are disposed on the right and left, and these are said to be united in Shechinah. But the complete integration of all branches of the sephirotic tree in Shechinah will not take place until He comes, Who shall be called Man, that is Adam or Shiloh (Zohar II, 165a; IV, 109; I, 25b; I, 160).

It follows that there is a sense in which Shechinah is in *Chokhmah*, because she is indubitably present in things that are united in her. Also because insofar as Shechinah represents sex, conceived transcendently, she is male and female; and because in the Supernals there is no distinction between her and the Holy One (ibid.).

It is of Shechinah that it is said: "She openeth her mouth in wisdom" (Proverbs 31:26). The reference there is to virtuous woman, and it accentuates in this manner the feminine aspect of Shechinah. We ought to remember that in the physical order, it is woman who conceives, contains, and brings forth, both male and female.

For the purpose of this attribution, Wisdom is the letter *hai* and all depends therefrom. This attribution, however, is casual and transient. For in the natural allocation of the Tree, it is the *yod* that is in *Chokhmah*. (Compare Assembly of the Sanctuary, Zohar II, 123b; III, 478.)

Shechinah in the above allocation is called "concealed and visible," conciliating the mysteries above and mysteries below. The hiddenness of Shechinah is in respect of the Supreme Degree of the Divine Essence, which exceeds understanding. Shechinah herself is revealed in Wisdom by the mode of the Law of Mercy, so that she is Mercy on one side, although Severity proceeds from her on the other. As the mouth, which is opened with wisdom, she is the *hai* final of the Sacred Name, and this is the word that emanates from wisdom (Zohar I, 145a; II, 171). Again it is said that Elokim is seated on the right side, suggesting that the Shechinah is in *Chokhmah*. Moreover, wisdom is the glory of and is revealed in the Tabernacle by Shechinah (ibid.). Elsewhere the Tabernacle is said itself to be Shechinah (Zohar III, 114; V, 285).

We must deal with the problem of understanding this, seeing that in another place Elokim "who is the Shechinah," is said definitely to designate *Binah*. Shechinah is known by many names as we are told in another place, sometimes as an angel simply, sometimes as an angel of HVYH (that is, God), and sometimes even as HVYH (Zohar III, 77b; V, 212; I, 113b; II, 58).

The truth is that Shechinah is on both sides of the Tree of Life, and the explanation is that she is the spirit of all the "Holy Assemblies" above and below (Zohar III, 103b; V, 262). It is in this sense only that *Chokhmah* is sometimes said to be female, and that *Chokhmah* is said to be that Mother, who is allocated alternatively to *Binah*, while she is Daughter, Sister, and Bride in the world below, because of the unity which obtains throughout the supernals. For the same reason she is now located in her manifestation at the foot of the Middle Pillar, that is to say in the fallen world. But we have also seen that Shechinah is also at the head and is therefore in *Kether*, that is to say, that "Eimma Elohim," covering the supernals with her wings. Hence it is mentioned that the Holy One is covered by His Shechinah, both within and without (The Faithful Shepherd; Zohar III, 243a; V, 581).

## REMINDER

We must recall here the symbolism of the White Head found in the Book of Mystery and in the Idras. The manifest Godhead is male and female; but this distinction is entirely lost in *Ain Soph* about which nothing can be posited, except that it is shown forth in *Kether*. These are Abba, being *Chokhmah*, and Eimma, being *Binah*, and there is *Daath*, overshadowing the lower Sephiroth (though other allocations are also made and stand at their value). These three are symbolized by *yod*, *hai*, and *vav*, in the Sacred Name, while the *hai* final, the Bride in manifestation is in *Malkuth* since the Fall, but so that the kingdom of this world may become in the fullness of the Messianic day, the kingdom of heaven. Outside these, there is *Kether*, the supernal sephirah, and HVYH abides in the deep hiddenness with Shechinah in that supernal sephirah. Shechinah is represented also by the initial letter of the word *Sabbath*, but this would be Shechinah below because of the Sabbatical year already mentioned. The seeming attribution of feminine description to Shechinah is because of her threefold aspect in her degrees and grades.

Everything proceeds from *Kether* in virtue of the union between God and His Shechinah therein. Also it is to be remembered that the Supernals are in unity (Zohar III, 243a).

## SHECHINAH, THE FIRST OF CREATED BEINGS

Shechinah herself in a state of distinction concerning her is either the first of created things or may be such when she assumes the vesture of Metatron (ibid.). We have already seen that Metatron is the vesture of Shaddai. But this Divine name is interchangeable with the Divine names and with Shechinah. They are so related because the numerical value of one name is the same as the other (Zohar III, 231a). In the state of ineffable union, Shechinah can only be eternal in that conception, like the Holy One. Safe insofar as the Holy One in time conception, postulated in *Kether*, and in respect of *Ain Soph* is the Inaccessible God and compared with Whom even the world of *Atziluth* is a conditioned state in respect to manifestation (ibid.).

## SHECHINAH, THE ARCHITECT AND BUILDER

In another connection we have mentioned already the work of Shechinah in creation. In "her" office, as the architect of this world, the Word was uttered to her and the Word was conceived by her and was brought or begotten into execution. We have also seen that Shechinah below concurred with the architect above and was also a builder; the Zohar does not explain fully in what sense. It is said, however, that she is the object of the mysteries, relative to the works of creation (Zohar I, 22a). Insofar as creation is symbolized as the history of the elect, it is obvious that this work remains unfinished until the great day of restitution. On the manifest side, this history begins in the Garden of Eden. Shechinah was the companion of human exile when Adam and Eve were expelled from the Garden as we shall see. For according to the Zohar, it was

Shechinah who walked with Adam in Paradise under the title Lord God (I, 76a, and I, 448). This is Shechinah in manifestation, the union above communicating to the union below, and prescribing the first law of life. But we know that the trespass followed, and that our prototypical parent Adam was driven out of the Garden—which might mean that he was cast out from under the wings of Shechinah.

## THE DOCTRINE THAT SHECHINAH SUFFERS WITH MANKIND

But Adam was not deserted in his need. Shechinah followed him into the captivity of the senses. This is the Zoharic doctrine that Shechinah suffered with mankind. This doctrine is put forth much more explicitly when it is said in the Zohar. Therefore the man was driven out and the mother was driven out with him (Zohar I, 120b: II, 84–85). The authority for this is the verse: "Behold for your iniquities have ye sold yourselves, and for your transgressions is your mother put away" (Isaiah 50:1).

This with Adam was her primal captivity, and many captivities followed wherein Shechinah shared. For it is said that she is the sacrifice which God had placed on His right and on His left hand and around Him (Zohar I, 256a).

There was a separation between the King and Matrona in respect of the outer world, and so came about a separation in the Divine Name. For the final *hai* was detached and came down on earth, the source of graces coming with her. It is expressly stated that the world could not exist until the *hai* final detached itself from the other three letters of the Divine Name and descended to earth. The authority for this, says the Zohar, is the verse in Psalms 89:2: "I have said Mercy shall be built up forever," which means says the Zohar, "the world shall be built on Mercy" (Zohar II, 554b; II, 600).

## SHECHINAH IN EXILE

Though it is forbidden to separate the Heaven Bride and Bridegroom even in thought, it is this which has come to pass by reason of the sufferings of Israel with whom Shechinah was destined to endure, even from the beginning. When Israel is in exile, the Shechinah is also in exile. It is for this reason that the Holy One will remember Israel. For the Lord will remember His covenant "Which is Shechinah." So compare Deuteronomy 30:3: "The Lord God will turn thy captivity and have compassion upon thee" (Zohar II, 9a).

The final statement is summed up, saying that the second *hai* was obscured and fell, becoming a symbol of penitence. She is weighed down by the sin of Israel. The meaning is that she is with the elect for better or for worse and as in their attainments so is she with them in their sins, though not after the same manner; for she is then on the wrath side. Her shame is the defiled body of man (Zohar II, 114b).

Again, Shechinah is in separation from the King, owing to the wickedness of man, and though she does not leave him, the sin of Israel causes her to turn away. To sum up on the subject, Shechinah was driven out of the Garden of Eden with Adam, like a wife sent away by her husband, but it was for the salvation of the world. Now then, it is written in Isaiah 26:13: "O Lord our God, other lords besides thee have had dominion over us; by Thee only will we make mention of Thy Name." The Zohar renders this, "But thanks to Thee we have remembered Thy Name only." This verse, says the Zohar, contains the supreme Mystery of Faith. HVYH Elokim is the source of highest mysteries and when Israel attains perfection, it will make no distinction between HVYH and Elokim. It is forbidden to separate these Names even in thought. Yet is there separation now on account of the sufferings of Israel, and because it is apart from God (Zohar III, 155a).

## THE SHECHINAH OF THE SUPERNALS AND THE ONE EXILED

In glancing at the concurrent teachings about Shechinah, considerable care is needed to distinguish between the allusion to her as Shechinah who is enthroned in *Binah* and never leaving the supernals, and the Shechinah who is the exiled servant of God. For there is a Shechinah called servant and a Shechinah called daughter of the King. The one is above the angels like the queen of all angels, and in respect of all other lights of creation is that, which soul is to body, though in relation to the Holy One she is as the body to the soul, notwithstanding that she is one with God. She is the mistress of the Celestial School called the Abode of the Shepherds, and this is a school of Metatron, understood as a vesture or form assumed by Shechinah (Zohar III, 223a).

In another aspect the Shechinah of the supernals is that great and wide sea mentioned in Psalms 104:25, and she embraces the whole world, which is concentrated in her. She is the jubilee of joy above (ibid.). All this is in the world of procession or emanation—the hypostatic world, which is *Atziluth*. But Shechinah is said otherwise to receive a body in Yetzirah, and so is empowered to manifest in Assiah, wherein among other titles, she is the Lady of Battles, who also obtains remission of the sins of Israel. It is obvious, of course, that Shechinah as daughter of the King did not fall into sin and hence, her exile is willing and as this text says, she is empowered. But, that of which she is prototype—incarnate womanhood—did fall, and that son who is incarnate manhood, fell with her (Zohar III, 109a).

## SHECHINAH AND THE PATRIARCHS

The Shechinah is said to connect in a particular sense with the patriarchal age.

It was after his circumcision that the letter *hai* was added to the name of Abram and it was also thereafter that he was united with Shechinah. Most of the Divine visions beheld by Abraham were visions and manifestations of Shechinah who dwelt constantly in the tent of Sarah. This is why Abraham, on appearing in the presence of Pharaoh, described Sarah as his sister, not as his wife. His reference was really to Shechinah, who bears this title, in respect of man, and who accompanied Sarah.

When Abraham went to rescue Lot, on leaving his house Abraham beheld Shechinah lighting the way before him and encompassed by many celestial legions (Gen. 14:14). She was present when Isaac blessed Jacob. It was Shechinah who conferred upon Jacob the name of Israel, and she was with him when he set up the mystic stone as a pillar.

When seeking a wife, it was with Shechinah that Jacob united his intention, and hence it is said that when Jacob married Rachel he united heaven and earth. Shechinah, however, did not forget or ignore Leah, but as the Holy Spirit inspired her so that she knew her part in the bearing of the twelve tribes (Zohar I, 93a).

## THE SHECHINAH IN EGYPT

Rachel died when the progenitors of these tribes were completed and her place was taken by Shechinah. But after the death of Leah, she removed to the house of Bilhah, so that she might be near Jacob, though she could not dwell in his house because as we know she resides only where the man is united to the woman. When Jacob lost Joseph, he lost the Shechinah also either because joy had left him or she dwells only with the glad heart, or because, it is said, he ceased to cohabit with his wife as a mark of grief and desolation. The part of joy returned to him after reunion with his son. Also Shechinah returned to him, for she accompanied Jacob and his family into Egypt, and forty-two sacred angels destined for her service came down with her, each bearing a letter belonging to the Divine Name of forty-two letters (Zohar I, 175b).

So long as Joseph was with the Israelites, the Shechinah was with them and the Egyptians did not enslave them. When the day came for him to die though, it is said that Shechinah departed and we know how it was with the people until the advent of Moses. It was Moses who again attracted the Shechinah to Israel. It is said that Shechinah never quitted him from the day of his birth. More even than this, one of the rabbis of the Zohar affirms that the father of Moses was espoused to Shechinah, or alternatively, that both his father and mother aspired towards Shechinah in their hearts during the intercourse which was followed by his conception. This is what the statement already cited meant, that the Shechinah reposed upon the nuptial bed of the parents of Moses (Zohar I, 184a).

## THE ALLEGORY OF SHECHINAH AND THE THREE HUSBANDS

About the nature of the union that subsisted between Moses and Shechinah, we hear that allegorically Shechinah had three husbands, namely, Jacob, Joseph, and Moses. But Jacob abode with his wives on earth and was only united with Shechinah after his death. The espousals of Joseph and Shechinah were not dissolved between them until the bones of Joseph were interred in Palestine. It was for this reason that Moses carried them out of Egypt, and they accompanied the children of Israel during their wandering in the desert. It was somehow by virtue of their presence that Moses was united to Shechinah, so that she dwelt by him, and in connection with this, it is observed that he detached himself from his wife. Though we know well the intimation that the Indwelling Glory (that is, Shechinah) abides only with man, insofar as he is wedded in the ordinary and lawful sense (see this whole narrative in Zohar I, 21b; and I, 133–35).

In another place it is said as we have already mentioned previously, that Moses failed to open the fiftieth Gate of Understanding because he had ceased to live with his wife.

Now the fact that the bones of Jacob were interred in Palestine means that they belonged to the celestial beings. It was otherwise with those of Joseph, and he was still counted as belonging to the earth. The bones are symbols of celestial legions, and these only needed to be interred in Palestine. The Shechinah dwelt with Moses and until his death she fulfilled his desire. After his death, Moses ascended to the degree of the Jubilee, which, as we have seen, is *Binah*, and the Shechinah in transcendence therein. She who was the spouse of Moses was the Shechinah in manifestation; and it is said that after the death of Moses the Shechinah returned to Jacob (Zohar I, 22a).

## A DIVERSIFIED VERSION

In one place the Zohar states the fact of Moses' separation from Zipporah, his wife, and does not count it exactly as righteousness. This point rests seemingly on a Talmudic tradition, recorded in the Tractate *Sabbath* of the Babylonian Talmud, concerning this separation of Moses from Zipporah (Zohar I, 234b).

On the other hand we find another account in opposition to all that which says the Holy One espoused Matrona to Moses and this was the first time that she made contact with the world below. In another place the remark is on the Daughter of God that until she became a Bride no one spoke with her face to face, this being another reference to the espousals of Moses and Shechinah. Before, however, we heard of her espousals to Abraham and to Jacob and of her presence in the world before its creation.

The meaning, of course, is that Shechinah was united with Moses after a new and more intimate manner than had been the case previously, just as God revealed Himself to Moses the lawgiver in another way and in a sense under a new name. The exodus brought about by Moses occasioned, moreover, the manifestation of Shechinah before the people of Israel, she being the pillar of fire by night and then cloud by day. It was through this cloud by day that Moses passed on his ascent of Mount Sinai.

Finally, and most important of all, Moses caused Shechinah to manifest in the Ark of the Covenant over the Mercy Seat, between the figures of the cherubim. The Tabernacle was erected to serve as the residence of Shechinah; and at the moment when it was set up by Moses, there was another erected in the world above. The Tabernacle became also the residence of Metatron, who connects so closely with Shechinah. Metatron was also that cloud which abode on the tent of the congregation, while the glory of the Lord filled the Tabernacle as it is recorded in Exodus 40:34–35 (Zohar II, 145a).

Alternatively, we are told that it was a cloud that rose up to veil Shechinah's presence and dissolved when she went forth. The Zohar calls it smoke because Shechinah was drawn into this world by the fire which burns in the hearts of the patriarchs. God is said to have spoken from the Tabernacle by the intermediation of Shechinah. The Tabernacle itself is called in an aspect of symbolism, Shechinah, much as the tent of Sarah is so called on occasion, because Shechinah the Divine Bride dwelt therein. Shechinah considered as the Tabernacle is in pledge for the sins of man (Zohar I, 76b).

## SHECHINAH IN THE TEMPLE OF SOLOMON

We know by scriptural account that the Shechinah continued to repose in the Temple of Solomon between the wings of the cherubim. She is described in the Zohar as resident throughout the Holy of Holies, yet is connected in a special manner with the western wall of the Temple. The Holy of Holies was guarded moreover by Metatron and was built for the union of the King and Matrona (Zohar II, 16b).

Now then, it is written in Isaiah 33:7: "Those of the country shall utter cries; and the angels of peace shall weep bitterly." This refers to the weeping of the angels when the Sanctuary was destroyed and the Shechinah was exiled into a foreign land. (Note: This is the Zoharic version of the verse in Isaiah. The authorized version is: "Behold their valiant one shall cry without; the ambassadors of peace shall weep bitterly.")

Shechinah underwent transformation and assumed another form than that which she had worn previously. So also the spouse of Shechinah reduced that light which enlightens the world, as it is written: "The sun at his rising shall be covered with darkness and the moon shall give no light" (Isaiah 13:10). This reference is the *vav* of the Sacred Name, Shechinah in manifestation being the second *hai* (Zohar I, 203a).

## SHECHINAH DID NOT FORSAKE ISRAEL IN EXILE

Now, the First Temple was destroyed because light failed therein, but the Second Temple seems never to have had the light. In the Second Temple the Shechinah had no part, though she had followed her people into the exile of Babylon and had helped them to remember Zion by its sad waters (Zohar II, 95b). Those were dark moments that followed the day of the destruction of the First Temple and likewise the destruction of Jerusalem left the nation with a sense of being deeply bereft. This mood and its clouds lifted, however, and deep in their own hearts they knew that they had not been deserted and that Israel was not forsaken by God. Also Shechinah the Betrothed of God was more vitally and efficaciously with them in the exile of Babylon and in the greater exile that followed, than she had been with the patriarchs of old. They knew that the Shechinah was married to them not less closely than to Moses, Prince of Lawgivers. They knew that she was realized better as a presence than when she sat between the cherubim. Ever in *Binah* her celestial fire abode on the Throne of Mercy for those who dwelt in her covenant; and by her mediation a union was still possible as indeed actual between the Holy One and Community of Israel. This is one of the senses in which the souls of Israel are said to be attached to Shechinah (Zohar III, 115b).

## ANOTHER VERSION MORE DESPAIRING

We find, however, also passages of despair in the Zohar. "Israel is dead for the Shechinah, which is above by the destruction of the First Temple it is dead a second time, for the Shechinah which is below by the destruction of the Second Temple" (Zohar I, 26a). And again, "The destruction of the two Temples dried up the sources of the Shechinah above and below" (Zohar I, 255a). Shechinah and Israel are in exile together, in sorrow and in loss together; and the path of penitence trodden by the one is the path of emancipation for both. Meanwhile, "the earth is the Lord's and the fullness thereof, the world and they that dwell therein" (Psalms 24:1). But, the fullness thereof is a reference to Shechinah, as a full moon enlightened over its surface by the sun. She is full also of celestial benefits like a treasury. And in her manifestation to Israel, she is a treasury that belongs to the Lord (Zohar II, 189a).

Moreover, the exile of Shechinah with Israel and her residence among other peoples has its train of extrinsic consequences in the peace and benefits which are enjoyed by the latter. This is the sense in which it is said that other nations have attracted the Shechinah towards them. Indeed, her perfection is throughout the whole earth and her benedictions are over the entire world, for Elokim is a mystery of life and the source of all life. Shechinah never separated from man so long as he observed the commandments of the Divine Law (Zohar I, 84b).

## COUNTERSTATEMENTS

We find however, a number of counterstatements. Every sin committed in public drives away Shechinah from the earth. The generation of Noah sinned in the sight of the whole world and the Shechinah was far from the world. Owing to the wickedness of the world, it was left by Shechinah and was deprived of all defenses and the severity of justice reigns therein. After the guilty have been exterminated, the Shechinah returns (Zohar I, 57b).

## SUMMATION

The wounds of the world and the wound of the congregation of Israel in the world may be wide and deep, but the congregation and the world go on. For ten persons in the House of Prayer constitute the body of Shechinah. In a true sense those ten are never wanting. The elect are everywhere in the true people of Israel, and it is thanks to Israel that Shechinah resides on earth, Israel being the bodyguard.

In thousands and tens of thousands of cases the entire wide world over, it is true and glorious that man acknowledges the kingdom of heaven and submits thereto; it is true that the Shechinah rests upon his head, assisting him in the quality of witness. She testifies before the Sacred Kin how this man proclaims the Divine Unity; or, in other words, that HVYH is Elokim—above and below twice every day. So far as these are concerned, the earth is perfect and all joy is found therein. Thus is Jerusalem rebuilt forever in the heart. The Shechinah goes up into the high mountain and announces its reconstruction to the patriarchs. In these also, she herself is delivered and they dwell together henceforward in the Holy Land. It is a foretaste of that time when all peoples shall enter under the wings of Shechinah, as also of the day to come when evil shall be exterminated entirely. There shall be the same solemnity of festival as when the Holy One, blessed be He, created heaven and earth. Let us therefore join our voices to those of the Masters who say the Covenant with Shechinah will endure forever (Zohar III, 126a).

## ADDITIONAL PARTICULARS OF THE COLLECTION ABOUT SHECHINAH

The Created or External Torah (Law) is called the garment of Shechinah, that is, the vesture of Shechinah as Metatron is also. It follows that Shechinah herself is dwelling within it as, for example, the Traditional Oral and Secret Law, which is not disclosed to the rank and file of believers because of the wickedness of the world. When the Created or External Law is broken below, it is as if the sinner rent or removed the vestments of Shechinah, while alternatively those who observe the commandments have the same merit as if they clothed the Shechinah in garments. The Mishnah is the servant of Shechinah and is also the helpmate for man that is promised in Scripture (Genesis 2:18). The Zohar text states further that the Mishnah was the spouse of Israel during his adolescence and spouse also during his exile, though sometimes for and sometimes against him. During the adolescent period, the Mishnah was preeminent over Matrona (that is, Shechinah), so that the Kin and Matrona were separated from the celestial spouse. It was the servant who took the place of the mistress. The meaning may perhaps be that the literal explanation in its excessive development clouded the spiritual sense of the Holy Doctrine. Who then is the mistress? The answer of the Zohar is that the Divine Oral Law is the image of Elokim; and this we know to be Shechinah (Zohar I, 23a–b).

One practical application of this doctrine concerning Shechinah may be summarized thus. It is prayer that attaches man to Shechinah and as the Holy One is united constantly to her, it follows that prayer attaches man to the Holy One (Zohar I, 24a). All the angels open their wings to receive the Shechinah by prayer and those on earth who wish their prayers to reach Heaven, should unite themselves with Shechinah (Zohar I, 279b). Whereas the gates to the palaces to which prayers ascend commonly have numerous guardians, those of the palaces of Shechinah have none and prayers enter unhindered (Zohar I, 24a).

## REPETITION OF THE THEOSOPHICAL SYMBOLISM AND MYSTICISM

We must not forget Shechinah's incorporation with the Divine Hypostases. We have seen that God and His Shechinah (HVYH—Elokim) are in *Kether* in a state of oneness; they reproduce themselves immediately below as *Abba* and *Eimma* referred to *Chokhmah* and *Binah*. But they are not in a state of separation in these sephiroth, but are one with these in *Kether*. We already made mention of the supernals; it follows that Shechinah is on both sides of the Tree of Life.

While working towards manifestation, Abba and Eimma beat *vav* in *Daath* from which thus extending through six of the lower sephiroth. They also beat the Bride at first implied in *vav*, but afterward repeated and extended with him through the three worlds below *Atziluth*.

In the later kabbalah, we find the conception of *yod* in *Chokhmah*, excogitated as Kin and Father. *Hai* in *Binah* as Queen and Mother; *vav* posited in the six *Briah* sephiroth, and in the six Yetzirah sephiroth, from *chesed* to *yesod* inclusive; but enthroned especially in *Tifereth*; while the *hai* final is in *Malkuth*. All this is based on Zoharic authority.

## TWO ALTERNATIVES CONCERNING THE TREE OF LIFE

We must bear in mind that there are two separate arrangements of the Tree of Life recognized in the text of the Zohar. There is the one we have followed, drawing largely from the Book of Mystery and the three Idras, and there is its alternative, which can be extracted from other parts of the text. According to this alternative, *Abba* and *Eimma* are in *Kether*. *Vav*, who is the Word, is in *Chokhmah*; the Daughter and the Bride is in *Binah*. Now the Divine Name attributed to *Kether* is *Yah*, formed of *yod* and *hai* primal, belonging to the Tetragram. It is said to mean the Unknown God for whom the Name in question is that, which the Propitiatory was for the Tabernacle—a summary of the male world above and the female world below. It is the Name of the Ancient of Ancients. It is the synthesis of all things above and below.

It follows in this alternative arrangement of the Tree of Life that the *vav* is referable to *Chokhmah*, and the *hai* final to *Binah*, who descended to *Malkuth* as the Bride or Shechinah in manifestation. Shechinah is really, therefore, in every part as well as on both sides of the Tree, the mistress of height and depth and over the four quarters of the universe of created things and all that led up thereto.

## SHECHINAH AND THE HOLY SPIRIT PERSONIFICATION

We find many references to the Holy Spirit in the Scriptures. David says, "Take not thy Holy Spirit from me" (Psalms). Isaiah says, that the people of Israel vexed "God's Holy Spirit" (Isaiah

62:10). He also exclaims, "Where is He, that put His Holy Spirit within Him?" meaning Moses. He also adds that the "Spirit of the Lord" caused Moses to rest (Isaiah 63:14). We find also the reference in Numbers: "The Lord put his spirit upon them, and that the Spirit rested upon them and they prophesied" (Numbers 40:29). We find "the Spirit came upon Amasai" (Chronicles I, 12:19). We find that by His spirit God garnished the heavens (Job 24:13); also that "God sends forth His spirit" (Psalms 104:30). Isaiah says the "Lord God and His spirit has sent me" (Isaiah 48:16); and he says also, "the spirit of the Lord God is on me" (Isaiah 61:1). Zechariah mentions, "God sent in His spirit by former prophets" (Zechariah 7:12). These and many more allusions to the Holy Spirit do we find in Holy Scriptures. We must keep them in mind in connection with Zoharic allusions which will follow. We also find a great many references to the Holy Spirit and passages of accounts of the Holy Spirit in both Talmuds (the Babylonian and Jerusalem).

## IS THE HOLY SPIRIT SYNONYMOUS WITH SHECHINAH OR NOT?

The Zohar asks what the significance is of the words: "And the Spirit returns to Elokim who gave it"? (Literally: "And the spirit shall return unto Elokim who gave it" [Ecclesiastes 12:7].) The answer is that one of the words designates Shechinah; that word being *Elokim*, while another word designates the Holy Spirit, the word *Ruach*—"Spirit." It seems therefore, that the Holy Spirit is not Shechinah but is in close connection therewith, like a breath that goes forth and returns (Zohar II, 97b; III, 390). Of course this is the mystic Zoharic interpretation; the plain meaning is that the spirit mentioned in that passage of Scripture is that of man. Again, it is said that when man is circumcised, he is joined to the sacred crown of Shechinah and the Holy Spirit rests upon him (Zohar III, 14b; V, 42).

In still another place of the Zohar three spirits are distinguished: 1) the Spirit below, which is called the Holy Spirit; 2) the Spirit of the Middle Way, which is that of Wisdom and Understanding; 3) the spirit which sounds the trumpet and unites the fire to the water, this being the Superior, concealed and Mysterious Spirit, whereunto are suspended all sacred spirits and all luminous countenances (Zohar III, 26a; V, 73–74). Now it is stated concerning this triad that these three are one in an inward unity, and that they form a holocaust that is the Holy of Holies (Zohar III, 26a). Elsewhere, this is explained to be Shechinah, for she is the sacrifice which God has placed on His right and His left hand and about Him (Zohar I, 24a; I, 149). Again, "she is the sacrifice of the Holy One" and prayer is the storm that in turn is offered to her (Zohar I, 256a; II, 604).

Once more, it is said that when Shechinah resided in the Holy Land, the impure spirit took flight and found refuge in the abyss. This occurred while the Holy Spirit diffused throughout the world, so that the one would seem to be associated closely with the other (that is, Shechinah with the Holy Spirit) (Zohar II, 269a). Again it is said that when Joseph saw Benjamin with the rest of his brethren, he is said by the Zohar to have discerned "by the Holy Spirit, that Benjamin would have part in the Holy Land, and that the Shechinah would reside therein" (Genesis 43:16). This might be interpreted as identification of both as one, or it may tend to the opposite (Zohar I, 202b).

In the last connection, the Holy Spirit is spoken of as the cloud that covered the Tabernacle; but the same cloud had been identified otherwise with Shechinah and with Metatron. These statements, therefore, seem indecisive.

There is, however, one memorable passage, which we must cite in extenso. A tradition tells us, "at the hour when Moses, the true prophet, was about to be born into the world; the Holy One caused the Holy Spirit to come forth from the

Tabernacle elsewhere. That seems to imply the abode of Shechinah as in transcendence. God entrusted her with all power together with five diadems, the splendor of which enlightened a thousand worlds. The Sacred King exalted the Holy Spirit in His palace and set Him above all celestial legions, even as Shechinah is placed above all angels. The angels were in great amazement for they saw that the Holy One was resolved to change the face of the world by the intermediation of the Holy Spirit." They began to inquire concerning Him and were told to prostrate themselves, because He would descend one day among men and the Law—until then hidden—should be revealed. They did homage accordingly, and thereafter the Holy Spirit ascended towards the King. The three letters *mem, shin,* and *hai* belonging to the name of Moses offered their worship also. Then the Holy Spirit, in fulfillment of what had been foretold, came down to earth bearing the arms necessary to smite Pharaoh and his entire country. On reaching this world, *hai* found the Shechinah already here, radiant of aspect and spreading light through all the house (Zohar II, 53b). It will now be observed that the last sentence is an unqualified and conclusive maker of distinction between the two, though in its absence and from what preceded in the extract one might have said that the Holy Spirit was actually a synonym of Shechinah. We hear of nothing more, however, of any office in distinction, for that which henceforward abode with the Lawgiver was not the Holy Spirit, but the Glory of Shechinah, his spiritual spouse, who had been with him from his beginning on earth.

## THE CONTROVERSY CONTINUED— THE HOLY SPIRIT, THE EQUIVALENT OR IDENTICAL OF SHECHINAH

To this single testimony on the negative side of the subject, there is also evidence in the contrary sense.

In the first place, it is said as we have seen already that the Holy Spirit inspired Leah concerning her work in connection with the foundation of the twelve tribes (Zohar I, 157a). But we know otherwise that it is Shechinah who presides over birth. Again in connection with the daughter of Yethro (father-in-law of Moses), the Holy Spirit is affirmed to have been always with Moses (Zohar II, 13b). This we may read in the light of another statement that the Shechinah was associated with the orders which Moses gave to the experts charged with building the Tabernacle, because such work could not be accomplished properly without the inspiration of the Holy Spirit (Zohar II, 179b).

Here again is at least the close connection, in virtue of which one is not without the other. This kind of nearness is illustrated more clearly by another passage which speaks of the day when God shall pour upon us the Holy Spirit of His Shechinah (Zohar III, 219a; V, 555). Once more it is said that the Holy Spirit is called "Zos," being the name which designates the sign of the Sacred Covenant imprinted on man. Zos (this) is in its opposition to *halah* or *hu* (that) which is understood as being of the (more) evil side. The Zohar cites a number of biblical passages. Now, we shall see that this sign is connected especially with Shechinah (Zohar I, 228a).

In the account of Bilaam, it is said that when Bilaam lifted up his eyes, he beheld Shechinah resting with poised wings above the twelve tribes of Israel, and so questioned how he could prevail against them (Numbers 24:2). He saw that the Holy Spirit was thus their stay and their protection. It is at the end of the Zohar, that we obtain a still more decisive voice on the affirmative side. The question there is one of alleged or suggested criminal relations between Esther and Achushveirush, (King Xerxes) which are there characterized as slander. The Zohar adds, "she was clothed with the Holy Spirit," as it is written, "Esther put on her royal apparel" (Esther 5:1).

The passage renders it "Esther clothed herself with royalty." The immediate interpretation of the Zohar follows thus: "The Holy Spirit is the Shechinah with which Esther clothed herself" (Zohar III, 275b). The great text adds there: "Woe unto those who feed upon the husk of the Law [Torah] while the grain of wheat is the mystical sense." From these references it would appear that the Holy Spirit is the equivalent of Shechinah or even identical with Shechinah, so that we might say of the Holy Spirit, this is Shechinah.

When then the Holy Spirit is allocated to *Binah*, the meaning is that Shechinah is also referred thereto. To that we must conclude the authority of the text of the Zohar itself in repeating at this point: "from the constant and ardent love of *hai* in *Binah*, for *yod* in *Chokhmah*, there issues *vav* in *Daath*, conceived of *hai*, by which also it is nourished" (Zohar III, 77b). But *vav* came into the world with a twin bearing the name of Grace, which is *Chesed*, because Grace is Chesed (mercy). The two took root on earth and constituted the *hai* final, that is to say, in *Malkuth*, because the male is not without the female, either above or below. Thus was *vav* united to the *hai* final. But in the completion, the harmony and the perfection of the Divine Name, letter by letter and letter within letter, all these are one at the root. There must be no separation proclaimed. But *yod*, *hai*, *vav*, and *hai* bear only witness to His unity. The full knowledge and understanding of this is limited only to but a few of the elect.

## THE INDWELLING GLORY, TERMED SHECHINAH, IN SCRIPTURE AND IN THE TEXT OF THE ZOHAR

We know that the Shechinah dwelt between the cherubim in the Tabernacle or ark of Moses. Now, the cherubim are said to have been male and female types in the sanctuary of Israel, of things manifested on earth, as types in their turn, of the union that is above. In Scripture we read, "Ye are children unto the Lord your God" (Deuteronomy 20). When we speak of God's fatherhood, He being our heavenly Father, we also find many statements making mention of Shechinah's divine motherhood, she being our divine Mother in the symbolism of this analogy. The Shechinah abides in the House of Prayer, of prayer in the stillness of unexpressed thought mentioned in the Zohar, for she is the Indwelling Glory. It is said that the Shechinah dwells in man, being in the hearts of those who seek after good works zealously. And more definitely it is said that man is the House of Shechinah (Zohar I, 166a).

Shechinah begins to inhabit man when man makes a firm effort towards self-amendment, for by such turning the Shechinah is drawn towards him. And to this condition are applied the words: "I am my beloved's, and his desire is toward me" (Song of Solomon 7:10). Those with whom she dwells are those who are humbled and even broken by suffering. Yet does she reign only where there is joy rather than sadness in spite of the trials and the suffering. The suffering in question is more especially that of which the root or cause is in love of the Divine: these are the brothers of Shechinah (Zohar I, 88b). Again it is said that the work of Shechinah below is comparable to that which the soul accomplishes in the body. Moreover, it is of the same order. Symbolically speaking, if the sacred body of man were termed Tabernacle, Shechinah is termed the soul of the Tabernacle (Zohar I, 181a).

Whosoever wrongs a poor person is guilty of wrong to Shechinah, because she is the protectress of the poor (Zohar II, 86b).

The point and center of the whole subject of the Indwelling Glory: Shechinah, is declared everywhere, but everywhere also is concealed. The aspect of its presentation is amidst great hiddenness. The Mystery of Sex is tied in with the Mystery of Shechinah. The entrance of the High Priest into the Holy of Holies once yearly on the Day of Atonement belongs to those mysteries, since the hour of entrance is when the Sacred King is united to Matrona (Zohar III, 66b).

The Zohar points out to us that the union of male and female is modesty, and title to behold the face of Shechinah is one of purity. It seems true to say that she is the Law of the Mystery. The Zohar then quotes concerning her: "When thou goes, it shall lead thee; when thou sleepest it shall keep thee; and when thou awakest, it shall talk with thee" (Zohar III, 145b). The study of this Law is life eternal, and as a law it implies also a covenant, and Joseph is said to be the image of this covenant, because of his continence in respect of the wife of Potiphar (Zohar I, 175b).

## THE SIN CAUSING THE EXILE

It is specified that Shechinah dwelt with Israel prior to the captivity in Babylon, and the sin which brought about this exile was equivalent to the uncovering of the hiddenness of Shechinah. We can understand the meaning by assuming that Shechinah in this connection signifies the Secret Doctrine insofar as it was a mystery of sex. The Zohar goes on particularizing that the sins were crimes of incest as some illegal and reprobate application of the six doctrines in accordance with the hermeneutics of the Zohar. Such were also the views of the Babylonian Talmud (Zohar I, 27b). Spiritually, this is to be understood as an assault on Shechinah, who is in a sense the sister of all men.

## STILL OTHER ASPECTS OF SHECHINAH

It is said further that the mystery of Shechinah comprises all women, and this is why she does not abide except with him who is united to a woman. She is fixed definitely in the house of man when he marries. This is why the *hai* and the *vav* follow each other in the alphabet, *vav* being the symbol of the male and the *hai* of the female principle. Husband and wife are one, and a ray of celestial grace covers them. It descends from *Chokhmah,* penetrates the male principle, and the latter communicates it to the female. And it is in this sense that Shechinah's shame is the defiled body of man, and this is how she is weighted by the sin of Israel. She is a virgin betrothed to the Middle Pillar. She passes ever into espousals below— as she is ever in espousals above—for the fulfillment of herself in humanity and of all humanity in her. The evidence is that when there is a just man on earth, the Shechinah cleaves to him and does not leave him henceforth. In one of her aspects she is the symbol of stainless womanhood (Zohar I, 228b).

## SHECHINAH IN THE SONG OF SONGS

The object of the above is to indicate that the dwelling of Shechinah in the house of those who are married is to bring about the descent of souls to animate children under the presidency of Shechinah (Zohar I, 122a).

Another instance to that purpose is the statement that on the day that the Song of Songs of Solomon was revealed below, the Shechinah descended quasi, as if for the first time, though we know that the Shechinah had been with man from the beginning and had shared in the whole of creation. The authority for the statement is in I Kings 7:11: "So that the priests could not stand to minister, because of the cloud; for the Glory of the Lord had filled the house of the Lord" (Zohar II, 143b).

The object of this statement, however, is to show that this glorious canticle is this world's history of Shechinah in man, the beginning and end of all, of all that belongs to the union, the mystery of the lover and the beloved. Throughout the ages of election, the free will inherent only among mortals. It is the summary of Holy Scripture. It is the work of creation, the mystery of the patriarchs, the exile in Egypt, the exodus of Israel, the Decalogue and manifestation on Sinai. It is the emblem of all events during the sojourn in the Holy Land and so forward to the building of the Holy Temple.

It is also a summary of the mystery contained in the Sacred and Supreme Name, of the dispersal of Israel through the nations, of its deliverance to come, the resurrection of the dead and the events leading up to that day which is called the Sabbath of the Lord. It is the story of Shechinah; it contains all that has been, is, and ever shall be, from the first verse, concerning the kisses of His mouth to the last rapture on the mountain of spices (Zohar II, 144b).

## OF COMMUNION

Now, it is said that there is desire on part of man to be united with the Mother in transcendence, as well as with the Mother below; to attain her by perfection and to be blessed on account of her (the meaning being integration) by the law of correspondences of the Zohar. This, a desire for divine communion, because HVYH is Elokim. The Zohar adds elsewhere that the memorable words "I am that I am" signify in their inward sense: "I, the Holy One, blessed be He, am, and the Shechinah" (Zohar I, 23a).

It is certain that the state of communion is deeper than the state of vision and differs generically therefrom. Attainment of such Divine Communion is rare in that proper sense of the term and very difficult, according to the Zohar. But it is implied in its implicit sense in many places, for we have seen that Shechinah is within. It is, however, more often vision which is promised to the worthy in the world beyond, to gaze upon the face of Shechinah. It is a substituted state of communion and to be entitled to it must be earned in this life by the following of the path of purity (Zohar II, 40b).

## OF SPIRITUAL COMMUNION WITH SHECHINAH

It is affirmed in reference to this that those only who quit the lower world in the grace of Shechinah are judged worthy of eternal life (compare also Tract. *Ketuboth* 111b). So also there are some who do not die as men die commonly but are ravished by the attraction which Shechinah exercises on their souls. The Mother in transcendence is, however, as the Mother below, and spiritual communion with her is so far as a worthy man has become a house or abode by attaching himself to the female (in marriage); it is then that the Divine Mother pours down her blessings on both (Zohar I, 82a). There, then, in the true sense of this term, is the spiritual common below for the sons of the Divine Secret Doctrine with Shechinah. The manner of realization of her presence is by spiritual apprehension only (ibid.). During their deep studies they are conscious then of the presence of Shechinah. It is usually the case while they study the hidden divine teaching of the Law (Zohar II, 166a). One required condition was to be married and united to a woman below. Another condition was that the master of this Hidden Doctrine of Law must watch over all his actions in every phase of life; otherwise he might be separated from the spiritual companionship of the Shechinah, putting a stop to the communion and rendering himself an incomplete being (Zohar I, 50a). The Master of the Secret Doctrine prayed always to the Holy One to preserve him in this holy state (Zohar I, 49a).

We have now considered the Indwelling Glory, Shechinah, in the light of all her attributes. We may call attention to the personifications of high, lofty wisdom in the books of King Solomon; the titles and offices of the Hebrew

*Chokhmah* there. We have seen Shechinah as the president of the Mystery of Sex and as the Holy Guide of Jewry. The Secret Holy Doctrine in Israel encompasses therefore many mysteries, aside from that of Shechinah and of sex, as, for instance, eschatology and the parts of the soul of man and many others with which we have dealt already at their value.

CHAPTER TWO

# The Mystery of Sex and of the Generation of Souls

In this division, I am upon a part of a task which is at once most difficult and most important. The simplest way is to proceed from small beginnings below and thence work upward to the highest point. I will cite in the first place certain great axioms proclaimed on the authority of the masters on this subject.

It is testified that the union of the male and female must be a perfect union in the Mystery of Faith. Another testimony states that the title to behold the face of Shechinah is one of purity; the scholium of which is that modesty is the union of the male and female, that is, concealment. It may be remembered that the most cryptic book in the Zohar containing the mysteries of the Divine is called the Book of Concealment (or Modesty) (Zohar I, 101b). Man is perfect only when he comprises male and female; it is then that he fears sins and the title of modest is conferred upon him (Zohar III, 145b).

## THE COMPLETE MAN

This being so, we may consider what is said on the subject of espousals, as these are known on earth. There is one definition that marriage is the union of the Sacred Name here below and its completion in each person (Zohar III, 7a). The thesis appertaining thereto is that circumcision is the symbol of all purity in sexual intercourse. On this account, Israel is placed in purity as a starting point and enters under the wings of Shechinah. Circumcision is the sacred sign of the covenant that constitutes the root matter of the Sacred Name and of the Mystery of Faith. As the sun enlightens the world, so the sacred sign of the covenant enlightens the body; as a buckler protects man, so does this. No evil spirit can approach him who preserves it in purity. But, as the advantage is greater with which the children of Israel begin their earthly life, so is the responsibility greater if they make the covenant of no effect in their own persons (Zohar I, Appendix III, Secrets of the Law; also I, 95a).

Now then, the Sacred Name is never attached to an incomplete man, one who is unmarried or who dies without issue. Such a man does not penetrate after death into the vestibule of Paradise on account of his incompleteness. He is like a tree that is rooted up and must be planted anew—that is to say, he must suffer rebirth as we have seen in order that the Sacred Name may be completed in all directions. The command to increase and multiply, which means the procreation and engendering of children, is to spread the reliance of the Sacred Name in every direction by collecting spirits and souls, which constitute the glory of the Holy One above and below. Whosoever fails to apply himself to the fulfillment of this command, diminishes the figure of his Master and prevents it descending here below; for man was made male and female in the likeness of Elokim (Zohar I, 48b).

It is said also that the paucity in the descent of souls is the reason why Shechinah does not come down into this world (Zohar I, 165a). The reference is, of course, to manifestation and not to immanence, for the presence of the Indwelling Glory throughout the whole creation is well affirmed, as we have seen. She stands at the door and knocks, but those who should welcome her in keep fast their precincts and lock their portals (ibid.). God blessed Adam and Eve because they were made together, male and female, and blessings are found only where male and female were united for the fulfillment of the purpose of creation, which, according to the counsel of Elokim, was to multiply and replenish the earth. It was not good for man to be alone, because this end was in a state of frustration. At first Adam and Eve, as male and female, were side by side, indicating they were not in a marital state. Afterward, they were face to face, signifying the fulfillment of the precept (Zohar I, 165a).

## THE NUPTIAL STATE

The doctrine was that no marriage is made on earth before it is proclaimed in heaven, and that the Holy One accomplishes unions in the world above before the descent of souls on earth (Zohar I, 229a). In this particular sense it is held that the union here below between husband and wife implies the sanctity and necessity of the act, since the union is the work of the Holy One, as well as from other considerations. The Divine overshadowing of the act is indicated by the statement in Genesis that man was formed in the image of God, and so man is formed below on the model of that which is above (Zohar I, 186b). This compares also with the statement in Numbers (23:10): "Or numbered the stock of Israel," which is held in Talmud to have the same meaning.

It follows that he who suffers his fount to fail and produces no fruits here, to use Zoharic terminology, whether because he will not take a wife, his wife is barren, or he abides with her in a way that is against nature, commits an irreparable crime (ibid.).

The words in Psalms 127:2: "It is vain . . . to sit up late," are words that designate those who do not marry until an advanced age, for it is woman who constitutes the repose of man; hereof is the peace of espousals (Zohar I, 187a). It is added that man shall participate in the world to come because he has entered during his life into the joy of living honorably with his wife. The reason is that the soul as well as the body shares in the unseparable esoteric grade from which children are engendered (Zohar I, 90b). It is said on the authority of Rabbi Eliezer, son of Rabbi Shimon, that the *hai* is the repose of beings above and below; above being the rest of the Shechinah in transcendence and below of the Shechinah in manifestation.

## THE MYSTERY OF PURIFICATION AND SANCTIFICATION IN MARRIAGE

The thesis is that whoever sanctifies himself at the moment of the practice of intercourse shall have children who will not fear the tempter spirit. Another consequence of such a holy marriage is the raising of the union itself into a spiritual degree; from the mode of Nature into the mode of Grace. It is added that herein the Holy One exercises such providence over man, that he may not be lost in the world to come. But the fulfillment of a particular precept is the condition attaching hereto and this is the raising of the heart and mind on the part of the lover and beloved to the most holy Shechinah, the glory which indwells and cohabits during this external act (Zohar I, 50a). Holiness enters then the body of the woman (Zohar II, 101b).

The statement in the Zohar of the mystery, in words of veiled meaning, intimates what can be accomplished in nuptials through the purification of body and mind towards the union of souls, so that two spirits are melted together and are interchanged constantly between body and body. The sexes are then interchanged above in a sense, as the sex of Metatron is said to be transformed instantaneously before the veil of palms and pomegranates, on the threshold of the inmost shrine, in the supernals. In the indistinguishable state that arises it may be said almost that the male is with the female, neither male nor female; at least they are both or either.

So is man affirmed to be composed of the world above which is male and of the female world below. The same is true of woman (Zohar II, 173b).

The Zohar quotes the words of the Song of Solomon 1:2: "Thy love is better than wine," also another rendition reads: "Thy breasts are better than wine." It refers to that wine, says the Zohar, which provokes joy and desire. Now seeing that all things are formed above according to a pattern which is reproduced faithfully below, it is held to follow that when desire awaked beneath, it awakens also on high in an alternative manner of language (Zohar I, 70a–b). Herein lies the sanctity of espousals on earth, and from here depends the need for exulting that sanctity and all that belongs to espousals into the highest grade.

## THE SECRET OF MATRIMONIAL UNION

There are, however, two classes whose respective duties differ with the degrees of their election. There are those who are termed ordinary mortals, meaning the rank and file of the people of Israel. But there are also the sons of the Secret Holy Doctrine, chosen among the chosen out of thousands. The counsel imposed on the first class is to sanctify their conjugal relations in respect of the time thereof which is fixed at midnight or forward from that hour. The reason is that God descends then into Paradise and the offices of sanctity are operating in the plenary sense. But this is also the time when the counsel is to the sons of the Secret Doctrine, that they should arise for the study of the Divine Doctrine (Torah), for union thereby with the community of Israel above, and for the praise of the Sacred Name of God (Zohar III, 81a). The sons of the Holy Doctrine are described as reserving conjugal relations for the night of the Sabbath, being the moment when the Holy One is united to the community of Israel. For God is one and as such it is agreeable to Him that He should be concerned with a single people. The question arises as to when man may be called one; the answer is that this comes about when the male is united to the female in a holy purpose. It is then that man is complete, is one, and is without blemish (Zohar I, 14a–b).

It is of this that the man and the woman must think at the moment of their union. It is in uniting bodies and souls that the two become one; man in particular is termed one and perfect. He draws down the Holy Spirit upon him and is called the son of the Holy One blessed be He (Zohar I, 81b).

We now see that beyond that process indicated by Genesis 2:24 "And they shall be one flesh" there is another and higher process in the fulfillment of which it is possible they shall be one soul. The following curious notion should be noted in this connection. It is affirmed that the words "In the beginning God created" (Genesis 1:1) conceal the same mystery as those other words, "And the rib which the Lord God had taken from man, made He a woman" (Genesis 2:22). In the words, "God created the heaven" (ibid. 1:1), the two last words conceal the same mystery as the words: "And brought her unto the man" (ibid. 2:23). All designate "the earth of life" (Zohar I, 50b). But it is said also that the words "the heaven" signify Shechinah above while the words "and the earth" denote Shechinah below, whose union shall be as perfect, on a glorious day to come, as the union of the male and female.

Then again, according to Rabbi Shimon, the relations of the Patriarchs with their wives were actuated by a supreme mystery. So long as Jacob was unmarried, God did not manifest to him clearly, and this mystery is familiar to those who are acquainted with the ways of the Divine Teachings (Torah). After marriage, Jacob arrived at the perfection that is below, and God manifested to him clearly. For, as intimated already, Supreme Wisdom is a Mystery of Sex.

Now we must consider another development curiously arising. The principle is that the male must be always joined to the female for the Shechinah ever to be with him. All holiness might be practiced, the Secret Doctrine might be studied by night and by day, and the illuminations thereof might overflow the intellectual part, but failing fulfillment of this radical counsel, a man was not on the way that leads into true life. He was in that condition in which "it is not good to be" alone, like Adam in the Garden as mentioned in Genesis 2:18.

But there seemed to be a certain dispensation for the students of the Secret Doctrine in respect to the fruit of intercourse. On the assumption that there was no issue, they appear to have been spared the penalty of return into incarnation. There were those during the Middle Ages who had the precept at heart and were therefore complete men by their union with woman on earth. They were real sons of Israel and true students of the Doctrine; but they were also travelers in search of wisdom and they were also men of affairs, workers in the vineyard of this world as well as in the Garden of God. The Zohar is full of their little journeys in the early beginnings of the Middle Ages. These journeys were taken, as far as possible, one with another that the Secret Doctrine might be studied on the way, and that the presence of Shechinah might be sacred thus for their consolation, protection, and instruction as they fared forward. Great adventures befell them in the sense of the Mysteries of the Doctrine; for strange people went about in those days, carrying unknown to one another the treasures of hidden knowledge. It seemed like an unincorporated fraternity. Initiation was by segregating principle, not by communication from a common center of knowledge. At times the son of an instructed great doctor might have advanced a great distance unknown to others. Also occasionally, an isolated student entered by his own reflections, and by grace descending into the heart, into a golden chain of tradition, so that he was not less in an illuminated state than if he had sat at the feet of Rabbi Shimon through the days and the years.

Now, journeys in search of wisdom or in the prosecution of business meant separation from the wife of the student's or the scholar's household, and this would seem at first sight to involve separation from Shechinah. Similarly, we find that the high priest had to be a man, completed and in a sense made perfect by union with a wife, before he could offer sacrifice on the Day of Atonement. So as to remove this difficulty, it was held as necessary that the scholar or student would pray the Holy One before starting the journey, and that He should watch over all his actions during the period of absence from home. He would not be separated then from the Shechinah, and he would not be rendered an incomplete being. This counsel should prevail not only abroad but also at home and should become an inculcated precept of life.

Also, concerning the Great Presence, it postulates the dwelling of Shechinah with man. It is said elsewhere, that Shechinah never separates from man so long as he observes the commandments of the Law (the Divine Doctrine).

Authority for this statement are the following verses: "Behold, I send an angel before thee, to keep thee in the way" Exodus 23:20; also: "I will send an angel before thee" (ibid. 23:2). This is held in the Zohar to be the Liberating Angel to whom Jacob made allusion (Genesis 48:16), who receives blessings from above and distributes them below.

It was obviously and of course only in an inward sense that the Shechinah (Indwelling Glory) accompanied the Sons of the Secret Doctrine in their recurring voyages and ventures. She was their overshadowing grace and power, realized spiritually. We find the Zohar teaching us comprehensively and precisely, in the name of Rabbi Shimon, that it is not in virtue of man being side by side with the woman that Shechinah abode with man, for contiguity is not union.

Nonetheless, after days and weeks of travel when the Son of Divine Doctrine returns to his home, he must procure nuptial gratification to the wife of his heart; seeing that he has had the advantage of union in his absence with Shechinah on high. (In the deepest understanding of the subject one belongs to the other; that which is without as that which is within. All the correspondences being aspects of one thing, seen and done upon different places of being.)

There is also a Talmudic authority that conjugal relations on returning from a journey constitute a good work. There is also a Zoharic statement that every pleasure resulting from a good work is shared by Shechinah, for she who suffers with Israel enters into joy with him. Furthermore, it is in such pleasure that the peace of the house is maintained. The Scriptural authority obtained is contained in words of Job 5:24: "Thou shalt know that thy tabernacle shall be in peace; and thou shalt visit thy habitation, and shalt not sin." To abstain from conjugal relations in such a case would be indeed sinful, depreciating the work of the companion on high who cleaves to the man, but thanks only to his own union with his wife. If, subsequently, there be fruit of this intercourse, the Heavenly Companion will provide a holy soul for the newborn child; the Shechinah being that covenant which is termed Covenant of the Holy One. The rule on return from a journey must be fulfilled; therefore, with the same zeal, as the ordinance suggested by the wise that the conjugal experience take place on the night of the Sabbath, unless of course, there are special reasons to engage at other times as well.

## COMMUNION BETWEEN MAN AND SHECHINAH VIA MARRIAGE

Finally, and this has been cited already as a unique counsel: when man has in view the Shechinah at the moment of his conjugal relations, the pleasure that he experiences is a meritorious work. The reason as explained is that the union below is an image of the union that is above. It is part of the contemplation of the higher and absent beauty, in union with that beauty, which, albeit lower, is present, manifest, and is or may become holy. It is also a memorial that the union, which is of time, may attain a part or has a part in the union which is eternal, described as the contemplation of the beauty of the Shechinah. The mystery of the whole subject is the dogma that the Mother in transcendence abides with the male only insofar as he has constituted himself a house by his attachment to the female. There must be a local habitation, a union below, to offer a point of contact with the union that is on high; and then the Divine Mother pours down her blessings therefrom—that is to say, a male and female in equal measures. It is said also that Shechinah does the will of the master of the house, the reference being to Moses.

So it is mysteriously said that the male below is said to be encompassed by two females, and all the ways of blessing in the two worlds are open before him. He reads the Secret Doctrine in the womanhood on earth, and it is read to him by her, who is between the Pillars of the Eternal Temple, with the Book of the Sacred Law lying open on her sacred knees. Compare it with the popular saying: the Holy Torah is the betrothed Bride of the Congregation of Jacob.

The illustration involved, as a whole, is that man in his union with woman becomes a house in which the Divine Presence can dwell. Here is another excellent illustration, admirable in its symbolism, namely, the eye of man is said to be an image of the world. The white of the eye is an image of the great ocean by which earth is encompassed. Earth itself is represented by the internal circle of the eye. Within this is another circle, and it is called the image of Jerusalem, center of the whole world. Finally, there is the pupil, which corresponds to Zion, and this is the abode of Shechinah.

So also, there are the arts of human personality, physical and mental parts, and there is the conscious center, wherein is the Divine Presence awaiting realization with us. The thesis being that marriage is a condition of realization.

The counsel concerning the Sabbath day and the relation therein offers also proof to the spirits of the evil side, respecting the superiority of those on the side of goodness, meaning mankind, who being provided with bodies can fulfill the duties of procreation. Whosoever has intercourse with his spouse on that day must obtain her consent beforehand with words of affection and tenderness. Failing consent, he should proceed no further, for the act of union must be willing and not constrained. Nuptial intercourse is interdicted during the day, because of the words in Genesis 28:2: "And he lighted upon a certain place, and tarried there all night, because the sun was set."

In view of the sanctity that the Zohar attributes to the sex act under the obedience of purity, which is marriage, there was a prohibition of its performance in complete nudity. Those who ignore it are subject to the visitation of demons and will produce epileptic children, obsessed by Lilith. This is the case more especially if the light of a lamp is used. The Talmud also concurs in these statements.

It is affirmed that blessed are those who sanctify the Sabbath day by intercourse with their wives. For the sons of the Doctrine it is a work consecrated to the Holy One, because the union of Matrona with the heavenly King has for its object to send down holy souls into this world. The colleagues on earth seek to attract these sacred souls into their own children. The theory of conception is that the Holy One and His Shechinah furnish the soul, while the father and mother provide the body between them. Heaven, earth, and all the stars of heaven are considered as being associated in the formation, together with the angels.

## HOLY SOULS WHICH CAN BECOME INCARNATE IN JEWRY

By the desire which the man experiences for the woman and the woman for the man at the moment of their intercourse, their seeds are interblended and produce a child which is said to have two figures, one within the other. The child in this way draws life from father and mother, and this is why there should be some kind of sanctification for all classes at the moment of conjugal union, so that the child about to be born may be perfect and complete in figure. The secret of Divine generation is, however, a secret of the Doctrine, and is reserved for the initiated therein. It is apparently they alone who draw down the holy souls which are the fruits of the union between God and His Shechinah. There are various kinds of generations of souls, however, some being superior to others. When the desire, apparently of ordinary man, provokes in an equal degree the desire of the male soul for the female soul, the child born of this union will have a soul superior to that of other men. Its birth has come about by desire of the Tree of Life.

This implies that the frigid, uninspired unions of proforma marriages are useless for the higher purposes; there must be mutual equilibrated desire springing up from love, and such desire must be transmuted by the tincture of Divine Aspirations.

In conclusion, it is affirmed that the sons of the Doctrine, knowing the mysteries of the Doctrine, turned all their thoughts to God and their children were called sons of the

King. But such cleaving is in virtue of love uplifted through all the worlds. Those whose marital relations were not encompassed with sanctity caused a breach in the world above.

It is said also that woman is the image of the altar (it would follow in symbolism that man should consider himself the priest making oblations). It is said further in this connection that divorce makes a breach in the altar, in the altar below because there is separation between male and female, and in the altar above by the hypothesis of correspondences between things above and below.

## MYSTERY OF ESPOUSALS AND THE GREAT MYSTERY OF FAITH

Earthly espousals are the part in manifestation of that which is called so frequently the Mystery of Faith. In the words "Male and female created He them" (Genesis 1:27), there is expressed the Supreme Mystery which constitutes the glory of God as inaccessible to human intelligence and as the object of faith. By this mystery was man created as also the heaven and the earth (Zohar I, 55b). It is inferred that every figure which does not represent male and female has no likeness to the heavenly figure. This is why Scripture says in Genesis 5:2: "God, blessed them and called their name Adam in the day when they were created" ( Zohar I, 55b). Compare also Genesis 1:27: "And God created man in His image, in the image of God created He him, male and female created He them."

The scriptural authority for the affirmation that there is a Mystery of Faith is drawn from several sources in the Zohar, all, however, of cryptic origin and mysterious. Here we shall group a few of them together.

1. Isaiah 25:1, "Lord, Thou art my God; I will exalt thee. I will praise Thy Name, for Thou hast done wonderful things. Thy counsels of old are faithfulness and truth."

2. Genesis 25:26, "And his hand took hold on Esau's heel" (Zohar I, 199a).

3. Genesis 2:1, "Thus the heavens and the earth were finished and all the host of them," et sequelae. This is said to be the Great Mystery.

4. Exodus 15:1, "I will sing unto the Lord, for He has triumphed gloriously; the horse and his rider has He thrown into the sea," et sequelae.

The intimations of the Zohar there seem designed to cover up and to hide the inner meaning of the passages cited. The Mystery is said to consist in the examination of good and evil, and then in cleaving to the good (Zohar I, 34a). It is said again to be contained in the fact, that Zion constitutes the foundation and beauty of the world, and that the world draws its nourishment therefrom. There is Zion, which is severity and there is Jerusalem, which is mercy; but the two are one (Zohar I, 206b).

In comment thereon we may say that goodness and mercy are on the male side of the sephirotic tree, while evil and severity are on the female side. These two must be united by the Middle Pillar, and this is entering under the wings of Shechinah. When they are thus joined, goodness, joy, and beauty are found everywhere.

## THE FORTY-NINE GATES OF UNDERSTANDING—THE GATES OF COMPASSION AND THEIR ESOTERIC METAPHYSICS

Now, we must go further and acquaint ourselves with a few less obdurate extracts. There are forty-nine Gates of Compassion which connect with the mystery of the perfect man, composed of male and female and with the Mystery of Faith (Zohar

I, 139b). These are the Gates of Understanding referable to *Binah*, wherein dwells the Spouse in the Transcendence, who is Shechinah. But there is a fiftieth Gate, which Moses did not open. This Gate is the Mystery of Espousals in the Divine World (Zohar I, 139b).

At this point it is desirable to collect the references to the Gates (which occur throughout the text of the Zohar) and their subjects in summary.

1. It is through fifty openings of the mysterious heavenly palaces that the world of *yod*, which is in *Chokhmah*, penetrates to the *hai* (in *Binah*) (Zohar I, 13b).

2. There is one gate which is the synthesis of all gates and one degree which is the synthesis of all degrees; by this Gate of Degree do we enter into the Glory of the Holy One (Zohar I, 103b).

3. This gate is unknown because Israel is in exile, and the result is that all the gates are shut.

4. The fifty Gates of Understanding are, or may become, salvation for the whole world (Zohar I, 13b; also Appendix I, omissions 260a).

5. The gates emanate from or are referable to the side of severity (Zohar I, 13b).

6. It is owing to the evil Samael that Moses could enter only forty-nine of the fifty Gates of *Binah* (Zohar II, 115a).

7. The union of the Father and the Mother produced five lights, which in their turn gave birth to the fifty Gates of Supreme Lights (Zohar II, 115a; Assembly of the Sanctuary, 122b–123a).

8. The light of the Master above reaches us by fifty gates (Zohar I, 137b).

9. He who devotes himself to the study of the Law opens the fifty Gates of Binah, which correspond to the *yod*, multiplied by the *hai* (Zohar III, 216a).

10. By such multiplication Moses attained these gates (Zohar III, 223b).

11. In the absence of these gates, Israel would have remained always in the bondage of Egypt. They are in the region called the Supreme Mother, who gives power to the Mother below (Zohar III, 262a). It becomes clear that the Zoharic Gates of Compassion belong to another mode of understanding than the one summarized in Section V.

## THE SEVEN DEGREES AND THE MYSTERY OF PERFECT FAITH

Another reference tells us that there are Seven Degrees above which are superior to all others, and they constitute the Mystery of Perfect Faith (Zohar I, 204b). The attachment of Israel to the good side is attachment to the Supreme Mystery, the Mystery of Faith, so Israel is one therewith.

We have already learned that the Mystery of Faith is also a Sex Mystery. It follows therefore that the practice of perfection therein, on the terms already indicated, should give a title to the knowledge of these degrees, and thereby the Mystery of Faith would pass into a Mystery of Experience. One might surmise that these seven Degrees are probably identical with the seven firmaments, the purpose of which are, as we are told elsewhere, to reveal the Mystery of Faith. They are also called "Seven Palaces" (see Section IV) (Zohar I, 205a). There is a kingdom to come after that which is symbolically termed the end of the world; it is a sacred region and this also is said to constitute the Mystery of Faith. We have also heard otherwise that the advent of Messiah means perfect conformity in the nuptial state, above as well as below. The Feast of the Paschal Lamb is also the containment of the Mystery of Faith (Zohar II, 134a–b).

Most of that which these citations tell us is: that there is a Mystery of Faith, and that it is concerned with the union of male and female. By the collation of some final references, we shall take the question one step further. The phylacteries with straps on head and arm designate the Supreme Mystery, because God is found in that man who wears them (Deuteronomy 11:18). It is the Supreme Mystery of Faith (Zohar I, 141a). Another image of the Mystery of Faith is the image of a spring that flows unfailingly. In this connection we shall remember the sex interpretation placed on the river which comes forth from Eden, to water the Garden and which was afterwards parted and became into four heads (Genesis 2:10). A well fed by a spring also symbolizes the Mystery of Faith, because it symbolizes the union of male and female (Zohar I, 141b). Here we ought to remember the verses in the Song of Solomon, the Song of Songs, Chapters 4, 12, and 15: "the fountain of Gardens . . . the Garden enclosed . . . is my sister, my spouse; the fountain sealed . . . the well of living waters and streams from Lebanon." Whoever contemplates such a well is said to contemplate the Mystery of Faith (Zohar I, 141b). Finally, the moon is said to be another image of the Mystery of Faith; and we know that this luminary is a symbol of Shechinah (Zohar I, 142a–b).

## OTHER REFERENCES AND IMPLICATIONS OF THE MYSTERY OF FAITH

We have by no means exhausted the references to the Mystery of Faith; we shall make further selections as follows:

1. That the Supreme Mystery that is synonymous with the Mystery of Faith is the Law of the whole world, is taught in the words; "These are the three sons of Noah: and of them was the whole earth overspread" (Genesis

9:19). The Zohar indicates that the event in question marked a new epoch in the mode of generation (Zohar I, 73a).

2. Jacob represents the Mystery of Faith (Zohar I, 138b).

3. Every word in Scripture conceals the Supreme Mystery of Faith, because all the words of the Holy One are based on equity and truth (Zohar I, 142a).

4. The Supreme Wisdom is by implication the Mystery of Sex (Zohar I, 150b).

5. The Mystery of Faith and all celestial sanctities emanate from the union of male and female principles (Zohar I, 160a).

6. One Mystery of Supreme Wisdom is, that the world's salvation must issue from the union of Judah and Tamar, as if there were a secret sanctuary somewhere in the world, which over-watched that true legitimacy belonging to the line of David.

7. The union of the worlds above and below is of the Mystery of Faith.

8. The Supreme Mystery concealed in the Law is the Secret of the Lord, and this is a secret of the Holy Covenant.

9. The Cup of Blessing comprises the Mystery of Faith, which embraces the four quarters and the Sacred Throne.

10. The Sacred Reign to come constitutes the Mystery of Faith (meaning union sanctified everywhere).

11. The Mystery of Faith is to know the HVYH is Elokim.

The two collections of references are admittedly obscure and call for considerable explanations. Others not quoted are even more so. But the nature of the Supreme Mystery of Faith becomes nonetheless clear to us. But the Zohar intends to communicate under this often used formula only a broad and general definition of what is symbolized and of the nature of the Mystery which is qualified as supreme and characterized as that of Faith.

## THE HIGHER EDEN RIVER, RIVER OF THE LIFE AND OF SOULS

We must therefore again go further to find the key to the matter before us. We will start by the collation of two passages, widely separated from each other and of another form of symbolism.

It is affirmed in the Zohar, Part I, 95a, as we have seen before that when the *yod* is united to the *hai*, they give birth to that river, concerning which it is said: "And a river went forth from Eden to water the Garden" (Genesis 2:10). Another extract tells us that from the union of the male and female come all souls that animate men. The meaning, of course, is the aspect of transcendence. It is further said there that the creation of man in the likeness of the Elokim is an allusion to the Mystery of the Male and Female Principles. The inference is that the Eden River is that of life, or synonymously, it is the river of souls. We must understand it in the sense that the Higher Eden is the place of Divine Nuptials, while the Garden, which was watered by the river, was the place of nuptials below with regard to Adam and Eve. Similar illustrations by various speaking images we found already in the higher degree for example, by the analogy instituted between Shechinah and the seed of Solomon; the tent of Grace, where the tent of Sarah is understood as the tent of Shechinah, and others. There are other instances: the Jerusalem above is said to be designated a tent (Isaiah 40:22) and to signify Shechinah. In the lower degree, we find such illustrations by the identification of the Garden with womanhood. It was also the Synod of Israel.

The Eden River is the river of life and of souls in the sense that it issues from the letter *yod*, regarded as the organ of the Covenant in the Supreme World. It is said elsewhere on the subject that at the moment of the union of the Spouse and Bride, all souls come forth from the Celestial River. The one is "the Sanctuary O Lord, which Thy hands have established" (Exodus IV, 17), and the other is the repose of man. They come forth male and female, descending confusedly.

## FURTHER PASSAGES ON THE PRODUCTION OF SOULS

It is said elsewhere that the union of male and female produces souls. It follows that they have a father and mother in God, even as their bodies have when they enter in incarnate life (see Zohar I, 207b–208a; II, 432, among other places). We learn also that all souls emanate from the Celestial Region called Iah which is explained to be God Unknown. The reference is to *Kether*, where HVYH is in union with Elokim or, God and His Shechinah are one. We must remember that the letters *yod* and *hai* primal are allocated to the sephirah *Kether*. We have seen already that this name is for God, that which the Propitiatory is for the Tabernacle; a summary of the male world above and the female world below.

We can understand now in what sense the Shechinah is termed so often the Supreme Mother. We can understand also why it is joy of heart to know that HVYH is Elokim, and why the attainment of such knowledge is the object with which the Holy One sends man into this world.

It is also said that Eden is on the whole the Mother above, and the Garden which was watered by the river coming forth out of Eden is the Shechinah or Mother below, while the river itself is the Middle Pillar of the sephirotic tree. It follows that descent into manifestation is by the central path that communicates between *Kether* and *Malkuth*. This is the path of

Shechinah, who is the first of all that is. It is testified there that Shechinah was destined from the beginning to suffer with Israel. This means that the mystical intercourse which was infinite and holy in the world above and which was pure spiritual and holy for a period in the world below, then descended through what is termed the Fall of Man into the region of the shells, alternatively, into the order of animal things.

The physical sign of the covenant is held to symbolize Shechinah because it symbolizes the path of purification by which man may return the perfection of spiritual union. It is also said that the covenant with Shechinah will endure forever.

We ought to mention that in one place in the text, it is said that in forming the prototypical Eve and placing her face to face with man, it was intended that the union between male and female should be accomplished in divine holiness, in the absence of any secular and impure sensation.

## ANOTHER ASPECT OF THE MYSTERY OF FAITH IN THE NARRATIVE OF THE SOUL ORIGIN

Let us now take another narrative of the soul-origin which is not quite in consonance with some things that have preceded. It postulates a continual generation, as fruit of the eternal union between the Father and Mother in transcendence (God is our Father in transcendence and Shechinah is our Mother in transcendence), in place of a creation of souls once and for all prior to the evolution of the created universe. Hence it is said that man—understood as male and female, is the synthesis of HVYH-Elokim.

What follows now is more in consonance with the Mystery of Faith and is one of its aspects.

It is said that at every birth new souls are created and detached from the Celestial Tree. It is repeated also that all souls issue from the Celestial Region called Iah, which is the source of wisdom. This is called the Holy Spirit, and all souls are comprised therein. According to another version, those souls that animate men issue or emanate from Him who is called the Just.

## THE UNIVERSAL HISTORY OF SOULS

Thanks to these new souls, the legions of heaven are increased, for which reason the Scripture says, "Let the waters bring forth abundantly the moving creature that has life" (Genesis 1:20), meaning the waters of the Celestial River, which has its source in the holy and eternal alliance. They are the waters of *Chokhmah* and *Binah*, the *yod*, and the *hai* in their union, or as another version has it, they are those waters proceeding from *Kether* under the presidency of the Divine Name Iah.

This aforementioned alliance which is the union of HVYH and Elokim has its correspondence below in the covenant between God and man on the basis of circumcision, as symbolizing the great postulate concerning purity.

The Scripture there adds, "And fowl that may fly above the earth" (Genesis 1:20) because at the moment when the newly created soul traverses the heavenly region called *living*—meaning the Land of Life—it is accompanied by many angels. These have followed it from the time that it was detached from the Tree of Heaven. Such is the notion expressed in semi-poetical adornment.

It further adds that those who abstain from practicing the precept "increase and multiply" (Genesis), they diminish—if it were permitted so to speak of the Celestial Figure—the centralization of all figures. They arrest the course of the Celestial River and defile the Holy Alliance. We have seen that this is a sin against God Himself. The soul of such a man will never penetrate into the vestibule of Paradise and shall be repulsed from the world above. We shall remember, however, that ex hypothesi, such a man returns to this life in another body, and he has a chance to do better (if unatoned).

In such terms as these does the Zohar narrate to us the cosmic history in the outward sense and in the internal sense so that there is a literal side to the first chapters of Genesis and an inner side to its essence.

## THE COSMIC SOUL OF THE GENTILES

The souls of all Gentiles emanate from the demons under circumstances which are not explained directly in the Zohar. The suggestion is sometimes that they are from the left side of the Tree. This question, however, is exceedingly obscure. For God and His Shechinah are present everywhere in the tree of the sephiroth, and though there is a sense in which God is allowed to have created evil, the position remained obscure. It remained for later kabbalism to explain this. It was revealed in the idea of postulating ten sephiroth in each of the four worlds as also in each sephirah, so that there is a repetition in the individual sephiroth.

It is however affirmed elsewhere on the contrary that souls of the Gentiles come from the Divine World. The literal statement is that all differences notwithstanding, human souls come from heaven.

## OF THE SOULS OF THE ONES CONVERTED FROM PAGANISM

Now the case of those Gentiles who converted to Jewry and fulfilled the whole Law thereafter, raises another question how they become reconciled on all planes after being received into the fold. It was postulated that after undergoing circumcision they entered under the wings of Shechinah and were separated from the side of the demons. There is one place in which the right and the left side seem to be two paths of coming out into manifestation, apart from the sephiroth. These converted ones did not participate in the world to come in the full beatitude of the elect, who were such by their right of birth; they remained under the wings of Shechinah. But the latter was like a chariot for Israel, in which Israel passed higher, namely, into the Land of the Living.

The Gentiles had no part in the Heavenly Tree and could not, therefore, return to it.

## THE TEN AVERSE CROWNS

We have already found connection of the sephirotic tree, and the Tree of Life. We may also in a sense interconnect the Tree of Knowledge of Good and Evil in this attribution; the good being the right side and the left the evil side.

Zoharic kabbalah recognized moreover an averse tree under the title of Inferior Crowns, in analogy with the Crowns that are above, namely, the true sephiroth.

The salient allusions are as follows:

a. There were ten averse Crowns, and they were in analogy with ten varieties of magic, all understood as infernal, for there are typically no such subtle distinctions as white magic as opposed to the black as mentioned in occult literature (Zohar I, 167a).

b. The inferior Crowns are manifestations of one and the same Tree (Zohar I, 177a).

c. The law of correspondence obtains in these things, for the empire of the demon is modelled, as we have seen, on that of God (Zohar II, 37b).

d. There is further a demoniacal triad in imitation of that triad which is Supernal (Zohar I, 40b).

e. These are also inferior palaces corresponding to the palaces that are above, and like these, they are seven in number (Zohar I, 245a).

f. There are hierarchies of demons, answering to the hierarchies of blessed angels; seraphim to seraphim, and so forth (Zohar I, 247b).

g. The titles of the averse Sephiroth are the same as those above, Wisdom and so forth; all the qualities being illustrated by their opposites (Zohar III, 70a).

h. It is said finally, that there are ten averse sephiroth on the right and ten upon the left, just as in the holy configuration. Here is another way of understanding the right and the left sides in the Zohar (Zohar III, 207a).

## OF THE GENERATION OF SOULS, CONTINUED

Returning to the generation of souls, it is said that there are three souls in superior degrees. The first is the Supreme Soul, which is unintelligible even to beings of high. It is the soul of all souls; it is concealed eternally, and all depends therefrom. The second soul is the female principle, and the union of these two manifests Divine Works shown to the whole world, even as all acts of the human soul are manifested by the human body. The third soul is that of all holy souls, emanating from the male and female in transcendence. We are reminded again of the symbolical modes of the Doctrine of that which proceeds by emanating from *Ain Soph* into the complete concealment. This is the comparative manifestation of the three supernal sephiroth: *Kether, Chokhmah,* and *Binah,* as we have seen long ago; so also in the present instance of the symbol of begetting emanation, as it were (Zohar I, 245a–b).

We also see, however, in this place the root-postulate belonging to the Mystery of Faith, that the union of male and female in the Ineffable causes conception and birth everlastingly: that which are born are souls, that these descend, and that they are male and female. One account says that at the moment of earthly marriage, the souls must sort themselves out, each male soul discovering the female who was its companion before incarnation. The implicit is that the male body contains a male-soul, and that the soul of a woman is female. Again there is a sense, though hidden and in the obscure, in which any soul is male to any material body, but is female to the degree which is above it (Zohar I, Appendix III).

Another implicit to recognize is that he who abodes in the true way will meet in marriage with the woman-soul, which was his prenatal companion. If he has deviated, it may happen that the soul predestined to him is espoused to another. But in the event of his repentance, a time will come when the alien male will disappear, thus yielding the woman to her true mate. Occasionally there is that time, in virtue of which a male-soul will come into this world without a sister-soul, and presumably vice versa. It is held that such a person will not marry and cannot therefore have children. But, in the event of his keeping the Law and proving worthy, he will find the means of rehabilitation in another earthly life.

In the alternative case he will be judged not worthy of a new transmigration. Now we have seen that reincarnation is not in itself desirable, but that it is justified by adequate reasons. It follows, ex hypothesi, that there is a less favorable alternative. That which is suggested, however, is only a sporadic, casual notion. It is part of the Divine Plan for the salvation and felicity of man, that a sister soul is not permitted to remain the wife of another, except in some unusual cases (Zohar III, 283b–284a).

## OF THE UNION OF SOULS IN THE WORLD TO COME

The union of humanity below, according to the manner of flesh, is in its consecration at least a reflection of Divine Union. It is to be supposed on another and higher side of the mystery that there should be a union of souls in the world to come, so that in the beatitude of the true region of life, they should continue to reflect the supernal work and its mystery.

This is why the union between God and the soul of the just is often in the sense of vision; though there are indications of deeper stages. That which is substituted is the union in heaven of souls who have been espoused on earth, being those who were espoused previously before the world began. Here, too, the triad obtains as elsewhere and it is a recurring subject of reference. There are:

1. Prenatal union;
2. Union on earth, and
3. Union in the risen life of the spirit.

We must observe first, however, that we hear nothing concerning marriage life after the resurrection, which is that state wherein the perpetuation of a physical envelope is to continue in existence. Following all the analogies, it would seem beyond doubt that the risen bodies will enter into the life of marriage because they are complete bodies.

Rav Saadiah Gaon in his work Creeds and Opinion deals in detail with this question and problems, and states definite opinions concerning them (Zohar I, 283b–284a; also ch. VII on Resurrection and ch. VIII on the Final Redemption).

Returning to the union between God and the soul in the sense of vision, we find it often said that the Blessed Vision is the sight of Shechinah and the contemplation of her Divine

Face. We are apparently to understand that the union of sister-souls is under the eyes of Shechinah and in her presence (Zohar II, 40b; also the Faithful Shepherd; III, 189–90).

It is further said that in the heights of heaven there is yet another union of two born of love and forever inseparable (Zohar II, 50b). It is contemplated by those who have part in the life to come (ibid.).

## OF THE GRAND MATRONA HERSELF

The ways that lead to the Tree of Life, the Tree that is kept by the cherubim and the Flaming Sword, are the Grand Matrona herself. She is the way of the Sacred City, the way of the Heavenly Jerusalem, the intermediary of communication between things above and below in both directions; she is the perfect Mediatrix, to whom all the Divine Powers are confided (Zohar II, 50b). This intimation is vague. But as we remember, the contemplation of Matrona sanctified nuptials below. So also is the path by which the elect enter into the sanctified higher nuptials as if they ascended that Middle Pillar of the sephiroth, so often said to be Matrona.

## OF ENOCH/METATRON ALSO CALLED PRINCE OF THE INNER

The same Divine Powers aforementioned are said to be entrusted to Enoch when he became Metatron. Concerning Enoch we will now collect the following references:

a. Enoch is charged with the government of the earth. He sets all his legions in motion by the power of a single letter in his name (Zohar I, 143a).

b. Enoch is the serpent above (Zohar II, 28a). This is explained elsewhere in a passage which says that he is favorable to man, when he is transformed into a wand, for example the wand of Aaron and Moses; but as a serpent he is against man (Zohar I, 27a).

c. The river which went out of Eden to water the Garden (Genesis 2:10) is Enoch who is called otherwise Metatron. But it is the Lower Eden and not that in the supernal world. It is the place called Pardes (Zohar I, 27a).

d. Enoch is not to the cohorts above apparently that which is Samael to the cohorts below. He is called Server and he embraces the six directions of space (Zohar II, 42a).

e. It is said that souls proceed from the side of Metatron and from the side of Shechinah, but it does not seem to be by the way of generation (Zohar II, 94b).

f. Metatron is also called Young Man and it was he who dwelt in the Tabernacle of Moses and helped to build the Tabernacle. He guarded the Temple of Solomon (Zohar II, 143a).

g. The School of Metatron is the School of the Holy One. The curtain of the Tabernacle was his symbol. He is like Michael, for he offers the souls of the just to God (Zohar II, 278a).

h. Enoch has the keys of Heaven. During the exile he has the government of the House; he is the rainbow and he is also called Shaddai. He is old and he is again young (Zohar III, 171b).

i. As we have already noticed, he is the vesture of Shaddai. As noted also, he is to Shechinah that which are the weekdays to Sabbath, as if he were activity and she rest. He is poor in exile, that is to say, in the exile of Israel and his nourishment is prayer (Zohar III, 231a).

j. Two other very mysterious and obscure passages concerning Enoch-Metatron are not quoted here. There he is called the Angel of the Sun, and he is connected with Matrona in *Binah* and with *vav*. Or else we find him interconnected with the Lesser Countenance and the tenth sephirah *Malkuth* and with *vav* and *hai* final (Zohar III, 64b). There are still a few more minor allusions and extracts concerning Enoch not mentioned here.

## THE SOULS AND THE SEVEN PALACES

Now we shall quote additional statements and information concerning the seven palaces of the Zohar.

When souls leave the lower world they enter into a certain palace which is above if they carry the proper warrants. Therein those souls, which are male, are again united to the female, in which union they radiate light, as in sparkles (Zohar II, 264a). This palace is said to be the throne of Faith. Perhaps it is the place of the Mystery of Faith. Yet, another story of palaces tells us that there are four palaces that are exclusive to women, or at least to holy mothers, but it is forbidden to reveal their nature (Zohar III, 167b).

During the day the females are separated from the males, but the spouses are in union at night, and in their mutual embrace the lights of both dissolve into a single light. The conclusion reached is that blessed is the lot of the just, male as well as female, for they shall enjoy all delights in the world to come (ibid.).

## ABOUT THE SOULS OF GENTILES CONVERTED TO JUDAISM, BORN OF CELESTIAL MOTHERS

In this manner we come to the great mystery of the subject concerning the souls of those Gentiles who become converted to the Law of Israel, as to which there are several testimonies.

It first rests on the witness of a testament bequeathed by Rabbi Eliezer the Great (it probably does not mean the son of Rabbi Shimon) that when the Holy One comes down into Paradise at midnight, the male souls are united to the female. Fecundation from the joy which they experience in contemplation of God results in the bringing forth of other souls which are destined to occupy the bodies of Gentiles, who will become converts to the Law of Israel (Zohar III, 168a).

In another place this is explained in a different manner. The souls born of celestial unions are reserved in a palace, and when a man is converted, one of them takes flight and comes under the wings of Shechinah, who embraces her because she is the fruit of the just. And she is sent into the body of the convert, where she or he remains; and from that moment the convert acquires the title of just (ibid.). This is the mystery of those words in Scripture: "The fruit of the just is the Tree of Life" (Proverbs 11:30). There is yet also another testimony, in the general sense, that the Holy One effects the union of twin-souls, so that they may engender other souls, themselves animated by those sacred forces which are above them (Zohar I, 168b).

We must not omit to mention that this does not refer to the state of the souls and their life in the world to come. This is defined clearly in the Faithful Shepherd, which says in the world to come there is neither eating nor drinking, there are no conjugal relations, and the beatitudes of the just, as we have seen, are to contemplate the beauty of Shechinah (Zohar II, 116a).

At this stage there remain a few minor points which may be mentioned. It is said that all depends on thought and intention; holiness is attracted by good thought. But he who defiles himself by thought and he who at the moment of fulfilling the act of intercourse with his wife thinks of another woman, changes the degree above—the Degree of Holiness—

into one that is impure. This is later followed by a curious statement saying: "Yet it would seem permissible, on occasion, to think of another, because in cohabiting with Leah, Jacob thought of Rachel, though unintentionally, as it is said" (Zohar I, Appendix III, Secret of the Law).

Another place points out that there are rare occasions when conjugal relations seem forbidden even on the Sabbath and periods of famine are a case in point. Now ordinarily we would assume the regulation was a question of doing penance, and as such it is presented in the Talmud. But, according to Rabbi Shimon, a supreme mystery is involved (Zohar I, 204a). The child born at such a season will be from the side of the demon (ibid.).

Last there is the question of virginity among women (Zohar II, 131b). A woman must not remain a virgin and live out an unmarried life. There is one Zoharic reference to virgins in an exulted state. It specifies that the third among several legions is composed of celestial virgins, who are in the service of Matrona, and adorn her when she is presented to the king; these are her maids of honor. These legions, however, do not consist of human souls (Zohar II, 131b).

## CONCLUSION

We have now arrived at the end of our inquiry into the Mystery of Sex, in our search for statements in the text of the Zohar. We have found that there is a mystery of nuptials, of which it has not entered into the heart of man to conceive in the ordinary ways and under the common motives of desire. The lawful act of life and the Law of Nature can be raised above their own degree by the consecration of motive, and the will of man in all its authorized ways and places can be united to the Divine Will. The holy scholars of the Zohar had an inward, spiritual, and goodly ideal on which they dwelt and by which they have accomplished transmutations below. They made all things holy in their lives, as it was handed down to them from the past.

We are told by records that the fruit of the mystical holy marriages throughout the many centuries of our Jewish history was the begetting of children from what is called the Holy Side, as against the side of the demons. The literal fact was that the children born of such unions belonged to another category than we are accustomed to meet in the streets and byways of daily life all the world over, or for that matter, in our own homes. They were children of Grace rather than what we call children of nature, for their parents' lives were consecrated, sanctified lives. They were not solitaires and ascetics. They were truly a company of scholars in the city and along the countryside, in village and in wilderness. For them the world of nature was Grace externalized. The Divine Presence was about them, therein, and in their hearts and minds fully attained.

In conclusion we shall say that they found the true meaning of the words of Genesis 2:18: "It is not good for man to be alone," and they found that there is a secret path in which "the joy of living honorably with his wife" may bring the completed man (male and female) into "the spiritual city of joy. The great city of praise, wherein is the joy of the Lord."[1] And in the words of the Zohar already quoted in the above, it may be added "that man shall participate in the World to Come, because he has entered during this life, into the joy of living honorably with his wife" (Zohar I, 90b).

So the souls go up, male and female, into the World Beyond. If they are prepared souls, they find one another, and the everlasting union begins in the light of God.

---

1. Jeremiah 49:25, Isaiah 24:19

SECTION IX

# The Written Word of Kabbalism: Third Period

CHAPTER ONE

# Zoharic Treatises and Expositors

The growth of kabbalistic literature is sketched in certain expository works as commentaries on the Zohar and in some independent tracts which connect with the tradition.

These works and tracts fall under two heads, namely, those destined to elucidate technical matters and those that may claim to be original expository treatises.

In the first are included "Words of Understanding," which is a Zoharic lexicon, the "Gates of the Eyes" which is concerned with the scriptural passages in the Zohar and "Ancient Supplements," and the "Zeir Zahav" meaning a Golden Crown, a wreath of gold.

The second section contains the famous "Garden of Pomegranates," "The Way of Truth" and its sequel "Fount of Wisdom," and a digest of the Zohar proper, "Vision of the Priest." There are still a few other texts which may be regarded as extensions or developments of Zoharic doctrine especially of that part which is concerned with spiritual essences.

Illustrious names in later kabbalism, especially, were several monumental abstract treatises, involving Zoharic commentaries, and other esoterically relevant developments in rabbinic thought. These arose primarily due to the Zohar and its many diverse doctrines.

## ZOHARIC EXPOSITORS: MOSES OF CORDOVA

The Zohar first became known in Spain toward the end of the thirteenth century. Then there was a lapse of two hundred fifty years before any literature followed. Hence, this literature may be regarded as a consequence of the Cremona and Mantua editions of the Zohar.

## ZOHARIC SCHOOLS IN PALESTINE

Two Zoharic schools were founded about the same time in Palestine, namely, the middle of the sixteenth century: the first by Moses of Cordoba and the second by Isaac de Luria.

Other history scholars assign Moses of Cordoba to the fourteenth century; but as it happens there is no question that Moses ben Jacob, called "Ramak," was born in 1522 and died on June 25, 1570.

He is the first commentator on the Zohar, except for Joseph ben Abraham Gikatilla called the Divine Kabbalist. Also Thaumaturge, who was of the time of Ferdinand and Isabella, was a writer on the sephiroth and connects with the Sepher Yetzirah rather than Zoharic theosophy, though he refers to the kabbalistic "Work of the Chariot." He was born in Old Castile, circa 1248 and died at Penafiel circa 1305 or 1306.

Moses of Cordoba was a Spaniard but he traveled to Palestine. It is conjectured that he was instrumental in founding the Academy of Safed in Upper Galilee. In either case he was one of its teachers and helped to make it illustrious, for he was regarded by his fellow theosophists as the greatest light of kabbalism since Shimon Bar Yochai.

The work by which he is known is of high authority in kabbalism. It is entitled "Garden of Pomegranates" (Pardes Rimonim), referring to the verse in the Song of Solomon 4:13. Paradise is derivative of this scriptural Pardes—Garden or Orchard, and the pomegranate with its innumerable seeds is a favorite object of symbolism. Here it is the treasury of Scriptural meanings, the Hebrew word by which it is described having four consonants PRDS.

The *P* signifies the literal sense (pshat), the *R* the mystical sense (remez), *D* the enigmatic sense (derash), and *S* the secret and concealed sense (sod).

It appeared in Crakow in 1591, and Samuel Gallico published an abridged version under the title of "Asis Rimonim."

## CONTENTS OF THE GARDEN

The "Garden of Pomegranates" is a difficult and complex treatise. Specimens of the subject matter here and there are the following: the attribution of the letters of the Tetragrammaton to the sephiroth, the mystical meanings of words out of their context, the names applied to sephiroth, the superincession of these and their union with *Ain Soph*, the mystery of the Throne and of Shechinah, and primeval Tohu and Bohu, the unknown darkness.

## HIS TRACT ON THE SOUL

But as the heart of this kabbalist was fixed with peculiar intentness on the eternal destinies of Israel and not on temporal concerns, so his chief interest was the soul, ever recurrent in his writings. A special tract in the "Garden of Pomegranates" (tract 31) is dedicated to many diverse aspects of the soul.

The tract discusses the region from which the soul emanates, its purpose in the world, the profit of its creation, and its union with matter. Also, its superiority over the angels, its chief divisions, their relation with one another, the sephiroth to which they are referred, and the places to which they resort after death. Also explained are the absence of one or both of the higher divisions in many individuals, and the good and evil angel which accompany each human being. All of these topics are discussed following Zoharic Doctrine.

## THE SIMULACRUM IMAGO

The tract devotes also a very curious chapter to the simulacrum which presides at generation, a phantasmal image of humanity that descends on the male head "cum copula maritalis exercetur inferius." It is affirmed to be sent from the Lord and no procreation can take place without its presence. It is not visible, yet might be seen if license were given to the eye. The phantom or imago is prepared for each man before he enters the world and he grows in likeness thereof. With the Israelites, the simulacrum is holy, and it comes to them from the Holy Place. To those of another religion it descends from the side of impurity, and hence the chosen people must not mingle their seed with that of the Gentile. This rests on the authority of the Zohar that states that the simulacrum is an emanation of the celestial form of each man, that is, *yechidah* (Zohar III, 107a Mantua edition).

## ZOHARIC EXPOSITORS: ISAAC D'LURIA

This kabbalist is referred by some to the seventeenth century and by others to the century which preceded it. As a fact, he was born in Jerusalem of German parentage in 1534 and died at Tzfas (Safed) in 1572. He was a pupil of David ibn Abu Zimri and has been regarded as the greatest rabbinical scholar of his period.

He himself had not published anything other than several Aramaic poems now often used in the liturgy. The great body of his doctrines, collected by his disciple R. Chaim Vital, has not been challenged, however. The modern orthography is Luria and the full name is Isaac ben Solomon Ashkenazi Luria, otherwise known as the acronym of his name, the Ari, of blessed memory or alternatively, as the Arizal.

## SIGNIFICANCE OF RABBI YITZHAK ASHKENAAZI LURIA—THE ARIZAL LURIA

It is certain that the Ari was not a mere reflection of prior teachings. He did innovate or extend, and he makes good reading. He is termed the eagle of the kabbalists. The writings in full form a vast thesaurus. A printed edition in full appeared at Volkiev in 1772. They include:

a. The first tract, so called the Liber Drushim, that is, the Book of Dissertations.

b. A commentary on the Book of Concealment forms the second tract.

c. The Book of the Revolutions of souls forms a large tract of the collection, which is said to be even larger than the original Zohar itself.

## THE ANSWER TO WHY CREATION?

The Liber Drushim is a metaphysical introduction to the kabbalah that discusses a variety of subtle questions. His first point is, as he tells us, one over which kabbalists late and early had outwearied themselves already, namely, for what reason was the world created and was their creation of necessity.

The answer of Isaac de Luria is that God cannot fail of perfection in all the works and names of His Magnificence, His Excellence, and His Glory. If, though, those works had been brought from potentiality into act, they could not have been termed perfect as regards either works or names. The name Tetragrammaton signifies perpetual existence, past, present, or future in the condition of creation, before the creation, and thereafter in the immutability of things.

But if the worlds had not been created with all that is in them, it could not have signified thus the continuity of existences in every instant of time, and Tetragrammaton would have been an empty formula. So also the name of Adonai or the Lord involves the idea of ministers or servants, and if there were no ministers, God could not be called by this title. But after creation of the worlds and the production of the divine works from potentiality into accomplishment, God has fulfilled His perfection in every operation of his powers and in all His Names without exception.

## WHY CREATION AT THAT GIVEN TIME OR EPOCH?

The next point discussed by Liber Drushim is why the world was created at the time and moment it was and not at an earlier or a later epoch. The answer is that the Supreme and most Excellent Light is infinite, exceeding comprehension and speculation, and that its concealed foundation is far from all understanding. Before anything was produced by emanation therefrom, there was no time of beginning.

This is also the solution to this difficulty that is offered by most official theology, and it could have no aspect of novelty of speculation at the late period of Isaac de Luria.

## EMANATION OF SEPHIROTH

But the kabbalist in Liber Drushim passes speedily into the transcendental region of the sephiroth including the "manner of their emanation" which later he tells us is another question which has involved all kabbalists in controversy.

Such speculations are as follows: Do they proceed from one another in the simplicity of a successive series or are their emanation in columns? There is authority for both views and also for a third, which represents them as a series of concentric circles.

## THE THREE PILLARS

These questions are hard and difficult to determine, says R. Isaac, but he offers a solution on the Zohar. Namely, that before the order of things was instituted, they were disposed one over the other, but after that time, they are in three Pillars, those of Mercy and Severity with the central column, of which *Kether* is the summit and *Malkuth* the base. The hypothesis in circles adopted by a German expositor in *Coelum Sephiroticum* is thus implicitly set aside.

## THE LIGHT OF THE SEPHIROTH

In subsequent chapters the sephiroth are considered under a dual aspect, namely, as regards the portion of Divine Light contained in each and as regards the containing vessel, while these again are distinguished in an ambient and an inward Light, and an external and internal vessel.

The existence of many worlds prior to the sephirotic emanations is affirmed herein following both Talmudic and Zoharic tradition. Several classifications of the sephiroth are finally considered in the last chapter.

## BOOK OF CONCEALMENT

The commentary of the Book of Concealment does not yield readily to an analysis of contents. It takes various paragraphs of the text and exposes their meaning consecutively with the help of the Idra Rabbah and Idra Zuta. The peculiar designation of the treatise is said to arise out of Proverbs 25:2: "It is the Glory of God to conceal a thing" (i.e., the Word), and, "with the lowly is wisdom" (ibid. 11:2). The second reference explains why the work has the meaning not only of concealment but also that of modesty.

## THE BALANCE PRINCIPLE AND THE PILLARS

On the authority of the Zohar, section Pekudei, the Balance Principle which has made this treatise so famous in kabbalism, is affirmed to represent the male and female principles, which indeed follows from the development of the Lesser Holy Synod. The male denotes mercy, the right hand pillar of the sephiroth, and the female, severity, the pillar on the left hand. These principles are termed the Father and the Mother, and in the Hebrew alphabet are referable to *yod* and *hai*.

The father is perfect love and the mother is perfect severity. The latter had seven sons, namely the Edomite Kings, who had no foundation in the Holy Ancient One. These seven are empty light dispelled by the source of lights concealed within the mother. Male and female are conformations of the Holy Ancient One, corresponding to *Kether* represented mystically by three heads, signifying: a) the unmanifested Wisdom which is so withdrawn, that it is as though it were not, in contradiction to that which is manifested in the thirty-two paths; b) the Supreme Crown which is the Holy Ancient One; and c) the Head, which neither knows nor is known, namely, *Ain Soph*.

Thus in one side of *Kether* is *Chokhmah* or Wisdom; this is the father, while on the other side is *Binah*, the mother or increment of Understanding; and above is *latens Deitas*.

These are instances of the Ari's skill in developing Zoharic symbolism like these of the three supernal sephiroth and are representative specimens of the whole commentary.

## ESSENCE OF PRAYER

The Arizal finally affirms as the sum total of the whole mystery that man in his prayers should fix his mind upon the foundation of all foundations, that he may derive to himself a certain influence and benediction from the depth of that source. In this manner his kabbalistic obscurities are redeemed at times by the simplicity and depth of the lesson which is extracted from them.

## THE SEVEN EDOMITE KINGS

His *Book of the Revolutions of Souls* follows his obscure exposition of the very obscure work the *Siphrah Do Zenioutha*; the system which it develops is quite involved.

The basis of its scheme is the doctrine of the Book of Concealment and its expository synods concerning the Seven Edomite Kings who emanated and passed away prior to the production of the present universe. In these kings there was good, as well as evil, and a separation was made: that which was good for the material of the four kabbalistic worlds as they are now constituted. Each of these worlds, according to R. Isaac Luria, has its Macroprosopus, Supernal Father, Supernal Mother, Microprosopus, and Bride, all derived from the Seven Kings.

## FIVEFOLD DIVISION OF SOULS IN THE FOUR WORLDS

A like origin is attributed to souls and they are disposed similarly in the four worlds. Some correspond to the Bride, some to Microprosopus, some to the Supernal Mother, and some again to Macroprosopus in the world of Assiah. The totality of these souls constitutes Psyche in Assiah, which has five parts (in reference to the supernal personalities of that world): 1) the Psyche, in the Psyche or *Nephesh* of Assiah (the mundane factions); 2) the medial Spirit or *Ruach* of the Psyche factiva; 3) the mens or *Neshamah*; 4) the Vitalities or *Chaya*; 5) the Sinularitas, individuality of *Yechidah*; all belonging to the Psyches factiva or *Nephesh* of Assiah.

There is a similar distribution through the other Three Superior Worlds, *Yetzirah* to *Ruach*; *Briah* to *Neshamah*; and *Atziluth* to *Chaya*. *Yechidah* would then belong to the World of Unmanifested Deity which is beyond *Atziluth*.

## THE FIVEFOLD DIVISION IN THE SEPHIROTH

Each of the five divisions is again attributed in the sephiroth scheme as follows:

1. *Nephesh* to *Malkuth*; the Kingdom, that is, the Bride.
2. *Ruach* to the six sephiroth of Microprosopus.
3. *Neshamah* to Mother, that is, *Binah*.
4. *Chaya* to the Father, that is, *Chokhmah*.
5. *Yechidah* to *Kether*, that is, the Crown.

It follows that each of the four worlds has the four worlds within it, and also the Ten Sephiroth tabulated in the authentic Tree of Life. Other Lurianic speculations show each sephirah as containing all sephiroth.

## THE PROTOTYPAL ARCHEPLASMIC ADAM

All these souls were contained in the archetypal or protoplasmic Adam at the time that he was formed, some corresponding to the head, others to the eyes, and so with all the members. But these souls are those of the Israelites who are *ens uncia in terra*. Concerning the origin of the souls of the nations of the world, however, we must look elsewhere.

## THE EDOMITE KINGS AND ADAM BELIAL

The recrements, the gross evil and other rejected parts of the Edomite Kings, are the cortices or shells which compose the averse Adam Belial, evolved in Luriamic kabbalism from rare Zoharic allusions to the sephiroth of the shadow.

When the Adam and Eve of Genesis partook of the forbidden fruit, their fall confounded the good with the evil of the cortices. Adam's was with the male shells of Samael or Adam Belial, and that of Eve with the evil of his bride Lilith, the extraneousnesses of the serpent. For the serpent had commerce even with Eve, a recurrent doctrine of the Zohar. It was after this Fall of Man that the souls of the nations of the world were produced from the shells.

To put it tersely, the souls of the Israelites were distributed in the members of the protoplasmic Adam, regarded in his mystical extension through the four worlds, and the souls of the Gentiles in the members of Adam Belial (that is, Samael), belonging to the averse Tree.

## OF THE FALL OF MAN

Had man remained in perfection would he have procreated and brought an Israel of superelection into the world? This is not seemingly affirmed. But the Fall at least was responsible for the souls of the nations taking flesh on earth. Liberation from the soul's mess and venom of the serpent is by generation and death only, whereby the good is separated from the evil, until all nations shall have been brought forth from the evil and the Israelites from the good kind.

## OF THE CONFUSION OF GOOD AND EVIL

Good and evil were thus confounded, and since then two things have been necessary: 1) The good man should be separated from the evil, 2) the portion of the good should be restored. The first is accomplished by observation of the prohibitive precepts, and the second by that of the affirmative. Both classes of precepts must be accomplished in all their number, in thought, word, and in deed by every soul, whose revolutions therefore must continue until the whole Law has been fulfilled. This Law must also be studied in each of its four senses, failing which the revolutions of the deficient souls will be further prolonged. The scheme of revolution is subject to certain mitigation as revolution proper is sometimes replaced by *status embroyonatus.*

## OF REVOLUTION OF SOULS

Revolution is the entrance of a soul into the body of an infant at birth to experience the pain and trial prepared for that body. The alternative condition is the entrance of a soul into the body of a grown man, who must be at least thirteen years old, the Jewish age of reason, that is, when he is obliged to fulfill the precepts.

The status embroyonatus is entered either because the soul in question has something to fulfill which was neglected in the preceding revolution or for the benefit of the man who is impregnated, that is, to justify and direct him.

## PURPOSE OF THE REVOLUTIONS OF SOULS

Revolutions occur 1) for the cleansing of sins; 2) for the fulfillment of a neglected precept; 3) for the leading of other sins to the right way, in which case the returning soul is perfect in justice; 4) to receive the true spouse, who was not deserved by the soul in the prior revolution.

Four souls may revolve in one body, but not more, while the status embroyonatus may associate three alien souls with a single man but again no more. The object of all revolutions and of all kabbalistic embryology is the return of the Israelites into the stature of the first Adam, all having been involved in his fall since he included all.

The kabbalistic doctrine of revolution of souls of Isaac de Luria is not a scheme of reincarnation peculiar to other theosophies; it is not Zoharic doctrine though it has a certain ground therein; it is greatly curious.

## ZOHARIC EXPOSITORS: RABBI NAPHTALI HIRTZ

This German kabbalist, known as Naphtali Hirtz ben Jacob Elhanan, was born at Frankfort on the Main in the second half of the sixteenth century. He is said to have lived in Palestine and presumably died there. His work is entitled "The Valley of the King." The first part was printed at Amsterdam in 1648, under the title of "Emek HaMelech." The second part of "Gan HaMelech" has remained in manuscript. Few biographical particulars concerning him are extant.

## THE WORK: ROYAL VALLEY

The first six sections of the treatise are designed as an introduction to the Zohar for the better comprehension thereof.

A considerable part of the remainder is concerned with the Book of Concealment and the two synods as a commentary on these works.

The author belongs to the school of Rabbi Isaac de Luria. He appears to have traversed a portion of the ground covered by the Lurian manuscripts of R. Chaim Vital. After the same manner that these develop Zoharic metaphysics, the Royal Valley extends kabbalistic cosmology.

## OF HIS KABBALISTIC COSMOLOGY

The *mindus prior* of kabbalism, that is, the emanation of the seven Edomite Kings, is termed the World of *Nephesh*. It was destroyed with the souls belonging to it, because evil prevailed therein.

The actual world is that of *Ruach*, in which good and evil are confused, but good comes out of the evil and at last all shall be good. Then a new world shall succeed that of *Neshamah*, and this will be the Sabbath of Grace.

It follows, therefore, that the present order must pass away, and this is symbolized by the death of the second Hadad, the eighth Edomite King, as recorded in I Chronicles 50:51. In the day of this destruction, the spirits of impurity, namely the shells, shall be burnt up entirely. God will establish a new creation and will bring forth from His glorious light the mystery of the *Neshamah* of His Great Name. The dominion of this *Neshamah* is the King who shall reign over Israel and in that day the Lord shall be one and his Name one.

## HOW CREATION TOOK PLACE

The hypothesis of the Creation of the World begins with the contraction of the Divine Presence producing that space which is termed primeval air. Before the emanations issued forth and the things which exist were created, the Supreme Light was extended infinitely. When it came into the Supreme Mind to will the fabrication of worlds, the issue of emanations and the emission as light of the perfection of his active powers, aspects, and attributes took place. Then that light was in some measure compressed, receding in every direction from a particular vacuum, and was left in mid-infinite, wherein emanations might be manifested.

## THE LIGHT OF RADIATION IN COMPRESSION, EXPRESSION, AND FORMATION OF THE WORLD

To this treatise owes kabbalism the curious conception of the evolution of sephiroth by a process of explosion through the excess of light which descended them. From the fragments of the broken vessels originated the four worlds, the shells both good and evil, and myriads of souls. This motion is fundamentally similar to that of Isaac de Luria.

I will still add that the Royal Valley regards *Kether* as containing in potentia all the remaining sephiroth so that originally they were not distinguishable therefrom.

Precisely as in man there exist the four elements, potent but indistinguishable specifically, so in this Crown there were all the remaining numerations.

It is added that in the second world, called that of restoration, the term *Kether* is also used as its reference, because the "cause of Causes" and the "ancient of the Ancients," were principles of the Divine which were active in its manifestation.

It seems then, according to this late school of kabbalism, that the first attempt at manifestation by the latens Deitas went astray and that the evil of the world is the result of this failure, a peculiar curiosity which is also found in the Talmud.

## ZOHARIC EXPOSITORS: ABRAHAM COHEN HERRERA

This Spanish Jew was another and late follower of the School of Luria, but tinctured by Platonic philosophy which he sought to harmonize with kabbalism in his "Gate of the Heavens." He is otherwise known as Abraham Cohen de Herrera and accurately, Alonzo de Herrera. He was of Spanish birth but died at Amsterdam in 1631.

His other treatise is "Beth Elohim—The House of God," containing three dissertations in exposition of Lurianic doctrines, but founded upon the metaphysical portions of the Faithful Shepherd, the Pekudah Section in the Zohar, and the ancient supplements of that work. It deals with kabbalistic psychology.

The first dissertation in the "House of God" rests chiefly on Zoharic utterances attributed to R. Shimon bar Yochai, who is termed the mouthpiece of holiness and the angel of the Lord. It recites the emanation of the sephiroth. It develops the system of the hierarchy of evil spirits, who are termed "cortices" or shells and of the ten sinister or impure numerations, otherwise the averse sephiroth.

In a special chapter it examined also the opinion of R. Isaac de Luria concerning eleven classes of shells and R. Moses of Cordoba concerning the connection of the angels with the Celestial Bodies and concerning the physical vestments.

The second dissertation treats of the different angelic orders and the seven heavens. The third deals with elementary spirits and the nature of the soul.

The "Beth Elohim" is a commentary and a development of considerable importance in its own sphere. Both works were written in Spanish and remained in manuscript until they had been translated into Hebrew, in which form they appeared at Amsterdam in 1665.

## ZOHARIC EXPOSITORS: ISSACHAR BEN NAPHTALI

This expositor of kabbalism seems to have been a contemporary of the Arizal, and like him was a German Jew. His chief work, the "Vision of the Priest," was printed at Cacovai in 1559. It is a synopsis of the entire Zohar and a methodized analysis of its contents; it is subdivided according to the Mosaic books.

It is designed only for the assistance of the scholar desiring to consult the Zohar on a given subject. The other works of R. Issachar are of similar character. There are no particulars concerning him—in traditional Jewish sources.

CHAPTER TWO

# Expositors of Other Works

When sketching the growth of kabbalistic literature in certain expository works or commentaries on the Zohar and in some independent tracts which connect with the general tradition, one must make mention of two other works chosen for separate consideration: one being on the mysteries of Love because of its general diffusion, and one on the application of kabbalistic apparatus to alchemy, because of the credit which it has formerly obtained.

### PURIFYING FIRE OF ALCHEMY

The treatise entitled "Aish Metzareph," which signifies purifying fire, is an instance of the application of kabbalistic apparatus to the purposes of alchemy. It seems to be the sole instance of its kind; not to speak of a work under the title of the "Philosophical Stone," which is attributed idly by Moses Botarel to R. Saadiah but which reference is deduced only by a single quotation by which the work is even known.

*402*

A few metallic allusions are to be found in the Zohar, which recognizes the existence of an archetypal gold and regards the metals generally as composite substances (as indeed they are in consideration of protons, electrons, and their quanta). These references, however, are almost less than incidental. It is needless to say that there is no cryptic chemistry whatever in the great theosophical storehouse.

The treatise "Purifying Fire" is said to have been written in Aramaic Chaldean. No information is given as to the Chaldee original and no evidence is available by which we can fix with any precision the period at which this treatise was composed. It quotes frequently the Zohar, and thus, of course, it is subsequent to the promulgation of the Zohar.

It is also subsequent to the "Garden of Pomegranates" by R. Moses of Cordoba, a treatise belonging to the middle of the sixteenth century, which it quotes. It borrows processes from R. Mordechai, a kabbalistic alchemist of unknown date. It refers also to the Latin treatises of "Geber." It may be placed conjecturally at the end of the sixteenth century. It contains expressions common to most of the Latin chemists, which were derived by them from the Greeks. It does not possess the interest of importance, though, that would attach to a chemical-kabbalistic treatise.

Dr. Gerhard Scholem, who published an interesting study of alchemy and the kabbalah in 1925 and reprinted it subsequently as a pamphlet, said that after examining every kabbalistic text which came within his reach, it is certain that alchemy and kabbalism cannot be reconciled. Yet that is only because gold is the perfect metal for the one and silver for the other. As to the "Aish Metzareph," it is concerned with producing silver rather than gold, but it is not a treatise on actual processes of transmutation (*Monstschrift fuer Geschichte und Wissenschat des Juden tums*, 1925).

It should be noted that according to Zohar II, 147 and IV, 65, gold is greatly superior, however. The Aish Metzareph is entirely anonymous. The original is said to be still extant. The myth attributing the work to a certain R. Abraham and calling it the "Book of Abraham the Jew" is entirely an invention.

The book is only a curious memorial. It has the common difficulties of purely hermetic books further complicated by the system of Gematria and the sephirotic correspondences of metals.

The alchemical root of the metal corresponds to *Kether*. All metals originate therefrom. Lead is referred to *Chokhmah*. Tin has the place of *Binah*. Silver that of *Chesed*. These three are the white metallic natures. Among the red, gold is in correspondence with *Geburah*, iron with *Tiphereth*, and the hermaphroditic brass (copper) with *Netzach* and *Hod*. Quicksilver is referred to *Yesod*, and the "true medicine of metals" to *Malkuth*.

The writer also cites another distribution. The thick water, that is, mercury, is *Kether*, salt is *Chokhmah*, and sulfur is *Binah*. *Netzach* is tin, *Hod* is copper, *Yesod* is lead, while *Malkuth* is the metallic woman, the Luna of the wise and the "field into which the seeds of secret minerals ought to be cased, that is, the water of gold, etc."

The peculiar genius of the work is illustrated in the third chapter where Daniel's vision of the beast with ten horns is interpreted alchemically by the help of Gematria.

## IN CONCLUSION

Such has our contemplation for now reached a plateau, and a gentle rest is therefore in order: a rest to marvel, and to ponder the mysterious philosophy, theosophy, and esoteric metaphysics of the mystical, holy kabbalah.

# INDEX

Aaron the Great, 84
Abba, 164, 200, 324, 337
Abba, Rabbi, 48, 96, 142
  Book of Concealment and, 102
  discourse of the aged man, 115, 116
  Greater and Lesser Holy Synod and, 105, 111, 112–113
  three Sabbath meals, 119
Abel, 249
Abraham
  Book of Adam and, 13
  *Chesed*, 167
  the Covenant of circumcision, 266–267
  Covenant with, 262–263
  history of, 263–264
  ideas which lie behind the circumcision, 268–269
  Melchizedek of Salem, 265
  metaphysical principle of the Covenant, 267–268
  and Sarah in Egypt, 264–265
  Sepher Yetzirah of, 32, 35, 56, 74
  and Shechinah, 329, 331
  Shetiah stone and, 186
  the sign of circumcision, 266
  three angels of, 128–129
  token of the Covenant, 265–266

Abraham ben David Halevi (Ben Dior), 37, 68
Abraham ben David HaLevi, the Younger (Raavad), 68, 69, 78, 81–82
Abraham ben David of Posquiere, 70
Abraham ben Samuel Abulafia, 50
Abraham, Rabbi, 78, 404
Abulafia, Abraham, 68–69
Achushveirush, 342
Adam
  Adam's gift book, 12
  and angel Raziel, 11–12
  fall of man, 240, 241, 242, 244, 245–246, 247–248, 249–250, 252–253
  loss of the gift book, 12–13
  making of man, 224–226
  Mystery of Sex and, 352
  prototypal archeplastic Adam, 395
  Shechinah and Adam, 325–326, 327
  the soul of the departed meets Adam and others, 296–297
Adam Belial, 395
Adam Primordial, 196
Aged man, discourse of the, 114–116
Age of the chief texts, 31, 34–35
Book of Formation
  known to Archbishop of Lyons, 33–34
  empire of the demons, 232–233
  historical data, 31–32
  Sepher Yetzirah in the Talmud, 34
  Sepher Yetzirah of Abraham the Patriarch, 32
  the tanna Rabbi Akiva, 32–33
Agobard of Lyons, Archbishop, 33–34
*Ain Soph*, 151, 154
  Book of Formation and, 78, 81–82, 83
  the Faithful Shepherd and, 121
  four worlds and, 161, 162, 172
  Moses of Cordoba on, 152–153, 155–156
  Shechinah and, 319–320, 324
  Ten Emanations and, 54
  Ten Sephiroth and, 158
  White Head and, 170, 171
  Zoharic teaching of, 152
"Aish Metzareph", 402–404

Akiva ben Joseph, Rabbi, 32–33, 56, 65
Albertus Magnus, 72
*Alphabet of Rabbi Akiva*, 33, 34, 65
Alphrag, Abu, 69
*Amain*, 301–302
Amalek, 237–238
Amsterdam Codex, 127
Ancient of Days, 8
Ancient texts, 61
Angel of Vindication, 300
Angels and demons and metaphysical doctrine, 12, 128, 161, 213
choirs of angels in Yetzirah, 214–215
divine intelligence and forces, 213–214
empire of the demons, 232–233
fall of the angels, 230, 233–234
hierarchy of angels and hierarchy of demons, 232
other demons, 236–239, 247–252
Samael and Lilith, 217–218
universe correspondences of the Sephiroth: cortices, spirits, and demons, 215–217

Aristobolus, 54
Aristotle, 37, 72
Ark of the Covenant, 256–257, 332
Ashi, Reb, 21
*Asis Rimonim* (Gallico), 387
Assembly of the Sanctuary, 90, 170
*Atziluth*, 126, 141, 161, 162, 169, 172, 328
Avicebron. *See* Ibn Gebirol, Solomon ben Yehudah
Aza, 234–235
Azael, 234–235
Azriel ben Menahem, 68, 77–78, 82, 118

Babel, Tower of, 259, 260–261
Babylonian Talmud, 34, 38, 46, 104, 292, 300, 304, 331, 339, 345
Bahir, 118–119
Balance Principle, 392–393
Barachiel ben Korba, 92
Bartholocci, Julius, 3, 84
Benjamin, 340
*Bereshith*, 143, 174
Bereshith Rabbah, 101
*Beth Elohim*, 153, 159
*Beth Elohim—The House of God* (Herrera), 400
Bible stories, hidden meaning of, 95

*Bibliotheca Magna Rabbinica, Roma 1678–1692* (Bartholocci), 3
Bilaam, 342
Bilhah, 329
*Binah*, 112, 135, 141, 158, 177
   fifty gates of, 10
   the Four Worlds and, 161, 163
   Gates of Understanding, 364
   Matrona and, 172
   the soul and, 200
   Ten Sephiroth and, 167, 168
B'nai Elokim, 213
"Book of Abraham the Jew", 404
Book of Concealment (Book of Occultation), 56, 65, 99, 139, 170, 350, 392, 393
   as a theogony, 99–103
   Book of Splendor and, 88, 90
   Greater Holy Synod and, 104–105
   Hai Gaon and, 80
   the soul in, 194
   and Zoharic teaching of *Ain-Soph*, 12
Book of Formation. *See* Sepher Yetzirah (Book of Formation)
*Book of Genealogies* (Zakut), 41
Book of Mystery, 173, 324, 338
Book of Occultation. *See* Book of Concealment (Book of Occultation)
"Book of Points" (Aaron the Great), 84
Book of Splendor, date and authorship of, 40–41
   account of the *Sepher Yuhasim*, 41–44
Book of Splendor, its contents and divisions
   Book of Exodus, Luminous Book, Book of Leviticus, others, 89–90
   Book of Genesis and its omissions and additions, 89
   Book of Numbers and the Idra Rabbah, 90
   commentaries on the Zohar and explanatory books, 93–94
   contents of the Zohar, 88–89
   Deuteronomy and the Idra Zuta, 90
   divisions of Zoharic contents, 89

the external parts as
understood by
Rosenroth, 92–93
hidden meaning of Bible
stories, 95
Latin and French
translations, 87–88
mythos of the rose, 97
a narrative, 95–97
nature of Zohar, 94
of Zoharic contents,
continued, 94
power of faith and
thought, 98
Rosenroth's scheme of
tabulation, 91–92
the voice and the word,
97–98
the wise and the unwise,
94–95
the Zohar and the Sepher
Yetzirah, 87
Book of Splendor, modern
criticism of, 36
attitude and contrariety of
Aristotelians and their
antagonists, 36–37
defense of Zohar by
recent thinkers, 37–38
hostility of Graetz, 38
impeachment of the
Zohar, 38–39
Solomon Munk's
convictions, 39

*Book of the Revolutions of Souls*
(I. Luria), 114, 211,
393
Botarel, Moses, 78, 402
Briah, angels of, 161, 213,
214, 216

Caanan, 301
Cahen, Samuel, 50
Celestial Chariot, 136
Celestial Palaces, 140
Celestial Tabernacle, 136
*Chain of Tradition*, 35
Chariot theosophy, 27
Chasdai, Abn-Yussuf, 67
*Chayah*, 79, 203
Cherubim, 343–344
*Chesed*, 165
  Ten Sephiroth and, 167,
    168
"Chesed Abraham", 94
*Chokhmah*, 112, 135, 141,
  158, 176, 184
  the Four Worlds and, 161,
    163
  Matrona and, 172
  the soul and, 200
  Ten Sephiroth and, 167,
    168
*Chokhmat Nistar*, 5
Christian mind, the
  kabbalah's sphere of
  influence on the, 59–
  60
Chronicles, Books of, 398

Circumcision, 218
  the Covenant of, 175, 266–269, 351
*Coelum Sephiroticum*, 391
*Cohain of the Kabbalah of Gedaliah*, 69
Colors
  color symbolism in Sithre Torah, 129
  symbolic colors of the Sephiroth, 83
  three colors of the rainbow, 128
Cosmology, doctrine of, 179
  creation and the instruments appertaining thereto, 186–188
  doctrine of Divine Immanence, 183–185
  final intimations in creation, 188–189
  letters of concealment, 180–183
  many worlds were made, arose, and decayed, 189
  mysterious stone Shetiah, 185–186
  the world created from thought, 179–180
Creation of the world, 186–189, 398–399
*Creeds and Opinions* (Saadya Gaon), 376

*Crown of the Kingdom* (Ibn Gebirol), 71
Crowns, ten averse, 373–374

Daath, 158, 172, 196
Daniel, Book of, 51, 170–171, 186
David, 13, 281
Death
  deathbed visions, 297–298
  of Moses, 277–278
  resurrection of the dead, 305–306
"Delineation of the Heavenly Temples", 67
Deluge, account of the, 254–255
  confusion of tongues after the Deluge, 259–261
  the holocaust, 257–258
  Noah's ark and the meaning of the ark, 256–257
  Noah's experiment, 258–259
  sins which brought about the deluge, 255–256
Deuteronomy, Book of, 90, 137, 203, 241, 278, 289
Dew of life, 307–308
Divine emanation and divine immanence, 157–159, 183–185

Divine Hypostases, 169–170, 173, 337
Divine Name, 326, 330
Divine Will, 156–157
Donoto, Sabbatai, 84
*Duties of the Heart* (Paqudah), 46

Earthly paradise narrative, 221–222
  formation of Eve, 226
  the ineffable nuptials, 227
  making of man and his exulted state of radiance, 223–226
  revolt of the spirits, 228–229
  Shechinah—Matrona, 222–223
  of the supernal and the inferior paradises, 223
  the tree of the garden, 227–228
Ecclesiates, Book of, 211
Eden River, 368–369
Edomite Kings, 106–108, 392, 393, 395, 398
Egypt
  Abraham and Sarah in, 264–265
  the Shechinah in, 329–330
Eimma, 164, 167, 200, 324, 337

Eleazer, Rabbi, 96, 102, 131–132
Elias, Rabbi, 251–252
Eliezer ben Hyrcanus, 66
Eliezer of Worms, 12, 72, 83–84
Eliezer, Rabbi (son of R. Shimon), 113, 142, 245, 249, 353
Eliezer the Great, 380
Elijah, 124, 180, 184
  Prayer of Elijah, 144–145
Enoch, 13, 259–260
Eschatology, Zoharic, 302, 309–310
Espousals, 351, 362–363
Esther, 342–343
Eve, 258, 325, 352
  and making of man, 224–226
  and fall of man, 241–242, 244, 245–246, 248–250
  formation of, 226
Exodus, Book of, 89–90, 198, 199, 275, 306, 363
External Torah (Law), 336
Ezekiel, 273
Ezekiel, Book of, 258, 287, 290

Faithful Shepherd, 90, 121–122, 151, 152, 176, 186
  manifestation of the Shechinah, 124–126

Faithful Shepherd (*continued*)
  Metatron, Satan, and
    Lilith, 126
  three chances for a
    repentant sinner, 124
  vicarious atonement, 122–124
*Faithful Shepherd* in *Beth Elohim*, 153
Feast of the Paschal Lamb, 233, 365
Fifty gates
  of *Binah*, 10
  fifty Gates of
    Understanding, 321
    and man, 322
Flaming Sword, 251, 316, 377
*Fountain of Life* (Ibn Gebirol), 71–72, 73
Fountain text, 160–161
*Fount of Living Water, The* (Abulafia), 69
Four Worlds, doctrine of, 160, 161–164
  doctrine concerning the sephirotic tree, 172–173
  the fountain text, 160–161
  male and female principles, 171
  Matrona, 171–172
  summary of correspondences of the Sephiroth, 166–168
  the theosophy of the word, 173
  of the three hypostases, 169–170
  Tree of Life, 164–166
  the White Head and the two countenances, 170–171
  the word (logos), 174–175
Franc, Adolf, 88
France, as first recipient of kabbalah, 57–58

Gabriel, 128, 213
Gallico, Samuel, 387
*Garden of Aromatic* (Moses Ibn Jacob ben Ezra), 68
*Garden of Delight* (Nahmanides), 83
Garden of Eden, 204, 221, 224–225, 247, 252–253, 325–326, 327
"Garden of Pomegranates" (Moses of Cordova), 387–388, 403
*Gate of the Heavens* (Herrera), 400
Gates of Compassion, 363–365
"Gates of Light", 156–157, 159, 177–178
Gates of Understanding, 321, 363–365
*Geburah*, 165, 167–168, 205

Gemara
  divisions of the, 23–24
  and Talmud, 20, 21
Gematria, 26–27
Genesis, Book of
  Abraham, 263, 265, 267
  coming of Messiah, 290
  fall of man, 245
  making of man, 223–224
  marriage, 227, 352, 360, 382
  Mystery of Faith, 362, 363
  and its omissions and additions, 89
  the soul, 203
Gentiles
  resurrection of the dead, 305–306
  souls of, 209–211, 372–373, 379–381
Ginsburg, C. D., 88
Good and evil, 231–232, 396
Graetz, Germany, 38
Graetz, Henrich, 42, 51
Great and Holy Assembly, 170
Greater Holy Synod, 104–105
  esoteric speculation and the symbolism of the Edomite kings, 106–108
  explanation and developments of the treatise, 106
  sublime touches in this treatise, 110
"Great French Bible" (Cahen), 50
Great Zohar, 91, 92
*Guide for the Sinner* (Eliezer of Worms), 84
*Guide of the Perplexed* (Maimonides), 6, 32, 70

*Habitaculum*, 173
Haggada, 23
*Hai*, 167, 168
Hai Gaon, 67–68, 78, 80
Halacha, 23
*Halachoth Olam*, 19
Hammarumnah, Rabbi, 124
Hamnuna, Rabbi, 96–97, 139
Herod the Great, 118
Herrera, Abraham Cohen, 400
Hidden Commentary, 146
Hidden things of the law, 127
  other intimations and excerpts, 129–130
  stages of mystical vision, 127–128
  three angels of Abraham, 128–129
*Hilchot Yetzirah*, 74
Hillel the Elder, 118
Hillel the Great, 33
Hirtz, Naphtali, 156, 397–398

*History of Freemasonry* (Gould), 37
History of Sabbatai Tzvi, 59
*Hochmah*, 12
*Hod*, 165, 168
Holy of Holies, 141, 186, 333, 340, 345
Holy Spirit
   Shechinah and the, 338–343
   soul-origin and, 371

Ibn Ezra, Abraham ben Meir, 37
Ibn Falaquera, Shem Tov, 68
Ibn Gebirol, Solomon ben Yehudah (Avicebron), 68, 71–72, 73
Ibn Wakkar, Joseph ben Abraham, 70
Idra De Maschcanah, 90, 102
Idra Rabbah, 90, 99, 392
Idras, three, 106, 173, 325, 338
Idra Zuta, 90, 99, 111, 392
Iow, Menahem Recauatian Ibahian, 118
Isaac, 329
Isaac ben Abraham, 146
Isaac ben Moses, 146
Isaac de Acco, 42–44, 48, 87
Isaac de Lettes, 118
Isaac, Rabbi, 111, 139

Isaac the Blind, 51, 70, 72, 82, 152
Isaiah, Book of, 184, 251, 286, 291, 294, 300–301, 327, 333, 338–339, 362
Israel
   exaltations of, 274
   exile of Shechinah and, 333–335
   golden calf and the downfall of, 274–275
   messianic expectation in, 286–287, 290–291
Issachar ben Naphtali, 401

Jacob, 185, 329–330, 331, 356
Jacob ben Naphtha, 143
Jarki, Solomon, 68
Jeremiah, 35
Jerusalem Talmud, 21, 339
Jescivah ben Joseph HaLevi, 19
Jewish literature
   Abraham and Moses recipients, 13
   Adam's gift book, 12–13
   after Moses and David, 13–14
   the Ancient of Days, 8
   *Bereshith* and the Secret Doctrine, 10–11
   days of Rabbi Shimon, 14
   to the esoteric student, 6
   the fifty gates, 10

incompleteness of the Secret Doctrine, 14–15
kabbalah, 4
kabbalistic philosophy, 5–6
of literal vesture and the esoteric, 7–8
magical and pratical kabbalah, 6–7
no *scientia kabbalistica*, 6
origin of the Secret Doctrine, 11–12
of the Pentateuch's stories, 8–9
post-Christian literature of the Jews, 3
research probing the human mind, 4
of the Secret Doctrine, 7
secret doctrine of kabbalism, 5
sixty methods and seventy modes of interpretation, 9
the supplementary soul, 9–10
*Jewish Quarterly Review, 1913*, 35
*Jewish Society* (Eldershein), 52
Job, 123–124
Joel, Book of, 290
Jonathan ben Uziel, 248, 249
Joseph, 329, 330, 331, 340
Joseph ben Todros, 44

Joseph ben Uziel, 35, 84
Joseph Gikatalia ben Abraham, 178, 386
Joseph, Rabbi, 58
Joshua, 279
Judah ben Barzillai, 84
Judah Ha Levi, 32, 68, 84
Judah, Rabbi, 139
Judah the Prince, 19

Kabbalah, 4
exponents of speculative kabbalah, 70
historical treatises with kabbalistic sounding names, 69
influence of kabbalah on Jewry, 59–60
kabbalistic philosophy, 5–6
kabbalistic schools, 72
magical and pratical, 6–7
no *scientia kabbalistica*, 6
opponents of kabbalah, 70–71
secret doctrine of kabbalism, 5
as secret tradition and a cryptic philosophy, 16–17
the soul in kabbalism, 193–199
Spain and France, the first recipients of, 57–58

Kabbalah and the Talmud
  antiquity of, 18–19
  compilation method, 19–20
  distinctions between kabbalah and Talmud, 24
  divisions and contents of the Mishnah and Gemara, 23–24
  forms of the Mishnah, 20
  Gemara and Talmud, 20
  jurisprudence and sociology of the Talmud, 21–22
  materials of the Talmud, 19
  mesorah and kabbalah, 24
  metaphysics of the kabbalah, 22
  some enigmatic metaphysics in Talmud, 22–23
  two Talmud versions, 20–21
*Kabbalah Denudata*, 87–88
Kabbalah, divisions of the
  distinctions between ceremonial ritual and kabbalah, 25–26
  gematria, notarikon, temurah, 26–27
  kabbalah confused with ceremonial magic, 25
  theurgy, talismans, and kabbalah, 26
Kabbalism, majesty of God in, 149, 154
  God's uttermost transcendence, 150–151
  kabbalistic idea of God and the evolution of the universe, 149–150
  Moses of Cordoba on *Ain Soph*, 152–153
  Raayah Mehemnah on the notion of God, 153
  Zoharic teaching of *Ain-Soph*, 152
Kabbalistic doctrines-alleged sources, 56
  Philo's writings and kabbalistic doctrine, 55–56
  Ten Emanations, Macroprosopus, and Microprosopus, 54–55
Kadmoth HaZohar (Luria), 37–38
*Kether*, 100, 107, 141, 172, 177
  the Four Worlds and, 161, 162, 163, 164
  Ten Sephiroth and, 159, 166, 167
  White Head and, 170, 171
*Kuzari* (Judah Ha Levi), 68, 84

*La kabbale* (Franck), 34
Lamentations, Book of, 146
Landauer, M. H., 50
Law
  External Law, 336
  hidden things of the, 127–130
  Moses and the Law, 273
  original Tables of the Law, 275–277
  the soul and, 205–206
Leah, 329
Lesser Holy Assembly, 170
Lesser Holy Synod, 105, 111, 392
  the Master's death and instructions, 111–112
  nuptial joys of the soul of R. Shimon, 112–113
Letters, Hebrew
  Abraham and letter *hai*, 266
  of the Divine Name, 326, 330
  fifty gates of *Binah*, 10
  of HVYH Elohim, 314
  in creation, 188–189
  letter *aleph*, 130, 154
  letters of concealment, 180–183
  letters of the Tetragrammaton, 101, 102, 169, 182, 186, 203
  Shechinah's relation to the letter of Tetragrammaton, 317–319
  three Divine Hypostases, 169–170
Levi, David, 45
Levita, Elias, 45
Leviticus, Book of, 89–90, 98, 199, 258
*Liber Drushim* (Luria), 389–390, 391
Lilith, 126, 217–218, 236, 249, 250, 251–252, 360, 395
*Lingula examinis*, 100
Little Zohar, 91
Lot, 329
Luminous Book, 89–90, 117–118
  contents of the Bahir, 118–119
  holy living creatures, 119
  significance of the three Sabbath meals, 119–120
Luria, David, 37–38
Luria, Isaac de, 81, 93–94, 100, 114, 211, 386, 388–390, 393, 398, 399, 400

Maaman, 251–252
Maaseh Bereshith, 32
Maaseh Merkavah, 32

Macroprosopus, 54–55, 101, 102, 106, 107, 108, 112, 173
Mahaltoth, 251–252
Maimonides, Moses, 6, 32, 37, 68, 70
*Malkuth*, 107, 140–141, 161, 164, 168, 172, 196, 215
Man
  the complete, 351–352
  fifty gates and, 322
  making of man and his exulted state of radiance, 223–226
Man, fall of, 240, 395–396
  Adam and Eve both begot children from demons, 249–250
  Adam and the serpent, 247–248
  alternative accounts of the kinds of temptation, 242
  another account, 244
  another account of female demon, 250–251
  of the beauty of Adam and Eve, 245–246
  cuirass of sacred letters, 244–245
  dire consequences caused by the temptation, 242–243
  finale of the expulsion from Eden, 252–253
  Lilith, Maaman, Ogereth, and Mahaltoth, 251–252
  loss of the celestial decorations and the substituted leaf coverings, 243
  making of man and his exulted state of radiance, 223–226
  man in his glory and hereafter, 240–241
  of the odors diffused in Eden for the vestures of the soul, 247
  Samael and Eve, 241–242
  Samael defiles Eve/Cain, 248–249
  separation caused by the trespass and death, 246
Marcus Aurelius, 20
Marriage, 382
  communion between man and Shechinah via, 359–361
  the ineffable nuptials, 227
  of Moses, 272
  mystery of purification and sanctification in, 353–354

the nuptial state, 352–353
secret of matrimonial union, 354–358
virginity among women, 381
*Mathnisim*, 90
*Mathnitin*, 137–138, 142
Matrona, 171–172
  celestial virgins in the service of, 381
  Mystery of Sex and, 377
  and resurrection of the dead, 307
  Shechinah and, 222–223, 316, 317, 326, 331, 333, 336, 345
Meimron, 174
Meir ben Simon, 117–118
Melchizedek, 265
Mercy, retribution and, 303–304
Mesorah and kabbalah, 24
Messiah, coming of the
  the advent of the Messiah in another version, 292
  a light of symbolism, 291–292
  the intruders, 289–290
  messianic expectation in Israel, 286–287
  the portent of the Messiah's advent, 292–293
  the present abode of the Messiah and his suffering, 293–294
  several Messiahs to precede the advent of the true King Messiah, 288–289
  the subject of the Messiah in Israel, 290–291
  symbolism concerning Messiah, 289
Metatron
  and coming of Messiah, 289
  of Enoch/Metatron, 13, 232, 377–379
  and Lilith, 126
  in Mathnitin, 138
  and resurrection of the dead, 307
  Shechinah and, 317, 332, 333
  and the Temple, 281
Meyer, Isaac, 37, 70
Michael, 128, 213
Microprosopus, 54–55, 101, 102, 106, 108–110
Midrash Conen, 66, 101
Midrash HaNealam, 90, 92, 131, 142
Midrash Rabbah, 278
Midrash Ruth, 142–143, 248
Midrash Talpiyoth, 287
*Mikubbalim*, 5

Mishnah
  compilation of the, 19–20
  divisions of the, 23–24
  forms of the, 20
  Shechinah and the, 336
"Mishnat" (Joseph ben Uziel), 84
Mishnayoth, 19
Mocha, Rabbi, 45
Mordechai, Rabbi, 403
Mordell, Phineas, 35
Moses, 13, 88, 121, 270–271
  death of Moses and his sepulchre, 277–278
  exaltations of Israel, 274
  the faithful shepherd, 273
  golden calf and the downfall of Israel, 274–275
  marriage of, 272
  Moses will return, 278–279
  the original Tables of the Law, 275–277
  the promulgation of the divine teaching—the law, 273
  and Shechinah, 330, 331, 332, 334
  the tragedy of the great lawgiver, 278
Moses Abraham ben Samuel Zakut, 41, 42
Moses de Leon, Zohar and, 39, 40–41, 42, 43, 44–45, 48, 49, 50, 51, 56
Moses Ibn Jacob ben Ezra, 68
Moses of Cordoba, 152–153, 386–387, 400, 403
Most Holy Mystery, 179–180
Munk, Solomon, 37, 39
*Mysteries of Shimon ben Yochai*, 53
Mystery in Transcendence, 221
Mystery of Faith, 350, 375
  creation and, 179–180
  the Deluge and, 256
  fall of man and, 242, 253
  mystery of espousals and the, 362–363
  other references and implications of the, 366–368
  Seven Degrees and the, 365–366
  the soul and, 194–195
  soul-origin and, 370–371
  the souls and the seven palaces, 379
  spirits and, 229
Mystery of Sex, 350, 381–382
  communion between man and Shechinah via marriage, 359–361
  the complete man, 351–352

cosmic soul of the
Gentiles, 372
Covenant with Abraham
and, 269
the Deluge and, 254, 257,
259
demons and, 238
downfall of Israel and, 274
in earthly paradise, 221,
222, 228
of Enoch/Metatron, 377–
379
fall of man and, 242, 250,
254
forty-nine Gates of
Understanding—the
Gates of Compassion,
363–365
of the generation of souls,
350, 374–375
of the grand Matrona
herself, 377
the higher Eden River,
River of the life and
of souls, 368– 369
holy souls which can
become incarnate in
Jewry, 361–362
male issue, 297
mystery of espousals and
the great Mystery of
Faith, 362–363
Mystery of Faith in the
narrative of the soul
origin, 370–371
mystery of purification
and sanctification in
marriage, 353–354
the nuptial state, 352–
353
other references and
implications of the
Mystery of Faith,
366–368
production of souls, 369–
370
secret of matrimonial
union, 354–358
seven degrees and the
Mystery of Perfect
Faith, 365–366
Shechinah and, 344–345,
349
the souls and the Seven
Palaces, 379
souls of Gentiles
converted to
Judaism, 379–381
of the souls of the ones
converted from
paganism, 372–373
ten averse Crowns, 373–
374
of the union of souls in
the world to come,
376–377
universal history of souls,
371–372
Mystery of Wisdom, 259,
260

Naamah, 235–236, 250, 251–252
Nagdilah, 71
Nahmanides (Ramban), 42, 43, 58, 67, 78, 82, 83, 118
Nazir, Jacob, 68
*Nefesh*, 199–202, 203, 205
Nehunya ben HaKanah, 118
*Nephesh*, 79
*Neshamah*, 79, 199–202, 203, 205
*Netzach*, 165, 168
*Niddah*, 195
Noah, 241, 256–257, 258–259, 335
Notarikon, 26–27
Numbers, Book of, 90

Obadiah, Book of, 293
Ogereth, 251–252
*Ohr Ain Soph*, 15
Onkelos, 174
Oral Law, 7, 8, 13, 41, 137, 273, 275–277, 315, 336, 337
*Order of the Generations*, 35

Palace of Love, 115
Palaces
  palaces above, 207–208
  seven, 206–207, 379
Palestine, Zoharic schools in, 386–387
Palestinian Talmud, 21

Paqudah, Behai ben Yoseph Ibn, 46
*Pardes*, 162
Paternity, doctrine of, 208–209
Paths of wisdom and the gates of understanding, 176–178
Patriarchs, Shechinah and the, 328–329
Pentateuch, 7, 8–9, 21, 88
*Pesachim*, 252
Philo, 54, 55–56
*Philosophy of Ibn Gebirol* (Meyer), 37
Phylacteries, 366
Physiognomy, 138–139
Pillars, three, 391
Pirke Haichaloth, 66
Pirke Merhavah, 66
Postel, G., 77
Prayer, 393
Prayer of Elijah, 144–145
Proverbs, Book of, 156, 392
Psalms, Book of, 243, 326, 328, 353
"Purifying Fire", 402–404

Raavad, 68, 78, 81–82
Raayah Mehemnah, 56, 90, 153
Raaya Mehemna, 56
Rabbina, 21
Rachel, 329
Rafon, David, 43

Raphael, 12, 128, 213
Rava, 74
Raze de Razin, 138
Raziel, Book of, 11–12
Reincarnation, 79–80, 208–209, 211–212
Rekanati, Menahem, 196
Resurrection, concerning
   concealment of the curative light, the dew of life, 307–308
   conclusion of Zoharic eschatology, 309–310
   the imperishable little bone, 308–309
   resurrection of the dead, 305–306
   tradition of the thesis of resurrection, 306–307
Retribution, 303
   and mercy, 303–304
Reuchlinus Riccius, 77
*Revolutions of the Souls* (I. Luria), 114, 211, 393
Rosenroth, 87, 88, 91–92, 93
*Rosh Hashanah* tractate, 300
"Royal Valley, The" (Hirtz), 156, 397–398
*Ruach*, 79, 199–202, 203, 205
Ruth, 142–143

Saadiah ben Joseph, 67
Saadya Gaon, 78, 79, 80, 376, 402

*Sabbath*, 104–105, 248, 271, 304, 331
Sabbath
   marriage and the Sabbath day, 360
   significance of the three Sabbath meals, 119–120
   supplementary soul of, 204–205
   task of lighting Sabbath candles, 317
Samael, 126, 217–218, 228, 236–237, 238, 241–242, 247–249, 395
*Sanhedrin*, 34, 74, 185, 292
Sarah, 264–265, 329, 368
Satan, 126, 217–218
Scholem, Gerhard, 403
School of Abulafia, 72
School of Eliezer of Worms, 72
School of Isaac the Blind, 72
*Scientia kabbalistica*, 6
Secret commentary, the, 131–132
   light of the supersubstantial bread, 132–133
Secret Doctrine, 53, 98, 175
   *Bereshith* and the, 10–11
   Canaan, 301
   incompleteness of the, 14–15

Secret Doctrine (*continued*)
  in kabbalistic philosophy,
    5–6
  Moses and the, 13, 277,
    278
  Mystery of Sex and, 355,
    356
  origin of the Secret
    Doctrine, 11–12
  of the Secret Doctrine, 7
  Shechinah and the, 345,
    348, 349
  the soul and the, 9–10
  Tree of Life, 227, 276
*Secrets of the Torah*
    (Nahmanides), 83
*Seder Ha kabbalah* (Abraham
    ben David HaLevi), 69,
    81
Sepher HaBahir, 90, 117–
    118, 136, 142
Sepher Ha-Zohar, 27
Sepher Yetzirah and the
    Zohar, Midrashim,
    precursors of the, 65–66
  chapters of R. Eliezer and
    the Midrash Conen,
    66
  exponents of speculative
    kabbalah, 70
  Gebirol and the Book of
    Formation, 72–73
  historical treatises with
    kabbalistic sounding
    names, 69
  kabbalistic schools of the
    period, 72
  opponents of kabbalah,
    70–71
  other authorities of these
    periods, 67–69
  Sepher Yetzirah (Book of
    Formation), 34–35, 36,
    52, 56, 61, 74–75, 166,
    176
  of Abraham the Patriarch,
    32
  Book of Concealment
    and, 100
  Book of Splendor and,
    87
  the character and the
    teachings of the
    commentary, 82–83
  the commentary ascribed
    to Hai Gaon, 80
  the commentary of R.
    Eliezer of Worms,
    83–84
  the commentary of the
    Raavad, circa 1100–
    1180 on, 81–82
  connections and
    dependencies of, 77–
    78
  first appearance in Spain
    and France, 58
  kabbalah and, 26, 27
  known to Archbishop of
    Lyons, 33–34

publications and versions of, 77
Rabbi Aziel's Yetzirah commentary, 82
the Ramban, Nahmanides, 83
Saadya's commentary, 78
the soul and reincarnation, 79–80
the tanna Rabbi Akiva, author of, 32–33
the ten categories: Saadya, 80
Ten Sephiroth and, 164
transcendental numerations, 75–77
*Sepher Yuhasim*, 40, 41–44, 51
*Sephira*, 159
Sephiroth
  emanation of, 391
  fivehold division in the, 394
  light of the, 391
  summary of correspondences of the, 166–168
Sephirotic tree, 172–173, 319–321, 322–324
Serpent, son of the morning, and the fall of the angels, 230
Aza and Azael and company, 234–235
empire of the demons, 232–233
first downfall of the angels, 233–234
God also the author of certain evil, 230–231
the great dragon, 237–238
hierarchy of angels and hierarchy of demons, 232
Naamah, 235–236
other demons, 238–239
Samael and his wife, the serpent, 236–237
second downfall of the angels, 234
spirit of good and the spirit of evil, 231–232
Seth, 13, 250
Seven heavens and seven earths, 140–141
Seven Palaces, 206–207, 365
Shabbethai ben Abraham ben Joel, 84
Shechinah
  abides everywhere, 315–316
  additional particulars of the collection about, 336–337
  allegory of Shechinah and the three husbands, 128–129, 270–271, 272, 329, 330–332
  alternative allocations of, 316–317

Shechinah (*continued*)
- the architect and builder, 325–326
- of communion, 347–349
- communion between man and Shechinah via marriage, 359–361
- counterstatements, 335
- did not forsake Israel in exile, 333–335
- doctrine that Shechinah suffers with mankind, 326
- in Egypt, 329–330
- in exile, 327, 345
- fifty gates and man, 322
- fifty Gates of Understanding, 321
- the first of created beings, 325
- and the Holy Spirit, 338–343
- the indwelling glory, termed Shechinah, in Scripture and in the Zohar, 343–345
- integration of the entire tree in, 322–324
- manifestation of the, 124–126
- mystery of, 313–314
- other aspects of, 345–346
- and the Patriarchs, 328–329
- place of Shechinah in the Sephirotic tree, 319–321
- relation to the letter of Tetragrammaton, 317–319
- reminder, 324
- repetition of the theosophical symbolism and mysticism, 337–338
- revealed to Abraham, 128–129
- Sarah under the protection of, 264
- Shechinah—Matrona, 222–223
- the sin causing the exile, 345
- in Song of Songs, 346–347
- of spiritual communion with, 348–349
- summation, 335–336
- of the Supernals and the one exiled, 328
- task of lighting Sabbath candles, 317
- in the Temple of Solomon, 332–333
- Tree of Life, 338
- various ascriptions and designations of, 314–315

Shem HaMeforash, 119

Sheol, doctrine concerning, 295
  deathbed events, 297–298
  of death—the soul body separation and departure, 296
  of hell everlasting or otherwise, 300–301
  importance of *Amain* response, 301–302
  issue of male issue, 297
  respecting Canaan, 301
  retribution, 303
  retribution and mercy, 303–304
  the soul of the departed meets Adam and others, 296–297
  version of another account, 298–299
  Zoharic flux of eschatology, 302
Shereerah ben Chanina, 67
Sherirah, Rabbi, 139
Shetiah, 185–186
Shimon bar Yochai, 19, 88, 184, 196, 210, 225, 231, 276, 302
  Book of Concealment and, 100, 102–103
  disciples of, 138–139
  discourse of the aged man, 114
  explanation of the term *Bereshith*, 143
  the Faithful Shepherd, 121, 151
  Greater Holy Synod and, 104–105, 107
  Lesser Holy Synod and, 111, 112–113
  Mystery of Sex and, 356, 357, 358, 381
  nine Celestial Palaces, 140
  Zoharic expositors and, 387, 400
  days of, 14
  mysteries of, 53
  Zohar and, 41, 44, 46, 48, 58
Shiur Komah, 65–66
*Siphrah De Zenioutha* (I. Luria), 90, 100, 393
Sithre Torah, 90, 127, 129, 142
Sohphonia, 261
Solomon, 185, 282, 348
Song of Solomon, 97, 142, 146, 171, 174–175, 287, 354, 366, 387
Song of Songs, 97, 346–347, 366
Soul of man, 193
  belief in the soul's immortality, 194
  *chaya* and *yechidah*, 203
  cosmic soul of the Gentiles, 372
  five-fold division of souls in the four worlds, 394

Soul of man (*continued*)
  of the generation of souls, 350, 374–375
  the higher Eden River, River of the life and of souls, 368–369
  holy souls which can become incarnate in Jewry, 361–362
  kabbalistic pneumotology, 194–199
  the law leads the soul, 205–206
  metapsychosis or revolutions of souls, 208–209
  Mystery of Faith in the narrative of the soul origin, 370–371
  other soul extensions, 203
  the palaces above, 207–208
  parable of the soul, 206
  parts of division of the soul, 199–202
  on preexistence of souls, 199
  production of souls, 369–370
  and reincarnation, 79–80, 208–209, 211–212
  resurrection and reincarnation, 211–212
  of revolution of souls, 396–397
  the soul in kabbalism, 193–194
  soul of the departed, 296–297
  the souls and the Seven Palaces, 206–207, 379
  of the souls of the ones converted from paganism, 372–373
  the supplementary soul, 9–10, 204–205
  transmigration of souls of gentiles, 209–211
  of the union of souls in the world to come, 376–377
  universal history of souls, 371–372
Spain, as first recipient of kabbalah, 57–58
Spirit of good and the spirit of evil, 231–232, 396
Supernals
  Shechinah and the, 324, 328
  Supernal and the inferior paradises, 223
*Supreme Mysteries*, 136
Supreme Mysteries, 206
Supreme Soul, 374
Szinessy, Schiller, 39, 48–49

Tabernacle, the, 332, 340–341, 342
Talmud
   Sepher Yetzirah in the, 34, 74–75
   *See also* Kabbalah and the Talmud
Targum, 27
Temple of Solomon, 332–333
Temples in Jerusalem, two, 280–281
   an alternative version concerning the sanctuaries, 282–283
   consolation and hope, 284–285
   first temple described by the Zohar, 281–282
   lamentations over the holy houses and places, 283–284
   Shechinah and, 334–335
Temurah, 26–27
Ten Emanations, doctrine of the, 54–55
Ten Sephiroth, 155–156, 164, 166, 176
   angels and, 214
   divine emanation and divine immanence, 157–159
   mystery of the operation of the mysterious divine will, 156–157
   summary of correspondences of the, 166–168
Tetragrammaton, 101, 102, 141, 167, 169, 182, 186, 188, 203, 317–319, 390
Thaumaturge, 386
Theosophy, 26
Theosophy Mystica, 52
Thomas Aquinas, 72
*Tikkunei HaZohar*, 92
*Tikkunim Chadashim*, 93
Tiphereth, 140–141, 165, 168
Tower of Babel, 259, 260–261
Tree of Knowledge, 228, 241, 244–245, 276
Tree of Life, 135, 164–166, 227–228, 229, 246, 276, 316, 338, 361
Tree of Trespass, 231, 241

Uriel, 213

*Valley of the King, The* (Hirtz), 397
*Vav*, 168
*Vestment of the Lord, The* (Eliezer of Worms), 84
Virginity among women, 381
*Vision of the Priest* (Issachar ben Naphtali), 401
Vital, Chaim, 93–94, 389, 398

"Voice of G-d in Its Power, The" (Hai Gaon), 68

White Head, 170–171, 324
Work of Creation, 32
Work of the Chariot, 31
Written Law, 7–8, 41, 137, 273, 275–277, 315

Yebba the Ancient, 114, 115
*Yechidah*, 79, 203, 388
Yehuda, Rabbi, 82
Yesod, 171, 172
Yetzirah, angels in, 214–215
Yochanon ben Eliezer, 21
Yochanon, Rabbi, 53
*Yod*, 167
*Yoma*, 185
Yonathan ben Uziel, 27
Yosi, Rabbi, 21, 96

Zechariah, Book of, 289, 339
Zeira, Rav, 74–75
Zipporah, 272, 331
Zohar, 6, 23, 61
   and account of the *Sepher Yuhasim*, 41–44
   Book of Splendor and, 87, 88–89, 91–94
   commentaries on the Zohar and explanatory books, 93–94
   contents of the, 88–89
   defense of Zohar by recent thinkers, 37–38
   divisions of Zoharic contents, 89
   first appearance in Spain and France, 58
   first temple described by the, 281–282
   impeachment of the Zohar, 38–39
   and kabbalah, 21, 22, 24, 26
   nature of, 94
   Oral Law and Written Law, 7–8
   the original, 9
   Rabbi Shimon and the, 14
   Secret Doctrine and the, 11
   Sepher Yetzirah and the, 35, 36
   Shechinah in the, 343–345
   transcription and antiquity of the, 40–53
   Zoharic eschatology, 302, 309–310
   Zoharic theosophy, 26, 27
   *See also* Sepher Yetzirah and the Zohar, Midrashim, precursors of the

Zohar, minor tracts of the, 134
   additions, 135–137
   ancient and latter supplements, 143–144
   discourse of the young man, 139–140
   God and his attributes, 145–146
   Midrash Ruth, 142–143
   omissions, 134–135
   Prayer of Elijah, 144–145
   repetitions: *mathnitin*, 137–138
   secrets of secrets—of human physiognomy, 138–139
   seven heavens and seven earths, 140–141
*Zohar Chadash*, 92, 136, 146, 249
*Zohar Eicha*, 93
Zoharic tradition, age of, 50–51
   antiquity of contents of Zohar, 52–53
   evaluation, 51–52
   Isaac the Blind, 51
   mysteries of Rabbi Shimon, 53
Zoharic treatises and expositors, 385–386
   Abraham Cohen Herrera, 400
   Balance Principle and the Pillars, 392–393
   Book of Concealment, 392
   of the confusion of good and evil, 396
   Edomite Kings and Adam Belial, 395
   emanation of sephiroth, 391
   essence of prayer, 393
   of the fall of man, 395–396
   five-fold division of souls in the four worlds, 394
   fivehold division in the sephiroth, 394
   "Garden of Pomegranates", 387–388
   how creation took place, 398–399
   Isaac D'Luria, 388–389
   Issachar ben Naphtali, 401
   the light of radiation in compression, expression and formation of the world, 399
   light of the sephiroth, 391
   Moses of Cordova, 386–387
   Naphtali Hirtz, 397–398

Zoharic treatises and expositors (*continued*)
  prototypal archeplastic Adam, 395
  purpose of the revolutions of souls, 397
  of revolution of souls, 396–397
  Royal Valley, 397–398
  seven Edomite Kings, 393
  the Simulacrum Imago, 388
  the answer to why creation?, 389–390
  the three Pillars, 391
  why creation at that given time or epoch?, 390
  Zoharic schools in Palestine, 386–387
*Zohar Shir HaShirim*, 93

## ABOUT THE AUTHOR

Rabbi Raoul Nass was well known during his life as a highly effective teacher of Torah. At one time, he was known in his community as the physician to the Lubavitcher Rebbe, Rabbi Menachem Mendel Schneerson.

## ABOUT THE EDITOR

Kalman Serkez, a disciple of the Orthodox path, as well as of new age ideas, discovered some of the wonderfully awesome and poetic teachings of mysticism while pursuing tradition, and has been most pleasantly distracted ever since. He has edited other inspirational works, including *The Holy Beggars' Banquet* (Jason Aronson Inc.). Mr. Serkez lives in the New York community of Monsey where he is a stockbroker by trade and a member of the local Lubavitch congregation.